WHEN THE TOWERS FALL

WHEN THE TOWERS FALL

A Prophecy of What Must Happen Soon

STEVEN J. ROBINSON

RESOURCE *Publications* · Eugene, Oregon

WHEN THE TOWERS FALL
A Prophecy of What Must Happen Soon

Resource Publications
An Imprint of Wipf and Stock Publishers
199 W. 8th Ave., Suite 3
Eugene, OR 97401

www.wipfandstock.com

PAPERBACK ISBN: 978–1-6667–3577–2
HARDCOVER ISBN: 978–1-6667–9320–8
EBOOK ISBN: 978–1-6667–9321–5

FEBRUARY 3, 2022 9:27 AM

Contents

THE FINAL BOOK | 1
    An introduction to John's Apocalypse and its place in the Bible.

AUTHOR'S TESTIMONY | 33
    An account of what led the author to undertake this work.

THE REVELATION OF JOHN | 42
    Translation of the whole text.

THE PROPHECY

ONE LIKE A SON OF ADAM | 65
    Revelation 1. The Son of Man is manifested as the universal King who
    is coming soon to take up his rule.

THE STATE OF THE CHURCH | 78
    Revelation 2–3. An assessment of how well each of the churches has
    been following him. An outline of Church history up to the present day.

A VISION OF THE THRONE | 97
    Revelation 4–5. A throne is seen in heaven, the centre of all power in
    the universe. But who is to exercise that power on earth?

THE SCROLL AND THE SIX SEALS | 111
    Revelation 6. The birth pangs of the kingdom of heaven in the 20th
    century and the wrath of God in the 21st.

THE 144,000 AND AN INNUMERABLE THRONG | 126

> Revelation 7. Where are the 12 tribes of Israel today? Why are 144,000 called out from them? And what is the great multitude now seen before the throne?

THE SIX TRUMPETS | 135

> Revelation 8–9. As a final warning fire is cast on the earth, then asteroids. Finally hordes of demons emerge from below. Few of earth's inhabitants repent.

THE TWO WITNESSES AND THE LAST TRUMPET | 148

> Revelation 10–11. Gentile powers again occupy the land of Israel, while two prophets teach the Jews about their Messiah and testify against the world.

THE WOMAN, THE MAN AND THE DRAGON | 165

> Revelation 12. The birth of the one who will overthrow the present ruler of the world. The Christianisation of Europe and the return of Jews to their ancestral land.

THE TWO BEASTS | 176

> Revelation 13. A second Antiochus at the head of an alliance of Middle Eastern states conquers Israel. Everyone under his rule must bow down before his image and be marked.

THE HARVEST OF THE EARTH | 186

> Revelation 14. A vision of the 144,000 in heaven, three messages, and the earth harvested.

THE SEVEN BOWLS OF GOD'S FURY | 199

> Revelation 15–16. Wrath is poured out on the world, culminating in the Day of the Lord.

BABYLON THE GREAT | 209

> Revelation 17. A prostitute seated on a beast: her identity and destiny.

THE FALL OF BABYLON THE GREAT | 216

> Revelation 18. The fulfilled prophecies concerning ancient Babylon, Jerusalem and Tyre give grounds for thinking that the days of modern civilization are also numbered.

THE MARRIAGE FEAST AND THE BANQUET OF GOD | 228
    Revelation 19. The Bride prepares for her marriage; the Bridegroom
    prepares by slaughtering his enemies. Jerusalem is delivered.

THE BEGINNING AND THE END OF THE KINGDOM | 239
    Revelation 20. The Devil is shut away. The saints come to life and reign
    on earth with Christ. After 1000 years the rest of the dead are judged.

THE HOLY CITY JERUSALEM | 254
    Revelation 21–22:5. The city that God has prepared for those who love
    him. Its gates are open, and the surviving nations live by its light.

CONCLUDING WORDS | 271
    Revelation 22. The final words of Jesus, the angel, John and the Bride.

SUPPLEMENTARY MATERIAL

DANIEL, THE COLOSSUS AND THE TREE | 277
    Nebuchadrezzar's dream of a colossus, why Daniel's book should be
    accepted as authentic, and the mystery of the tree.

DANIEL'S SEVENTY YEARS AND SEVENTY TIMES SEVENS YEARS | 285
    Daniel's prediction of when the Messiah would come, and when he
    would be killed and put an end to sacrifice.

APPENDIX 1 | 293
    References to creation in both the Old and the New Testament.

APPENDIX 2 | 298
    References to resurrection in the Old Testament.

REFERENCES | 305

The Final Book

The Bible begins with the Creation. The Lord God made man out of the dust of the earth, breathed into him the spirit of life, and planted a garden of trees in which he set the man and appointed him to look after it. Just like the man himself, the deity was a being who spoke and could be spoken to. He told the man he was free to eat from any of the trees except one: if he ate from that, he would die. Three days later God put him to sleep and out of his side made a female companion for him. Although both were naked, they felt no shame. God surveyed the world that he had made and found no evil in it. In creating man he had created the possibilities of relationship: living souls learning about each other, interacting with each other and relating with him, their All.

On the eighth day an angel entered the garden. Manifesting himself in the body of a serpent, he suggested to the woman that she might profitably disregard what God had commanded her husband. Innocent and unsuspecting, she plucked some of the fruit on the forbidden tree and ate it. The man did the same. At once they knew that they were naked. In their act of spiritual unfaithfulness they became guilty of sexual unfaithfulness and instinctively feared their Maker. Tearing off some leaves to cover their loins, they hid themselves. But God sought them out and explained the consequences of what they had done. He covered their sin by slaughtering some animals in their place, clothed them with the skins, and since they were no longer innocent, expelled them from the garden. They had learned about evil; he taught them how to deal with it.

As humanity increased, the feeling of shame that followed disobedience diminished. Alienated from God, people gave themselves up to violence and sexual promiscuity, until only one righteous man remained. God resolved to destroy the earth and told him to build a huge ark. No one took any notice. They mocked, and carried on eating, drinking, marrying, and planning for the next generation. Then the day came when God shut Noah and his family in. All the springs of the great deep exploded, the land above the deep foundered and asteroids rained on the planet. All terrestrial animals apart from those in the ark were obliterated. As became apparent in the 1970s, the moon was hit by the same group of asteroids. Some impact craters, still visible with the naked eye, were the size of France. On earth the suddenly molten material beneath the impacts welled up to become cratons, kernels of today's continents. As the water receded, the land began to renew itself, but remained unstable for tens of thousands of years. From the ancestral pairs on the ark animals multiplied and diversified, as they were programmed to do, evolving new forms in adaptive response to environments that were themselves evolving. Fossils today bear witness to earth's recolonization.

Three genealogies span the prehistoric period, highly abbreviated and centered on the Near East, where the biblical author himself lived. Initially Noah's descendants stayed together: it would have made no sense to venture into lands barren of vegetation and incapable of sustaining animal life. But eventually they spread abroad, making tools along the way by chipping at stones picked up from the ground. The skill took time to master, and at first the tools were crude. By the Neolithic their craftsmanship was exquisite. Other aspects of material culture— wood and bone implements, clothing, rope, huts, boats—became lost to the archeological record as the materials decayed. We also know next to nothing about their beliefs.

In the 5th millennium BC, along the Fertile Crescent that stretched from the Nile to south-east Iran, some gave up their hunter-gatherer way of life to domesticate animals and cultivate land. As settlements grew, work became more specialized and society more organized. Something recognizable as civilization developed. Genesis associates this development with the rise in Mesopotamia of the world's first kingdom. Comprising many cities, it was subsequently disrupted, not to be reunited until Sargon of Akkad. A second kingdom arose in Egypt. Men lost their fear of the Creator and instead feared demons, objectified by means of idols. Each city had its god, who resided in a house or temple in the heart of the city and ruled through a king. The king in turn was supported by a ruling class of priests and administrators, beneath them a middle class of artisans and traders, and beneath them an underclass of food-producers and slaves. By the 3rd millennium BC the whole civilized world worshiped idols. In North America, sub-Saharan Africa, Australasia and most of South America civilization did not develop until the arrival of Europeans.

The rest of Genesis tells how God set in motion a plan to reclaim the earth. He called one man out of urban Babylonia, named him Abraham, and created from his descendants a new nation, named Israel. Within a few generations the family had moved to the eastern side of the Nile Delta and settled there as herders. However, they were not allowed to become fully Egyptian, and as they multiplied they began to be seen as a threat. They ended up enslaved, at the bottom of the hierarchy. Eventually God intervened. Revealing himself by the name Yahweh, he brought upon Egypt a series of plagues to force Pharaoh to release the Israelites and, when the king pursued them, destroyed his army in the Red Sea. Seven weeks later he entered into a solemn covenant with Israel. He gave them laws setting out right behavior. Provided they obeyed, he would grant them a land of their own; he would bless the fruit of the ground, of their womb, and of their livestock, and he would cause those who rose against them to be defeated. Like the first human couple, all they had to do was be faithful.

Forty years later the Israelites began to take possession of the land. But they did not live up to their high vocation, and after centuries of conflict they demanded a human king like the other nations had, an intermediary between the divine and human. God acquiesced, but warned them that their kings would exploit and oppress them. He gave them Saul, then David, who between them subdued Israel's remaining enemies, then Solomon. With the country now at peace, Solomon's reign was a golden age. However, he turned away from Yahweh to worship the gods of his many foreign wives. Unfaithfulness proved to be the nation's besetting sin. Despite prophets repeatedly reminding Israel of their covenant, the power of the flesh was almost always too strong. With their rituals of fornication and sacrifice, they worshiped the same demons that the other nations worshiped, even sacrificing their children. Regulation proved insufficient; each individual needed to be regenerated.

So, as he had warned would happen, God took away the land that the Israelites thought was theirs forever and returned them to a condition of slavery and landlessness: the northern tribes in 721 BC when they were deported to Assyria, the southern tribes—the Jews—in 586 when they were deported to Babylonia, homeland of their progenitor. Only then did they realize that the prophets' warnings had come to pass and

God was not to be trifled with. After 49 years he gave part of the land back to a remnant of the southern tribes, with limited autonomy, first under the Persians, then the Greeks. They learned to obey the law given at Mount Sinai and waited for God to restore the kingdom. In 142 they gained a measure of independence. In 63 they became a client kingdom of Rome. Where the nation was headed long-term was far from clear.

Fragmentary stela from the city of Dan which the Syrian king Hazael erected in 841 BC to commemorate his victory over Jehoram "king of Israel" and king Ahaziah "of the house of David." The inscription ties in with the account in 2 Kings 8:28. Israel Museum (photographer: Oren Rozen).

The last prophet to speak to Israel had been Malachi. It was not until more than four centuries later, in AD 26, that a prophet named John broke the silence. He urged the people to repent and be baptized, in preparation for the coming of a far greater prophet who would baptize with holy spirit and fire. Soon afterwards the heralded Messiah appeared. Demonstrating his power through many signs, he challenged society's religious traditions and ideas about the kingdom of God. He even revived the dead. But when he was arrested most of the Jews rejected him. They persuaded the Roman governor to crucify him as a rebel.

However, God meant it for good. Christ's death brought about a sacrifice that enabled anyone, whatever his status, sex or culture, to begin to be regenerated. As set out in the Bible's opening pages but thereafter little reflected on, mortality was the consequence of human sin, of not accepting our Maker as our Master. Christ, the sinless son of God, had made atonement on a tree with his own naked body; he had died in the place of all who would look upon him and believe. By reason of that self-giving, God raised him to his right side in heaven and granted him authority over all kingdoms and authorities. One day he would exercise that authority in person.

"I am coming soon"

The Bible divides into the 36 books of the Old Testament (the first three quarters) and 27 books and letters of the New Testament (the remaining quarter). "Testament" here means "covenant," the old one referring to the covenant that God made with Israel at Mount Sinai, the new to the covenant that Jesus concluded with his disciples in Jerusalem. The last book in the Bible is John's Revelation. It renews the prophecies set forth in the Old Testament and sums up all that remains to be fulfilled. John was told not to seal up its words, for Christ would soon be coming back.

Paul in his earlier letters expected his return within a generation or two. Peter cautioned that our own sense of time was not the same as God's but similarly affirmed, "The end of all things has drawn near." So did James. Today, however, such words are problematic. Whether we think of history as beginning from the earliest writing of history c. 1400 BC (by Moses—the Greeks were much later) or from the rise of civilization c. 3400 BC, a delay of two thousand years seems anything but "soon." Or perhaps we should be thinking of the interval in relation to the whole of history rather than from when Jesus was speaking? According to Paul, history consisted of many undefined "ages" (e.g. Rom 16:25, Eph 3:9, 1 Tim 1:17), ages of whose existence we ourselves became aware only much later, through investigating the non-verbal record of Earth's rocks. The end was near in that we were now living in the last of those ages (1 Cor 10:11). On the other hand, the "conclusion" or "completion" of that age was still some way off (Matt 13:39, 28:20). When he came back, it would be like a nobleman returning after a long absence.

Christ's second coming is a major component of the gospel, and we are meant to keep it as a focus of hope and longing, the hope (would man but come to his senses) of all the world. In actuality, we expect to die of senility and only hope to be spared the tribulation that is forecast before he appears. It would be very unfortunate if ours happened to be the generation in which things came to an end, especially when advances in medicine, technology and opportunities to travel have left many of us feeling that life is more comfortable than ever. We eat well, we live in good houses, our wealth increases. Instead of seeming more imminent with each passing year, his coming recedes further and further into the future.

Our theology reflects this state of ease. The Church tells the world, "Jesus loves you; he accepts you just as you are." By contrast, Revelation speaks of a day when many will cry, "Hide us from the face of the one seated on the throne, and from the wrath of the Lamb." We have a different understanding of Jesus: different not only from John's but from all the New Testament's. One doesn't have to go far before being confronted with unpleasantness. "Anyone who is angry with his brother without cause will be liable to judgement." "Wide is the gate and easy the way that leads to destruction, and many are those who enter by it." "Many will say to me on that day, 'Lord, Lord, did we not prophesy in your name and perform many miracles in your name?' And then I will assure them, 'I never knew you.' " On the whole, Christians pass over the parts that are unsettling and do not see why he might be angry with the present world. They would prefer that it went on forever, and that the end was just the moment we individually died and went to heaven.

Acceptance in the Canon

The penultimate book of the Bible stresses the need to defend the "faith once for all delivered to the saints." "Delivered" implies inerrantly delivered by God himself. Since he is hidden, knowledge of him can only be founded on what he has verbally revealed. Christ himself stressed the importance of written revelation. Mere tradition—beliefs and practices hallowed by age—had no divine authority and often worked against the word.

After his departure, a true knowledge of Christ depended on the testimony of the apostles as they went about preaching, confirmed by signs and the internal witness of the Holy Spirit. Paul as apostle "delivered" (past tense of *paradidwmi*) what he had directly received from Christ (Gal 1:16f, 2:1f), even with regard to such well known details as the words spoken at the Last Supper. He dictated his letters, because he spoke as God directed, and what came out did not need correction; he understood himself to be composing Scripture on a par with the Tanakh (1 Cor 7:10, 14:37, 1 Thess 2:13). Christ had appointed him "an assistant and witness, of what you have seen and of things I'll appear to you about" (Acts 26:16), including "visions and revelations" so overwhelming that he needed a thorn to keep him from becoming conceited (2 Cor 12:1–7). His policy was to adhere strictly to the terms of his commission. That is why we find so little overlap between his writings and the gospel accounts, which, apart from John's, may already have been written by the time of his first letter.[1] The only tradition, *paradosis* (the noun from *paradidωmi*), that he could vouch for was the teaching that orally and by letter he himself had delivered as having come from God (2 Thess 2:15). Anything else would not have been by way of witness. The leader of the apostles confirmed that Paul's letters had the status of Scripture (2 Pet 3:16).

As with the Old Testament, the books making up the New Testament were accepted as canonical on the basis that God had inspired them and that they represented the totality of the faith once delivered. Agreement as to which were authoritative came more quickly for some than for others, but once this was achieved, tradition had no further role. Christ's witnesses having passed away, the written word took the place of what had been orally transmitted.

Even more plainly than Paul, John indicated that his book came from God; he was merely the scribe. Our earliest informants tell us he was the apostle John, son of Zebedee and author of the gospel and letters bearing his name, though none of these expressly identified him as the writer. He received his vision in the 14th year of the reign of Domitian, Emperor of Rome (AD 81–96), by which time he was in his eighties and the only apostle living. Jesus told him to send the revelation to seven churches in the Roman province of Asia. Part of the book consisted of messages specific to each. The believers at Ephesus, where for many years John himself had dwelt, no longer loved God with all their heart, mind, and strength. The believers at Laodicea, a town almost totally flattened in 60 by an earthquake, knew better than most how disaster could come like a thief in the night, yet there, just two generations after Pentecost, the church had lost sight of their Savior. Other churches were experiencing persecution. Whether by way of reassurance or admonition, they needed to understand that Jesus was coming soon.

In the western Empire the book quickly became widely known and accepted, despite its weirdness and unlikeness to any other New Testament work. In the East too it must have been widely accepted (concrete

---

1. Wenham, *Redating Matthew, Mark and Luke.*

evidence is lacking), for although John had his detractors, the churches
there knew the writer. He was so well known that the title did not need to
state which John the name referred to. Later, in the second half of the 2nd
century, they began to have doubts, apparently because of a sect known
as the Montanists, some of whom were prophesying that New Jerusalem
was about to descend on a mountain not far away. That did not happen.
Nor did the many predictions that piggy-backed on John's in succeeding
centuries, including those of Adventists and Jehovah's Witnesses in the
comparatively recent past. As the prophecy can only be fulfilled once,
whereas false predictions of its fulfillment can be made any number of
times, it is easy to dismiss the notion that Revelation speaks about real
events in the future.

Revelation has always been troublesome and controversial. Diony-
sius, leader of the Egyptian Church from 248 to 264, admitted that he did
not understand much of it but was certain that Christ would not reign
on earth for a thousand years, as the book stated. In the preface to his
translation, Martin Luther wrote: "My spirit cannot accommodate itself
to this book. . . . There is no prophet in the Old Testament, to say nothing
of the New, who deals so exclusively with visions and images. . . . Christ
is neither taught nor known in it." Later his opinion softened, and he saw
part of it as prophetic of the Church of Rome. Not all modern commentators think highly of it, for the book is about the destiny of nations as
much as of individuals, and frequently conflicts with modern notions
of what edifies. Among the most damning comments is Harold Bloom's:
"Resentment and not love is the teaching of the Revelation. It is a book
without wisdom, goodness, kindness, or affection of any kind. Perhaps it
is appropriate that a celebration of the end of the world should be not only
barbaric but scarcely literate."[2] Reasons for liking it are not always the
best. It is arcane, and one can be consumed by its lurid mysteries. Scores
of commentaries have been written on it, "so diverse," wrote George Caird
in 1966, "as to make the reader wonder whether they are discussing the
same book."[3] Scores have been written since, to say nothing of what may
be found on the web. Many are put off by its harshness and obscurity. You
rarely hear sermons preached on the middle chapters.

Revelation's obscurity must be intentional, for all time is present to
the one who sees the end from the beginning and he could have described

2. Bloom, *Revelation of St John the Divine*, 4.

3. Caird, *Commentary on the Revelation of St. John*, 2.

the future more plainly. Nor can we say that the Church has been greatly disadvantaged by paying the middle chapters little heed. These mostly tell of things that only the last generation will experience. While we need to keep in mind that Jesus will come again, we get this awareness chiefly from reading Matthew, Mark and Luke, where Jesus speaks about this often, and often with greater clarity. Further material is found in the epistles and the Old Testament prophets.

"My thoughts are not your thoughts, nor your ways my ways." It is as well to remember that, as the veil lifts on a world of angels and demons. The book subverts at every level: word order, grammar, tense, genre, narrative structure, Christology, ideas about heaven, ideas about judgement. Metaphors are presented as if they were real. It is one thing for a prophet to point to "the Lamb of God" when everyone can see that the lamb is a man; it is quite another to be taken to the center of the universe and see such an animal sitting on the throne. The Bible concludes its revelation of God with a series of visions foreign to all normality. Some of them, we know, relate to the familiar geopolitical world where, sooner or later, they must be fulfilled. Others give us insight into the spiritual world behind the visible.

Confronted with so many competing interpretations, the reader must determine for himself how best to read the work. Jesus advises us to avoid interpretations that do not keep to the actual words. The words of the prophecy, he emphasizes, are "trustworthy and true," a statement that itself can be true only if the words communicate meaning that is capable of being false and not open to multiple interpretations, several or all of which might be "valid." Parts of the book undoubtedly are difficult: challenging sometimes to understand and challenging, because of what they communicate, to take in. Nonetheless, he lays on us an obligation to wrestle with them and "hear what the Spirit is saying to the churches." Those who do so, he says, will be blessed.

When will these things be?

The message "I am coming soon" is a call to keep awake. Jesus might have said, "I will not be back for thousands of years. But be vigilant, for as individuals you will live only decades, not knowing the day and the hour when you will die." Would the warning have been heard in the same way? Probably not. We live for our children and grandchildren as well as ourselves, and get our sense of identity and meaning, partly, from being members of the human race, which we hope will go on forever even though individuals die. So he gives no timescale, and the message "I am coming soon" is for all down the centuries. Some may scoff, and reply, "Where is the promise of his coming? Man has been on the earth for millions of years, and the earth will continue until the Sun becomes a red giant." The message in that case is, he will come sooner than you think.

We are faced with a paradox. John is told, "Do not seal the prophecy," yet the book does not give up its meaning easily. That it has been as good as sealed is why interpretations of it abound. Maybe the answer is that Jesus intended it primarily for believers at the end of the age (hence e.g. the exhortations at 13:9f and 13:18). Only they would need to understand its contents, and these would become easier to understand as the day approached and the events described began to occur. Revelation as a whole is not unlike the scroll in chapter 5, which remained sealed until near the end. Naturally, most scholars who write about it are more positive. Contrary to what the book itself says, they maintain that it is not primarily about the future, and it has always been intelligible. The two beliefs tend to go together: Revelation is "not a coded collection of secrets that will finally become intelligible at the end of time."[4]

The case can be made that the end is not now distant. In the USA this view is common enough, and the ideological and theological revolutions that have overcome both the western and non-western world over the past century seem not inconsistent. Paul warns that the final generation will be characterized by people who are lovers of self, lovers of money, disobedient to their parents, ungrateful, unholy, lovers of pleasure rather than lovers of God, having the form of piety but denying its power. They will accumulate teachers who affirm their sensual desires and not listen to teachers who do not affirm them (2 Tim 3–4). This is a description of non-Christian society, but the Church too embodies the decay, with consequent drifting away from the gospel all round. In the USA, adult church membership since 2000 has been in rapid decline, overall by 28%, and chiefly because fewer young people identify as Christians (Gallup). Over the last decade, the annual rate of decline was 4%. In England, a country not untypical of western Europe, the number of 20–44 year-olds who worshiped regularly fell in the period 1980 to 2015 by half, from 2.2% of the population—already a tiny number—to just 1.1%.[5] Judges

4. Koester, Revelation *and the End of All Things*, 40.
5. Brierley, https://www.brierleyconsultancy.com/.

and legislators trample on what remains of Christianity while bishops hold their peace.[6]

In general terms, when would it make sense for him to come: when the world was still half empty or when it was filled, as Genesis more or less says was the end-goal? When man was subduing the earth cooperatively with nature or cutting its forests down, depleting its soils and driving innumerable species to extinction? When the Church was fulfilling its role of making disciples or unwilling even to talk about sin, righteousness and judgement? When the world was receptive to the gospel or hostile to it? If the prophets still speak, it is to tell us that the axe falls when a civilization that knew God forgets about him and turns to other gods (Jer 18:15f).

Here are some other considerations:

- The Book of Daniel contributes extensively to Revelation. It deals with the future of the Jews, from the 6th century BC to "the time of the end." The angel who imparted its final vision told Daniel to seal the book until that time. As a result of archeological discoveries and other scholarly study over the last hundred years, most of it is now well understood. It can no longer be regarded as sealed.

- In particular, the colossus that Nebuchadrezzar dreamt about is widely acknowledged to represent the succession of empires or civilizations that would follow his own before a kingdom set up by God obliterated them all. These empires were: Persia, Greece, Rome and Europe, the latter divided and incohesive. The kingdom to come would rule the whole earth and last forever. We are more than a thousand years into the history of that last empire.

- Towards the end of Jesus's ministry, his disciples asked, "What will be the sign of your arrival and of the conclusion of the age?" Things that had to take place first included the appearance of false Messiahs and the outbreak of wars in Judaea. Then would come "the beginning of the birth pangs": nation would rise against nation, kingdom against kingdom, and there would be famines, infectious disease and great earthquakes. It is not difficult to see the world wars and famines of the 20th century and the earthquakes of 2004–2014 as fulfilling this prediction, in which case the horsemen of the Apocalypse in chapter 6 have come and gone.

6. Hill, *Reshaping of Britain, Church and State*.

- The return of Jews to the land of Israel, the Arab-Israeli wars of 1967 and 1973, and the growing persecution of Christians are arguably all referred to in chapter 12, in which case we stand at the juncture between chapter 12 and chapter 13.

- Jesus told his disciples to reflect also on the parable of the fig tree. A man planted a fig tree in his vineyard, but it bore no fruit, so he told the vinedresser to cut it down. The worker said, "Let me feed it one more year, and if it still bears no fruit, then cut it down." A little earlier, Jesus had cursed an actual fig tree because it bore no fruit, and it immediately withered, indicating that the nation God had planted among the Gentiles would be uprooted and the kingdom given to a people who would repay his labor. In the Jewish-Roman wars of AD 66–73 and 132–35 the Jews were exiled from their land. In 1948 the fig tree was re-established: Britain's mandate over Palestine came to an end and the Jews who had migrated there declared the establishment of the state of Israel. "As soon as its branch becomes tender and puts out leaves," Jesus intimated, "you know that summer is near. So also, when you see all these things, you know that he is near, at the doors. Amen, I tell you this generation will not pass away until all these things take place." Life expectancy in Israel is currently 82 years.

The reader must test everything and judge for himself. Some understand "this generation" to refer to Jesus's contemporaries. However, he had already stated what would befall his own generation (Matt 23:34f). Thereafter would come a succession of false Messiahs and a period of birth pangs. Some time after the start of those pangs the fig tree would sprout again and signal that he was near, and once all the events of Matthew 24:9–29 had come to pass, the world would know that he was very near.

In his best-seller *The Late Great Planet Earth*, Hal Lindsey asserted (without scriptural backing) that a generation was about 40 years. Accordingly he predicted that 'all these things' would happen by 1988 or thereabouts. What he must have had in mind was Israel's time in the wilderness, during which the nation was made to wait until all who had not trusted in Yahweh had died out (Num 14:29–35). He assumed that "this generation" was a unit of time defined by the wilderness period, that a generation, so understood, did not begin until the age of 20, and that all the Israelites alive at the start of the period died except Joshua and Caleb.

Unfortunately, the assumptions and consequently the predictions based upon them were false, resulting in confusion and no little skepticism. People say, "No one knows the day or the hour," and ignore the pains Jesus took to indicate when he would be near. The danger in his mind was not that people would be overly precise about the timing, but that they would be asleep—that delay would lead to complacency. To be fair, Lindsey eventually admitted his mistake and pointed out that in other respects his interpretation of Matthew 24:32–34 was unaffected.

The 2020/21 coronavirus crisis, well reviewed in Laura Dodsworth's book *A State of Fear* and in articles by Alex Gutentag and Ole Skambraks, also seems significant. The crisis is not mentioned in the Bible and generally, like the fall of the tower of Siloam, pandemics do not have theological significance. If this one does, it is firstly because man synthesized the virus, in the course of clandestine "gain-of-function" research funded by western agencies and China's Wuhan Institute of Virology (and Revelation does speak of merchants getting rich from *pharmakeia*). Man was in effect "playing God," but for evil purposes rather than good. The same philosophy underlay the mRNA vaccines. Secondly, in its determination to appease a fear that had no rational basis, western civilization gave up the freedoms it had previously considered inalienable and in effect enacted its own dissolution. Pandemic scenarios with code-names such as "Dark Winter" and "Event 201" (the latter simulating, in October 2019, the outbreak of a novel coronavirus) had been rehearsed in exercises for twenty years, so those involved, at increasingly higher levels of government and supranational organizations, knew what to do. Citizens were instructed to stay in their homes on pain of large fines and exhorted to perceive others as a potential threat; all but essential retail businesses were shut, some never to reopen; schools and universities were shut; street protests were suppressed and democratic systems of accountability suspended; scientists concerned about the quality and interpretation of the data, or about the safety and efficacy of the vaccines (the only medicine authorised outside the hospitals), were vilified, even censored. Meanwhile, medical care was withdrawn from those too old to look after themselves and minimized for everyone else that had a health condition other than covid itself. For the first time in history, churches shut down throughout the world, for the most part willingly. When the State granted them permission to re-gather, though not to sing, they came before God in masks, uncritically accepting that masks would materially inhibit transmission. Their fear of death, and understanding of what was happening behind the scenes, was no different from the world's. Fear of God had long since gone.

During the period 1880–2019, life expectancy in the USA doubled, from 39.4 years to 78.9 (in the UK from 43.0 to 81.3).[7] When adjusted for this aging trend, mortality was lower in 2020 than in every year up to 2004 (UK: up to 2009), and the median age of those who died from or with covid in 2020 was around 78 (UK: 81). People with pre-existing health conditions—obesity, for example, which is widespread in the West and causes as many deaths as covid[8]—had good reason to take precautions; others below the age of 65 had a negligible risk of dying from it. Nonetheless, at every level of authority fear was played up, even among children. And all for nothing. As became apparent from the experience of Sweden and states in the USA that refused to follow China's totalitarian example, the sacrifices were futile, the doomsday scenarios false. Those who bore the heaviest cost of governments wanting to be seen to do something were the young and the very poor. Globally around one hundred million more people were made "poor or extremely poor," i.e. reduced to living on less than US$3.20 per day in purchasing power parity terms,[9] while the wealth of the 400 richest Americans grew by 40%, or $1.3 trillion.

The disease is a respiratory disease, and spiritually we have long been breathing unwholesome air. By means of the virus God exposed the rottenness of our civilization, in order that he might be justified and prove blameless when he brings it to an end. The name "coronavirus" is also significant, but I leave that until commenting on the first trumpet (Rev 8:7). As we approach the two thousandth anniversary of Christ's departure, the key point, more than ever, remains. "I am coming soon."

Revelation's purpose

The purpose is to prepare and equip the Bride of Christ for his return. Here in the West we are not in that position at the moment. The gospel, as given by Matthew, Mark and Luke, has been cheapened and distorted.

---

7. https://ourworldindata.org/life-expectancy; https://data.oecd.org/chart/6w7F

8. In the USA 42% of adults were classified as obese in 2017–18 (UK: 28%). Deaths attributed to obesity annually exceeded 300,000. Only 5-6% of the death certificates mentioning covid in 2020 and 2021 gave covid as the sole cause of death (England and Wales 11%). Most died because early treatment using generic drugs was prohibited.

9. Kühn, *World Employment and Social Outlook.*

In their accounts the word for "love" (*agapaw*) is used of Jesus just once in total, when he advises the rich ruler to sell all he has, give it to the poor and follow him; in loving him, he didn't accept him just as he was. In John's gospel the Savior's love for the world is mentioned once and for his disciples several times, but the point is that we should love others likewise. In Acts the word does not appear at all.

Agapaw is used of Jesus's love for us two times in Revelation (1:5 and 3:9). But occurrence of the word is not everything. The whole book is sent out of God's love for the Church, and promise after promise expresses the substance of his love without using the word (e.g. at 21:7). The crucial question is not whether he loves us but whether we love him; whether, when the Bridegroom comes, there will be oil in our lamps. When we understand that God has come to us in mercy and will come again in judgement, the appropriate response is fear (11:18, 14:7, 15:4). Then fear may lead to repentance, and repentance to forgiveness and peace with our Maker; to knowledge of him and therefore love. God's wrath, *orgē*, or rage, *thumos*, is also an important theme. The main purpose of Scripture is to "convict, rebuke, and exhort . . . for the time is coming when people will not endure sound teaching" (2 Tim 3:16, 4:2f). We must take care not to be seduced by interpretations whose only merit is to satisfy palates brought up on sugar.

A heresy is a doctrine damaging to the health of the Church and contrary to Scripture. Are the following teachings heresies? At any rate, they are not countenanced by Revelation, and they are widely held.

1. *"Everything in the universe—the earth, the sun, the planets, the plants and animals on the Earth—had a natural origin."* Cosmologists say that the solar system—the earth some time after the sun, the moon later still—did not form supernaturally in the beginning, but naturally two thirds through the history of the universe. Revelation re-affirms what is declared throughout the Bible, that God created the heavens and the earth. If "create" means anything, the word means to form or bring into existence that which Nature by itself cannot bring into existence. Only when God speaks does anything happen. As everyone outside the peculiar world of theology recognizes, a process whereby everything evolves into being is the opposite of creation: God plays no role, although he may, 13.8 billion years ago, have lit the touchpaper. The soul, in this view, is simply highly organized matter. Followers of Jesus need to understand that

the wisdom of the world is at enmity with God, and they have to make a choice. If they agree with what the world teaches, they are choosing the wrong side. The universe is not false in bearing testimony to its Creator; in Psalms 8 and 19 David states what is merely obvious. Even Richard Dawkins admits that living things appear to have been designed.

2. If Christians no longer understand who God is, many also do not understand who Jesus is. On the human side, they say that *he is not "the son of Adam, son of God"* (Luke 3:38) and not the physical image or representation of God (2 Cor 4:4, Col 1:15), since he had an evolutionary ancestry and his bodily form derived from the apes, all the way back to bacteria. On the divine side Christ cannot be the Son of God because he is coeternal with him; he is his son only in a "spiritual" sense, distinct from the physical and literal. As the BBC says on its website, "the Trinity is a controversial doctrine; many Christians admit they don't understand it, while many more Christians don't understand it but think they do. In fact, although they'd be horrified to hear it, many Christians sometimes behave as if they believe in three Gods and at other times as if they believe in one." As will be discussed, the doctrine comes from the Creeds rather than Scripture.

3. *"Satan is not a real spiritual being."* After Jesus was baptized, he immediately went into the wilderness and was tempted by the Devil. Not long afterwards he healed those possessed by demons, and taught his disciples to pray, "Do not lead us into temptation, but deliver us from the evil one." Near the end, he urged the Father directly, "Keep them from the evil one" (John 17:15). An understanding of life that does not recognize the spiritual reality of evil will be inadequate for the days ahead. "Whoever makes a practice of sin is of the Devil, because the Devil has been sinning from the beginning. The reason the Son of God appeared was to undo the works of the Devil." (1 John 3:8) The Devil was a murderer from the beginning (John 8:44) because man was in existence from the beginning and sinned, not at his own initiative, but at the Devil's prompting, and thus death came into the world (Rom 5:12).

4. *"The God revealed in the Old Testament is different from the one revealed in the New: Yahweh is wrathful and vindictive, Jesus is loving and kind."* At its most extreme, the antithesis (a revival of

Marcionism) suggests that many church leaders do not know God at all. In truth, the Old shows the justice of God, his constant desire to bless, and his great patience; the New announces as good news his willingness to grant forgiveness—exemption from punishment, not merely an attitude—on the basis of the justice satisfied on the cross. God does not change; rather, by the gift of his holy spirit he changes us. Because we were once his enemy ourselves, we are to imitate him by loving our enemy and praying for those who persecute us. Or even the other way round: "Father, forgive us our sins, as we forgive those who sin against us." When Jesus returns, he will avenge himself on his enemies. Then the carnage, Revelation confirms, will be greater than in any Old Testament battle, and he will enforce the justice of the law.

5. *"The Church has replaced Israel as God's chosen people. Assurances under the old covenant that he would eventually bless Israel and restore the exiled nation to the land of their forefathers are really promises of blessing to the Church."* The promises, it is maintained, are to be spiritualized, on the grounds that all the promises of God find their Yes in Christ; whoever believes in him inherits the promises. However, this is to ignore what they specifically say. The ark of the covenant was never destroyed, and its heavenly counterpart still acts as a reminder of what God promised to Israel under the covenant. The temple and, within it, the altar, the bowls of incense, the lamps and the ark are all seen in John's vision. The promises to Israel come to pass when the Messiah leads them into the land and reigns over them. He could hardly be more emphatic: "If the heavens above can be measured, and the foundations of the earth below be explored, then will I cast off all the offspring of Israel for all that they have done" (Jer 31:37). The promises relate to them (Rom 9:4), and extend to us only inasmuch as we are grafted into Israel.

6. *"Sexual intercourse is fundamental to a person's humanity, and therefore need not be restricted to marriage."* In marriage, man and woman become one flesh, and the relationship is holy because in the beginning God blessed it as the means of carrying on his work of bringing life into the world. Any sexual relationship outside such a union is unholy, and no one will inherit God's kingdom unless he is holy (1 Cor 6:9). "Those who are Christ's have crucified the flesh with its passions and desires." Much of the western Church is now

disinclined to understand holiness in these terms, unaware that in Revelation sexual promiscuity is the principal charge laid against the civilization about to be destroyed.

7. *"Christian believers go straight to heaven when they die."* In truth, we lie in the earth, unconscious like everyone else until the day we rise. We don't go to heaven as a disembodied soul and then—if we believe in an appointed day at all—slip back to earth just before the resurrection. The idea that our immediate and final destination is heaven etherializes the life to come, reinforces a bias against the physical, historical and literal, and promotes individualism. "Your kingdom come on earth" is the Church's goal and mission. We are members of one body, and having been in Christ when he rose, we shall rise as one (Rev 20:4). Why should we look forward to the Lord's return if our own personal resurrection does not depend on his coming back? Whether he comes soon or in a million years becomes a matter of indifference.

8. *"Make an initial commitment to Jesus and your eternal destiny is secure."* At the end of each letter to the churches Jesus makes his promise of eternal life conditional on our remaining faithful. We are saved through faith, but that faith, that salvation, is proved in the way we live. David Pawson spells this out in *Once Saved, Always Saved?* The Sower sows his seed: some falls on good soil, some gets choked by thorns, some falls on soil with no depth. Without a root, we wither away. Minimizing the importance of working out our salvation goes with a general devaluation of intimacy with Christ (need a believer always be listening for his voice?), a devaluation of service (need a believer serve God and man in practice?) and a devaluation of reward (will he really differentiate between one follower and another?). "See, I am coming soon, and my wages with me, to pay everyone for what he has done."

9. *"Theological knowledge is not important."* This is not so much a belief as an affirmation of non-belief, of the acceptability of luke-warmness. Jesus told the Pharisees, "Well did Isaiah prophesy of you when he said, 'This people honors me with their lips, but their heart is far from me.' " His main criticism of the Sadducees was, "You know neither the Scriptures nor the power of God." He expected his followers to know both, and to love God with all their heart and

all their mind. Indifference is not the right response to his having overcome the world.

The Puritan divines who did much to revive Britain's churches in the 17th century also had to contend with indifference. In his *Treatise of Conversion* (1657) Richard Baxter exhorted the people of Kidderminster:

> 1. Every man that hath a reasonable soul should know God that made him, and the end for which he should live, and know the way to his eternal happiness as well as the learned. Have not you souls to save or lose as well as the learned have? 2. God hath made plain his will to you in his word; he hath given you teachers and many other helps, so that you have no excuse if you are ignorant; you must know how to be Christians if you are no scholars. You may hit the way to heaven in English, though you have no skill in Hebrew or Greek, but in the darkness of ignorance you can never hit it. 3. Will not God judge you as well as the learned? And will not he require an account of the talents which you possess? He hath set you on his work as well as others, and therefore you must know how to do his work. If you think therefore that you may be excused from knowledge, you may as well think that you may be excused from love and from all obedience, for there can be none of this without knowledge. . . . Were you but as willing to get the knowledge of God and heavenly things as you are to know how to work in your trade, you would have set yourselves to it before this day, and you would have spared no cost or pains till you had got it. But you account seven years little enough to learn your trade, and will not bestow one day in seven in diligent learning the matters of your salvation.

Lifelong learning is defined by the European Commission as "all learning activity undertaken throughout life, with the aim of improving knowledge, skills and competences within a personal, civic, social and/or employment-related perspective." It is something the Commission commends. There is no equivalent culture in the churches, at least in Britain. Content to remain in infant school Sunday by Sunday, we do not understand the Way as one of lifelong discipleship. Going deeper into the Word is seen as an academic occupation.

The teachings highlighted are expressions of spiritual laxity, and, ironically, of a hermeneutic that thinks the reader closer to God if he "spiritualizes" the seemingly untrue, or unacceptable, or inapplicable. How we read the first chapter of Genesis determines how we read the rest of the Bible. Some allege that it tells us why, rather than how, God made the universe, "how" being a scientific question beyond the competence of the text. Spiritual truth is thereby recovered from statements that, taken literally (scientifically and historically), are embarrassing, for God as much as for us. I must hope the reader sees that this thinking is anything but spiritual. Indeed, the theologians who invoke the "spiritual" typically deny the existence of evil spirits and deny that man has a spirit (cf. Job 27:3, 32:8, 34:14f). Although advanced as a higher kind of reality, "spirit" is for them no more than a figure of speech. The re-interpretation is not even correct on its own terms, for Genesis 1 tells us *how* God brought things into being (by divine fiat) and says almost nothing about why (why he created what we believe he did not create).

Such thinking certainly will not equip the reader to understand the book of Revelation. The rule is, "first the physical, then the spiritual" (1 Cor 15:46). Spiritual significance is not intended to nullify the physical, but to fulfill it. Mount Zion functions as an image for God's spiritual dwelling-place in heaven, because it was also once a literal hill where God dwelt on earth; it still has a literal existence, and he will dwell there again. Where Revelation appears to describe physical events, that is what they are, notwithstanding their immensity and horror. "A third of the earth was burned up, and all its vegetation was burned up." An earthquake shakes the planet "such as has never been since man was on the earth." The spiritual significance of such events is that they express God's rage. The bowls that the angels pour over the Earth and the Sun may be figurative, but the havoc wreaked is not. As mentioned, the preliminary horrors have already occurred (Rev 6:1–8).

Literal and spiritual are not necessarily opposites. When John enters heaven, he sees an actual, visible throne. An astronaut looking for it will look in vain, but when Jesus returns, he will sit on that throne of glory in physical Jerusalem (Matt 25:31). True, the throne is a symbol, signifying kingly power, but it is in the nature of a throne to symbolize kingly power; it is not the less real for being a symbol. By contrast, when John sees seven lampstands, he has to be told that these symbolize churches, for of themselves lampstands do not symbolize churches. The same applies to the numbers: the actual number of the armies of demonic horsemen is 200,000,000 (John expressly confirms the number); we know that the 1260 days during which the two prophets prophesy is the actual duration because it coincides with Jerusalem's occupation by Gentiles for 42 months; 666 is an actual number because it has to be computed.

Some commentators ask whether John even had a vision. "Ordinary readers . . . assume that John had some sort of vision, and that what we have is a more or less straightforward description of what he saw."[10] The implication is that ordinary ways of reading are not to be trusted. After all, a politician who says, "I had a dream," does not mean that he really had a dream. John's description of a rainbow "in appearance like emerald" cannot represent what he actually saw; rather, he chose words for their (undisclosed) symbolic significance. The weaving in of more than 500 references to the Old Testament, as well as many references to the New, is thought to show that he was no mere reporter but played a major part in the book's composition. And consider how many times important words or phrases occur in the text. "The Lord God the Almighty," "our God," "Jesus," "Christ" (as a separate name), "coming quickly," "endurance," "prophecy," "prepared/made ready" (same word), "time" (*kairos*), "altar," "reign," "kingdom," "son," "blessed," "every people, tribe, language and nation," "cloud," "abyss," "earthquake" all occur seven times. "For ever and ever," "scroll/book," "write," "servant," "saint," "Jesus," "trumpet," "star" and "woe" each occur fourteen times; "sun," "power," "elder," "written," "temple," "bowl," "smoke," "plague" and "repent" twelve times, "worship" and "Lord" twenty-four times, "Lamb" (excluding 13:11) twenty-eight times.

Given the emphasis on true and faithful witness in Revelation, we should be slow to infer that John himself did not bear true witness. According to his own testimony, the revelation came from God, and John wrote down what he saw and heard, writing as he went along. Afterwards he must have expanded what he jotted down, and what that involved we can only surmise. My own surmise is that, as he relived the experience, words that he sensed to be right just came to him. It was the Spirit that embroidered the account with repeated allusions to the Old and New Testaments, much as the angels and other heavenly voices did their own speech. The vision and the precise words used to communicate it were one, as if he had digested an invisible scroll with the words. It seems ridiculous to imagine John counting key words and phrases and revising the text until he had the number he wanted. Rather, the numerological patterns are evidence that God was the ultimate author, just as—and here is the really difficult thought—numerological patterns in history (e.g. 2 Chr 36:21, Dan 9:24–27) show that he is ultimately the author of all

10. Paul, *Revelation*, 22.

things, past and future. Everything is timed to the "hour, the day, the month and the year." "The ages were fashioned by the word of God" (Heb 1:2, 11:2).

Faithful translation of the word of God

Writing materials such as papyrus and vellum were perishable, so manuscripts of the New Testament, as with all ancient texts, exist only as copies, even if some are very old. Copying resulted in errors, and determining which variant reflects the original is not straightforward; the oldest copy is not necessarily the truest. Further differences arose through copyists deliberately amending, adding or deleting words to accord with what they regarded as a better reading—and therefore probably the correct one—on the basis that they were undoing a previous copying error. Translations also exhibit this tendency of adding, amending and deleting.

The Greek text used for the commentary is the Textus Receptus, as set out with an interlinear translation in *The Englishman's Greek New Testament* (archived on the web). A variant reading is adopted only when supported by at least five of the seven other editions surveyed in that work, in which case it is usually the Griesbach edition that tips the balance. Indeed, where Griesbach adopts a variant, he is usually supported by at least four of the other editors. In most cases this rule results in the same reading as the English Standard Version (2001), the ESV having stepped back from the textual revisionism that characterized the Revised Standard Version (1952). One example to the contrary is Revelation 5:9, "You ransomed people for God," spoken by the elders. The reading accepted by the ESV has no object for the verb and "people" has to be supplied, whereas the Textus Receptus has "You ransomed [i.e. purchased] us for God." The principle that the less obvious reading is likely to be the correct one is known as *lectio difficilior* and is particularly manifest in Revelation, which has a tendency anyway to break grammatical and stylistic norms. "You purchased us for God" is the less obvious reading because, disconcertingly, the elders later in the sentence speak in the third person, but it gives us the essential clue as to who the elders are: "they" stand for "us," those whom God has purchased.

While not to be exaggerated, the textual issue affects all the New Testament. Another example is John 1:18, "No one has ever seen God. The only-begotten Son [*ho monogenes huios*], who is in the bosom of the Father, he has made him known." The ESV, following a reading (*monogenes theos*) attested by only one of the other editions, translates "the only God" and ends up with nonsense ("the only God [Jesus] . . . has made God known"). A manuscript known as P72—preserving the oldest known copy of Peter's two letters—has a similar alteration, substituting *theos* in 1 Peter 5:1 for *Christos*. Here the weight of manuscript evidence is sufficient to discredit the reading, so we know that corruption in this direction did occur (also at 1 Tim 3:16) and that earlier copies are not necessarily more accurate than later ones. A third example is 2 Peter 3:10, which says that the earth and man's works on the day of the Lord "will be burned up"; the alternative reading, "will be found," supported by only one editor, is close to meaningless. In my judgement, the rule never results in an intrinsically inferior reading, and no one should think that describing a voice as "what seemed/sounded like a voice" is divinely inspired (Rev 6:6 ESV/NIV). That said, in the vast majority of cases variant readings are insignificant (e.g. spelling differences).

"Heaven and earth will pass away; my words will not pass away." Jesus was referring to all Scripture (Isa 40:8), including that which at the time had not been written. Every iota, he said, was as intended, not simply the general sense. Accurate theology therefore requires a literal approach to translation. As soon as we paraphrase, we move away from the words and begin to lose their inspiration. Revelation itself warns us not to add to or take away from them. The truth is found by meditating on and wrestling with the Logos, not attempting to change it in accordance with what we think the truth is.

With regard to Revelation the best translations are those in the direct line of descent from the King James Version, notably the ESV at the end of the line. The NIV is not quite as good overall, and sometimes chooses a less obvious rendering just to be different from the KJV revisions. A faithful translation cannot help resembling the ESV much of the time. That said, the ESV could be better than it is. Even it adds words "for clarity," and changes the meaning of a word where it is not understood (Rev 14:15, 18:2, 18:5).

Paraphrases are interpretations, somewhere between translation and commentary, and can be helpful so long as one is aware they are not translations. However, the prophetic books are another matter. These are difficult to understand chiefly because the Holy Spirit scrambles his message, leaving the reader repeatedly having to pick up verbal allusions to other utterances and use these clues to piece things together (the procedure known as *gezerah shawah*). The specific words must therefore be retained.

Detecting the cross-references in Revelation requires a depth of knowledge that cannot be expected of most readers—hence the need for commentaries—and following them up requires diligence. But the effort will repay. Paradoxically, the disjointedness is itself evidence that the books were inspired, for typically the prophets did not understand what they were saying (2 Pet 1:21) and made no attempt to order their utterances into something clearer and more sequential. As sketched by different prophets at different times, the total picture remains coherent.

Translation issues are discussed, sparingly, in the relevant part of the commentary, but a few may be worth elaborating on. They illustrate how choice of words affects theology, and how even the smallest words can have significance.

- *porneia*—this common word in the New Testament means sexual intercourse outside marriage. Unmarried women were expected to be virgins and married women to be faithful to their husbands. Ancient Greek and Roman society did not hold husbands to the same standard; if they were unfaithful, it was generally with a prostitute (*pornē*) or slave. Christian teaching insisted that husbands should be equally faithful.[11] Since Scripture considers all copulation outside marriage unclean, the word should be translated "fornication" (so the RSV), not "sexual immorality" (which, in begging the question what sexual immorality is, is unlikely to challenge readers). It occurs seven times in Revelation.

- *kai* ("and," occasionally "also")—New Testament Greek uses the conjunction *kai* slightly more often than English does, perhaps partly because the written language had no commas or full stops (the translator must decide how to punctuate). But in Revelation John also uses the connective more often than other New Testament writers do, or John himself in his gospel. Known as parataxis, the linking of clauses by addition is characteristic of Hebrew writing, and is consistent with Revelation's many allusions to the Old Testament. It is also part of John's minimalist apocalyptic style—minimalist because he is concerned to write only what he has seen and heard. Details keep piling up, every one of them significant, and while interpretation is not eschewed, it is either provided by his guide or he gives it as on a par with the things he has seen and heard. Modern translations tend to omit the connective, or translate it "so,"

11. Harper, *From Shame to Sin*.

or "then." (The Greek word for "then," next in time, does not occur at all in Revelation but occurs 54 times in the NIV!) Occasionally I have done the same. However, I have resisted the temptation to replace "and" with "but" where a reader would expect the adversative, on the grounds that an ancient reader would also have expected "but," and "and" must therefore be deliberate. Again, "and" where one would expect "but" is a Hebraism.[12] In one place (Rev 17:6 ESV, NIV) omission of the word mistakes the meaning: "the blood of the saints *and* the blood of the witnesses of Jesus." The two groups of people are distinct, namely Jews and believing Gentiles. Omission of the word is also culpable at 11:8, which speaks of the city "where also [*kai*] their Lord was crucified," implying that, like the apostle Peter in the first century and not a few since, some of his witnesses will be crucified.

- *hagioi*—that "saints" (holy ones) in some contexts refers to the people of Israel is clear from the equivalent in Daniel 7, Daniel 12 and numerous psalms. "They shall be called the holy people" (Isa 62:12). The NIV's "people of God" or "God's people" is simply a mistranslation.

- *zwon*—this is the normal word for "animal" ("ω" in transliterations is the vowel omega, pronounced "awe"). "Living creature" is wrong. The word denotes both the animals ("living souls") created in the beginning and the four animal-like beings beneath the throne of God, which are not creatures. In both Greek and Hebrew the root idea is "life." The root of the English word is *anima*, Latin for soul, which every animal was intuitively perceived to have.

- Where possible, translations should use the same word each time the same Greek one occurs. "Purchase," "ransom" and "redeem," for instance, are distinct ideas and should be restricted to the corresponding Greek words. The word in Rev 5:9 is "purchase" (NIV), not "ransom" (ESV); in 14:3, it is "purchase," not "redeem" (ESV, NIV). The word translated "seduce" in Rev 2:20 is *planaw*, the normal word for "deceive," as in 12:9 and elsewhere. "As slaughtered" in 13:3, describing the beast, echoes the same phrase in 5:9, describing the Lamb. *Phwnos* means "voice" or "sound" (between which the translator must choose) but in some places is translated "rumblings"

---

12. Steiner, "The Biblical Hebrew Conjunction," 249–67.

(e.g. 8:5, ESV, NIV). Such inconsistencies are motivated by a desire to add color, but in a minor way they too contravene the warning not to add to or take away from the words of the prophecy. John compensates for complexity of structure and symbolism by keeping the language simple, and uses other ways to ring the changes. Revelation is vivid enough.

- Disregard for word order can also be a failing. One example, discussed in the commentary, is Rev 13:8. Another is Rev 5:9:

> and you purchased us for God by your blood
> from every tribe and language and people and nation,
> and you made them for our God kings and priests . . .

In the Greek, "for (our) God" precedes "by your blood" and "kings and priests," and the semantic emphasis falls on these final phrases. Scripture's writing is skilled, and reading it is also a skill.

Why another commentary?

The inference that Christ is returning soon puts the present work at odds with most published commentaries. In my view Revelation will not unlock its mysteries until he is imminent and unless we then understand that he is imminent. Furthermore, its teaching is at variance with modern theology as critiqued above, whereas many scholars are comfortable with it. If the purpose of Revelation is to prepare and equip the Bride for his coming, this must also be the purpose of any exposition of the book.

Followers of Christ are identifiable by their witness. They bear testimony to what he did and who he is, and to the truth that he is coming. I give a brief account of my life and formal qualifications after this introduction, and in particular describe how I reached the conclusion that what we know from geology, paleontology and archeology agrees with the Bible's account of early history.

The elders in John's vision declare that God is worthy to assume kingship over the nations because he created all things: heaven, earth and the life that they contain, visible and invisible. Acceptance of what the elders say is requisite if one wishes to understand the prophecy. Christ is coming to judge the world because Western civilization, the part that has received the most light scientifically and theologically, denies that he together with the Father created all things. Much of the rest of the world is dominated by Islam. It believes in God (Allah) but denies that Jesus is his son, denies that he rose from the dead, and persecutes his followers. Another part worships images. Another is in thrall to spirits. They too will be judged.

Notwithstanding the atheistic bias of historical science, the physical sciences must be allowed to inform our understanding of the phenomena described. That the earth will be burned with fire is clear from several parts of the Bible; Revelation elaborates on this in some detail, enough for us to see that the fire is not to be spiritualized into an innocuous metaphor. The visions describe global hazards that the world is increasingly worried about: fierce heat, wildfires, asteroids tearing through the atmosphere, coronal mass ejections. Understanding Scripture in the light of contemporary knowledge is part of what it means to "interpret the signs of the times" and apply his word to the world in which we live. We are not meant to shut ourselves within a theological bubble.

The final reason for offering yet another commentary is that, for all the prodigious output of divinity schools, Old Testament prophecy remains largely sealed. One purpose of Revelation is to open it up: to "bear witness to the word of God." Concerning the future yet to take place, the Old Testament has only one major theme: the fulfillment of God's promise to Abraham to give to his offspring the land from the Euphrates to the Nile. The judgement of the nations, which will take place synchronously, is a minor theme. By contrast, in Revelation the judgement is the major theme and the fulfillment of the promise a minor one (having been treated at length in the Old Testament). Revelation brings Old Testament prophecy to life by helping us see that it is not primarily about the first coming of Christ. The redemption of Israel, the wrath of God and the kingdom of God still lie ahead, and they will come to pass on this present earth.

Despite Scripture's testimony to the contrary, we have a habit of non-contextual reading that writes Jewry out of history. When we pick out a verse such as, "I know the plans I have in mind for you, plans for well-being [shalom] and not evil, to give you a future and a hope," and read this as God speaking to us, we are interpreting history as if the Jews, to whom God was actually speaking, ceased to exist after most of them rejected Christ. But in the same passage (Jer 29:11–15), God declares that he will not forsake his people. After their punishment he will bring them back to the land promised to them and, much later, gather all the Jews from every nation, not just Babylonia, and restore them permanently to the land. Those are his "plans." Again there is a translation issue. "A future and a hope" in the Hebrew is more literally "an eventual hope," referring to the hope of a future at the end of the age (as in Deut 4:30, Prov 23:18 and most pertinently Jer 30:1–24). "I will consume all the nations among whom I have scattered you, but you I will not consume. . . . I will restore you to health, and your wounds I will heal, Yahweh declares, because they have called you an outcast: 'It is Zion, for whom no one cares.' " A little later God repeats (31:17), "You have the eventual hope that your children will come back to their own borders." Having hardened their hearts for our sakes, God will have mercy on them (Rom 11:28–32 RSV).

The libretto of Handel's *Messiah* contains probably the sum total of the prophecies most Christians are familiar with. It starts with Isaiah 40:

> Comfort, comfort my people, says your God,
>   speak tenderly to Jerusalem and cry to her
> that her warfare is ended,
>   that her iniquity is pardoned,
> that she has received from Yahweh's hand
>   double for all her sins.
> A voice of one crying in the wilderness:
>   "Prepare the way of Yahweh,
>   make straight in the desert a highway for our God.
> Every valley will be lifted up
>   and every mountain and hill be made low;
> the uneven ground will become level
>   and the rough places a plain.
> The glory of Yahweh will be revealed,
>   and all flesh will see it together."

Matthew and Mark tell us that John the Baptist was that voice, apparently fulfilling Isaiah's ancient prophecy. John himself believed he was fulfilling the prophecy, speaking in terms so apocalyptic that he later found it difficult to understand how Jesus matched up. Another prophet, Malachi, had spoken of an Elijah-like figure who (in contrast to the social divisions described in Micah 7:5f) would bring young and old back together "before the great and terrible day of the Lord." But then John was killed. In the light of that setback, others too began to have doubts: was Jesus really the Messiah? Jesus confirmed that John was the voice crying in the wilderness and said that he himself would suffer the same fate. That still left matters unclear. Three of them had seen his glory on the mount of transfiguration, but when would "all flesh" see it?

The problem of how to read the prophets continues to this day, and is resolved only when we recognize that there would be two advents and two periods of preparation. Isaiah was speaking chiefly about the second, in the wilderness of exile. Judah and Jerusalem were soon to be destroyed by the Babylonians (Isa 6:11f, 39:6f), would be destroyed again by the Romans (Isa 6:13, Zech 11:1–3, 13:8), and would be conquered yet again at the end of the age (Isa 52:5). By then they would have received double for their sins, once for their idolatry under their own kings, and again for preferring their own righteousness to the Messiah's under the Romans. The latter retribution was the wrath that John the Baptist warned about—he was not speaking hyperbolically. Nonetheless, God would restore their fortunes (Deut 30:3, Jer 29:14). Literally, the words mean "reverse their captivity." He would lead them out of slavery and exile back to the land (Ezek 20:43). An earthquake would shake the planet and bring even mountains crashing down. All humanity would see the glory of the Lord. The libretto goes on to quote the prophet Haggai: "I will shake the heavens and the earth and the sea and the dry land. And I will shake all the nations." Also Malachi: "Who can endure the day of his coming, and who can stand when he appears? For he is like a refiner's fire," consuming evildoers like stubble. The fire is a simile referring to the real fire that will scorch the earth.

After Isaiah's prophecy that a maiden would conceive and bear a son named Immanuel, the oratorio reverts to the time when all humanity will see him:

> Go up onto a high mountain,
>   you who bring good news to Zion;
> lift up your voice with vigor,
>   you who bring good news to Jerusalem.
> Lift it up, do not fear;
>   say to the cities of Judah, "Behold your God!"

While "good news" may have evoked the gospel in Handel's mind, here it is the news that the Messiah, now glorified, will come in power to deliver Judah. Isaiah continues:

> Behold, the Lord—Yahweh—comes with strength,
>   his arm ruling for him.
> Behold, his wages are with him
>   and his reward before him.
> He will tend his flock as a shepherd;
>   he will gather the lambs with his arm.

The promise is repeated in Isaiah 51 and 62. The mighty "arm" of the Lord—first outstretched to deliver Israel in the time of Moses—is his servant the Messiah (Isa 53:1). He will dash the nations in pieces like a potter's vessel.

So the oratorio begins with a message to the Jews that, when all seems lost, God himself will come to them in glory. The middle part then reminds us that he has already come, in the person of one who was wounded for our transgressions and crushed for our iniquities. We who listen to the music await his coming in hope. Death has been swallowed up in victory, and will be swallowed up at the last trumpet, at the resurrection of the dead. Handel concludes with words from the final book: "Blessing and honor, glory and power, be unto him that sitteth upon the throne, and unto the Lamb, for ever and ever"—the cry of every creature under heaven.

Revelation's structure

Apart from the difficulty of taking in the sheer magnitude of the events, the greatest challenge is discerning the book's chronology. The general direction of travel is of course forwards. Events are described in the order in which they happen, but with pauses for excursions which set forth some aspects in more detail. The scroll with the seven seals reveals its contents as it is opened one seal at a time. The first four encompass a series of disasters that are now behind us; the fifth is being fulfilled; the sixth and seventh represent the final wrath. The period from the fifth seal to the end of the wrath is elaborated upon in chapters 7 to 19. Chapter 12, at the center of the book, summarizes all history, from Creation to the return of Jews to Palestine in the modern era. The Lamb claims his inheritance after the scroll is fully opened. He is married to his bride. Chapter 20 summarizes the millennial reign of Christ and his people, expanded on in chapters 21 and 22.

The blasts of the trumpets are God's final warnings before the full force of his wrath. The natural disasters bring civilization to its knees. Some Christians receive divine protection in order to make one last appeal to the world to be reconciled to God. Then the sky dims and demons invade the earth, initially to torment, subsequently to kill. Meanwhile, Jerusalem is conquered by a coalition of Gentile powers and for three and a half years two prophets explain the significance of what is coming on the world. At the end of their testimony they are murdered.

Many Israelis are killed, enslaved and sent into exile. One more trumpet is blown. Believers who have survived are taken off the earth. The dead in Christ rise from their graves. The earth is plunged into darkness and given over to fire, the Sun's fire.

God uses an intensification of the solar wind and a world-wide seismic convulsion to destroy civilisation. The nations around Israel gather at Megiddo to confront the Messiah they know is coming, but the flesh falls from their bones. Finally Christ returns with the saints and rules for a thousand years. He establishes peace, enforces righteousness and restores the physical creation. After his reign, those who did not die in Christ are raised and judged according to their deeds. Earth and heaven are dissolved, and those who are granted eternal life will live on a new earth. Death will be no more.

Daniel was told that the end of the age for the Jews would consist of 7 years split into two three-and-a-half-year periods. The first of these were the years AD 26–30, when John the Baptist and the Messiah prophesied to the nation. Then came an interval elided in the prophecy when the Jewish people were mostly indifferent or hostile to what was offered and the gospel went out beyond Judaea. The second half of the 7 years, still to come, is the three-and-a-half-year period described in chapters 11 and 13 of Revelation. An interpretation of Daniel's prophecy is given at the end of this book.

Daniel indicated that there would also be a 7-year period for the Gentiles, when civilization would be chopped down like a tree and stripped bare, until men understood that the Most High was the supreme ruler. That period is interpreted to begin with the first trumpet and end with the final bowl of wrath, shortly after the 42 months of chapters 11 and 13.

How to read this book

Revelation is designed to be read sequentially, the earlier chapters cumulatively informing the later ones. The commentary is designed to be read the same way. The first time through, ignore the scriptural references in brackets, and if the first chapter seems difficult, persevere; the rest is easier. Then go back and read the commentary again, studiously look up the references, and use these as an aid to understanding the revelation of God which is in all Scripture. The appendices are also suitable for devotional study. Finally, just read the text (or even start with this if you have not read the book for a while). Spread the word. Hard times lie ahead, but the prophecy is intended to equip us for them. "Everyone who hears these words of mine and does them I will liken to a wise man who built his house on the rock. And the rain fell, and the floods came, and the winds blew and beat on that house, but it did not fall, because it was founded on the rock."

Author's Testimony

My father was half-English, half-Welsh, my mother Dutch. They met a few years after the war in Exeter youth-hostel, he a customs officer, she a nurse. I was born in 1954. Soon afterwards we moved to the Isle of Man, then an idyllic place for a new family. The sea was close by, and not much further were the mountains, clad in bracken, gorse and heather. A few hundred yards along the road was a small farm, which for me meant cows, haystacks in the summer, the daily sound of a cockerel crowing. The Customs House where my father worked and where I sometimes passed by after school overlooked the harbor. Although the industry was in decline, fishing boats still trawled for herring and other fish, small cargo ships delivered coal, and for a few years there was the added interest of offshore Radio Caroline. In the shops people knew who you were and had time to chat.

At the age of eleven I went to a boarding school in the south of the island. I was a bright boy, and my parents thought that the fees, mitigated by a scholarship, would be money well spent. But I was deeply unhappy, suddenly wrenched from home and thrown into the constant society of boys much more gregarious and worldly-wise than I. In letters home I expressed my misery. My parents urged, "Persevere a little longer, and if you are still unhappy, we'll take you away." Gradually I got used to the regime, and in my fourth year began to enjoy it. We had chapel every morning, I sang in the choir, and at age 14 I got confirmed, not knowing that I had never been baptized. Subsequently I went through a religious phase, but heard nothing about the personal knowledge of God called conversion. I left school an atheist.

After a year off, I went to university and studied English Literature. My supervisor at Cambridge was something of a free spirit (he never dined at high table), imparted his love of Shakespeare and taught me to read intelligently and avoid cliché. The college chaplain, who doubled as my "tutor" and was devoting what time he could to a commentary on Revelation, kept a kindly eye on me but had no effect on my somewhat bolshie temperament. I remember some dark months when I was overwhelmed by the realization that one day I would die. Ultimately, even the Earth would die, the Sun swelling into a red giant and gobbling it up. As existentialist novelists said, life was ultimately meaningless. Some time later a student in the year and floor above introduced me to the philosopher Friedrich Nietzsche, famous for pronouncing God dead. I found Nietzsche's aphoristic writing intoxicating. He used the word "life" in a way which seemed to reclaim some meaning.

After graduating I spent fifteen months in Mainz, teaching English and learning something of West Germany's language and culture. In 1977 I returned to Cambridge. In an effort to understand the wisdom reached by humanity's best minds, I dipped into the writings of other philosophers. I felt out-of-place in modern society and did not know what to do for a living. I spent three years translating into English hexameter the satires of Juvenal, a Roman poet of the 2nd century AD. Almost as soon as the work was published (in 1983), I became deeply dissatisfied with it. I also attended Peter Jones's newly launched *Reading Greek* course.

I lodged for several years with a single Christian lady, who had a strong, quiet faith. At the back was a vegetable plot, a few flowers, and an apple tree. What was this thing "life," I mused, as bees buzzed in the sunshine. The idea that it was no more than highly organized atoms seemed false: I was a conscious being; animals were conscious beings. And where did the beauty of the flowers come from? As part of my program of self-education, I read one of the gospels, and to my surprise began thinking, "I agree with what this man was saying." Then came another thought: "If you do, doesn't that entail that you accept what he said about himself?" I replied, "I suppose that follows." It was a dim dawning. I didn't agree with everything in the New Testament, and my basic line was, "I'll decide what is true or not." As when Jesus called his first disciples, the cross, repentance, the Spirit, came later.

Soon afterwards, in February 1980, Billy Graham held a mission in the city and I went along, now content to call myself a Christian. His words made no impression, but at the end of the meeting a volunteer from the Round Church engaged me in conversation and asked me where I stood spiritually. I said, "There's no need to concern yourself;

I'm already a Christian." He asked whether I went to a church. "No, not regularly—here at St Mary's, now and again." He asked for my name and address, and a few days later paid a visit. I was out, but on learning that he had taken the trouble to look me up, I decided that Sunday to try his church, a more evangelical fellowship than the university church. Over time I fell in with others my age, joined a home group and discovered that there were intelligent people who believed that the Bible was, as they put it, the inspired Word of God.

I struggled with this. Reading through the Bible, I wrestled with four questions: (1) Did the world come into existence by creation, (2) Could God foretell the future, (3) Was there such a being as the Devil, and (4) How could one possibly accept the book of Revelation? About six months into my journey I again had a thought that did not seem mine: "Come, are you setting yourself as judge over God, dismissing as untrue whatever you don't like or understand, or will you submit to the mind of God and let him judge you?" That proved a pivotal moment. Convicted, I accepted that the Bible was his definitive revelation of himself and ceased to set myself over it. Christ, I saw, was the Word in his own person: to know one was to know the other. The more difficult passages began to open up—even Revelation to some extent. I began to address God as "Lord." Eleven years after being confirmed, I got baptized.

Another significant event was a visit by Dr Arthur Jones, a biologist by training but then working as a missionary. Over one weekend he held a series of seminars at St Matthew's in which he argued that scientific evidence for creation—for biological design, for discontinuities in the fossil record—was plentiful. I lapped it up. The perception that the Earth was not billions of years old was like a second conversion. The world suddenly took on a new appearance: everything was God's handiwork, albeit hugely changed from its original state. God was not distant. Just as the beginning of the world was not billions of years in the past, neither was the end of the age billions of years in the future.

Unknowingly I had embarked on a long odyssey into the unknown. At school, history had been a subject dropped at the earliest opportunity; now, as I learned that God was directing it towards some final goal, I was gripped by it. Surrounded by libraries, I acquainted myself with the course of the major civilizations—Egypt, Crete, Greece, Rome, Europe— and tried to understand what each one, as it came to an end, passed on to its successor. In each case I thought three phases could be discerned, one in which a distinct people settled in a new land, another in which they explored the world of the spirit, and a third in which reason superseded spirit and reached a dead-end. Exhausted, the civilization was eventually judged. But the work came to nothing, and my failure to get it published, on top of the collapse of an engagement to be married, hit me hard. I was to go through a very similar crisis twenty years later.

I was a sensitive, emotionally immature young man, and it took me a long time to settle to any sort of career. Penniless and spiritually adrift, I got a job inspecting business VAT records. Two years later I started a three-year program to train as a tax inspector.

In my spare time I became interested in problems of Egyptian chronology and how these affected the reconstruction of histories only known from archeological remains. In this field the main workers were Peter James and David Rohl, the latter building on the work of John Bimson. Bimson had demonstrated that the destructions in Palestine near the end of the Middle Bronze Age closely matched the conquest of Canaan in the Hebrew record, with the consequence that the Exodus was better dated to the 15th century than the 13th. James and co-authors argued that the misdating of Egypt's Third Intermediate Period had resulted in Palestine's archeology being misaligned with the Hebrew record by over two hundred years. Rohl made a similar case in relation to Egypt's Second Intermediate Period. All these authors were raising important and fascinating questions. The academic establishment, however, resisted their proposals, and there was little scope for me to contribute.[1]

Going back in time, I began to explore the human fossil record. Could everything in the historical and prehistoric record up to the present day truly be squeezed into just 5000 years, as some were teaching? I did not see that it could. Through the forest of my own ignorance I hacked further back, into geological periods before the oldest human fossils. How did they all relate to the biblical record? I was helped in this by three Christian geologists who were asking much the same question and took me along on field trips. While, like all creationists, they believed that Noah's Flood—called the Cataclysm in the New Testament—had to be an important part of the answer, they did not accept that all fossils could have formed then. Much of the record consisted of trace fossils— burrows, tracks, nests—showing that animals were very much alive at the time. Worse still, the traces might be in sediments miles above the level where the pre-Flood world was purportedly located. How could those

---

1. I have set out what I consider the correct solution in "Bronze and Iron Age Chronology Recalibrated."

animals have been living seemingly normal lives after that amount of sediment had been dumped on their world? What about the fossil reefs occurring at various levels, the oyster beds, the roots and tree stumps buried in growth position, the vast deposits of oil and coal? Reluctant to conclude that fossils had nothing to do with the Flood, they proposed that some formed then, whereas others resulted from residual catastrophism after the Flood. I was impressed by their arguments, and persuaded the then editor of Creation Ministries International's *Technical Journal* to devote a special issue to the new interpretation. That was in 1996. About the same time I started going on field trips run by a small consultancy company in the Pyrenees. From this very different perspective I learned about mountain uplift and denudation as the Iberian plate rotated anti-clockwise into Eurasia. I learned how it was possible to infer from the bedforms, grain size and associated fossils the environment in which the sediments formed. I saw plant roots extending into dried-up channels, *in-situ* coral and bivalve reefs, a dinosaur nesting site littered with egg fragments, dinosaur footprints.

I wrote several articles for the *Technical Journal*. In retrospect it was like a blind man trying to lead the blind; except that part of me knew I was blind. As I sought to become better informed, I began to question some tenets of creationism. If fossils formed during the Flood and the Flood was a judgement on humanity, why at the base of the record were there no human remains: buildings and other artifacts, as well as bones? Why were the fossilized terrestrial animals so different from those of the modern world if today's animals descended from those on the ark? Why did the first four-fifths of the sedimentary record consist of rocks barren of fossils apart from microbes and algae? Why should any fossils be expected if, according to Genesis, all animal life had been obliterated and not simply destroyed? However, dialogue proved impossible, and my concerns were rebuffed. Even my British geologist friends did not wish to ditch the paradigm completely.

Rightly or wrongly, I felt God saying: "Brush the dust off your feet and move on. The subject is important, but you will need to research it alone." Eventually, I came to a radically different interpretation of the rock record. In summary, this: In the beginning the Earth was created with a deep subterranean ocean, from which springs watered the land. The rate of radioactive decay was then much faster than today. Over time the heat from this radioactivity caused the interiors of the rocky planets to melt. Either their surfaces became completely drowned in upwelling magma (Mercury, Venus and Mars) or, in the case of bodies larger than the Earth, they exploded and ended up as asteroids. Even the ancient gray-white rocks of the Moon gave evidence of a magma ocean. Within the Earth, however, the deep acted as a buffer. Eventually, under the thermal pressure the springs of the deep exploded and overwhelmed the land (Gen 7:11). Simultaneously, fragments of the planet formerly between the orbits of Mars and Jupiter pounded Earth and its satellite. God destroyed the original land and, as with the other planets, resurfaced it with volcanic rock. Some of Earth's oldest rocks were sedimentary, showing that the planet straight after the Cataclysm was covered by water. The impact sites became the granitic cores of new land, and since these were less dense than the basaltic rocks around them, they gradually emerged above the water. Slowly life began to recover, marine life first, then terrestrial, as the animals preserved on the ark multiplied and spread abroad. Fossils told the story of that recovery: large-scale, pre-programmed, within-phylum multiplication of species, diversifying as they adapted to environments that were ever changing. In that limited sense they evolved. Animals did not appear until the last fifth of the sedimentary record because time as measured by radioactivity was continually slowing down. In real time the last fifth was much longer than the preceding four fifths.

Thus, much of the story presented by orthodox geology was sound. The points on which I dissented were the vast timescale, the origin of the solar system's asteroids, the definition of life so as to exclude consciousness (spirit), and the idea that all forms of life evolved from a single ancestor. These were matters of interpretation rather than fact. Since no extant rocks, on Earth or on any other planet, went back to the Creation, creation in six days was not problematic. Nothing that could be sampled and analysed in the lab went back that far.

Perhaps the greatest implication of accepting that Genesis was true was the recognition that science (natural philosophy) really was in conflict with religion (scriptural revelation), as the Bible more or less said (1 Cor 3:18–20). Scientists were not exempted from the condition of being "darkened in their understanding, alienated from the life of God." Geology, evolutionary biology and cosmology were philosophically committed to the belief that matter was all there is and that the world was capable of creating itself. The law of increasing entropy was thought somehow not to apply to the story of life. To suppose therefore that scientists reasoned impartially regarding questions of origin was naive. The one thing they were not skeptical about was their own atheism.

That said, the questions thrown up by geology, biology and cosmology are complex, and anyone inquiring into them needs to be more than ordinarily honest, curious, careful, open to the thoughts of others, willing to test all things and willing to face head-on whatever resists one's favored hypothesis. The Bible does not provide any short-cut to scientific understanding. Along the way I myself made many mistakes and wrong assumptions.

It is a hopeless situation. Christians working professionally in these fields accept the story advanced by their atheistic colleagues, since science cannot lie, but stress that the world at least had a beginning in the Big Bang. Bishops and theologians believe and pass on what the scientists tell them. When they say that "man was created in the image of God," they mean that man became like God in certain non-physical respects by a process of evolution. Those who believe that the story is deeply flawed are left to argue their case from the sidelines, without the expertise and procedures of validation that universities provide. Commercial publishers not unreasonably prefer the work they handle to be academically accredited, so dissenters are forced to self-publish and, since they cannot agree with each other, the naturalistic world-view prevails without credible opposition. Nor does it help that conservative churches discourage difficult questions for fear of impiety, and embarrassed that they do not have the answers. Christian culture has become more anti-intellectual as it has become more marginalized.

At a conference in 1998 I met Anthony Bush. He had sensed a call to convert part of his farm into a zoo that would tell the story of Noah's Flood, and was about to open it, but now I, a believer in creation, was arguing that the creationist explanation of Earth history ought to be abandoned. Disconcerting though this was, he listened, asked questions, and gradually came round. As the zoo grew, he designed, with my help, posters promoting a "recolonization" explanation of the fossil record and displayed them on the walls. Most importantly, he sponsored the design and running costs of a website (earthhistory.org.uk) which set out the arguments in more detail. In his autobiography *Building Noah's Ark* Anthony hailed me as a "modern Galileo." Be that as it may—he was, with one exception, a lone voice in that respect—his belief that sooner or later the new account of Earth history would be vindicated was an encouragement. Meanwhile the zoo went from strength to strength, despite various campaigns to have the business closed down. In 2018 Anthony retired. His successor took down the posters.

In 2001 I joined one of the "Big 4" accountancy firms and dropped to a 3-day week. On the other days I began investigating the tradition about the confusion of language. This was another important moment in the biblical narrative. Again I was fortunate to have access to specialist books and journals, mostly at the Bodleian. I concluded, after several years, that the event was linguistically and archeologically well supported. The historical setting was the end of the Late Uruk period, carbon-dated to c. 3200 BC, by which time Uruk was the dominant city-state in Mesopotamia and ruled by a "mighty man" depicted as a hunter and tamer of lions. Under him the cities were uniting to become the world's first empire, extending even into Egypt and ancient Iran, and at Babylon (*Babel* in Hebrew) men were building its capital. They got as far as to construct a brick tower with a stairway and a gate at the top, inviting God to come down and bless the work.

God did come down, but not to bless. He disrupted the project by causing each clan to speak a different language. Forced to disperse, the builders turned the judgement on its head. They told the peoples that their occult powers and languages had come from God: they were apostles sent to civilize the earth, and those who learned their heavenly languages would be similarly anointed. Thus originated the earth's linguistic macrofamilies, around two dozen in total, within which evolutionary variation (e.g. diverging pronunciation) and degradation (loss of grammatical complexity) gradually produced the 6000 languages spoken in modern times. Only the Afro-Asiatic macrofamily predated the confusion. Perhaps the strongest evidence for the event was the co-existence in Mesopotamia c. 2500 BC of two completely unrelated languages, Akkadian and Sumerian. Within 800 miles of Babel there were no fewer than eight unrelated languages.

It was obvious by this time that I needed academic credentials more relevant to these fields of research, and that would entail going back to university. I inquired about the possibility at two such institutions. One cursorily dismissed my application. Royal Holloway University of London invited me for interview and, despite my age, took me in. Thus in 2008 I gave up paid employment and started a degree in geology. I learned a lot, though the new knowledge did not fundamentally disturb my understanding of Earth history. Three years later I commenced postgraduate research at University College London into the evidence for "Snowball

Earth," the purported glaciation of the whole planet shortly before the first appearance of animal fossils. I completed the doctorate in 2016.

In 2018 a friend lent me a book on biblical prophecy, focusing particularly on the last days. It provoked me into writing down my own thoughts on Revelation. My life story is undoubtedly a peculiar one, but it could be seen as one long preparation for the present work. Training in literary criticism (hermeneutics) enabled me to distinguish between the literal and metaphorical, among other skills. The experience of translating Latin verse impressed on me the importance of verbal accuracy. Acquaintance with the cultures of Rome and the Ancient Near East, which were part of the Bible's cultural world, sensitized me to the dangers of reading the Old Testament and Revelation as if they were modern texts. My interest in science enabled me to recognize that many of the phenomena described in Revelation were natural phenomena. And most critically, my understanding of what happened geologically at the end of the Hadean impressed on me how God might be prepared once again to bring the world to a dreadful end. When it comes to the last things, theology cannot remain divorced from science, any more than, with respect to the first things, science should isolate itself from theology.

REVELATION OF JOHN

1 A revelation of Jesus Christ, which God gave him to show to his servants what must happen speedily. And he communicated it by sending through his angel to his servant John, [2]who bore witness to the word of God and the testimony of Jesus Christ, to everything that he saw. [3]Blessed is he who reads and those who hear the words of this prophecy and keep what is written in it, for the time is near.

[4]John to the seven churches that are in Asia: Grace to you and peace from who is, and who was, and who is to come, and from the seven spirits before his throne, [5]and from Jesus Christ the faithful witness, the firstborn of the dead, and the ruler of the kings of the earth.

To him who loves us and has washed us of our sins in his blood [6]and made us a kingdom, priests to his God and father, to him be glory and dominion for ever and ever. Amen. [7]Behold, he is coming with the clouds, and every eye will see him. So will those who pierced him. And all the tribes of the earth will wail because of him. Yes. Amen.

[8]"I am the Alpha and the Omega," says the Lord God, "who is, and who was, and who is to come. The Almighty."

[9]I, John, your brother and partner in the tribulation and kingdom and endurance of Jesus Christ, was on the island called Patmos on account of the word of God and the testimony of Jesus Christ. [10]I went into the spirit on the Lord's day, and I heard behind me a voice, loud as a trumpet, [11]saying, "Write what you see in a book and send it to the seven churches, to Ephesus, to Smyrna, to Pergamum, to Thyatira, to Sardis, to Philadelphia and to Laodicea."

[12]And I turned to see the voice that was speaking to me. And on turning I saw seven golden lampstands, [13]and in the midst of the seven lampstands one like a son of man, clothed in a robe, girt toward his breasts with a golden belt, [14]and his head and hair white as wool, white as snow, and his eyes like a flame of fire, [15]and his feet like burnished bronze, glowing as in a furnace, and his voice like the sound of many waters, [16]and in his right hand seven stars, and issuing

from his mouth a sharp two-edged sword, and his face like the sun shining in its power.

[17]And when I saw him, I fell at his feet as though dead. And he laid his hand on me, saying, "Do not fear. I am the first and the last, [18]and the living one, and I became dead, and behold, I am alive for ever and ever, and I have the keys of Death and Hades. [19]Therefore write down what you have seen, and what is, and what is to happen after this. [20]As for the mystery of the seven stars that you saw on my hand and the seven golden lampstands, the seven stars are angels of the seven churches, and the seven lampstands are seven churches.

2 "To the angel of the church in Ephesus write: 'Thus says the one who holds the seven stars in his right hand, who walks in the midst of the seven golden lampstands.

[2]" 'I know your works, and your toil, and your endurance, and how you cannot suffer bad people, and have tested those who call themselves apostles and are not and have found them to be false. [3]You have endurance, and you have suffered for my name's sake, and have not grown weary. [4]But I have this against you, that you have abandoned the love that you first had. [5]Remember therefore from whence you have fallen and repent, and do as you did first. If not, I will come to you soon and remove your lampstand from its place. Unless you repent. [6]But this you have, that you hate the works of the Nicolaitans, which I also hate.

[7]" 'He who has an ear, let him hear what the Spirit says to the churches. To him who conquers I will give to eat from the tree of life, which is in the paradise of God.'

[8]"And to the angel of the church in Smyrna write: 'Thus says the first and the last, who became dead and lived.

[9]" 'I know your works and your tribulation and your poverty—but you are rich—and the slander of those who say they are Jews and are not, but are a synagogue of Satan. [10]Do not fear what you are going to suffer. Behold, the Devil is going to cast some of you into prison, so that you may be tested, and for ten days you will have tribulation. Be faithful unto death, and I will give you the crown of life.

[11]" 'He who has an ear, let him hear what the Spirit says to the churches. The one who conquers will not be hurt by the second death.'

[12]"And to the angel of the church in Pergamon write: 'Thus says the one who has the sharp two-edged sword.

[13]" 'I know your works, and where you dwell, where Satan's throne is; and you hold fast my name. And you did not deny my faith even in the days of Antipas my faithful witness, who was killed in your midst, where Satan dwells.

[14]But I have a few things against you: you have some there holding the teaching of Balaam, who taught Balak to put a stumbling block before the sons of Israel, to eat food sacrificed to idols and to fornicate. [15]So you too have some holding the teaching of the Nicolaitans, which I likewise hate. [16]Repent, therefore. If not, I will come to you soon and war against them with the sword of my mouth.

[17]" 'He who has an ear, let him hear what the Spirit says to the churches. To him who conquers I will give of the hidden manna, and I will give him a white pebble, and on the pebble a new name written which no one knows except the one who receives it.'

[18]"And to the angel of the church in Thyatira write: 'Thus says the Son of God, whose eyes are like a flame of fire, and his feet like burnished bronze.

[19]" 'I know your works, and your love and faith and ministry and endurance, and that your latest works exceed your first. [20]But I have this against you, that you tolerate the woman Jezebel, she who calls herself a prophetess, and she is teaching and deceiving my servants to fornicate and eat food sacrificed to idols. [21]I gave her time to repent of her fornication, and she did not repent. [22]Behold, I will cast her onto a bed and those who commit adultery with her into great tribulation, unless they repent of her works. [23]And I will kill her children with pestilence, and all the churches will know that I am he who searches the inward parts and will give to you each according to your works. [24]To you I say, the others in Thyatira who do not support this teaching, those who have not known what some call the deep things of Satan, I do not cast on you any other burden. [25]Only hold fast what you have until I come.

[26]" 'The one who conquers and who keeps my works until the end, to him I will give authority over the nations. [27]And he will shepherd them with a rod of iron, as when earthen pots are smashed, even as I myself have received from my father. [28]And I will give him the morning star. [29]He who has an ear, let him hear what the Spirit says to the churches.'

3 "And to the angel of the church in Sardis write: 'Thus says the one who has the seven spirits of God and the seven stars.

" 'I know your works, that you have a name for being alive and are dead. [2]Be vigilant, and strengthen the remainder, what was about to die, for I have not found your works sufficient before my God. [3]Remember therefore how you received and heard. Keep it, and repent. If you are not vigilant, I will come upon you like a thief, and the hour I come upon you will take you unawares. [4]Yet you have a few names in Sardis who have not soiled their garments, and they will walk with me in white, for they are worthy.

[5]" 'The one who conquers will be clothed in white garments, and truly I will not wipe out his name from the book of life, and I will confess his name before my father and before his angels. [6]He who has an ear, let him hear what the Spirit says to the churches.'

[7]"And to the angel of the church in Philadelphia write: 'Thus says the one who is holy, who is true, who has the key of David, who opens and no one will shut, and shuts and no one opens.

[8]" 'I know your works: behold, I have set before you an open door, which no one can shut. Because you have little power and have kept my word, and have not denied my name, [9]behold, I will cause those from the synagogue of Satan who say they are Jews and are not, but lie—behold, I will make them come and bow down at your feet, and know that I have loved you. [10]Because you have kept my word of endurance, I will keep you from the hour of trial that is coming on the whole world to try the inhabitants of the earth. [11]I am coming soon. Hold fast what you have, so that no one takes your crown.

[12]" 'The one who conquers, I will make him a pillar in the temple of my God, and never shall he go out of it. And I will write on him the name of my God, and the name of the city of my God, the new Jerusalem, which comes down out of heaven from my God, and my own new name. [13]He who has an ear, let him hear what the Spirit says to the churches.'

[14]"And to the angel of the church in Laodicea write: 'Thus says the Amen, the faithful and true witness, the beginning of the creation of God.

[15]" 'I know your works: you are neither cold nor hot. Would that you were either cold or hot! [16]So, because you are lukewarm, and neither hot nor cold, I am going to spew you out of my mouth. [17]For you say, I am rich, I have become rich and need nothing, and do not realize that you are wretched, and pitiable, and poor, and blind, and naked. [18]I counsel you to buy from me gold refined by fire, so that you may become rich, and white garments, so that you may clothe yourself and the shame of your nakedness not be apparent, and salve to anoint your eyes, so that you may see. [19]Those whom I love, I reprove and discipline. Be zealous therefore, and repent. [20]Behold, I stand at the door and knock. If anyone hears my voice and opens the door, I will come in to him and dine with him, and he with me.

[21]" 'The one who conquers I will grant to sit with me on my throne, as I also conquered and sat with my Father on his throne. [22]He who has an ear, let him hear what the Spirit says to the churches.' "

4 After these things I looked, and behold, an open door in heaven, and the trumpet-like voice that I first heard spoke to me, saying, "Come up, and I

will show you what must happen after this." ²At once I was in spirit, and behold, a throne stood in heaven, and one seated on the throne, ³and the one seated similar in appearance to diamond and carnelian, and a rainbow encircling the throne similar in appearance to emerald, ⁴and encircling the throne twenty-four thrones, and seated on the twenty-four thrones twenty-four elders, clothed in white garments, with golden crowns on their heads. ⁵And from the throne issue lightning, and sounds, and thunder; and before the throne seven lamps of fire burning, which are the seven spirits of God; ⁶also before the throne what seemed to be a glass sea, like crystal. And in the midst of the throne and around the throne, four living beings, full of eyes in front and behind: ⁷the first like a lion, the second like a calf, the third having the face of a man, the fourth like an eagle flying. ⁸And the four living beings, each with six wings, are full of eyes all around and within. And they have no rest, day and night, saying,

> "Holy, holy, holy is the Lord God, the Almighty,
>   who was, and is, and is to come!"

⁹And when the living beings will offer glory, and honor, and thanksgiving to the one seated on the throne who lives for ever and ever, ¹⁰the twenty-four elders will fall down before the one seated on the throne and worship him who lives for ever and ever and cast their crowns before the throne, saying,

> ¹¹"Worthy are you, our Lord and God,
>   to receive glory, and honor, and power,
> because you created all things,
>   and by your will they existed and were created."

5 And I saw in the right hand of the one seated on the throne a scroll, with writing inside and out, sealed up with seven seals. ²And I saw a mighty angel proclaiming with a loud voice, "Who is worthy to open the scroll and break its seals?" ³And no one in heaven, or on earth, or under the earth was able to open the scroll, nor to look at it. ⁴And I wept much because no one was found worthy to open the scroll, nor to look at it. ⁵And one of the elders says to me, "Do not weep. Behold, the Lion who is from the tribe of Judah, the Root of David, has conquered, to open the scroll and its seven seals."

⁶And I saw in the midst of the throne and the four living beings and in the midst of the elders a lamb standing, as one slaughtered, with seven horns and with seven eyes, which are the seven spirits of God sent into all the earth. ⁷And he came and took the scroll from the right hand of him who was seated on the throne. ⁸And when he had taken the scroll, the four living beings and the

twenty-four elders fell down before the lamb, each holding a lyre and golden bowls full of incense, which are the prayers of the saints. ⁹And they sing a new song, saying,

> "Worthy are you to take the scroll and open its seals,
> for you were slaughtered,
> and you purchased us for God by your blood
> from every tribe, language, people and nation,
> ¹⁰and you made them for our God kings and priests,
> and they will reign on earth."

¹¹And I looked, and around the throne and the living beings and the elders I heard the voice of many angels, numbering myriads of myriads and thousands of thousands, ¹²saying with a loud voice, "Worthy is the Lamb who was slaughtered to receive power and riches and wisdom and strength and honor and glory and blessing!"

¹³And I heard every creature in the heaven and on the earth and under the earth and on the sea, all that is in them, say, "To him who sits on the throne and to the Lamb, blessing and honor and glory and dominion for ever and ever!"

¹⁴And the four living beings said, "Amen!" And the elders fell down and worshiped.

6 And I looked as the Lamb opened one of the seven seals. And I heard one of the four living beings say with a voice like thunder, "Come!" ²And I looked, and behold, a white horse. And its rider had a bow, and a crown was given to him, and he went out conquering and in order to conquer.

³And when he opened the second seal, I heard the second living being say, "Come!" ⁴And there went out another horse, fiery red. And it was given to the rider to take peace from the earth, so that men should slaughter one another, and he was given a great sword.

⁵And when he opened the third seal, I heard the third living being say, "Come!" And I looked, and behold, a black horse. And its rider had a pair of scales in his hand. ⁶And I heard a voice in the midst of the four living beings say, "A quart of wheat for a denarius, and three quarts of barley for a denarius! And do not harm the oil and the wine."

⁷And when he opened the fourth seal, I heard the voice of the fourth living being, saying, "Come!" ⁸And I looked, and behold, a pale horse. And its rider's name was Death, and Hades followed close behind. And they were given authority over a fourth of the earth, to kill with sword and with famine and with pestilence and by the beasts of the earth.

⁹And when he opened the fifth seal, I saw under the altar the souls of those slaughtered for the word of God and for the testimony they had borne. ¹⁰And they cried with a loud voice, "How long, Master, holy and true, before you judge and avenge our blood on the inhabitants of the earth?" ¹¹And each was given a white robe, and they were told to rest a little longer, until the number of both their fellow servants and their brothers should be fulfilled who were to be killed as they had been.

¹²And when he opened the sixth seal, I looked, and there was a great earthquake, and the sun became black like hair sackcloth, and the full moon became like blood, ¹³and the stars of heaven fell to the earth as when a fig tree sheds its unripe fruit on being shaken by a gale, ¹⁴and the heaven disappeared like a scroll being rolled up, and every mountain and island was moved from its place. ¹⁵And the kings of the earth, the great ones, the generals, the rich, the strong, every slave and free man, hid themselves in the caves and among the rocks of the mountains, ¹⁶calling to the mountains and the rocks, "Fall on us and hide us from the face of the one seated on the throne and from the wrath of the Lamb, ¹⁷for the great day of his wrath has come, and who is able to stand?"

7 After this I saw four angels standing at the four corners of the earth, controlling the four winds of the earth so that no wind might blow on the earth or on the sea or against any tree. ²And I saw another angel coming up from the rising of the sun, bearing the seal of the living God, and he cried with a loud voice to the four angels to whom it was given to harm the earth and the sea, ³saying, "Do not harm the earth or the sea or the trees until we have sealed the servants of our God on their foreheads." ⁴And I heard the number of the sealed, 144,000, sealed from every tribe of the sons of Israel:

> ⁵12,000 from the tribe of Judah sealed,
> 12,000 from the tribe of Reuben,
> 12,000 from the tribe of Gad,
> ⁶12,000 from the tribe of Asher,
> 12,000 from the tribe of Naphtali,
> 12,000 from the tribe of Manasseh,
> ⁷12,000 from the tribe of Simeon,
> 12,000 from the tribe of Levi,
> 12,000 from the tribe of Issachar,
> ⁸12,000 from the tribe of Zebulun,
> 12,000 from the tribe of Joseph,
> 12,000 from the tribe of Benjamin sealed.

⁹After these things I looked, and behold, a great throng which no one could number, from every nation and tribes and peoples and languages, standing

before the throne and before the Lamb, clothed in white robes, and with palm branches in their hands. [10]And they cry with a loud voice, "Salvation to our God who sits on the throne, and to the Lamb!" [11]And all the angels stood around the throne and around the elders and the four living beings, and fell on their faces before the throne and worshiped God, [12]saying, "Amen! Blessing, and glory, and wisdom, and thankfulness, and honor, and power, and strength to our God for ever and ever! Amen."

[13]And in answer one of the elders said to me, "These clothed in the white robes: who are they, and where have they come from?" [14]And I said to him, "My lord, you know."

And he said to me, "These are the ones coming out of the great tribulation. They have washed their robes and made them white in the blood of the Lamb. [15]Therefore they are before the throne of God, and minister to him day and night in his temple; and he who sits on the throne will shelter them. [16]They will hunger no more, nor thirst any more, nor will the sun, nor any heat, beat down on them; [17]for the Lamb in the midst of the throne will shepherd them, and he will lead them to fountains of waters of life. And God will wipe away every tear from their eyes."

8 And when he opened the seventh seal, there was silence in heaven for about half an hour.

[2]And I saw the seven angels who stand before God. And they were given seven trumpets. [3]And another angel came and stood at the altar with a golden censer, and he was given much incense to add to the prayers of all the saints at the golden altar before the throne. [4]And the smoke of the incense, with the prayers of the saints, went up from the hand of the angel before God. [5]And the angel took the censer and filled it with fire from the altar and cast it on the earth. And there occurred sounds, and thunder, and lightning, and an earthquake.

[6]And the seven angels who had the seven trumpets got ready to blow them.

[7]The first blew his trumpet, and there was hail and fire, mixed with blood, and these were cast on the earth. And a third of the earth was burned up, and a third of the trees were burned up, and all green grass was burned up.

[8]The second angel blew his trumpet, and something like a great mountain, burning with fire, was cast into the sea, and a third of the sea became blood. [9]And a third of the creatures in the sea died that had life, and a third of the ships were wrecked.

[10]The third angel blew his trumpet, and a great star fell from heaven, burning like a torch, and it fell on a third of the rivers and on the springs of the waters. [11]The name of the star is Wormwood. And a third of the water became

wormwood, and much of mankind died from the water, because it had been made bitter.

[12]The fourth angel blew his trumpet, and a third of the sun was struck, and a third of the moon, and a third of the stars, so that a third of them should be darkened and a third of the day should not shine, and the night likewise.

[13]And I looked, and I heard one eagle say with a loud voice as it flew overhead, "Woe, woe, woe to the inhabitants of the earth, at the sound of the other trumpets that the three angels are about to blow!"

9 And the fifth angel blew his trumpet, and I saw a star fallen from heaven to earth, and he was given the key to the shaft of the abyss. [2]And he opened the shaft of the abyss, and out of the shaft rose smoke like that of a great furnace, and the sun and the air were darkened by the smoke of the shaft. And out of the smoke came locusts onto the earth, [3]and they were given power like that of the earth's scorpions. [4]And they were told not to harm the grass of the earth or any green plant or any tree, but rather those of mankind who did not have the seal of God on their foreheads. [5]And it was given, not that they should kill them, but that they should torment them for five months. And their torment was like the torment of a scorpion when it stings a man. [6]And in those days men will seek death and fail to find it. They will long to die, and death will flee from them.

[7]And in appearance the locusts were like horses prepared for battle. And on their heads were what looked like crowns of gold, and their faces like human faces. [8]And they had hair like women's hair and teeth like those of lions. [9]And they had breastplates like breastplates of iron, and the sound of their wings was like the sound of many horse-drawn chariots rushing into battle. [10]And they have tails and stings like scorpions, and in their tails is their power to harm mankind for five months. [11]They have a king over them, the angel of the abyss. His name in Hebrew is Abaddon, and in Greek, Destroyer.

[12]The first woe has passed; behold, two woes are yet to come.

[13]And the sixth angel blew his trumpet, and I heard one voice from the four horns of the golden altar before God [14]say to the sixth angel who had the trumpet, "Release the four angels who are bound at the great river Euphrates." [15]So the four angels, who had been prepared for the hour, the day, the month and the year, were released to kill a third of mankind. [16]And the armies of the horsemen numbered two hundred million; I heard their number. [17]And this was the appearance of the horses and their riders in the vision: their breastplates were fiery and hyacinthine and sulfurous, and the heads of the horses were like lions' heads, and fire, smoke and sulfur came out of their mouths. [18]From these three plagues a third of mankind was killed, by the fire, smoke and sulfur coming out

of their mouths. [19]For the power of the horses is in their mouths and in their tails, for their tails are like snakes, having heads, and by them they harm.

[20]And the rest of mankind, who were not killed by these plagues, did not repent of the works of their hands so as not to worship the demons and the idols of gold and silver and bronze and stone and wood which cannot see nor hear nor walk. [21]And they did not repent of their murders, nor of their drug-taking, nor of their fornication, nor of their thefts.

10

And I saw another mighty angel coming down from heaven, wrapped in cloud, and the rainbow on his head, and his face like the sun, and his feet like pillars of fire, [2]and holding in his hand a little scroll, open. And he set his right foot on the sea and his left on the land, [3]and he cried with a loud voice, like a lion roaring. And as he cried, the seven thunders also gave voice. [4]And as the seven thunders spoke, I was about to write. And I heard a voice from heaven say, "Seal what the seven thunders have spoken, and do not write it down." [5]And the angel whom I saw standing on the sea and on the land raised his right hand to heaven [6]and swore by him who lives for ever and ever, who created the heaven and what is in it, the land and what is in it, and the sea and what is in it, that no more time would be given, [7]but in the days of the trumpet to be sounded by the seventh angel, the mystery of God would also have been fulfilled, as he announced to his servants the prophets.

[8]And the voice that I heard from heaven spoke to me again, saying, "Go, take the little scroll that is open in the hand of the angel standing on the sea and on the land." [9]So I went to the angel and said to him, "Give me the little scroll." And he says to me, "Take, and eat it up; it will make your stomach bitter, but in your mouth it will be as sweet as honey." [10]And I took the little scroll from the hand of the angel and ate it up. And it was as sweet as honey in my mouth. And when I ate it my stomach became bitter. [11]And he says to me, "You must again prophesy about many peoples and nations and languages and kings."

11

And I was given a rod-like reed, and told, "Rise, and measure the temple of God and the altar and those who worship in it, [2]and exclude the court outside the temple; do not measure it, for it was given to the nations, and they will tread the holy city for forty-two months.

[3]"And I will give to my two witnesses, and they will prophesy for 1260 days, clothed in sackcloth." [4]These are the two olive trees and the two lampstands that stand before the Lord of the earth. [5]And if anyone would harm them, fire issues from their mouth and consumes their enemies, and if anyone would harm them, thus must he be killed. [6]These have authority to shut the heaven, so that no rain falls during the days of their prophecy, and they have authority over the

waters to turn them into blood and to strike the earth with every kind of plague, as often as they will.

[7]And when they have finished their testimony, the beast that rises from the abyss will make war on them and conquer them and kill them, [8]and their corpse will lie on the street of the great city that is spiritually called Sodom and Egypt, where also their Lord was crucified. [9]And for three and a half days some from the peoples and tribes and languages and nations look at their corpse and refuse to let their corpses be placed in a tomb. [10]And the inhabitants of the earth rejoice over them and make merry and will send presents to one another, because these two prophets tormented the inhabitants of the earth.

[11]And after the three and a half days a breath of life from God entered them, and they stood on their feet, and great fear fell on those watching them. [12]And they heard a loud voice from heaven say to them, "Come up." And they ascended to heaven in the cloud, while their enemies watched. [13]And at that hour there was a great earthquake, and a tenth of the city fell, and seven thousand individuals were killed in the earthquake. And the rest became fearful and gave glory to the God of heaven.

[14]The second woe has passed; behold, the third woe is coming soon.

[15]And the seventh angel blew his trumpet. And there were loud voices in heaven, saying, "The kingdom of the world has become the kingdom of our Lord and of his Christ, and he shall reign for ever and ever."

[16]And the twenty-four elders who sat on their thrones before God fell on their faces and worshiped God, [17]saying, "We give thanks to you, Lord God, the Almighty, who is and who was, for you have taken your great power and reigned. [18]And the nations were wrathful, and your wrath came, and the time for the dead to be judged, and for paying the wages of your servants the prophets and the saints and those who fear your name, the small and the great, and for bringing to corruption the corrupters of the earth."

[19]And the temple of God in heaven was opened, and the ark of his covenant was seen in his temple. And there occurred lightning, and sounds, and thunder, and an earthquake, and great hail.

12 And a great sign appeared in heaven: a woman clothed with the sun, and the moon under her feet, and on her head a crown of twelve stars. [2]And being pregnant, she cries out in travail and torment of giving birth.

[3]And another sign appeared in heaven. And behold, a great red dragon, with seven heads and ten horns, and on his heads seven diadems. [4]And his tail drags a third of the stars of heaven, and he cast them to the earth.

And the dragon stood before the woman about to give birth, so that when she should bear her child he might devour it. [5]And she gave birth to a son, a male, who is to shepherd all the nations with a rod of iron. And her child was caught up to God and to his throne. [6]And the woman fled into the wilderness, where she has a place prepared by God, so that she may be nourished there 1260 days.

[7]And war arose in heaven. Michael and his angels warred with the dragon, and the dragon warred, and his angels, [8]and did not prevail, [9]and place was no longer found for them in heaven. And the great dragon was thrown, the ancient serpent who is called the Devil and Satan, the deceiver of the whole world—he was thrown to the earth, and his angels thrown with him. [10]And I heard a loud voice in heaven say, "Now has come the salvation and the power and the kingship of our God and the authority of his Christ, for the accuser of our brothers has been thrown down who accuses them day and night before our God. [11]They have conquered him by the blood of the Lamb and by the word of their testimony, and they did not love their lives unto death. [12]Therefore rejoice, you heavens and you who sojourn in them! Woe to the earth and the sea, for the Devil has come down to you in great fury, knowing that he has little time!"

[13]When the dragon saw that he had been thrown down to the earth, he pursued the woman who had given birth to the male. [14]And the woman was given the two wings of the great eagle, so that she might fly from the presence of the serpent to the wilderness, to her place, where she is nourished for a time, and times, and half a time. [15]And out of his mouth the serpent cast water like a river after the woman to carry her away. [16]And the earth helped the woman, and the earth opened its mouth and swallowed the river that the dragon cast out of his mouth. [17]And the dragon was angry with the woman and went off to make war on the rest of her offspring, on those who keep the commandments of God and have the testimony of Jesus.

13 And I stood on the sand of the sea. And I saw a beast coming up from the sea, with ten horns and seven heads, and with ten diadems on its horns and blasphemous names on its heads. [2]And the beast that I saw was like a leopard, and its feet like a bear's, and its mouth like the mouth of a lion. And to it the dragon gave his power and his throne, and great authority. [3]And one of its heads was as slaughtered to death, and its fatal wound was healed. And the whole earth marveled after the beast. [4]And they worshiped the dragon, because he gave his authority to the beast, and they worshiped the beast, saying, "Who is like the beast, and who can war against it?"

[5]And it was given a mouth speaking great things, and blasphemies. And it was given authority for it to exercise for forty-two months. [6]And it opened

its mouth to blaspheme against God, blaspheming his name and his tabernacle, those who sojourn in heaven. [7]And it was given to it to make war on the saints and conquer them. And it was given authority over every tribe and people and language and nation. [8]And all the inhabitants of the earth will worship it, those whose names have not been written in the book of life of the Lamb who was slaughtered from the foundation of the world.

[9]If anyone has an ear, let him hear. [10]If anyone is to be taken captive, to captivity he goes; if anyone kills with sword, with sword he must be killed. Herein is the endurance and the faith of the saints.

[11]And I saw another beast, coming up from the earth. And it had two horns like a lamb, and it spoke like a dragon. [12]It exercises all the authority of the first beast in its presence and makes the earth and its inhabitants worship the first beast, whose mortal wound was healed. [13]And it performs great signs, even making fire come down from heaven to earth in front of people. [14]And it deceives the inhabitants of the earth by the signs it was given to perform in the presence of the beast, telling the inhabitants of the earth to make an image for the beast that was wounded by the sword and lived. [15]And it was given to it to give breath to the image of the beast, so that the image of the beast might even speak and cause those who would not worship the image of the beast to be killed. [16]And it causes all—both the small and the great, the rich and the poor, the free and the slave—to give themselves a mark on their right hand or on their forehead, [17]so that no one can buy or sell unless he has the mark, the name of the beast or the number of its name. [18]Herein is wisdom. Let him who has understanding calculate the number of the beast, for it is a man's number, and his number is 666.

14 And I looked, and behold, the Lamb, standing on Mount Zion, and with him 144,000 who had his name and his father's name written on their foreheads. [2]And I heard a sound from heaven like the sound of many waters, and like the sound of loud thunder. And the sound I heard was like lyre-players playing on their lyres. [3]And they sing a new song before the throne and before the four living beings and the elders, and no one could learn the song except the 144,000 purchased from the earth. [4]These are the ones who did not defile themselves with women, for they are virgins. These are the ones who follow the Lamb wherever he goes. These were purchased from mankind as first-fruits for God and for the Lamb, [5]and in their mouth no falsehood was found, for they are blameless.

[6]And I saw another angel flying overhead, with eternal good news to deliver on those who were seated on the earth, and on every nation and tribe and language and people, [7]saying with a loud voice, "Fear God and give him glory,

because the hour of his judgement has come, and worship him who made the heaven and the earth, and sea and springs of water."

[8]And another, a second angel, followed, saying, "Fallen, fallen is Babylon the great, who made all the nations drink from the wine of her raging fornication."

[9]And another angel, a third, followed them, saying with a loud voice, "If anyone worships the beast and its image and receives a mark on his forehead or on his hand, [10]he himself will drink from the wine of the fury of God, served unmixed in the cup of his wrath. And he will be tormented with fire and sulfur before the holy angels and before the Lamb. [11]And the smoke of their torment goes up for ever and ever. And they have no rest, day and night, the worshipers of the beast and its image, and whoever receives the mark of its name."

[12]Herein is the endurance of the saints, those who keep the commandments of God and the faith of Jesus.

[13]And I heard a voice from heaven say, "Write: Blessed are the dead who die in the Lord from henceforth." "Yes," says the Spirit, "that they may rest from their labors. Their works follow them."

[14]And I looked, and behold, a white cloud, and seated on the cloud one like a son of man, with a golden crown on his head, and a sharp sickle in his hand. [15]And another angel came out of the temple, crying with a loud voice to the one seated on the cloud, "Send forth your sickle and reap, for the hour to reap has come, for the harvest of the earth is dried up." [16]So he who was seated on the cloud swung his sickle over the earth, and the earth was reaped.

[17]And another angel came out from the temple in heaven, he too holding a sharp sickle. [18]And another angel came out from the altar, having authority over the fire, and he called in a loud voice to the one who had the sharp sickle, "Send forth your sharp sickle and harvest the clusters of the vine of the earth, for its grapes are ripe." [19]So the angel swung his sickle across the earth and harvested the vine of the earth and threw it into the great winepress of the fury of God. [20]And the winepress was trodden outside the city, and blood flowed from the winepress up to the horses' bridles, for 1600 stadia.

15

And I saw another sign in heaven, great and wondrous: seven angels with seven plagues—the last, for with them the fury of God is finished.

[2]And I saw what seemed like a glass sea mingled with fire, and those conquering, from the beast and from its image and from the number of its name, standing on the glass sea holding lyres of God. [3]And they sing the song of Moses, servant of God, and the song of the Lamb, saying,

> "Great and wondrous are your deeds,
>   Lord God, the Almighty!

Just and true are your ways,
>> King of the nations!
[4]Who should not fear you, Lord,
>> and will not glorify your name?
For you alone are sinless;
>> for all nations will come and worship before you;
>> for your righteous acts have been manifested."

[5]And after these things I looked, and the temple of the tabernacle of the testimony in heaven was opened, [6]and out of the temple came the seven angels with the seven plagues, dressed in pure, bright linen, and with golden belts around their chests. [7]And one of the four living beings gave to the seven angels seven golden bowls full of the fury of God who lives for ever and ever. [8]And the temple was filled with smoke from the glory of God and from his power, and no one could enter the temple until the seven plagues of the seven angels had ended.

16 And I heard a loud voice from the temple telling the seven angels, "Go and pour out the seven bowls of the fury of God onto the earth."

[2]So the first went and poured out his bowl onto the earth, and a noxious and evil sore came on the people who had the mark of the beast and worshiped its image.

[3]And the second poured out his bowl onto the sea, and it became blood, like a corpse's, and every living soul died that was in the sea.

[4]And the third angel poured out his bowl onto the rivers and onto the springs of water, and they became blood.

[5]And I heard the angel of the waters say, "Righteous are you, who is, and who was, sinless one, for thus you have judged; [6]for they poured out the blood of saints and prophets and you have given them blood to drink. They are worthy of it." [7]And I heard the altar say, "Yes, Lord God the Almighty, true and just are your judgements!"

[8]And the fourth poured out his bowl on the sun, and it was given to it to scorch men with fire. [9]They were scorched by the great heat, and they reviled the name of God who had power over these plagues, and did not give him glory by repenting.

[10]And the fifth poured out his bowl on the throne of the beast, and his kingdom became dark. And they gnawed their tongues in pain [11]and reviled the God of heaven because of their pain and their sores, and they did not repent of their deeds.

[12]And the sixth poured out his bowl on the great river, the Euphrates. And its water was dried up to prepare the way for the kings from the rising of the sun.

[13]And I saw out of the mouth of the dragon and out of the mouth of the beast and out of the mouth of the false prophet three unclean spirits, like frogs. [14]For they are demonic spirits, performing signs that go out to the kings of the whole world to gather them for battle on the great day of God the Almighty. [15]("Behold, I am coming like a thief! Blessed is he who is vigilant and keeps his garments, lest he go about naked and be exposed to shame.") [16]And he gathered them at the place that is called in Hebrew Armageddon.

[17]And the seventh poured out his bowl on the air, and a loud voice came from the temple, from the throne, saying, "It is done!" [18]And there occurred lightning, and sounds, and thunder. And there was a great earthquake, such as has never been since man was on the earth, so great was that mighty quake. [19]And the great city split into three parts. The cities of the nations fell, and God remembered Babylon the Great to give her the cup of the wine of the fury of his wrath. [20]Every island fled, and mountains were not to be found. [21]And great hailstones about a hundred pounds weight come down from heaven on mankind. And they reviled God for the plague of the hail, because its plague is very great.

17 And there came one of the seven angels who had the seven bowls, and he spoke with me, saying, "Come here, I will show you the judgement of the great prostitute who is seated on the many waters, [2]with whom the kings of the earth have fornicated, and from the wine of whose fornication the inhabitants of the earth have become drunk." [3]And he carried me away in spirit to a wilderness, and I saw a woman seated on a scarlet beast that was full of blasphemous names and had seven heads and ten horns. [4]And the woman was clothed in purple and scarlet and gilded with gold and jewels and pearls, holding in her hand a golden cup full of abominations. And I saw the uncleanness of her fornication, [5]and on her forehead a name written, a mystery, "Babylon the Great, mother of prostitutes and of earth's abominations." [6]And the woman was drunk from the blood of the saints and from the blood of the witnesses of Jesus.

And I marveled greatly when I saw her. [7]And the angel said to me, "Why did you marvel? I will tell you the mystery of the woman, and of the beast carrying her, with its seven heads and ten horns. [8]The beast that you saw was, and is not, and is to rise from the abyss and go to destruction. And the inhabitants of the earth whose names have not been written in the book of life from the foundation of the world will marvel when they perceive the beast that was, and is not, and will arrive.

[9]"Herein the mind that has wisdom. The seven heads are seven mountains on which the woman is seated; [10]they are also seven kings, five of whom have fallen, one is, the other has not yet come, and when he does come he must remain

a little while. [11]The beast that was and is not, it is also an eighth but belongs to the seven, and goes to destruction. [12]And the ten horns that you saw are ten kings who have not yet received kingship, but will receive authority as kings for one hour together with the beast. [13]These are of one purpose, and give their power and authority to the beast. [14]These will make war on the Lamb, and the Lamb will conquer them, for he is Lord of lords and King of kings, and those with him are called, and chosen, and faithful."

[15]And he says to me, "The waters that you saw, where the prostitute is seated, are peoples and throngs, nations and languages. [16]And the ten horns that you saw, they and the beast will hate the prostitute, and will cause her to be laid waste, and naked, and will eat her flesh and burn her up with fire. [17]For God has put it into their hearts to carry out his purpose, and to be of one purpose, and to give their kingship to the beast until the words of God are fulfilled. [18]And the woman that you saw is the great city that has kingship over the kings of the earth."

18 After these things I saw another angel coming down from heaven, having great authority, and the earth was illumined from his glory. [2]And he cried with a mighty voice, "Fallen, fallen is Babylon the Great! She has become an abode of demons, and a prison of every unclean spirit, and a prison of every unclean and hated bird. [3]For all the nations have drunk from the wine of her raging fornication, and the kings of the earth have fornicated with her, and the merchants of the earth have got rich by the power of her luxury."

[4]And I heard another voice from heaven, saying,

> "Come out of her, my people,
>> lest you participate in her sins
>> and in her plagues you share;
> [5]for her sins have been glued together as far as heaven,
>> and God has remembered her iniquities.
> [6]Pay her back as she herself has paid back
>> and render double for her deeds;
>> in the cup she has mixed mix double for her.
> [7]As she glorified herself and lived in luxury,
>> in like measure give her torment and mourning,
> since in her heart she says,
>> "I sit a queen, no widow am I,
>> and mourning may I never see."
> [8]For this reason her plagues will come in a single day,
>> death, and mourning, and famine,
> and she will be burned up with fire,
>> for mighty is the Lord God who judged her."

[9]And the kings of the earth, who fornicated and lived in luxury with her, will weep and wail over her when they see the smoke of her burning, [10]standing far back for fear of her torment, and saying, "Woe, woe, the great city, Babylon the mighty city! For in a single hour your judgement has come."

[11]And the merchants of the earth weep and mourn for her, because no one buys their cargo anymore: [12]cargo of gold, and of silver, and of precious stones, and of pearls, and of fine linen, and of purple, and of silk, and of scarlet, and every aromatic wood, and every article of ivory, and every article of costly wood and of bronze and of iron and of marble, [13]and cinnamon, and cardamom, and incense, and myrrh, and frankincense, and wine, and oil, and fine flour, and wheat, and mules, and sheep, and of horses, and of carriages, and of bodies and souls of men.

[14]And the fruits which your soul desired are departed from you, and all the sumptuousness and the splendor are destroyed from you, and they will be found no more.

[15]The merchants who got rich from her will stand far back for fear of her torment, weeping and mourning, saying, [16]"Woe, woe, the great city that was clothed in fine linen, purple, and scarlet, and gilded with gold, and jewels, and pearls! [17]For in a single hour all this wealth has been laid waste."

And all shipmasters and seafarers and mariners and all who traded on the sea stood far back [18]and cried seeing the smoke of her burning, saying, "What compared with the great city?"

[19]And they threw dust on their heads and cried, weeping and mourning, saying, "Woe, woe, the great city, in which all who had ships at sea grew rich by her wealth! For in a single hour she has been laid waste." [20]Rejoice over her, heaven, and the saints, and the apostles, and the prophets, for God has passed your judgement on her!

[21]And one mighty angel took up a stone like a great millstone and threw it into the sea, saying, "Thus with violence will Babylon the great city be thrown down, and let it be found no more. [22]And let the sound of lyre-players and singers and pipers and trumpeters be heard in you no more, and craftsmen, of whatever craft, be found in you no more, and the sound of a mill be heard in you no more, [23]and the light of a lamp shine in you no more, and the voice of bridegroom and bride be heard in you no more! For your merchants were the great ones of the earth, for all the nations were deceived by your drug-dealing [24]And in her was found the blood of prophets and saints, and of all the slaughtered on the earth."

19 After these things I heard what seemed like the loud voice of a great throng in heaven, saying, "Alleluyah! The salvation and the glory and the power of our God! [2]For his judgements are true and just; for he has judged the great prostitute who was corrupting the earth with her fornication, and has avenged the blood of his servants from her hand." ³And a second time they cried, "Alleluyah! Her smoke goes up for ever and ever."

⁴And the twenty-four elders and the four living beings fell down and worshiped God who is seated on the throne, saying, "Amen. Alleluyah!" ⁵And a voice came from the throne, saying, "Praise our God, all his servants and all who fear him, the small and the great."

⁶And I heard what sounded like a great throng, like the sound of many waters, and like mighty thunder, saying, "Alleluyah! For the Lord God the Almighty has reigned. ⁷Let us rejoice, and exult, and give him glory, because the marriage of the Lamb has come, and his wife has made herself ready, ⁸and it was given her to clothe herself in fine linen, bright and pure. For the linen is the righteous acts of the saints."

⁹And he says to me, "Write this: Blessed are those who are invited to the marriage feast of the Lamb." And he says to me, "These are the true words of God." ¹⁰And I fell down at his feet to worship him. And he says to me, "Don't do that. I am a fellow servant with you and your brothers who have the testimony of Jesus. Worship God." For the testimony of Jesus is the spirit of prophecy.

¹¹And I saw heaven opened, and behold, a white horse, and its rider, called faithful and true, and in righteousness he judges and wars. ¹²His eyes were like a flame of fire, and on his head many diadems, and he had a name written which no one knew but himself, ¹³and he was clothed in a garment dipped in blood, and his name was called The Word of God. ¹⁴And the armies of heaven, dressed in fine linen, white and pure, were following him on white horses. ¹⁵And from his mouth issues a sharp sword with which to strike the nations, and he will shepherd them with a rod of iron. And he treads the winepress of the fury of the wrath of God the Almighty. ¹⁶And on his garment and on his thigh he has a name written, King of kings and Lord of lords.

¹⁷And I saw an angel standing in the sun, and he cried with a loud voice to all the birds flying overhead, "Come, gather for the banquet of God, ¹⁸to eat the flesh of kings, the flesh of captains, the flesh of mighty men, the flesh of horses and their riders, the flesh of everyone, both free and slave, small and great." ¹⁹And I saw the beast and the kings of the earth with their armies gathered to make war against the rider on the horse and against his army. ²⁰And the beast was captured, and with it the false prophet who had performed in its presence the signs by which he had deceived those who received the mark of the beast and worshiped its image. The two were thrown alive into the lake of fire that burns

with sulfur. [21]And the rest were killed by the sword that issued from the mouth of the rider on the horse, and all the birds filled themselves with their flesh.

20 And I saw an angel coming down from heaven, holding the key to the abyss and a great chain in his hand. [2]And he seized the dragon, the ancient serpent who is the Devil and Satan, and bound him for a thousand years [3]and threw him into the abyss, and shut and sealed it over him so that he should no more deceive the nations until the thousand years had ended. After this he must be released for a little while.

[4]And I saw thrones, and people sitting on them, and judgement was given to them, and the souls of those beheaded for the testimony of Jesus and for the word of God, and those who did not worship the beast or its image and did not receive its mark on their forehead and hand. And they lived, and reigned with the Christ for a thousand years. [5]The rest of the dead did not live until the thousand years had ended. This is the first resurrection. [6]Blessed and holy is he who has a share in the first resurrection. Over these the second death has no authority, but they will be priests of God and of Christ, and they will reign with him for a thousand years.

[7]And when the thousand years are ended, Satan will be released from his prison [8]and go out to deceive the nations at the four corners of the earth, Gog and Magog, to gather them for battle, their numbers like the sand of the sea. [9]And they went up over the breadth of the earth and surrounded the camp of the saints and the beloved city. And fire came down from heaven and consumed them, [10]and the Devil who deceived them was thrown into the lake of fire and sulfur where both the beast and the false prophet were. And they will be tormented day and night, for ever and ever.

[11]And I saw a great white throne and him who was seated on it, from whose presence the earth and the heaven fled, and no place was found for them. [12]And I saw the dead, the great and the small, standing before the throne of God, and books were opened. And another book was opened, that of life. And the dead were judged by what was written in the books, according to their works. [13]The sea gave up the dead that were in it, and Death and Hades gave up the dead that were in them, and they were judged, each according to their works. [14]And Death and Hades were thrown into the lake of fire. This is the second death, the lake of fire. [15]If anyone was not found written in the book of life, he was thrown into the lake of fire.

21 And I saw a new heaven and a new earth, for the first heaven and the first earth have gone, and the sea is no more.

²And I saw the holy city, new Jerusalem, coming down out of heaven from God, prepared as a bride adorned for her husband. ³And I heard a loud voice from heaven saying, "Behold, the tabernacle of God is with men, and he will sojourn with them, and they will be his peoples, and God himself will be with them, their God. ⁴And he will wipe away every tear from their eyes. Death will be no more; neither will there be mourning, or crying, or pain anymore; for the former things have gone."

⁵And he who was seated on the throne said, "Behold, I am making all things new." And he says, "Write, for these words are trustworthy and true." ⁶And he said to me, "It is done! I am the Alpha and the Omega, the beginning and the end. To the thirsty I will give from the spring of the water of life without payment. ⁷He who conquers will inherit these things, and I will be God to him and he will be a son to me. ⁸As for the cowardly, and faithless, and abominable, and murderers, and fornicators, and drug-dealers, and idolaters, and all liars, their share will be in the lake that burns with fire and sulfur, which is the second death."

⁹And there came one of the seven angels who had the seven bowls full of the seven last plagues, and he spoke to me, saying, "Come, I will show you the Bride, the wife of the Lamb." ¹⁰And he carried me away in spirit to a great mountain, and showed me the holy city Jerusalem, coming down out of heaven from God, ¹¹having the glory of God, her radiance resembling a precious jewel, like diamond, crystalline, ¹²and with a great, high wall, with twelve gates, and at the gates twelve angels, and names inscribed of the twelve tribes of the sons of Israel, ¹³to the east three gates, to the north three gates, to the south three gates, and to the west three gates, ¹⁴and the wall of the city having twelve foundations, and on them twelve names of the twelve apostles of the Lamb.

¹⁵And he who spoke with me had a golden reed with which to measure the city, and its gates, and its wall. ¹⁶The city lies foursquare, its length the same as its width. And he measured the city with the reed at 12,000 stadia. Its length and its width and its height are equal. ¹⁷He also measured its wall: 144 cubits, a man's measure being an angel's. ¹⁸And the structure of the wall was diamond, and the city pure gold, like clear glass. ¹⁹And the foundations of the wall of the city were adorned with every kind of jewel: the first foundation diamond, the second sapphire, the third agate, the fourth emerald, ²⁰the fifth onyx, the sixth carnelian, the seventh chrysolite, the eighth beryl, the ninth topaz, the tenth chrysoprase, the eleventh jacinth, the twelfth amethyst. ²¹And the twelve gates twelve pearls, each of the gates being of one pearl, and the street of the city pure gold, like pellucid glass.

²²And I saw no temple in the city, for the Lord God the Almighty is its temple, and the Lamb. ²³And the city has no need of the sun or the moon to shine on it, for the glory of God gave it light, and its lamp is the Lamb. ²⁴And the nations will walk by its light. And the kings of the earth bring their glory and honor into it. ²⁵And at no time will its gates be shut, for there will be no night there. ²⁶They will bring the glory and the honor of the nations into it. ²⁷And nothing common may enter it, nor anyone who does what is abominable or false, but only those who are written in the Lamb's book of life.

22 And he showed me a river of water of life, bright as crystal, flowing from the throne of God and of the Lamb, ²in the middle of its street; and on either side of the river a tree of life producing twelve fruits, each month yielding its fruit, and the leaves of the tree for healing of the nations. ³And there will be no curse anymore. And the throne of God and of the Lamb will be in it, and his servants will minister to him. ⁴And they will see his face, and his name will be on their foreheads. ⁵And night will be no more. They will need no lamp, or light of a sun, for the Lord God will illumine them, and they will reign for ever and ever.

⁶And he said to me, "These words are trustworthy and true. And the Lord God of the spirits of the prophets has sent his angel to show to his servants what must happen speedily. ⁷And behold, I am coming soon. Blessed is he who keeps the words of the prophecy of this book."

⁸I, John, am the one who heard and saw these things. And having heard and seen, I fell down to worship at the feet of the angel who showed them to me. ⁹And he says to me, "Don't do that. I am a fellow servant with you and your brothers the prophets, and with those who keep the words of this book. Worship God."

¹⁰And he says to me, "Do not seal the words of the prophecy of this book, for the time is near. ¹¹Let the wrongdoer still do wrong, and the filthy still be filthy, and the righteous still do right, and the holy still be holy."

¹²"Behold, I am coming soon, and my wages with me, to pay to each as his work deserves—¹³I, the Alpha and the Omega, the first and the last, the beginning and the end."

¹⁴Blessed are those who do as he commands, so that they will have the right to the tree of life and may enter the city by the gates. ¹⁵Outside are the dogs, and the drug-dealers, and the fornicators, and the murderers, and the idolaters, and everyone who loves and practices falsehood.

¹⁶"I, Jesus, have sent my angel to testify to you about these things to the churches. I am the root and the offspring of David, the bright morning star."

[17]And the Spirit and the Bride say, "Come." And let whoever hears say, "Come." And let whoever is thirsty come. Whoever desires, let him take the water of life without charge.

[18]I testify to everyone who hears the words of the prophecy of this book: if anyone should add to them, God will add to him the plagues described in this book. [19]And if anyone should take away from the words of the book of this prophecy, God will take away his share in the tree of life and in the holy city, which are described in this book.

[20]He who testifies of these things says, "Yes. I am coming soon." Amen. Come, Lord Jesus!

[21]The grace of the Lord Jesus be with all the saints.

One like a Son of Adam

Revelation 1. The Son of Man is manifested in his glory as the firstborn of the dead and the King of Kings who is coming soon.

REVELATION OF JOHN

A revelation of Jesus Christ, which God gave him to show to his servants what must happen speedily. And he communicated it by sending through his angel to his servant John, who bore witness to the word of God and the testimony of Jesus Christ, to everything that he saw. Blessed is he who reads and those who hear the words of this prophecy and keep what is written in it, for the time is near.

"REVELATION" (*APOKALUPSIS*, WHENCE the word "apocalypse") has the sense of an unveiling. The subject is the events that "must" happen, climaxing with the revelation of Christ to all the world (1 Cor 1:7, 2 Thess 1:7). The book is a prophecy, and makes good his promise that the Spirit would declare to his disciples what was yet to come (John 16:14). It is not directed to unbelievers or to those who think it sufficient to hold right belief, but to those who serve him . It reveals him as the Christ, the anointed king. Flesh and blood cannot see him; only his father can make him known, the veil-removing Spirit (Matt 16:17). But the vision will unsettle even those who thought they knew him.

In writing down what he heard and saw, John added his witness to the witness of Christ in all Scripture. The book is not a work of human composition. Its words come from God, whether or not John understands what he reports. And it is to be read out, so that the whole congregation receive it. Whoever hears it and lives by it will know God's blessing. Jesus testified: "Man shall not live on bread alone, but on every word that issues from the mouth of God" (Matt 4:4). In quoting Deuteronomy to resist the Devil, he demonstrated what living by every word meant. He regarded all Scripture as the voice of God, and through it God spoke to every reader (Matt 22:31).

Whether Scripture is to be accorded this degree of authority is not a minor issue. Nineteen centuries after the revelation, we might question whether the foretold events can be considered near, seeing that they have still not happened. "Near" most naturally means within decades. In the AD 60s Christians in Rome had been tortured and killed, Jerusalem's Christians had fled the city, and now there was again persecution: Jesus seemed to be saying that the suffering would soon be over. We can no longer take that view. While it is true that we might die at any time, regardless of when he returns, the nearness of his return must relate to some greater totality than the last two millennia.

Revelation concludes the entire Bible, not just the New Testament. Its scriptural allusions are many, and most refer to the Old Testament, from Genesis to Malachi. The last two chapters refer to the Bible's first two chapters. It gives a summation of the whole purpose of him who encompasses all history, from Alpha to Omega (the first and last letters of the alphabet), from the Creation to the new Creation. Reflecting on God's patience, and perhaps also on how patiently Israel had had to wait for prophecies of Christ's first coming to be realized, Peter cautioned that we should take the long view (2 Pet 3). According to Christ himself, his return would be delayed, even though justice would be given soon (Matt 25:5, Luke 18:8). From every perspective, "soon" seems best understood in relation to the ages of all created time.

John to the seven churches that are in Asia: Grace to you and peace from who is, and who was, and who is to come, and from the seven spirits before his throne, and from Jesus Christ the faithful witness, the firstborn of the dead, and the ruler of the kings of the earth.

"From," *apo*, normally takes the genitive, whereas "who is and who was and who is to come" is nominative, as if the whole phrase is a name. God told Moses that his name was Yahweh, or "I am" (Heb. *ehyeh*, Exod 3:14f), the supreme being who transcended time. Now the future is distinguished from the past by an action: the one on the throne is coming. The greeting is threefold, but the New Testament is emphatic that God is one (Mark 12:29–32, Rom 16:27, 1 Cor 8:6, Gal 3:20, Eph 4:6, 1 Tim 2:5, 6:15f, Heb 2:11, Jude 25), re-affirming the Old Testament's solitary declaration (Deut 6:4) many times. In letter after letter, Paul greets his readers, "Grace and peace from God our father and the Lord Jesus Christ," distinguishing between God and his son and seeing no need to add "and the Holy Spirit." Peter and John in their letters likewise. But here the salutation does seem to include the Holy Spirit. Why he is sevenfold will become apparent later.

According to the Nicene Creed, agreed by a church council in AD 325, Jesus Christ was "begotten from the Father, light from light, very God from very God, begotten, not made." But if this indicated that he had an origin, the declaration ended by warning, "Those who say that the Son of God once was not . . . or say that he is created, the holy catholic and apostolic Church curses." They were having the same trouble understanding how God could have a son as the Jews had and as Muslims would have. In 381 another council withdrew the anathema and added "before all the ages" after the first "begotten." Later still the amended phrase was translated "eternally begotten," in accordance with the so-called Athanasian Creed (late 5th or early 6th century) which, contrary to the earliest understanding of the Church,[1] declared that Christ was "coeternal" with his father. Like the beginning and end of the original Nicene formulation, "eternally begotten" was, by normal logic, a contradiction in terms and amounted to a denial of his sonship, for begetting is necessarily an action in time. But by then such controversies had lost sight of the simplicity of the words from heaven, "This is my beloved son."

Jesus himself attested that he received his life, and with it his glory, from the Father, before the foundation of the world (John 5:26, 17:24). He was the firstborn of all creation (Col 1:15, Rev 3:14), created before anyone or anything else. God had brought many sons into being (Job 38:7), but he preceded them; he was the *prwtotokos*—from *prwtos*, first, and *tiktein*, to give birth—in the same literal sense that he was later Mary's firstborn (Luke 2:7). Through him—the one to whom God spoke at Creation—all things were created, including all institutions of authority and power, in order that in everything he might be pre-eminent, *prwteuwn* (Col 1:18). God alone, whom no one has ever seen, or can see, has immortality in the sense that he never came into being (1 Tim 6:16). To speak of three persons, coeternal and coequal, is to speak of three gods, a notion that might have been acceptable to the pagan world but makes no sense in the modern. Indeed, polytheism was a corruption of the more ancient

1. Miller, *Letters on the Eternal Generation*.

understanding that God, the Creator of the world and father of many sons, was one God.[2]

Today the New Testament's revelation that God involved his first-born in creation is complicated by another creed that denies that he created the universe at all. To affirm otherwise is lip service if what we have in mind is particles ordering themselves into atoms, and atoms organizing themselves over billions of years into plants and animals. Are we, with Pope Francis, to scorn the idea that God acted supernaturally, on the grounds that this would be to believe in "a magician, with a magic wand able to do everything," and instead believe that creation itself is the magician, that it over time does everything? If "create" means letting Nature do the forming and the breathing of life into forms, do we think that God, unbeknown to science, is still creating? Even with a Christian gloss, Darwinism abolishes the Father and the Son quite as much as the Athanasian Creed does.

God called himself "Yahweh of hosts" because a vast army of angels belonged to him, and he was at the head of them. But the commander of this army was a man (Josh 5:13), an angel having the appearance of a man, who would go before Israel to fight for them in the name of Yahweh (Exod 23:20–23, Isa 63:9). Joshua, when he saw who he was, worshiped him as God and was not rebuked. Rather, the commander said, as God had said to Moses, "Take off your sandals, for the place where you stand is holy." Even the Hebrew word for "God," El, can be plural, Elohim, though it normally takes a singular verb. The plural reflects the fact that he is Yahweh of hosts. As his sons, the angels share in his divinity (Ps 8:5, 97:7, Heb 2:7).

The Old Testament refers to the commander as "the angel of Yahweh," the definite article highlighting his uniqueness. He was the only angel in whom all the fullness of God was pleased to dwell (Exod 23:21, Zech 12:8), and by implication there existed a time before God chose to impart his fullness to another being. He was the angel who appeared to Moses in the midst of a bush, for the text goes on to say, "God called to him out of the bush." He is also portrayed as one with Yahweh in the passages telling of his appearance to mistreated Hagar (Gen 16), to Abraham in the dialogue about Sodom (Gen 18, where the angel is accompanied by two others), to Abraham as he moved to strike his son (Gen 22) and to doubting Gideon (Judg 6). He was of the same nature as God, just as a

---

2. Schmidt, *Origin and Growth of Religion*; Schmidt, *Primitive Revelation*.

son is of the same nature as his father and in that sense equal with him (John 5:18, and the next verse). Scripture describes the divine in terms of the human relationship because the human reflects the divine (Eph 3:15). Christ was *theos* (John 1:1, Rom 9:5, without the definite article) because he was God's son, a son in the same sense, his genealogy indicates, as Seth was Adam's son (Luke 3:38).

He was begotten three times: once at the beginning, once in the incarnation, and once at his resurrection, that in everything he might be first. It was at the incarnation that Yahweh said to him (Heb 1:5):

> "You are my son,
> I, today, have begotten you."

Psalm 2, which Hebrews quotes here, is the only place in the Old Testament that refers to the begetting of the Messiah (unless we accept, in the light of Luke 11:49 and Matt 23:34, that the personification of Wisdom in Proverbs 8 refers to him, equivalent to the Logos of John 1). "Today" does not, of course, mean "eternally" or "continually." The psalm looks ahead to the "today" when Mary would conceive her child by holy spirit (without the "the"), by the spirit of Yahweh: "Therefore the begotten holy one will be called Son of God" (Luke 1:35). He alone among the angels became the human son of God: of the one God, excluding any idea whereby Jesus was one third the son of himself, or, as per the Nicene Creed, whereby the Holy Spirit rather than the "one God" was his father![3] So the angel's words to Joseph (Matt 1:20) were: "What is begotten of spirit in her is holy," that is, not of another man's flesh, which could not be holy. He was the *monogenes* (John 1:14, 3:16), the only-begotten in the sense of being God's only human son. Evidently Jesus was not the only son, since Scripture repeatedly testifies that before the incarnation there were many sons (Gen 6:2, Deut 32:8, Job 1:6, 38:7, Ps 29:1, 82:1, 89:6), albeit to the discomfort of translators who substitute "heavenly beings" for "sons of God." How could the angels not have been sons if they had an origin, and if we, as his sons, shall be like them in the resurrection?

As the only divine son to live among us as a man, Jesus Christ bore witness to the Father, emphasizing repeatedly that he was subordinate to him, not coequal (John 4:34, 5:19–36, 6:37f, 6:57, 8:28, 8:42, 8:54, 10:18, 10:29, 12:49f, 14:10, 14:16, 14:26–28, 15:15, 17:2f, 17:24, 20:17). "My father is greater than I." "All things have been delivered to me by

---

3. "We believe in one God, the Father . . . and in one Lord Jesus Christ . . . who was incarnate by the Holy Spirit . . . "

my father" (Luke 10:22, John 3:35, 17:7)—things that in the beginning he did not have. Dying and rising again, the first son of creation thereby also became the first son of the resurrection (Luke 20:36, Rom 1:4) and was exalted to the highest position of power and authority, at the right hand of power. Only then did all authorities and powers become subject to him (Matt 28:18, Acts 2:36, Heb 1:2–4). Only then did he receive from his father the promise of the Holy Spirit, to pour onto, and breathe into, his disciples (John 15:26, 20:22, Acts 2:33). We are priests to "his God and Father." Eventually, having subdued the earth, he will deliver the kingdom back to his father: the Son will be subjected to him who subjected all things under him (1 Cor 15:24–28), for we are Christ's, and Christ is God's (1 Cor 3:23, 11:3). God is the head of Christ. Although one with God, Christ modeled the obedience of a son and servant. On what authority then do we undermine that model and substitute another Jesus, with all that that implies for our walk with him (Heb 3:1f, 1 Pet 2:21, 1 John 2:6)?

Points of translation are not necessarily academic quibbles. "Beget" translates *gennaw*, the usual word for "bear, produce, bring into existence." It is the same word as when Jesus says (translated from Aramaic), "You must be born from above," with Nicodemus replying, "Can a human being enter his mother's womb a second time and be born?" Jesus might equally have said, "You must be begotten from above." At his death, he surrendered his spirit to the Father (Luke 23:46) in order that he might be brought into existence anew and receive the glory that he had before the world existed; and we likewise (John 17:22). Psalm 2 was therefore also fulfilled in his resurrection when he became the "firstborn from the dead" (Acts 13:33, Col 1:18). Our lives of faith are a kind of gestation, during which we retain our mortal bodies but are inwardly renewed; the moment of birth is the resurrection, when we emerge from the sleep of death into eternal life. It is then the waters break.

Christ was the first to be begotten anew of Holy Spirit. He who repents and believes in the Son becomes a child of God like him (1 John 3:2) and "puts on" Christ like a garment, even as he is "in" Christ, having been chosen in him before the foundation of the world (Eph 1:4). His beginning is also our beginning. We are begotten through the seed of God's word (1 Pet 1:23, 1 John 3:9), so that it may be said of us too, "What is begotten in us is of spirit." In this way God becomes our father. It is not that we have two divine parents, the Father and the Holy Spirit.

God is spirit (John 4:24) and he has always been holy. In the Old Testament the "Holy Spirit" is mentioned only as his, Yahweh's, spirit (Isa 63:10f, 63:14), in the same way as we might speak of our own spirit without implying another person. He inspired the judges and the prophets (e.g. Judg 3:10, Neh 9:30, Heb 10:15), was a constant presence in the life of David (Ps 51:11, Acts 1:16), and was present in John the Baptist even from his mother's womb (Luke 1:15). He who inspired them was also Christ (1 Pet 1:11). At his baptism God endued him with power, so that Luke describes him as full of the Spirit, again signifying the Spirit of Yahweh (Isa 11:2, 61:1). Jesus was not from this point, if not from birth, two persons, Son and Holy Spirit, as Trinitarianism would imply; he was the Son of God because the spirit in him came from God.

As a separate person the Holy Spirit originated from the time that God gave him to the Church. The gift was the gift of God's own spirit (Joel 2:28, Matt 10:20, 2 Cor 1:22, 1 Thess 4:8), not the visitation of another person of the godhead, unable, despite his co-equality, to give himself. When Jesus assured his disciples that they would be given the words to say before kings and governors, he said, according to Matthew, that the Father would speak through them (10:20); according to Mark (13:11), that the Holy Spirit would; according to Luke (21:15), that he himself would. When he rejoiced in spirit ("holy" is not well attested) that his disciples saw things hidden from the wise and understanding, he thanked the Father for revealing such mysteries (Luke 10:21f, cf. John 11:33). When he spoke of blasphemy against the Holy Spirit, he was referring to the "Spirit of God" (Matt 12:28) in himself (Mark 3:30); the blasphemy consisted of attributing his acts of power to the work of demons. In us the Spirit begets, searches, convicts, sanctifies, comforts, inspires, empowers, reveals. He is distinct by virtue of having been given, of being sent. He is separate because he dwells in us, even though we remain one person. When Jesus referred to him as the *Parakletos* (John 14:16, 16:7), the Advocate who stands alongside and intercedes with the Father, he was telling us his function, not his name. In reality, the Paraclete is Christ (1 John 2:1); it is he who comes to us and intercedes for us (John 14:17f, 20, 16:25, Rom 8:34). The Holy Spirit who forbade Paul from speaking the word in Asia and Bithynia was "the Spirit of Jesus" (Acts 16:6f). Christ being in the Father and the Father in him, both make their abode in us (John 14:23). We know the Father through receiving of his spirit, and his Son's spirit (John 5:26, Gal 4:6).

> You are not in flesh but in spirit, if in fact God's spirit dwells in you. If anyone does not have Christ's spirit, he is not of him. (Rom 8:9)

> I bow my knees before the Father . . . ˈprayingˈ that he may grant you to be strengthened with power through his Spirit in the inner man, Christ dwelling through faith in your hearts . . . (Eph 3:14–17)

The fellowship of the Holy Spirit (2 Cor 13:14) is explicitly fellowship with the Father and the Son (1 John 1:3).

Therefore, sharing in that Spirit, we too are sons of God. We are baptized into the one name of the Father and the Son and the Holy Spirit—the name of the Lord Jesus—because all three are involved in regeneration (Acts 2:38f, 19:5f). It really does not help our understanding to think of the Spirit as a separate person coequal and coeternal with the Father and the Son. He has no personal name and no independent authority (John 16:13), and while Revelation refers to the Spirit a number of times, it avoids the term "the Holy Spirit"; the focus is on Christ.

Right belief is not a matter of salvation, for "if anyone loves God, he is known by him" (1 Cor 8:3). Nonetheless we should not be intimidated by anathemas and false claims of orthodoxy. Knowledge is not a matter of reciting what we do not comprehend. Many believers speak only of Jesus, because they have lost sight of the truth that the Son came to show the Father. Having only the vaguest concept of the Creator and of what he did through time to prepare for his son, they sound like a sect. Jesus is left without witness and testifying only about himself.

To him who loves us and has washed us of our sins in his blood and made us a kingdom, priests to his God and father, to him be glory and dominion for ever and ever. Amen. Behold, he is coming with the clouds, and every eye will see him. So will those who pierced him. And all the tribes of the earth will wail because of him. Yes. Amen.

"I am the Alpha and the Omega," says the Lord God, "who is, and who was, and who is to come. The Almighty."

There will be much suffering in the future if we have not yet experienced it, so we need to know that Jesus loves us and we are clean before him. Our role is to serve him as priests by making God known. As such, we are his kingdom (Ex 19:6, I Pet 2:9), in advance of the day when the whole earth will be his kingdom.

When he comes, every people will see him (Matt 24:30). "All the tribes of the earth" (or "ground"—the same word in Greek) alludes to Genesis 12:3, when God promised that in Abraham "all the tribes of the ground [*adamah*]" would be blessed. "Tribes" (bigger than family, smaller than nation) alludes to the peoples that spread across the earth after the Flood-Cataclysm; "ground" alludes to the dust from which Man was taken. Temporarily the blessing will have gone. The Gentiles will wail because they have rejected him and on them has come the day of wrath. The clouds (Dan 7:13) will not be ordinary clouds—why would they be significant?—but clouds that envelop the whole planet. John emphasizes that these things must be, and assents to it.

The Jews will wail because their forefathers pierced their Messiah with nails. But God will pour on them a spirit of grace and supplication (Jer 31:9, Zech 12:10). It will be a godly grief:

> They will look on me whom they pierced and mourn for him as one mourns for an only child, and grieve for him as one grieves for a firstborn.

They pierced "me": God himself. The prophecy refers to both the day of crucifixion (John 19:37) and that future day.

God himself reiterates that he is, and was, and is to come. In the Greek Old Testament as in English translations, "LORD God" is the rendition of *Yahweh Elohim*, where "Lord" (capitalized) replaces the personal name. The title is transitional. With the appearing of the Messiah, the two terms, Lord and God, become distinct: "There is one God, the Father, from whom were all things and for whom we exist, and one Lord, Jesus Christ, through whom were all things and through whom we exist" (1 Cor 8:6), as Jesus himself affirmed (John 17:3). The very first sentence of Revelation distinguishes between God and his Christ.

But Thomas, seeing the healed wounds, cries, "My Lord and my God!" (John 20:28). The substitution of "Lord" for "Yahweh" conveys the same mystery: it was the Son, the image of the Father, who breathed into Adam's nostrils and walked in the garden; hence the shift from "God" in Genesis 1 to "LORD God" in Genesis 2. It was through the Son that the Father appeared to Abraham as both Yahweh and the Word of Yahweh, and delivered the Law to Moses (Acts 7:38). The Father and the Son have always worked as one—both are Lord (Luke 2:9, 2:11). When God exalted his son, he devolved his lordship to him: "God has made him both Lord and Christ" (Acts 2:36, 2:39). Nonetheless, in the last book the title "Lord God" returns, and refers specifically to God the Father.

The essential question is not whether Jesus is coeternal and coequal, but whether he, a man, is God at all. Israel was faced with much the same question. In the confrontation between Elijah and the prophets of Baal, Elijah told the people: "If Yahweh is God, follow him; if Baal, follow him." Although Yahweh had made it clear that he was God Almighty, maker of heaven and earth, it was open to Israel to see him as just one deity among many. He did not force himself on them. Again and again, Israel preferred the life of the flesh to the spirit. They did not understand how far God had stooped when he redeemed the nation to make them his own. At Mount Carmel he showed his power, as before on Mount Sinai, and then they understood. They fell on their faces and cried, "Yahweh, he is God; Yahweh, he is God." It was precisely Thomas's cry. Only, when the fire came down there was no personal knowledge; there was fear, but no love.

I, John, your brother and partner in the tribulation and kingdom and endurance of Jesus Christ, was on the island called Patmos on account of the word of God and the testimony of Jesus Christ. I went into the spirit on the Lord's day, and I heard behind me a voice, loud as a trumpet, saying, "Write what you see in a book and send it to the seven churches, to Ephesus, to Smyrna, to Pergamum, to Thyatira, to Sardis, to Philadelphia and to Laodicea."

John is saying that tribulation and the need to endure are normal aspects of life in the kingdom. The book will enlarge on these aspects. Patmos, to which John, according to Irenaeus, was banished, lies 33 miles off the coast of Asia, now known as western Turkey, and the order in which the churches are listed follows the road connecting them, from Ephesus north as far as Pergamum and thence south-east towards Laodicea. Ephesus was where John lived and the city nearest Patmos.

John hears a voice behind him just as Ezekiel did when he was in exile (Ezek 3:12). But the voice has the loudness of a trumpet (a ram's horn in Old Testament times) rather than a great earthquake, recalling what Isaiah was told: "Lift up your voice like a trumpet; declare to my people their transgression" (Isa 58:1). What the churches will hear will be similar to what Isaiah was charged to tell Israel, beginning with an assessment of their spirituality, continuing with prophecies about the Messiah's salvation, vengeance, and restoration of Israel, and ending with the new Jerusalem (Isa 58–66).

"In [the] spirit" (also 4:2, 17:3, 21:10) signifies that John was transported outside his body, but he still sees, hears, speaks, writes, turns, falls prone. In Ezekiel's case, spirit (no definite article, and "of God" implied) entered him and lifted him up (e.g. Ezek 2:2, 3:14). Hebrew never refers to "the" Spirit of God.

The "Lord's day" is most naturally understood as the first day of the week, when Christ rose. According to a roughly contemporary text called the *Didachē* (Teaching), believers were already meeting for a meal and the sacrament of bread and wine on a day known as the "Lord's." The command to rest and to remember God's deliverance every seventh day still holds. John, one supposes, was meditating on the Scriptures and seeking God in prayer when the vision came.

And I turned to see the voice that was speaking to me. And on turning I saw seven golden lampstands, and in the midst of the seven lampstands one like a son of man, clothed in a robe, girt toward his breasts with a golden belt, and his head and hair white as wool, white as snow, and his eyes like a flame of fire, and his feet like burnished bronze, glowing as in a furnace, and his voice like the sound of many waters, and in his right hand seven stars, and issuing from his mouth a sharp two-edged sword, and his face like the sun shining in its power.

"Son of man," a common phrase in the Old Testament, is a Hebraism. In Greek and English the phrase makes no sense, because one cannot be the son of a collective noun; it makes sense in Hebrew because man, *Adam*, has three possible meanings: "mankind" (Gen 1:26, 6:1), "human being" (Gen 2:7), and the name Adam (Gen 3:17). "Son of Adam" in Hebrew thus means descendant of the first man or simply "man"—Ezekiel is so addressed 93 times in total. By styling himself "the" Son of Man, Jesus indicated that he was the archetypal man, "the man" (John 19:5), and thus representative of all mankind. He was typologically the son of Adam given to Eve in place of the one who was slaughtered (Gen 4:25). Here, while his form is human, imaging the female as well as the male, he is transfigured. The same similes of snow and wool are used to describe the garment and hair of the "Ancient of Days," also the angel's appearance on the bank of the Tigris (Dan 10). The Ancient of Days is God, and as a consequence of receiving his glory and authority, the "one like a son of man" in the vision becomes the Ancient of Days, for it is the latter who comes at the end of the age (Dan 7:22). Narrative consistency is violated in order to convey the idea that the coming of the one like a son of man will be that of God himself. The paradox has already been conveyed in v. 4.

The long robe (*poderes*) is a garment particular to the chief priest (Exod 28:4 LXX[4]), a role Christ fulfills on our behalf. The belt is golden, like the angel's (Dan 10:5), but worn as a woman would wear it, below the breasts (*mastoi*). The glowing bronze evokes the metal in the midst of the fire in Ezekiel's vision of God (Ezek 1:4), and the voice evokes the cherubim in the vision, for they sounded like "many waters, like the sound of the Almighty" as well as like an earthquake. The same sound will be heard when Yahweh comes again (Ezek 43:2). The weapon in his mouth is a *rhomphaia*. In the Septuagint, *rhomphaia* commonly renders "sword," though *machaira* is more common. In the only New Testament occurrence outside Revelation, it refers to the effect on Mary of her son's violent death (Luke 2:35). It symbolizes here the deadly power of the Messiah's tongue (Isa 11:4, 49:2) rather than the living power of Scripture (Heb 4:12).

And when I saw him, I fell at his feet as though dead. And he laid his hand on me, saying, "Do not fear. I am the first and the last, and the living one, and I became dead, and behold, I am alive for ever and ever, and I have the keys of Death and Hades. Therefore write down what you have seen, and what is, and what is to happen after this. As for the mystery of the seven stars that you saw in my hand and the seven golden lampstands, the seven stars are angels of the seven churches, and the seven lampstands are seven churches."

John's prostration, the touch of the hand and the words "Do not fear" imply that the unnamed speaker is the person Daniel saw at the Tigris. In Isaiah (44:6), Yahweh king of Israel was "the first and the last," but here Jesus takes the title, being before Abraham and also the last Adam (1 Cor 15:45). Having submitted to death, he stands before John in assurance of the resurrection. He who gave Adam temporary life has received authority to confer eternal life. The Holy Spirit is not "the Lord" or "the giver of life," as the Nicene Creed declares (misunderstanding 2 Cor 3:17f), nor does the New Testament ever represent him as worshiped or glorified; rather, the Spirit glorifies Christ (John 16:14).

4. "LXX" denotes the Septuagint, the Greek version of the Old Testament produced in the 3rd and 2nd centuries BC.

Belief in resurrection goes back a long way. Buried with Egypt's 1st Dynasty king Djer were 318 servants killed so that they could accompany him into the afterlife. It is implicit in the sacrificial system that God instituted for the first human beings (Gen 3:21, 4:4). When Moses asked God to blot him out of his book if he would not forgive Israel, he was referring to the book that contained the names of those destined for eternal life (Exod 32:31–33). The Psalms abound in references to the life hereafter, and there are more references in Job, Proverbs, Isaiah, Ezekiel, Daniel, Zechariah and Malachi (Appendix 2). When the book of Kings states that such-and-such a king died and slept with his fathers, it implies that one day they will awake. It was despite the testimony of the Scriptures that the Sadducees did not believe in the resurrection. In Jesus the hope was validated.

Hades is the resting place of the dead, equivalent to Hebrew Sheol (Gen 37:35 etc). "Death and Hades" is one idea, denoting both the condition of death and the place (Hos 13:14). "Hell" (KJV), connoting consciousness and torment, is not an accurate translation. David was not condemned to torment when, like the rest of humanity, he ended up in Sheol/Hades (Acts 2:25–29). Until the resurrection, the dead know nothing (Eccl 9:5, 9:10).

John is told to record (1) the things he has seen already, (2) the state of things now (the subject of chapters 2–3) and (3) the things that will take place in the future (the subject of chapters 4–22). The lampstands are seven churches; there were others, so not "the" seven (although "the" in v. 11). The Holy Spirit is sevenfold because he indwells the sevenfold Church, a single body composed of many local congregations. Jesus Christ, in the midst of them, shines with the brightness of the sun, but is seen only by his servants. The light that people beyond their circle see is the light of their burning oil, be it bright or dim.

THE STATE OF THE CHURCH

Revelation 2–3. Jesus's assessment of how well each of the churches is following him. An outline of Church history up to the present day.

"CHURCH," *EKKLESIA*, MEANS CONGREGATION or assembly, from *ekkalew*, to call out. In the Christian context the assembly is the people called out of spiritual Egypt and Babylon into the fellowship of the Son. In the first century, fellowships mostly met in people's homes,[1] and usually over a meal. There were no denominations, though there might be factions. The church in a city simply consisted of the inhabitants who were Christians, one with "all who in every place call on the name of the Lord Jesus" (1 Cor 1:2, Acts 9:21). Seven are singled out as representing the whole Church.

One approach to understanding the letters—first proposed by certain Franciscans in the 13th century—is to read each community as encapsulating a particular age: the churches are successive just as the seals, trumpets and bowls of wrath within their sevens are successive. Naturally such an interpretation, if valid, will not become fully apparent until all the ages have come to pass. While recognizing that the letters also had contemporary relevance, the present author shares this perspective. In the scheme tentatively proposed here the community at Ephesus represents the immediately post-apostolic

Location of the seven churches.

---

1. Hughes, *Ecclesial Solidarity in the Pauline Corpus.*

Church (AD 70–140), Smyrna the Church up to the time of Constantine (140–320), Pergamon the Church that lived through the fall of imperial Rome (320–530), Thyatira the medieval Church (530–1530), Sardis the Church of the Reformation era (1530–1740), Philadelphia the Church that experienced a revival of spiritual life and doctrine (1740–1920) and Laodicea the Church of the present day.

The letters are performance appraisals, reminding us that Christ is jealous over the faithfulness of the bride he will marry, and he knows her inside out. Revelation is about to close the biblical canon, but he still has particular things to say to individual congregations. Judgement begins with the house of God (1 Pet 4:17), the letters exemplifying what we may expect at his judgement seat. Five of the seven churches are found wanting. The message to them is the same as to the world: repent. Indeed, only they are explicitly told to repent. An eternal reward is promised for those who endure, do his work, and keep themselves pure.

"To the angel of the church in Ephesus write: 'Thus says the one who holds the seven stars in his right hand, who walks in the midst of the seven golden lampstands.

" 'I know your works, and your toil, and your endurance, and how you cannot suffer bad people, and have tested those who call themselves apostles and are not and have found them to be false. You have endurance, and you have suffered for my name's sake, and have not grown weary. But I have this against you, that you have abandoned the love that you first had. Remember therefore from whence you have fallen and repent, and do as you did first. If not, I will come to you soon and remove your lampstand from its place. Unless you repent. But this you have, that you hate the works of the Nicolaitans, which I also hate.

" 'He who has an ear, let him hear what the Spirit says to the churches. To him who conquers I will give to eat from the tree of life, which is in the paradise of God.' "

Aggelos, angel, literally means "messenger," just as *aggelia* means "message" and *euaggelion* the "good message" or "gospel" (-*gg*- pronounced "-ng-"). Thus John the Baptist was the *aggelos* who prepared the way before the Lord (Mark 1:2), and the Lord himself was the *aggelos* of the covenant who suddenly came to his temple (Mal 3:1 LXX, Luke 19:45). "You" is consistently singular, and the stars are angels symbolically distinct from the churches. Nonetheless, while addressed to them, the letters are sent to the churches, as if they, the messengers of the gospel, were identical to the angels. Each church has a common life; it is not a group of mere individuals. Jesus, who is the Spirit, speaks first to the community, then to each member. Each person is to listen to what he says to all the churches, not just his own, and understand its relevance to himself.

In the Septuagint, "Thus says" typically introduces the direct speech of Yahweh; by implication, Jesus is Yahweh. He walks among the lampstands as God once walked in the midst of the Israelites (Deut 23:14). Nothing is hidden from him. The Ephesians are commended for their discernment, their perseverance, and their faithfulness in the face of persecution—important virtues. In his farewell speech Paul warned that fierce wolves would come and seek to distort his teaching (Acts 20:29f). Apparently they took the warning to heart and saw through these false apostles.

Nonetheless, the church is in decline, for they do not love him as once they did. "Love" here is *agapé*. While it has an emotional element, it is primarily evinced in deeds (works). "If anyone has the world's wherewithal and sees his brother in need, yet closes his heart against him, how does God's love abide in him? Children, let us not love in word, with the tongue, but in action and truth." (1 John 3:18) Jesus counsels them to remember the love they had when Paul founded the community ("first" in time and putting him first). They were once excited, grateful, full of zeal; now the new life seems stale, though they continue to behave commendably. What is lacking is love of himself. That John's own church should be criticized in this respect is rather shocking, for the apostle repeatedly stressed the primacy of the commandment to love God. Did this teaching itself now seem stale? Without such *agapé* (praying, meditating on the word, listening for his voice, seeking his will, rejoicing in him) love of one's neighbour does not have the same depth. If the church does not repent, Jesus will bring it to an end. If this applies to Ephesus, not the most criticized of the churches, it applies to every church that is found wanting. A congregation that cannot repent walks in darkness.

Although we know almost nothing about the Nicolaitans, the name means a follower of *Nicolaos* (one tradition identifies him as the Nicolas of Acts 6:5). From the letter to the church at Pergamon we learn that the sect considered it permissible to eat food sacrificed to idols and to lie with cult prostitutes.

The verb "conquer," *nikaw*, always used in a spiritual sense when applied to believers, can also be translated "overcome." We expect an object, but none is given (not until 12:11). Each must listen to the Spirit to find out what his particular adversary or adversity is. It might be the desires of the flesh, the opinion of others, love of money; it might be the burden of looking after a disabled child. Whatever the challenge, we overcome most successfully by trusting in the one who went before us. "This is the victory (*nikė*) that has overcome the world: our faith" (1 John 5:4). Whoever conquers will be granted the right to eat of the fruit that imparts immortality. He will enjoy fellowship with God.

"And to the angel of the church in Smyrna write: 'Thus says the first and the last, who became dead and lived.

" 'I know your works and your tribulation and your poverty—but you are rich—and the slander of those who say they are Jews and are not, but are a synagogue of Satan. Do not fear what you are going to suffer. Behold, the Devil is going to cast some of you into prison, so that you may be tested, and for ten days you will have tribulation. Be faithful unto death, and I will give you the crown of life.

" 'He who has an ear, let him hear what the Spirit says to the churches. The one who conquers will not be hurt by the second death.' "

The city's name means "myrrh," its main export. Among other uses, the aromatic resin was used for anointing (Exod 30:22–32) and embalming (John 19:39).

Jesus says nothing against the community. It is doing good work, despite tribulation and its material poverty and opposition from Jews in the city. For a little while the persecution is going to intensify. Some will die. But if they remain faithful and do not deny their Master, they will come out with the prize of eternal life, just as victors were crowned with a laurel wreath at the games (2 Tim 2:5, 4:8). They will not suffer death again when they rise at the judgement.

About sixty years later several of Smyrna's Christians were martyred, famously its 86-year-old bishop, Polycarp. He had been a disciple of John's and, as bishop, a vigorous opponent of the philosopher Marcion, who maintained that the God of the Old Testament was different from the loving God revealed by Jesus. In AD 155, in the space of a few days, twelve Christians were executed for refusing to call Caesar "Lord." Polycarp was the last. The account of his martyrdom says that Jews were among the crowd demanding blood.

Christians were frequently persecuted in the period before Emperor Constantine. Were it not for the example of the twelve apostles, all but one of whom were martyred for their testimonies, the Church at this critical stage might have been snuffed out. They showed that the truth was more important than prolonging their mortal lives. Under Trajan (AD 98–117), Decius (249–251) Valerian (253–260), Diocletian (284–305) and Maximinus (310–313) many of the Christians who did not submit to paganism were executed.

One of the oldest references to Revelation comes from Irenaeus, who wrote in his book *Against Heresies* that the vision was received "almost in our day, towards the end of Domitian's reign." Irenaeus had been taught by Polycarp, and Polycarp by John, so the statement was on good authority. The vision cannot have been much earlier, since the church of Smyrna did not exist when Paul was active in Asia (before AD 62).

"And to the angel of the church in Pergamon write: 'Thus says the one who has the sharp two-edged sword.

" 'I know your works, and where you dwell, where Satan's throne is; and you hold fast my name. And you did not deny my faith even in the days of Antipas my faithful witness, who was killed in your midst, where Satan dwells. But I have a few things against you: you have some there holding the teaching of Balaam, who taught Balak to put a stumbling block before the sons of Israel, to eat food sacrificed to idols and to fornicate. So you too have some holding the teaching of the Nicolaitans, which I likewise hate. Repent, therefore. If not, I will come to you soon and war against them with the sword of my mouth.

" 'He who has an ear, let him hear what the Spirit says to the churches. To him who conquers I will give of the hidden manna, and I will give him a white pebble, and on the pebble a new name written which no one knows except the one who receives it.' "

"Satan's throne" is an allusion to the spiritual reality behind Pergamon's so-called Altar of Zeus. Zeus was the head of the Greek pantheon and chief god of the city, and members of the community were expected to offer sacrifice to him. Today we admire the sculpture and architecture; in John's time the monument—probably a visualization of Zeus's palace on Mount Olympus[2]—was where citizens unknowingly worshiped Satan, the god behind all paganism. Most Christians resisted the pressure, but some were persuaded that participation in pagan rites was not incompatible with faith in Jesus.

---

2. Picón and Hemingway, *Pergamon*, 50.

Pergamon's "Altar of Zeus," relocated to the Pergamon Museum in Berlin.

Balak was the king of Moab at the time the Israelites entered his territory to cross into Canaan. Fearing them, he asked the Assyrian mystic Balaam to curse the Israelites, but the angel of Yahweh stood in his way with a drawn sword. God put his own words into his mouth, and Balaam could only prophesy blessing on them. Later Balaam advised Balak that he could weaken Israel a different way, by getting them to participate in sacrifices to Baal and fornicate with Moabite women (Num 25:1-5, 31:16). Some did, and in his anger God had them put to death. Jesus indicates that he looks on such practices in the same light. The issue had cropped up before, in relation to whether Gentile believers were bound by the Law of Moses. The apostles decided they were not, except that they should abstain from food sacrificed to idols, from blood products, from animals that had been strangled and from fornication (Acts 15:29). Now some are disregarding this instruction and teaching the very things the leader of the apostles had said would be ruinous (2 Pet 2). The congregation needs to repent. If they do not, Jesus will "war" with the offenders (as in Num 25:17, 31:1-16) with his sword (*rhomphaia*, a distinctly Old Testament word—see on 1:16). Similar language near the end of the book (19:11-15) indicates that he will strike them down, not merely admonish them. On past occasions, behavior offensive to the Holy Spirit provoked disease, blindness, even death (Acts 5:1-10, 1 Cor 11:30).

The Church has always had to battle the temptation to adulterate "the faith once for all delivered to the saints" (Jude 3) in the hope of winning acceptance. Antipas is unattested, but evidently he died upholding the truth—a faithful witness of Jesus even as Jesus was a faithful witness of God. From Constantine onwards the temptation took on a different guise. Persecution came to an end and the Church began to occupy a privileged position in society. This was a good thing in the main. Gladiatorial games and crucifixion were abolished, Sunday became a day of rest, polytheistic worship was discouraged. In 380 the State adopted Christianity as the official religion. A State religion of some kind there had to be: it would be anachronistic to suppose that institutional polytheism could have withered and Christianity remained a network of local churches. So a professional, tax-exempt class of priests was set apart to stand between the laity and God, the Bishop of Rome replaced the Emperor as the Empire's *Pontifex Maximus* or Chief Priest, and the Nicene Creed determined orthodoxy. Peter's teaching that all believers were priests, serving God and making him known, became obsolete—indeed, it was already fading in the 3rd century. Temples were converted into Christian places of worship and church buildings erected *de novo*, complete with altars and the idea that a priest was needed to consecrate and re-offer Christ's body and blood. The Lord's Supper ceased to be a communal meal. Opponents to the Nicene Creed were vilified and their writings destroyed.

In principle, the function of the State religion was to maintain the *pax deorum*, the goodwill of heaven on which earthly peace depended. The new religion proved of no avail. In 410 Rome was sacked by the Visigoths and again in 455 by the Vandals. The western part of the Roman Empire disintegrated. But the Church survived. Although the Visigoths and the Vandals tore up the Empire's borders, their rulers already confessed the Christian faith and in that respect there was no change. In addition, the Church was respected for its literacy and learning, its organizational skills, its spiritual discipline. In due course it would be the Church that gave rulers their legitimacy. The eastern part of the Empire remained intact.

He who conquers is promised participation in a mystery greater than that of the cult: not food offered to idols but the bread of life, and a token granting admission into the sanctuary of the one true God. A jar within the ark of the covenant kept a quantity of the manna that sustained Israel in the wilderness (Exod 16:33). The promise of a new name extends the promise made to Jerusalem (Isa 62:2, 4). We are given a name after we are born, and again after we are reborn.

"And to the angel of the church in Thyatira write: 'Thus says the Son of God, whose eyes are like a flame of fire, and his feet like burnished bronze.

" 'I know your works, and your love and faith and ministry and endurance, and that your latest works exceed your first. But I have this against you, that you tolerate the woman Jezebel, she who calls herself a prophetess, and she is teaching and deceiving my servants to fornicate and eat food sacrificed to idols. I gave her time to repent of her fornication, and she did not repent. Behold, I will cast her onto a bed and those who commit adultery with her into great tribulation, unless they repent of her works. And I will kill her children with pestilence, and all the churches will know that I am he who searches the inward parts and will give to you each according to your works. To you I say, the others in Thyatira who do not support this teaching, those who have not known what some call the deep things of Satan: I do not cast on you any other burden. Only hold fast what you have until I come.

" 'The one who conquers and who keeps my works until the end, to him I will give authority over the nations. And he will shepherd them with a rod of iron, as when earthen pots are smashed, even as I myself have received from my father. And I will give him the morning star. He who has an ear, let him hear what the Spirit says to the churches.' "

The church at Thyatira may have taken root after Lydia was converted and spread the gospel (Acts 16:14). "Inward parts" translates *nephrous kai kardias*, "kidneys and hearts," reflecting the belief that these were the core of a person's moral being. "I, Yahweh, search the heart and test the kidneys, to give to each man according to his ways, according to the fruit of his deeds" (Jer 17:10). As in every letter, Jesus mentions works first among the things he knows about the church, for they are the fruit by which he judges. In this respect the church is progressing, and overall the message is positive. He does not question its love, its faith, or its steadfastness. The only criticism concerns the issue faced also at Pergamon: the pull of the flesh.

Jezebel was a daughter of Ethbaal, king of Sidon (1 Kgs 16:32) and exemplified what happened when Israelite men married foreign women. Jezebel married Ahab, king of Israel. A sorceress and adulteress (2 Kgs 9:22), she induced him to build a house for Baal, supreme god of the Phoenicians, and in it to place a wooden pillar symbolizing the tree of life, to which Asherah, Baal's consort, was thought to vouchsafe access. Four hundred and fifty prophets of Baal and four hundred prophets of

Asherah ate at the royal table. The cult was demonic (hence the ability to prophesy), and entailed an understanding of Yahweh as a sexual being and corresponding practices (idolatry, prostitution, child sacrifice) that were an abomination to him. The cult was so popular that all but seven thousand in Israel bowed the knee to Baal. Thus Ahab did more to provoke God's anger than all the kings before him.

Old Testament history is repeating itself. Calling herself a prophetess, the new Jezebel claims to be a conduit for words and insights that come direct from God. The church has been warned about her promiscuity before but has failed to rebuke her, so Jesus warns that he will take action himself, as at Pergamon. Retribution will be so clear that all the churches will hear of it.

While judgement is rarely immediate, no one should think that there will not be a final reckoning. He is coming, and when he does, he will repay each person according to his works (Prov 24:12, Isa 62:11, Matt 6:1–18, 16:27, Luke 6:38, 14:11–14, 1 Cor 3:8–13, 2 Cor 9:6, Gal 6:9, Eph 6:8, 1 Pet 1:17). "Each one's work will become manifest." This is a vital part of Christian doctrine. Having wiped the slate clean, he expects us to be zealous to do good and incentivizes us, the flesh being weak, with promise of reward. He even treats good deeds as if they created a debt on his part. "So we aspire, whether at home or away from home, to be pleasing to him. For we must all appear before the judgement seat of Christ, so that each may receive back what he did in the body, whether for good or evil." (2 Cor 5:9f) Church leaders especially are reminded to live up to their calling (Luke 12:42–48).

The closing exhortation reiterates that the life to come is not in heaven but among the nations on earth. We will be given positions of responsibility.

> He proceeded to tell a parable, because he was near Jerusalem and because they supposed that the kingdom of God was to appear immediately. He therefore said, "A certain nobleman went into a far country to receive for himself a kingdom and then return. Calling ten of his servants, he gave them ten minas, and said to them, 'Engage in business until I come.' But his citizens hated him and sent a delegation after him, saying, 'We do not want this man to reign over us.' When he came back having received the kingdom, he ordered these servants to whom he had given the money to be called to him, so that he might know what they had gained by doing business. The first came before him, saying, 'Lord, your mina has produced ten minas more.' He

said to him, 'Well done, good servant! Because you have been faithful in very little, you shall have authority over ten cities.' And the second came, saying, 'Lord, your mina has made five minas.' He said to him, 'And you shall be over five cities.' And another came, saying, 'Lord, here is your mina, which I stored away in a handkerchief; for I was afraid of you, because you are a severe man. You take what you did not deposit, and reap what you did not sow.' He says to him, 'Out of your own mouth I will judge you, you wicked servant! You knew that I was a severe man, taking what I did not deposit and reaping what I did not sow? Why then did you not put my money in the bank, and at my coming I might have collected it with interest?' And he said to those who stood by, 'Take the mina from him, and give it to the one with the ten minas.' And they said to him, 'Lord, he has ten minas!' For I tell you that to everyone who has, more will be given, but from the one who has not, even that which he has will be taken away. 'Moreover, as regards those enemies of mine who did not want me to reign over them, bring them here and slaughter them before me.' " (Luke 19:11–27)

A lot is communicated in this parable. Jesus likens his future absence to a long journey; he is not coming back soon in the usual sense; and during this absence his *douloi*—his slaves, so called because he owns them, though he chooses to pay them at the end—are to look after his affairs on his behalf; they are to "keep his works." The freeborn do not accept his rule. When he returns, he asks his slaves what they have done with the resources entrusted to them, and remunerates them accordingly. After the resurrection we will be able to recall our former lives. To one he gives authority over ten cities, to another five, for he will rule the nations with a rod of iron (Ps 2:9) and there will be work to do. Perhaps most startling is the confirmation that anyone who thinks that the master (*kurios*) does not mean what he says will be dealt with severely, just like the nations will be. It is not enough just to know who he is; one must do something with the knowledge. Therefore it must be stressed that the translation "servant" for *doulos* is by concession; the meaning is slave, "bondservant" (Mark 10:44). A believer is expected to serve his lord (*kurios*). The slaughter of the freeborn—and here Jesus steps half outside the parable—refers to what happened in AD 70, just forty years later; the freeborn were the Jews.

The last four letters, beginning with Thyatira, vary the epilogue by putting the promise of reward before, rather than after, the injunction to hear what the Spirit is saying, and there are explicit references to the Lord's return. The churches at Thyatira, Sardis and Laodicea, although addressed successively, continue to the end. The "morning star" is Venus. For half its orbit round the Sun it is an evening star, becoming brighter as it moves from behind the Sun closer to Earth. Near its closest and brightest point it becomes invisible, rising eight days later as a morning star, just as when Jesus rose before the dawn.

If the churches at Pergamon and Thyatira seem very similar, the difference is that the Moabites tempted Israel from without in order to weaken her; Jezebel tempted Israel from within. She used religion to strengthen spiritual and political power. In the course of the Middle Ages the Roman Church did much the same, maintaining that kings were subject to her supreme authority and that the Pope ruled as Christ's vicar, his king-making representative. In 754 Pope Stephen II anointed Pepin king of the Franks and in return received title to the territories in northern Italy that subsequently became the Papal states, making him a temporal as well as spiritual ruler. Kings had an interest in who occupied the papal throne. In 1305 a French king ensured the election of a French Pope who was well disposed towards his country. The Pope transferred the papal court to Poitiers, four years later to Avignon. It continued there until 1377, when Gregory XI brought it back to Rome. The following year he died and the crisis only worsened. From then until 1417 there were at least two claimants to the throne, one based in Rome, the other in Avignon. Among the spiritual abuses was the dispensing of papal indulgences in return for good works, such as a financial contribution to the rebuilding of St Peter's Basilica. The Church, overcome by venality and lust for power, was sick.

The threatened chastisement (*thanatos*, death, but here pestilence, as in 6:8) perhaps alludes to the Black Death, the most catastrophic pandemic in human history. More than 60 million people died. Clergymen were hit worst because of their contact with the sick and dying. While one hesitates to attribute so indiscriminate a plague to the hand of God, its magnitude was unprecedented, though over time tuberculosis killed many more people.

Meanwhile the Byzantine Empire—the former Roman Empire to the east—was being eaten away by the might of Islam. Following the battle of Manzikert in 1071, most of Anatolia fell to invading Turks. In the 13th century Mongols took control, followed in the 14th by the Ottoman Turks. Muslims have ruled the peninsula ever since. Byzantium itself—also called Constantinople, later Istanbul—fell to Islam in 1453. Thereafter the Eastern Orthodox Church allied itself with the Russian state. In Turkey it continued to have a substantial presence until the early 20th century, when it was all but wiped out.

"And to the angel of the church in Sardis write: 'Thus says the one who has the seven spirits of God and the seven stars.

" 'I know your works, that you have a name for being alive and are dead. Be vigilant, and strengthen the remainder, what was about to die, for I have not found your works sufficient before my God. Remember therefore how you received and heard. Keep it, and repent. If you are not vigilant, I will come upon you like a thief, and the hour I come upon you will take you unawares. Yet you have a few names in Sardis who have not soiled their garments, and they will walk with me in white, for they are worthy.

" 'The one who conquers will be clothed in white garments, and truly I will not wipe out his name from the book of life, and I will confess his name before my father and before his angels. He who has an ear, let him hear what the Spirit says to the churches.' "

The church is dead. Even the part of it that might not be dead is moribund. Once more, Christ's emphasis is on deeds. As at Ephesus, the church is counselled to look back to when it listened to his voice with eagerness. It has grown complacent. The reference to his unexpected return recalls the parable of the ten maidens (Matt 24:42f, 25:1–13).

> "The kingdom of heaven will be like ten maidens who, having taken their lamps, went out to meet the bridegroom. Five of them were prudent and five foolish. The foolish, when they took their lamps, took with them no oil, but the prudent took flasks of oil with their lamps. As the bridegroom was delayed, they all became drowsy and slept. But at midnight there was a cry, 'Look, the bridegroom is coming, go out to meet him!' Then all those maidens rose and trimmed their lamps. And the foolish said to the prudent, 'Give us some of your oil, for our lamps are going out.' But the prudent answered, 'There will not be enough for us and for you; go instead to the dealers and buy for yourselves.' While they were going off to buy, the bridegroom came, and those who were ready went in with him to the marriage feast, and the door was shut. Afterwards the other maidens also came, saying, 'Lord, Lord! Open to us.' But he answered, 'Truly, I say to you, I do not know you.' Be vigilant, therefore, for you do not know the day nor the hour."

Two men will be in the field; one will be taken and the other left. Two women will be grinding at the mill; one will be taken and the other left. Once that has happened, it will be too late to repent.

That Jesus should call God "my God" is unsettling if one supposes that he was somehow coeternal with his father, but it is characteristic of the Messiah (Ps 18, 22:10, 40:8, 45:7, 69:3, 89:26, Isa 49:4f, Mic 5:4, Rev 1:6) and is but the first-person equivalent of Paul's own understanding (Rom 15:6, 2 Cor 1:3, Eph 1:3). On the cross he cried, "My God, my God, why have you forsaken me?" The appellation expresses the intimacy of sonship. After the resurrection he told his disciples, "I am ascending to my Father and your Father, to my God and your God." The psalm has him say, "I will tell of your name to my brothers; in the midst of the congregation I will sing your praise" (Ps 22:22). We are children of one Father.

White garments betoken holiness. Garments clothe our nakedness because we are all stained with evil, and in the flesh we cannot please God (Rom 8:8). Garments are his provision, covering our sin, and figuratively speaking need to be kept clean. In the life to come the immortal body itself will clothe our naked souls (2 Cor 5:1–4). The "book of life" contains the names of those appointed to eternal life (Acts 13:48), but their names can be erased (Exod 32:33, Ps 69:28, Heb 6:4–6, 2 Pet 2:20f). The parable about the ten maidens itself gives a hint of that.

It is not difficult to see the Protestant churches in the indictment of being only reputedly alive. The Reformation went only so far. Its works were inadequate, and Luther, for one, struggled to understand how works, the fruit of repentance, might be inseparable from faith. Despite his emphasis on justification by faith, he believed, like his opponents, that faith sufficient for salvation was latent even in infants. Infants were to be "baptized"—sprinkled on the forehead (the proper meaning of *baptizo* is fully immerse)—on the grounds that the rite was equivalent to circumcision, a mark of inclusion in God's covenant (though Christ was both circumcised as a child and baptized as an adult). They were baptized because their parents were in his covenant, parents who had themselves been baptized as infants. The Reformed churches in the countries where they replaced the supranational Roman Church were State churches, and for a long time hostile to those who believed in adult baptism; some Anabaptists, as they were called, were even executed. Christianity was a matter of social identity rather than faith, though faith might follow. In Britain, Puritanism from the mid 16th century onwards was a response to the perception that much remained unreformed. Parliament after the Cromwellian Interregnum did what it could to suppress it. Its Act of Uniformity of 1662 resulted in the ejection of around two thousand non-conformist ministers from the established Church. By the end of the 17th century Puritanism had lost its power, and in many places Christianity was dead. It was dead in most of Europe, though Pietism kept a small flame burning.

Revelation is about the coming of the kingdom of God. The Church's own understanding of this is reflected in its relationship with the State. For most of its history theologians saw the State as God's instrument for establishing his kingdom. The relationship went through five phases.

Phase	Characterization
Early post-apostolic Church	Separate from, and sometimes persecuted by, the State
Emperor Constantine (313) onwards	Christianity becomes the imperial religion
Donation of Pepin (756) onwards	The Roman Church becomes a supranational State in its own right
Reformation (16th century)	In some countries the Church becomes a State church
Growth of free churches	Some congregations break away from State affiliation (mostly in the UK and USA, later South America and China)

Table 1. The relationship of Church and State through Church history.

Whatever the outward forms of rule, God exercises his kingship primarily in the heart of the believer. But time does not stand still. As the world turns away, the Church becomes forced to choose whether to please the world or stick to the truth as delivered and please God. It is difficult for the pastor of a State church to say, "Jesus Christ will destroy all the kingdoms of the earth." The State claims ever more authority over its subjects, and at the end of the age, God says, "Come out of her, my people, lest you participate in her sins and her plagues become yours." The kingdom belongs to those who respond to this call.

"And to the angel of the church in Philadelphia write: 'Thus says the one who is holy, who is true, who has the key of David, who opens and no one will shut, and shuts and no one opens.

" 'I know your works: behold, I have set before you an open door, which no one can shut. Because you have little power and have kept my word, and have not denied my name, behold, I will cause those from the synagogue of Satan who say they are Jews and are not, but lie—behold, I will make them come and bow down at your feet, and know that I have loved you. Because you have kept my word of endurance, I will keep you from the hour of trial that is coming on the whole world to try the inhabitants of the earth. I am coming soon. Hold fast what you have so that no one takes your crown.

" 'The one who conquers, I will make him a pillar in the temple of my God, and never shall he go out of it. And I will write on him the name of my God, and the name of the city of my God, the new Jerusalem, which comes down out of heaven from my God, and my own new name. He who has an ear, let him hear what the Spirit says to the churches.' "

"Philadelphia" means brotherly love, implying that believers see each other as equal and as kindred. The preamble refers to the occasion when God told the self-serving steward of the house of David that Eliakim would take over its key and assume responsibility for its administration (Isa 22:20–25, 2 Kgs 18:18). Jesus reveals the typological significance, for now he has charge of the house of David, and he has become a throne of glory to his father's house (1 Chr 17:12, Luke 1:69). He will exercise his authority so as to open a door for effective work in the kingdom. Some of the Jews—followers of Satan rather than real Jews (Rom 2:28f)—have been opposing the church's witness, but they will find the church is not weak. As with the community at Smyrna, Jesus has no word of criticism. Philadelphia is the only church to hear that he has loved them.

"Hour of trial" recalls the words Jesus used to describe his own hour of crisis (Matt 26:41–45). Circumstances can arise which test a person's worth, whether by suffering or by temptation, including temptation to deny Jesus if that will obviate suffering. Knowing what they have gone through, he will keep the Philadelphians from tribulation of the kind described later in the book. But they should not rest on their laurels: the crown will only be theirs if they remain steadfast; it is possible to lose the prize.

The "temple of my God" is his dwelling-place in heaven. Whoever remains faithful will be part of that habitation (Isa 56:5); he will know God intimately. The new Jerusalem, God and man together, will come down from heaven, and he will be amongst its citizens.

An open door suggests an opportunity to share the message about the kingdom with those who will listen (1 Cor 16:9, Col 4:3). Here again we may discern a historical parallel. Spanish and Portuguese missionaries had been working in South America from as early as the 16th century. The Moravians in the 18th also sent missionaries far beyond Europe. Amongst those they influenced were John and Charles Wesley, who, along with George Whitefield, Jonathan Edwards and Howell Harris, travelled in Britain and North America far and wide to bring the gospel to millions who had never heard it, whether or not they went to church. Undeterred by violent mobs, they asked, "Do you desire to flee from the wrath to come, and to be saved from your sins?" Many repented and heeded the call to holiness, and goodness. Like the Jews in Philadelphia, clergy in the established Church opposed the preachers, and few congregations welcomed the converts.

Although there was some faltering around the end of the 18th century, the revival resumed in the 19th, reaching its acme in the third quarter of that century as it affected all parts of the Church and all levels and sections of society, particularly in Britain and North America.[3] In terms of works the effect was enormous: dramatic falls in murder, gambling, prostitution and alcoholism, the founding of schools, hospitals and orphanages, statutory constraints on child labour, reform of the prison system, the abolition of slavery (chiefly of negroes). Because of the revival, political ideals of freedom, equality and fraternity included more of a Christian understanding than in Europe, and there was less inclination to attribute the success of Western civilization to race. The gospel went out into Asia and South America afresh. Huge efforts were made to translate the Bible into native languages. One of the earliest pioneers was William Carey. Noting that "multitudes sit at ease and give themselves no concern about the far greater part of their fellow sinners, who to this day, are lost in ignorance and idolatry," in 1792 he founded the Baptist Missionary Society. The following year he emigrated to India, where he translated the New Testament into Bengali and other languages and helped to outlaw infanticide and the immolation of widows. Other missionary societies sprang up. Men and women of extraordinary faith but little power took the gospel to far-flung lands, at great personal cost. Carey himself did not see anyone converted for seven years. He lived in penury, contracted malaria, his five-year-old son died of dysentery,

3. Thomas, *The Nation's Gospel.*

his neglected, grief-stricken wife became mentally ill, and his printing presses were destroyed by fire.

Philadelphia is the only church to be reminded that Jesus is coming soon, and it is by way of comfort, not admonition. The reminder makes best sense if the church lives in a period before the tribulation coming on the world.

"And to the angel of the church in Laodicea write: 'Thus says the Amen, the faithful and true witness, the beginning of the creation of God.

" 'I know your works: you are neither cold nor hot. Would that you were either cold or hot! So, because you are lukewarm, and neither hot nor cold, I am going to spew you out of my mouth. For you say, I am rich, I have become rich and need nothing, and do not realize that you are wretched, and pitiable, and poor, and blind, and naked. I counsel you to buy from me gold refined by fire, so that you may become rich, and white garments, so that you may clothe yourself and the shame of your nakedness not be apparent, and salve to anoint your eyes, so that you may see. Those whom I love, I reprove and discipline. Be zealous therefore, and repent. Behold, I stand at the door and knock. If anyone hears my voice and opens the door, I will come in to him and dine with him, and he with me.

" 'The one who conquers I will grant to sit with me on my throne, as I also conquered and sat with my Father on his throne. He who has an ear, let him hear what the Spirit says to the churches.' "

Christ is the Amen—a Hebrew word related to "faithful"—for he is in total accord with his Father. "May Yahweh be a true and faithful witness against us if we do not act according to everything he says" (Jer 42:5): effectively a paraphrase of "Amen," and a reminder that Christ is not always a witness in our favor. He is the beginning (same word as in John 1:1 and Mark 13:19) and originator of God's creation, something the Laodiceans particularly need to comprehend (Col 1:15–18, 4:16). He was created before all else, and through him all things were created. The statement is the first of three variations on "I am the first and the last" (1:17), the others being at 22:13 and 22:16.

Recently excavated Laodicea was founded in the mid 3rd century BC by Antiochus II of Syria and named after his wife, Laodice. It got its wealth from banking and from garments which it made from a prized black wool—hence the references to money and clothing. It also had a medical center in which blindness was treated with an eye-salve. Water was supplied by an aqueduct. Warmed under the sun, it was neither refreshingly cool as at Colossae, nor pleasantly hot like the springs at nearby Hierapolis, where there was also a church.

Material wealth had deceived the fellowship into thinking that they were spiritually rich. That was not the case. Of treasure in heaven—and no other treasure will outlast our bodies—the Laodiceans had nothing. Forty years previously Paul had impressed on them the importance of putting on Christ, but they had lost their covering. Unlike Eve and Adam when they sinned, they did not even know that they were naked. They needed to hear his voice, open their hearts and allow him in. Without him their works amounted to nothing. Unless they bought from him atonement and sight-giving ointment (to speak their language, for of course such things cannot be bought), they could not be considered Christians at all.

The same complacency will be encountered in the woman who symbolizes mercantile civilization at the end of the age. Dressed in expensive clothes and adorned with gold and jewels, she says, "I am a queen, I will never be a widow"; but before long she will find herself naked and desolate. The western Church resembles the world around her. The Church of England is a typical example: an institution wedded to the State, still hierarchical, still ritualistic (where it does not replace formality with the banal), still concerned, when a choice must be made, to please man rather than God. As prophesied of society in the last days, it "has the form of piety, but denies the power of it." The non-State churches also languish.

To allege that denial of one's own blindness is evidence of blindness may seem a circular argument. How can one argue against it? But it may still be true (John 9:40f). The Council of Laodicea, representing the churches of Asia in AD 364, accepted the canonicity of all the books in the New Testament except Revelation. Today all the western churches accept it, but reject most of what it teaches, just as they reject the testimony of the prophets and the Lord himself concerning the beginning of creation (Appendix 1). The beginning and end hang together. The Council also banned Christians from celebrating the Lord's Supper in private homes. As hierarchy took over, it became difficult for the Lord to come in and dine with them. In AD 494 the city was completely levelled by an earthquake.

"Gold refined in the fire" is faith purified by tribulation (Job 23:10) until it redounds to praise and glory and honor at the revelation of Jesus Christ (1 Pet 1:7). The coming tribulation will either purify the church or result in its being extinguished. Those whom he loves (*philw*, expressing affection), he rebukes and disciplines, just as under the old covenant (Heb 12:5–11). He disciplines us for our good, that we may share in his holiness. We should treasure such love.

The Church is intended to preserve society from its natural tendency to rot. Her role is to speak prophetically about the judgement and salvation of God, to promote the good and oppose what is evil, to set an example of peace, kindness and obedience. If she loses her saltiness, she is not fit for anything but to be thrown out and trampled under men's feet. She becomes like Jeremiah's loincloth, rotting in the river of the nations (Jer 13:1–11), and God withholds destruction no longer. That is why faithless Laodicea is the last of the seven churches.

Yet he keeps back his most astonishing promise until this point: he who conquers will reign alongside him, just as he reigns alongside his father.

A Vision of the Throne

Revelation 4–5. A throne is seen in heaven, the center of all power in the universe. The question is: who is to exercise that power on earth?

After these things I looked, and behold, an open door in heaven, and the trumpet-like voice that I first heard spoke to me, saying, "Come up, and I will show you what must take place after this." At once I was in spirit, and behold, a throne stood in heaven, and one seated on the throne, and the one seated similar in appearance to diamond and carnelian, and a rainbow encircling the throne similar in appearance to emerald, and encircling the throne twenty-four thrones, and seated on the twenty-four thrones twenty-four elders, clothed in white garments, with golden crowns on their heads. And from the throne issue lightning, and sounds, and thunder; and before the throne seven lamps of fire burning, which are the seven spirits of God; also before the throne what seemed to be a glass sea, like crystal.

WE PASS FROM CHRIST'S review of the churches to "what must take place after these things" (1:19), the subject of the rest of the revelation. "After these things I looked" refers to what he saw next, not necessarily to the chronology of the events themselves. "I looked, and behold" echoes Daniel's phraseology (Dan 2:31, 7:2). If the human heart is entered through a door (3:20), so too is the heart of heaven. Transported thither, John sees a throne, the throne to which Jesus has just alluded. Only prophets (including David) and the first Christian martyr were privileged with the sight.

Although we know who is seated there, John does not describe a person. His only observation is that he has the appearance of certain gemstones. "Diamond" translates *iaspis*, which could mean "jasper," but in 21:11 it is described as crystal-like. Diamond and carnelian, a brownish-red

97

stone, were the last and first of the twelve stones encrusting Aaron's breast-plate, one for each of the twelve sons of Israel (Exod 28:17–20). They bring to mind the radiant purity of God and his shed blood.

A rainbow was a sign of the promise that the waters of the deep would never again destroy the earth, but this rainbow (or "halo," Gk. *iris*) is dominated by the color green. We should therefore be thinking of another atmospheric phenomenon, the northern and southern lights, which are typically emerald as a result of electrons exciting molecules of oxygen, but also streaked with other colors. The significance of the aurora will become apparent later.

Around the throne on subsidiary thrones are twenty-four human beings. Strangely, they are described as elders rather than kings, but are not otherwise identified. The vitreous sea (Exod 24:10), celestial counterpart of the bronze basin before the entrance of the Tabernacle and the much larger bronze sea before the entrance of the Temple, signifies the primeval waters whose eruption destroyed the antediluvian world. "Yahweh is seated like the *mabbul*," David declares—like the waters of the cataclysm upon the earth (Gen 6:17, Ps 29:10). It is a perpetual reminder of former wrath. The lightning (*astrapē*, denoting any flashing light), the sounds, and the thunder (distinct from the sounds) hint at future wrath. The lamps correspond to those on the seven-branched lampstand in the Tabernacle and have a searching function (Prov 20:27, Zeph 1:12). They burn before the throne, but are also aspects of the king himself. Like the lightning and thunder, they indicate that the surroundings are dark (1 Kgs 8:12).

And in the midst of the throne and around the throne, four living beings, full of eyes in front and behind: the first like a lion, the second like a calf, the third having the face of a man, the fourth like an eagle flying. And the four living beings, each with six wings, are full of eyes all around and within. And they have no rest, day and night, saying,

> "Holy, holy, holy is the Lord God, the Almighty,
> who was, and is, and is to come!"

More and more the description evokes Ezekiel's commissioning at the beginning of his prophecy. As a storm approaches, he sees a large cloud surrounded by brightness, and a blazing fire, and appearing from the midst of the fire something like glowing metal. Also in the fire four living beings; not creatures, for both in Hebrew and Greek the single word means simply "living one" or "animal" (Heb 13:11, 2 Pet 2:12). They seem like burning coals, like constantly moving torches, with wings stretched out towards each other. And over their heads something crystal-like, analogous to heaven's ice-enclosed firmament. Above that, a throne. As the vision gets closer, he sees that the apparition of glowing metal occupies the throne and, from the waist up, resembles a man, surrounded by fire. The brightness all around is like a true rainbow. Ezekiel has seen the likeness of the glory of the maker of heaven and earth. In John's vision the living beings proclaim his holiness, as they do in Isaiah's vision. The revelation establishes John as the successor of Ezekiel and Isaiah.

The beings represent life on earth: wild and domesticated quadrupeds, man (the only tailless terrestrial biped) and flying animals. But they have six wings, like the fiery beings Isaiah saw, and they are full of eyes, before, behind and within, sharing in the divinity of him who sees everything and never sleeps. They are in the center of the throne yet also around it, as if the throne were translucent. They manifest something of the otherness of God, are part of him yet distinct from him. Something of the Creator appears in earth's creatures—the mighty lion (Amos 3:8), the lowly ox (Matt 11:29, but here a young bovine as was often prescribed for sacrifice), the man (Gen 1:26), the soaring eagle (Exod 19:4)—for they originate from the plenitude of God's imagination, not Earth's self-evolution. Man is not the only embodiment of nobility. Jesus was pleased to liken himself even to a domestic hen (Matt 23:37), an animal we farm under artificial light and in such packed conditions that it cannot express its natural behavior, so alienated are we from the author of life. When Ezekiel later sees the glory abandoning the Temple, he realizes that the animals under the throne are the cherubim, the only supernatural beings described as having wings. Two cherubim overshadowed the mercy seat on the ark, and two spanned the inner sanctuary of the Temple where the ark was later housed (1 Kgs 6:23, 8:6). God was seated (not specifically "enthroned") above the cherubim (2 Sam 6:2), residing in darkness behind a cherubim-embroidered veil. Theirs was the one likeness of a heavenly being that God sanctioned. In the old world they guarded the way to the tree of life.

When God first made himself known to Moses, he told him not to come near. He revealed his name as Yahweh, "I am who I am," existing in and beyond time, "who inhabits eternity, whose name is holy" (Exod 3:14f, Isa 57:15). After the terrible Exodus judgement he revealed more, that he was compassionate, gracious, slow to anger, abounding in truth and goodness (Exod 34:6). The cherubim might therefore have proclaimed these aspects of his character. But they speak only of his holiness, affirming in heaven what we pray on earth: "Hallowed be your name. Your kingdom come." Defined by the supreme fact of his existence, he is coming to manifest himself in person. The tenses shift from past to present.

The world's scientists and philosophers say, "There is no God," but it is the heart that schools men in such folly. Eternal nothingness is easy to conceive of; existence is a mystery. We might conceive of one simple thing having always existed, without origin, but how can we conceive of two identical things having always existed? The universe consists of countless trillions of atoms, and atoms consist of quarks and leptons, of which, in each case, there are six types. How can six different but mutually compatible types of quark have come into existence or always have existed—let alone trillions of identical quarks of each type? How can six different but mutually compatible types of lepton have always existed? With their ability to bind themselves into protons and neutrons and combine with electrons (a type of lepton), quarks make atoms possible, and make diverse elements possible. The hypothesized existence of dark matter, capable of interacting with atoms, only adds to the mystery, should one wish to believe in the existence of a physical thing that has never been detected. God was one from the beginning; his creation was multipartite from the beginning. Even if we are blind to the witness of God in the order and beauty of the world, in the wonders of the human body, in the mystery of our own consciousness and free will, in the history of Israel, in the resurrection of Jesus Christ, atheism is a doctrine devoid of substance.

The elders are a completely new presence.

And when the living beings will offer glory, and honor, and thanksgiving to the one seated on the throne who lives for ever and ever, the twenty-four elders will fall down before the one seated on the throne and worship him who lives for ever and ever and cast their crowns before the throne, saying,

> "Worthy are you, our Lord and God,
>   to receive glory, and honor, and power,
> because you created all things
>   and by your will they existed and were created."

The tenses become future (not the usual tense after *hotan*, when), then present, then past. On behalf of all creation the cherubim will express thankfulness to God for the gift of life. The truth that God exists leads to the truth that the world came into existence by his will. He is eternal; all things owe their existence to him; he created them; over them he is lord; and one day he—God himself—will come to the earth to receive the glory, honor, and power due to him as Creator. These attributes of kingship belong to him because everything belongs to him (1 Chr 29:11f, Dan 2:37f); the nations will give back what is his. As throughout the Bible, "worship," *proskuneō*, means to bow down, to kiss the ground in a physical act of homage (3:9), and hence to acknowledge with the lips, in spirit and in truth, that he is worthy to be king. This is the worship he seeks, and requires (John 4:23f).

The throne which we have seen is in heaven, not on earth. While it is true that "he does according to his will among the host of heaven and the inhabitants of the earth" (Dan 4:35), his kingdom has not yet come.

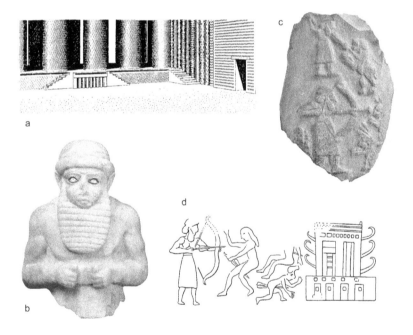

(a) Drawing of the Pillar Hall in Uruk, level IV (c. 3000 BC). (b) Figurine of the priest-king of Uruk IV, identifiable as the legendary En-merkar and biblical Nimrod (National Museum of Iraq). (c) The Lion Hunt Stele from Uruk, showing the priest-king spearing and shooting lions (cf. Gen 10:9). (d) Rendition of a seal from Susa contemporary with Uruk IV, showing the priest-king as a "mighty man" conquering Elam (Louvre Museum). The horned building is a temple built by the colonizers.

When the Flood-Cataclysm destroyed his dwelling-place, God withdrew to heaven. For a long time men remembered why wrath had come on the earth and saw no need for a human ruler.

Some, as they migrated, began to colonise Eden-like Mesopotamia, the plain between the Tigris and Euphrates. One settlement dwarfed and overshadowed the others: Uruk in southern Mesopotamia (the *Erech* of Gen 10:10). In order to feed its increasingly specialized workforce, it began exacting tribute from the surrounding villages. Eventually all Shinar came under Uruk's control. With the aid of proto-cuneiform markings on clay tablets, administrators regulated the labor of every household, whether it was food production or craft production, in the city or in the fields. In return the citizen got a daily ration, doled out in a beveled-rim bowl. Fortified outposts were established upstream to guard trade routes and claim some sort of ownership over northern Mesopotamia. Syria, Elam (immediately east of Shinar) and Egypt were also colonized. Seeing the need for a more centrally located capital to control this empire, Uruk's lord (*en* in Sumerian) founded another city, called Babel. At its heart was a brick-built mountain to induce God to come down and dwell among them, while the *en* would rule in his name as king and chief priest. But God was not pleased. Coming down, he confounded their language and forced them to disperse.

However, they did not forget their ability to manipulate the spirit world through idols, sacrifices and incantations, and as they dispersed, they took their knowledge with them. The earth divided into multiple centers of power, ruled by multiple gods. God intervened no further. He waited until the whole world had shut him out, then made himself known to one man in polytheistic Shinar and told him to leave the country. He renamed him Abraham, "father of a multitude," even though the man was childless. Only when his wife was long past child-bearing did God give them a son. Time passed. Their descendants settled in the midst of the world's other great power, Egypt, and multiplied, to the point where the pharaoh began to kill the male infants and make the parents toil as slaves. Eventually God brought them out from there too and gave them a land of their own. He pledged himself to Israel exclusively, their king and national god, in the same sense that his sons ruled other nations.

> When the Most High gave to the nations their inheritance,
>   when he separated the sons of Adam,
> he fixed the borders of the peoples
>   according to the number of the sons of God.

> For Yahweh's portion was his people,
>> Jacob the bounds of his heritage. (Deut 32:8f)

In return, they were to worship him exclusively, make no image of him and live according to his law. He dwelt amongst them initially in a tent, later, when on their insistence human kings ruled on his behalf, in a house next to the king. To David he promised,

> "I will raise up your offspring after you, one of your sons, and I will establish his kingdom. He shall build a house for me, and I will establish his throne for ever. I will be to him a father, and he shall be to me a son." (1 Chr 17:11f)

In the first instance the house (*beth*) was God's temple or palace (*hekal*)—the temple being his palace—on Mount Zion in Jerusalem. When it was finished, in 961 BC, his glory entered the building as the people looked on. Next to the temple was the king's house (*beth*, often translated "palace"), and within that the throne from which he gave judgement. "To build a house" also meant to establish a family (Ruth 4:11). The Jews never entirely lost sight of this promise.

The king was meant to be the people's representative before God, and God's representative before the people. But that is not how things turned out. Beginning with Solomon, king and people alike lusted after gods who cared nothing for their souls. Throughout the land Israel worshiped idols, performed fertility rites with cult prostitutes, summoned up the dead, practiced human sacrifice. They would not listen when God pleaded with them to repent. After more than three hundred years his patience ran out. He quit the Temple, the ark of the covenant with its cherubim was removed, and in 586 BC he allowed the Babylonians to destroy the city. Of those who survived, all but the poorest were deported. The kingdom was abrogated. Although some returned and rebuilt the Temple, as Isaiah prophesied, God did not return to it, and the nation continued to be subject to foreign kings. In AD 70 that second Temple too was demolished.

God had no wish to be ruler of Israel merely on the grounds that he was the all-powerful Creator and everything belonged to him. He wished the relationship to be one of marriage. He courted the people for their affection, sought to demonstrate that he deserved their love, and hoped that they would respond. But although he lived among them, he was too distant. They wanted an image that made him visible and close, a stone block that they could invest with their own conception of divinity.

And I saw in the right hand of the one seated on the throne a scroll, with writing inside and out, sealed up with seven seals. And I saw a mighty angel proclaiming with a loud voice, "Who is worthy to open the scroll and break its seals?" And no one in heaven, or on earth, or under the earth was able to open the scroll, nor to look at it. And I wept much because no one was found worthy to open the scroll, nor to look at it. And one of the elders says to me, "Do not weep. Behold, the Lion who is from the tribe of Judah, the Root of David, has conquered, to open the scroll and its seven seals."

Although the Lord God is worthy, some other person must come forward to open the scroll: otherwise, whatever is written in it will not come to pass. But no one anywhere is qualified, not even in heaven or among the dead. Except one. He is not named, but the title suggests he fulfills Jacob's enigmatic prophecy that someone from lion-like Judah would one day command the obedience of the peoples (Gen 49:10). Much later Isaiah foresaw a time when a man of perfect righteousness, filled with the Spirit of God, would rule the earth, and he would be not only a shoot from the stem of Jesse but "the root of Jesse" itself (Isa 11:1, 10). Jesse was David's father, from the tribe of Judah. Jesus, born of Mary, was descended from him, and by his own testimony was in existence before Abraham (John 8:58).

The idea of conquering has particular resonance after the letters to the churches. In total the word occurs eight times before this chapter and eight times after it, and Christ himself is associated with the verb three times (3:21, 5:5, 17:14). This is the first of Revelation's three central statements: his having conquered entitles him to open the scroll (or book, *biblion*).

In a different context Ezekiel too was presented with a scroll inscribed on both sides. Such documents are known from archeology: the inner contents were reproduced or summarized on the outside and then sealed to prevent alteration.[1] What the contents were in John's vision is debated. Arguably they are the details narrated in chapter 6 as the seals are broken. There is no further reference to the scroll.

And I saw in the midst of the throne and the four living beings and in the midst of the elders a lamb standing, as one slaughtered, with seven horns and with seven eyes, which are the seven spirits of God sent into all the earth. And he came and took the scroll from the right hand of him who was seated on the throne. And when he had taken the scroll, the four

---

1. Welch, "Doubled, Sealed, Witnessed Documents."

living beings and the twenty-four elders fell down before the lamb, each holding a lyre and golden bowls full of incense, which are the prayers of the saints. And they sing a new song, saying,

> *"Worthy are you to take the scroll and open its seals,*
> > *for you were slaughtered,*
> *and you purchased us for God by your blood*
> > *from every tribe, language, people and nation,*
> *and you made them for our God kings and priests,*
> > *and they will reign on earth."*

We expect to see a lion if not a human being, but instead, in the center of the throne and of the whole gathering, we see a lamb, previously unnoticed. Horns were symbols of power in the ancient world, and the lamb has seven horns, one more than the maximum in nature and therefore signifying supreme power. In some respects he is like the cherubim: he stands in the same place, is portrayed as an animal, and has many eyes. The eyes are the seven spirits of God, an attribute of the Almighty (1:4, 4.5). Zechariah saw a golden lampstand with seven lamps, symbolizing "the eyes of Yahweh, which range through the whole earth." Like God himself, the lamb searches even the unconscious parts of our being (2:23). From his position alongside the one on the throne he comes forward and takes the scroll, given at the point that the birth pangs preceding its arrival must now come on.

John the Baptist hardly knew what he was saying when he hailed Jesus. "Behold the Lamb of God, who takes away the sin of the world." How could Israel's Savior be a lamb? And how could he take away the sin of the whole world, of Gentiles as well as Jews (though Gentile soldiers were among his listeners)? As Paul was to point out when writing to the Romans, we fall short of God's goodness. We are not fit for the life to come, where there is no sin or death. But God offers a solution: renewal on the basis of forgiveness, and forgiveness on the basis that we accept the sacrifice provided, the Lamb who lived without sin and endured the agony of crucifixion in order that justice might be satisfied, no matter how heinous our offenses—even the offense of crucifying God's son.

> He was pierced for our transgressions,
> > crushed for our iniquities;
> the chastisement that was our peace fell upon him,
> > and by his wounds we were healed. . . .
> He was oppressed, and was afflicted,

> yet he does not open his mouth.
> As a lamb he is led to the slaughter,
>   and as a sheep is silent before its shearers
>   he does not open his mouth. (Isa 53:5, 7)

The atonement was prefigured in Abel's offering of the firstborn from his flock already at the beginning of history (Gen 4:4). It was prefigured when Abraham prepared to sacrifice his only son as a burnt offering, until God provided the substitute of a lamb (Gen 22:8, 13f). It was prefigured again at the Exodus. Before redeeming his people, God commanded every household to sacrifice a young sheep or goat without blemish and smear its blood on their doorposts. Egypt was ripe for judgement. But for the blood, the children of Israel also would have perished, since they were idol-worshipers (Ezek 20:7f).

"Saints" is the plural of *hagios*, holy [one]. Whoever believes in the Lamb is imputed holiness as an unearned gift of the Holy Spirit (Acts 26:18, 1 Cor 6:11), without which we cannot enter the presence of God (Isa 6:3–7). This is the sense in Revelation; the saints are not an elite group in heaven, and one does not become a saint by being "canonized." But holiness is also something for which the Spirit urges us to strive (Heb 12:14). God has called into being a holy nation such as Israel was called to be. That those purchased are also a "kingdom of priests" (Exod 15:16) is therefore no idle metaphor. God will be their inheritance as he was for the Levites, whom he set apart to serve as priests in cities throughout Israel. Whoever explains the truth about God to those estranged from him performs a priestly role (Rom 15:16). In the resurrection they will rule over cities amidst the tribes of all the earth. They will be priest-kings after the order of Melchizedek (Heb 7:11–17, Gen 14:18), mediating between the peoples and the Lord God in Jerusalem.

"Us for God" becomes "them for our God": he possesses us, then we possess him. "Us" refers to the twenty-four elders, becoming "them" as the elders identify with the unseen multitude that the Lamb has purchased from every division of humanity. "Every tribe, language, people, and nation," the first of seven variations of the phrase, refers to the progressive ethnogeographic division of mankind after the Cataclysm and the linguistic division at Babel. As the motif repeatedly reminds us, the events of Genesis 10–12 are the deep-time context of this final prophecy.

God had promised that every tribe on earth would be blessed through Abraham's offspring. He would make Abraham into nations; kings would issue from him (Gen 17:6). Isaac was the type and Christ the antitype. In due time God's firstborn son would become the substitute for all Israel, God's firstborn son (Exod 4:22). He would redeem souls from every tribe, language, people and nation and make them one in himself, who was the true Israel (Isa 49:3, Matt 2:15).

Nisan	Day	The Exodus	Passion Week
10	Sun	A lamb is taken and kept until Nisan 14	Jesus enters Jerusalem on a donkey.
13	Wed	At the end of the day (beginning of Nisan 14, Jewish reckoning) the lamb is slaughtered and eaten.	Jesus celebrates the Passover; he is arrested the same night.
14	Thu	Egypt's firstborn die. The Israelites leave Egypt. That night they camp at Succoth.	Jesus is crucified. The Jews celebrate the Passover at the end of Nisan 14.
15	Fri	The Israelites travel on, camping at Etham.	Special sabbath (Exod 12:16, John 19:31)
16	Sat	The Israelites reach Migdol, where they camp but do not rest.	Weekly sabbath (Luke 23:56).
17	Sun	During the night they cross the Red Sea. Egypt's pursuing army is drowned.	Jesus rises from the dead before dawn.

Table 2. The chronology of the Exodus and of the week prior to Christ's resurrection compared.

The chronology of Israel's escape from Egypt in 1447 BC is summarized in Table 2. The week in which Jesus offered up his life followed precisely that chronology. In accordance with the first created day, days began and ended in the evening. On the 10th day of the month Nisan (Abib), Jesus rode into Jerusalem and presented himself as the paschal lamb. The lamb was to be killed "between the two evenings" of sunset and nightfall on the 14th day (Exod 12:6). That the beginning of the day was meant was clear enough from the instruction to eat the flesh that night and not let any of it remain till morning. However, the temple authorities interpreted the phrase to mean the end of the day. So it happened that, crucified on the afternoon of the 14th day, he became the paschal lamb for the whole nation at the very time the Jews slaughtered their paschal lambs (John 19:14). God himself made atonement (Ezek 16:63).

Israel crossed the sea in the night of the 17th day. They passed, as it were, from death to life, following which their enemies perished. They, not the Egyptians or Mesopotamians, were the people God had chosen. Seven weeks later God came down not to the base of a brick-built ziggurat but to the top of a real mountain, burning and shrouded in darkness, and there made himself known. He was to be their king, they his people, provided that they kept his covenant. After three days and nights, Christ rose from the dead. Seven weeks later, the Holy Spirit came down. Foreign visitors to Jerusalem each heard the disciples speaking in their own language and were "confounded." Pentecost signalled the beginning of the reversal of man's division at Babel.

Jesus told his disciples: "Take heart, I have overcome the world." Because he had overcome without force, his followers were also not to use force. "You know that the rulers of the nations lord it over them, and their great ones exercise authority over them. It shall not be so among you, but whoever would become great among you must be your servant." He had shown them the way to greatness:

> He emptied himself, taking the form of a servant [*doulos*], born in the likeness of men. And having been found as a man in appearance, he humbled himself and became obedient even to death, death on a cross. Therefore God has supremely exalted him and granted him the name that is above every name. (Phil 2:6–9)

Although he was Jerusalem's king (Zech 9:9), he entered the city on a donkey, not as military conqueror on a warhorse. He defeated man's greatest enemy by surrendering his life (Heb 2:14), knowing that he could trust his father to give it back. Thereby he propitiated God's wrath toward sin for anyone who believed in him, and earned the right to rule the earth and judge the souls of all mankind. Having descended to Hades (Eph 4:9, 1 Pet 3:19), he ascended to the place of ultimate authority, the right hand of God in heaven, to abide there until the day of his return. For the first time he sat on the throne.

We have been bought for a price, redeemed from a slave-owner who has had to let us go. "Purchase" is *agorazw*, the regular term for buying in the market place (*agora*). Our new master has left his seal on us until the day he comes back to complete the purchase (Luke 21:28, Eph 4:30). Once slaves to sin, we now serve righteousness (Rom 6).

"Elder" is a term of leadership but not hierarchy, first used of Israel's leaders. Hierarchy was discouraged in the early Church. Papias, a disciple of John's, even called the apostles elders, as did the apostles themselves (1 Pet 5:1, 2 John 1). Their number might suggest the twelve sons of Israel and twelve apostles, but the former were never described as elders, while the latter included John himself, who is here an onlooker, not one of the twenty-four. Their identity is conveyed in their own words: "you purchased us for God from every people and nation." They represent the redeemed, keeping their place before the throne in anticipation of the resurrection (Eph 2:6). The saints whose prayers fill their golden bowls are not seen because that day has not yet occurred. Even the apostles will not be raised until that day (Phil 3:11). The golden crowns (wreaths, not diadems) symbolize the prize given to those who have fought the good fight (2 Tim 4:7f, Rev 2:10). The thrones symbolize that they will one day reign on earth. Their number, also symbolic, indicates that they represent the redeemed under the old covenant as well as the new.

And I looked, and around the throne and the living beings and the elders I heard the voice of many angels, numbering myriads of myriads and thousands of thousands, saying with a loud voice, "Worthy is the Lamb who was slaughtered to receive power and riches and wisdom and strength and honor and glory and blessing!"

And I heard every creature in the heaven and on the earth and under the earth and on the sea, all that is in them, say, "To him who sits on the throne and to the Lamb, blessing and honor and glory and dominion for ever and ever!"

And the four living beings said, "Amen!" And the elders fell down and worshiped.

Suddenly we hear the "thousands of thousands" that David saw on the mountain of God (Ps 68:17) and the "thousand thousands and ten thousand times ten thousand" that Daniel saw around the throne. Like John, Daniel saw other thrones, but empty, then "one like a son of man" coming with the clouds of heaven, who was presented before the Almighty and given "dominion and glory and kingship" over all peoples. That day is not far off.

The Lamb is worthy because of his perfect faith, his perfect love, his unblemished holiness. When the elders proclaim that the one on the throne is worthy to receive glory and honor and power because he created all things, the implication is that God alone is worthy. But in this too the Lamb qualifies. For "all things came to be through him, and not one thing that is came into being without him" (John 1:3). When God spoke, it was the Son who executed the commands. He was the appointed heir, the image of God who at the end of the ages would bring God near (Col 1:15).

Therefore the angels declare that glory and honor and power are due no less to him than to the Father. And they invoke still more: wisdom and riches and benediction, just as David blessed God in the presence of the assembly and acknowledged that the kingdom belonged to him, for everything in heaven and on earth belonged to him. All the assembly blessed God and worshiped, before God and king alike (1 Chr 29:11–22). The angels are the celestial counterpart of that congregation, the Lamb the celestial counterpart of that king. They express the mystery of the faith of Israel, that the son of David would be like Solomon, yet greater than Solomon (Ps 72, Isa 11:1–10).

> Give the king your judgements, O God,
>> and your righteousness to the king's son.
> He will judge your people with righteousness
>> and your poor with justice. . . .
> Let them fear you as long as the sun
>> and as long as the moon, before all generations. . . .
> May he have dominion from sea to sea,
>> and from the River to the ends of the earth.

All creation has been groaning, awaiting release from the bondage of decay, and now every creature—winged, terrestrial, burrowing, aquatic—joins in the cry. His worshipers joyously assent to the glory, majesty, dominion and authority which are rightfully his. As yet, he reigns in heaven, not on earth. It is important that there be a people on earth, drawn from every tribe and nation, that assents to his reign, for the world hates him and does not want him to rule over them. Who we worship—Satan in human form, or God in human form—will be a critical question.

The Scroll and the Six Seals

Revelation 6. The scroll is opened, precipitating the birth pangs of the kingdom in the 20th century and the wrath of God in the 21st.

OF THE FOUR GOSPEL writers, only John did not record what Jesus said about the end. The visions in Revelation 7–16 make good the omission and do so by adding material provided nowhere else. Chapter 6, on the other hand, expands on what Matthew, Mark and Luke record. In those gospels, as he drew his teaching to a close, Jesus warned that one day the magnificent Temple built by Herod would be demolished. In response, his disciples asked him two questions: when would the building be demolished, and how would his followers know that his arrival as king was imminent?

In reply to the first, he said he would send prophets and scholars expert in the Scriptures to Jerusalem, and they would be persecuted with such hatred that the Jews would end up being held accountable for all the innocent blood shed on earth since Creation (Matt 23:34–36). Retribution, including the destruction of the Temple, would happen in their lifetimes (Matt 24:1f). In Luke's account, Jesus gave the same warning somewhat earlier (11:49–51). As he approached Jerusalem he wept, and added (19:43): "Your enemies will build a rampart around you and encircle you and hem you in on every side. They will dash you to the ground, you and your children in you, and not leave one stone upon another."

The second question he answered on the Mount of Olives, where Yahweh was to set his feet at the end of the age (Zech 14). Many, he said, would come in his name and claim to be the Messiah, announcing, "The time is near." There would also be wars and reports ("rumors") of war.

Nonetheless, such troubles would not even be the beginning of the "birth pangs."

These things came to pass. As orthodox Jews waited for a Messiah other than Jesus, would-be Messiahs appeared sporadically throughout history, most catastrophically one Simon bar Kochba, leader of the war against the Romans in AD 132–35. "Reports of wars" imply a time when the Jews would no longer be in Palestine but the land still be in dispute, as when Muslims wrested control of it from the Byzantines and crusading Europeans in the period 1095–1272 tried to take it back.

Matthew 24	Revelation 6
Nation will rise against nation and kingdom against kingdom ...	1st & 2nd seals: a rider with a crown, bent on conquest; people kill one another
	3rd seal: grain in short supply
	4th seal: killing by war, famine, pestilence and beasts
Famines, disease and earthquakes	
Followers ("you") imprisoned and killed	5th seal: people killed for their witness to the gospel
Terrors and great signs from heaven, stars falling to the earth	6th seal: the sun becomes black and the moon red; stars fall to the earth

Table 3. What must happen before Christ returns.

The metaphor of a woman in travail refers to the day when God's wrath visits the earth (Isa 13:8, 1 Thess 5:3) and Israel's forbears at the end of that tribulation rise from the dead (Mic 5:3). The events of Revelation 6 correspond to the birth pangs, and are foretold in the same order.

And I looked as the Lamb opened one of the seven seals. And I heard one of the four living beings say with a voice like thunder, "Come!" And I looked, and behold, a white horse. And its rider had a bow, and a crown was given to him, and he went out conquering and in order to conquer.

The rider ignores that the Lamb has already conquered. Like the warrior at the end of the period encompassed by the seals (19:11), he sits on a white horse; but he wears a *stephanos*, a victor's laurel wreath or crown rather than many *diademata*, and his weapon is a bow rather than a sword (though both are symbolic of war). Roman conquerors were awarded a laurel crown and rode in triumphal processions on chariots drawn by white horses, but apart from being summoned with a voice like thunder there is nothing obviously portentous in the manifestation. Some interpret the rider as an Antichrist figure, but the other riders symbolize events, not individuals. Unlike the one who spilt no blood but his own, he symbolizes an episode of military aggression or empire-building.

That being so, how far back should one go for a historical parallel? Russia's territorial expansion dates to the 15th century, and its empire, now known as the Russian Federation, still survives; the Spanish and Portuguese empires lasted from the 16th to the 19th century; the Mongol empire, the creation of Genghis Khan, sprang up in the 13th century and disintegrated in the 14th. All these empires were larger than Rome's at its zenith. In the context of the Apocalypse, however, what is indicated is the latest such conquests, those of the late 19th and early 20th centuries. Here an obvious starting point is the Franco-Prussian War of 1870–71, which resulted in the unification of the German states and the almost immediate transformation of Germany into an imperial power.

There were two waves of European colonization. The first was the subjugation of North and South America, India, Siberia and Indonesia. The second was the drive by Britain, France, Belgium, Portugal and newly unified Italy and Germany to conquer Africa and Indochina. Russia meanwhile pressed into the Caucasus, central Asia and south-eastern Siberia down to Vladivostok. All these countries were in competition, but after the Franco-Prussian war they sought to increase their military, commercial and industrial might without fighting each other, by grabbing as much territory as possible outside Europe. Technological advances in transport, communication and weapons enabled them to spread their civilization—their commercial practices, technologies, arts, sciences and philosophies—across the world. Only China, Japan, Thailand, Turkey, Ethiopia and Iran escaped subjugation. On the continent itself states protected themselves by a network of alliances.

Eventually, the tensions became too great. In 1914 a Bosnian Serb assassinated the heir to the throne of Austria-Hungary because of the latter's annexation of Bosnia-Herzegovina. In retaliation Austria-Hungary attacked Serbia, and its ally, Germany, attacked Serbia's ally, France. Britain sent troops to defend France and Belgium. Russia, its empire bordering Germany and Austria-Hungary, attacked Germany in defence of its ally, Serbia. Within weeks most of Europe, including Turkey's Ottoman Empire, was at war.

And when he opened the second seal, I heard the second living being say, "Come!" And there went out another horse, fiery red. And it was given to the rider to take peace from the earth, so that men should slaughter one another, and he was given a great sword.

"Nation will rise against nation, and kingdom against kingdom." There have been wars for as long as there have been nation states and kings, so the prophecy implies conflict on a much larger scale than the wars with which Jesus's listeners would have been familiar. Those of the 20th century offer unambiguous fulfillment. In the First World War some 10 million soldiers and 7 million civilians died, to say nothing of the wounded or deaths from disease and famine. More millions were slaughtered in Russia's civil war of 1917–1921, which was partly provoked by the huge losses inflicted by Germany. In the Second World War 21–25 million soldiers and 50–55 million civilians died, including 19–28 million from disease and famine. They were instances of "total war," affecting the whole of industry and the whole of society, while the power of the State grew ever bigger. And they reverberated through every level of creation: under the sea, the surface of the sea, the land, the air. Heaven became a place from which droning and screeching flying machines rained down bombs. Terrified civilians sought shelter underground as their homes were pulverized.

Countries beyond Europe were also sucked in: Canada, the United States, Australia, New Zealand, the Caribbean, India, parts of Africa, parts of south-east Asia, Japan, the Middle East, most of them because they were European colonies. Why would one not regard these wars as fulfilling Jesus's prediction? But they now seem far in the past, and since then Europe has enjoyed a period of peace and security (cf. 1 Thess 5:3). In retrospect they seem like a false alarm.

And when he opened the third seal, I heard the third living being say, "Come!" And I looked, and behold, a black horse. And its rider had a pair of scales in his hand. And I heard a voice in the midst of the four living beings say, "A quart of wheat for a denarius, and three quarts of barley for a denarius! And do not harm the oil and the wine."

Wheat, barley, oil and wine were staple foods in Palestine (2 Chr 2:10). A denarius was typically a day's wages and would buy around 16 quarts of wheat or 30 quarts of barley; hence the better off tended to eat wheat bread, poorer people barley bread. Whether because prices rise or earnings fall, both become almost unaffordable.

In the 20th century large-scale famines were frequent, though not unprecedented. Those after the First World War include the following:

Year	Region	Deaths
1921–1922	Russia	5 million
1921–1922	Tatarstan	0.5–2 million
1928–1930	North China	3 million
1932–1933	USSR, Ukraine	4.5–8 million
1936	Sichuan	5 million

Table 4. Large-scale famines in the interwar years.

Outside China, the worst famines were the direct result of economic policies pursued by the Communists after the Russian Revolution. Even at the height of the 1921–22 famine, the Russian government preferred to export grain rather than feed its own people. The Sichuan famine was aggravated by civil war between Communists and Nationalists. Over time we forget about such tribulations, if we were ever aware of them.

In Germany, massive war debts and crippling war reparations led to hyperinflation. A loaf of bread costing half a mark in 1918 cost 200 billion marks by the end of 1923. In the United States the stockmarket crash of October 1929 precipitated the Great Depression and soon spread to other countries. Worldwide gross domestic product fell by 15%. While prices dropped, so did real income, and unemployment soared.[1] Drought in the Great Plains of the United States subsequently reduced the land to a dust bowl.

In France—the principal wine producer and consumer—prices were depressed by the United States' prohibition of alcohol from 1919 to 1933. Perfect weather in 1933 produced the biggest grape crop in French agricultural history. Bumper harvests and increasing cultivation in countries beyond Europe resulted in a glut. "Wine production," concluded an official in 1939, "is in the process of destroying itself by its own excesses."[2] Europe was also the main market for olive oil, as it still is. In the principal olive-growing countries—Italy, Spain and Greece—the milling and pressing of olives became increasingly mechanized, and better methods were developed of storing oil. Again, there was no shortage in the interwar years.[3] The production of other oil-yielding crops also rose.

1. Crafts and Fearon, "Lessons from the 1930s," 285–317.
2. Paxton, *French Peasant Fascism*, 21; Pinilla and Ayuda, "The Wine Market 1850–1938," 179–99.
3. Ramon-Muñoz, "Modernizing the Olive-Oil Industry," 71–88.

World production of groundnuts, copra and soya beans increased around 95% between 1910 and 1939.[4]

The prophecy is quite specific: some staples, such as wheat and barley, will be in short supply, others, such as oil, will not.

And when he opened the fourth seal, I heard the voice of the fourth living being, saying, "Come!" And I looked, and behold, a pale horse. And its rider's name was Death, and Hades followed close behind. And they were given authority over a fourth of the earth, to kill with sword and with famine and with pestilence and by the beasts of the earth.

The series of the horsemen climaxes with the appearance of Death himself. Since he is distinct from Hades riding just behind, he must be the personification of an equivalent place, namely Tartarus. According to Homer, Tartarus was a region "as far beneath Hades as heaven is above earth." It was where the demons could expect to be confined and tormented (Matt 8:29, Luke 8:31). Hades and Tartarus were also the names of the gods in charge of their respective regions.

View of Dresden from the townhall after British and American bombing raids on the city, Allegory of Goodness in the foreground, 1945 (photograph: Richard Peter).

4. Neumark, "World Situation of Fats and Oils," 192–203.

Twice as many died in the Second World War as in the First, and while the trenches were hellish, the Nazi death camps and concentration camps were even more so. The horsemen kill by God's archetypal judgements: war, famine, pestilence, vermin (Ezek 14:21 LXX). "Sword" translates *rhomphaia*; the modern equivalent might be the rifle. "Pestilence" is *thanatos*, the normal word for death, as in the sentence preceding. English has an analogous use of the word in "Black Death," referring to bubonic plague. "Beasts of the earth" echoes Gen 1:24, where it refers to all animals apart from quadrupeds and animals with wings; "wild" is not in the Greek. Typhus was transmitted in concentration camps by the human body louse and, as in Russia's Civil War, killed millions. Japan used bombs to spread plague and other bacterial diseases.[5]

The world can be likened to a field in which some men sow wheat and others sow darnel, a weed that resembles wheat (Matt 13:24–30). The darnel comes to fruition independently of the good seed. The history of 19th-century Europe illustrates this. Pre-eminently in Britain and North America, the gospel transformed society, giving individuals a new understanding of reality and access to a fountain that, having cleansed the soul, inspired much well-doing. At the same time others were sowing different seed, thinkers such as Charles Darwin, Karl Marx, Friedrich Nietzsche and their disciples. Although they were in some respects children of their time, their ideas disseminated with the force of newly revealed truth. After centuries of Christianity, the discovery (as it seemed) that there was no God opened up new worlds. There was "grandeur" in the idea that natural selection brought about new life; the overthrow of capitalism would usher in a millennial reign of justice and peace when religion would wither; the death of God would make way for a new Man to emerge, free to choose his own values.

"What is good?" Nietzsche asked in *The Antichrist* (1888). "Everything that heightens the feeling of power in man, the will to power, power itself. What is bad? Everything that is born of weakness." A dictator might be "left-wing" or "right-wing," it hardly mattered. Russia's internal war, lasting 30 years off and on, in which Stalin killed tens of millions by execution, starvation, deportation and forced labor, was as ideologically driven as Hitler's determination to restore Germany's greatness by genocide and foreign war. In this "age of social catastrophe"[6] Europe

5. Harris, *Factories of Death.*
6. Gellately, *Lenin, Stalin and Hitler.*

reaped what it had sown and came face to face with the abyss in its own soul. Entire cities were levelled to the ground. Hundreds more were half-ruined. A thousand years of cultural history—palaces, museums, opera houses, churches, town halls—went up in flames.

In the 6th century BC the prophet Zechariah received a vision of four chariots emerging from between bronze mountains and heading out to the four winds of heaven. The first was drawn by red horses, the second by black horses, the third by white horses, the fourth by grizzled horses. Only two directions were specifically mentioned: the chariot with black horses went to the north country, Babylonia, while the chariot with dappled horses went to the south country, Egypt. Their function was to patrol the earth and report back. All the countries were at rest. With the return of some exiles from Babylonia, God's spirit there was also at rest. Although having the same colors, the horses of the Apocalypse have a different function. They issue forth one by one, separated by time rather than geography, and they bring unrest to the nations. The whole earth is disturbed.

The horses suggest a rapid succession of events. Accordingly the First World War brought to fruition the "survival of the fittest" philosophy that inspired the jostlings for power of the previous decades. The causes of the Great Depression are debated, but certainly war debt and the reparations imposed on the loser played a part. The reparations fostered resentment, and along with fear of Bolshevik revolution they enabled Hitler to win wide electoral support for his extreme solutions. Parliament itself voted for him to govern by decree. Just 22 years after the armistice in 1918 acknowledging Germany's defeat, France signed another armistice acknowledging its own defeat. The events let loose by the fleet-footed animals took place within a single lifetime.

In the gospels, Jesus spoke of wars between nations without chronological distinction. In Revelation, large-scale slaughter occurs in two phases: that of the second seal and, after an interval, that of the fourth, corresponding to World War One and World War Two. Large-scale famine is associated with the third and fourth seals. The second is the only one to be opened without the phrase "I looked, and behold," suggesting continuity with the first. World War One was the direct consequence of Europe's imperialism in the preceding century. After World War Two the colonial empires crumbled. Bankrupted Europe had neither the strength nor the will to hold on to them. The United Nations, founded in 1945, reflected a new world order in which the increasing cost of weaponry and the deterrent effect of nuclear weapons rendered large-scale wars of conquest all but inconceivable.

Matthew mentions famines, infectious diseases (*loimoi*) and earthquakes as among the beginning of the birth pangs. Mark has "disturbances" instead of disease and mentions earthquakes first. Luke has great earthquakes, famines and infectious diseases. Famines after the Second World War were as catastrophic as between the wars.

Year	Region	Deaths
1947	Soviet Union	1–1.5 million
1959–1961	China	15–23 million
1967–1970	Biafra, Nigeria	1–2 million
1968–1972	Sahel	1 million
1974	Bangladesh	Up to 1.5 million
1983–1985	Ethiopia	1 million
1991–1992	Somalia	300,000
1996	North Korea	600,000
1998–2004	Congo	3.8 million

Table 5. Major famines following World War Two

The famine in China was a direct result of the policies of Mao Zedong, described in Jung Chang's book *Wild Swans*. Since 1961 most of the famines have occurred in Africa, often in association with war and disease. Famines continue to this day, but international and non-governmental agencies have generally become better at delivering relief.

The phrase *edothe autwi/autois*, "it was given to him/them," occurs five times in chapter 6. It indicates something willed, not merely allowed, for in a non-arbitrary sense the will of God governs all things (Eph 1:11) and the horsemen come at the command of the cherubim. Nonetheless, the wars, famines and epidemics of the 20th century were as much symptoms of a general disorder as they were judgements, their immediate causes natural and human.

Since 1900 the frequency of great earthquakes (now technically defined as moment magnitude ≥ 8.0) has been out of the ordinary only in the decade 2004–2014.[7] The quake that triggered the Boxing Day tsunami in 2004 killed 230,000 people, the Haiti earthquake of 2010 85–220,000

7. Lay, "Surge of Great Earthquakes 2004–14," 133–46.

people. The most powerful earthquake ever recorded was the Chilean earthquake of 1960.

We are all under sentence of death. Life is given so that we might seek him and find him, and of our own volition choose good rather than evil, life rather than death. The many acts of temporal judgement on cities and nations in the Old Testament—Sodom and Gomorrah (Gen 19), Egypt (Exod 12, 14), Canaan (Lev 18:25), Israel (2 Kgs 17), Judah (2 Kgs 25) and the neighbors of Judah (Ezek 25–32)—came after wickedness had run its course, after society had become so corrupt that nothing good remained in it (Gen 15:16, Jer 13:10). That was not quite the case in the 20th century. The scriptural examples were types of a global judgement yet to come.

Europe saw the Great War as confirmation that there was no God. The kind of Christianity taught in the churches did not enable it to cope with the horrors. Half a century earlier, doubts concerning the foundations of the Christian world-view—concerning Creation, the existence of Satan, the historicity of the biblical narrative, the ability of God to foretell the future—had been robustly countered, as witness the response to *Essays and Reviews* published a few months after *The Origin of Species*.[8] By the end of the 19th century such doubts were becoming commonplace, in the Church as well as society. The Church could not understand what was going on when philosophers and scientists posed the age-old question, "Did God really say . . . ?" She did not wish to acknowledge that there even was a distinction between Church and society. Whenever a consensus emerged that what she had routinely commended, on the authority of the Bible, was in fact wrong, she gave ground, on the authority of those who were in fact her enemies. Man's wisdom and God's wisdom were assimilated. She wanted peace with society and to that end continually absorbed its doctrines. When finally people asked, "How can there be a God in the face of such misery?" the Church had little to say, not even after the Second World War, which was even more obviously the consequence of an atheistic, God-hostile understanding of reality.

And when he opened the fifth seal, I saw under the altar the souls of those slaughtered for the word of God and for the testimony they had borne. And they cried with a loud voice, "How long, Master, holy and true, before you judge and avenge our blood on the inhabitants of the earth?" And each was given a white robe, and they were told to rest a little longer, until the

---

8. Altholz, "The Mind of Victorian Orthodoxy," 186–97.

number of both their fellow servants and their brothers should be fulfilled who were to be killed as they had been.

In contrast to the preceding seals, the opening of the fifth discloses no new development. The martyrs are described as souls because they have not yet risen. (The vision is a dramatization. In reality, those who die in Christ "sleep" or, as Revelation puts it, "rest"; they have no existence as disembodied souls, and they are not confined under an altar.) Not previously noticed, the altar is where the servants of God present their offerings. We offer ourselves, living sacrifices, willing if necessary to die. Christians are martyred for their unashamed "testimony of Jesus," associated with the word of God also in 1:2, 1:9, 12:17 and 20:4. Their brothers are the Jews (13:10, 17:6).

The Spirit urges, "Bless those who persecute you. Never avenge yourselves but leave room for wrath, for it is written, 'Vengeance is mine, I will requite.' " "Vengeance" in Greek and Hebrew means the righting of a wrong; there is no sense of exacting more than is due (Luke 18:2–8). When Zechariah, son of Jehoiada, lay dying, stoned in the court of Jerusalem's Temple, he said, "May Yahweh see and avenge!" (2 Chr 24:22). Despite his censorious last words, Stephen cried, "Lord, do not hold this sin against them." Persecution reaches such a pitch that the martyrs' patience is exhausted. They cry for justice.

Over half of the Christians martyred since the birth of the Church were killed in the 20th century, mostly under fascist and communist regimes. Since the 1980s the greatest persecutor has been militant Islam. Believers are killed not so often at the hands of the State—though in twelve states the death penalty is prescribed for leaving Islam—as at the hands of a brother or a father who thinks that killing an apostate is a matter of honor (Luke 12:53), at the hands of an incensed mob, or suicide bombers at a church service (John 16:2), or in civil war. Fulani herdsmen cry "Allahu akbar!" as they surround Christian villages in northern Nigeria, then cut down the adults and children as they flee. Some are kidnapped, enslaved, raped, imprisoned, tortured. Contrasting with the courage of the martyrs is the attitude of leaders who, seeing what can happen to those who criticize Islam, choose to appease it, lest criticism cause offense. Everywhere worship of the true God is being closed down—in Europe and the United States voluntarily, as congregations decline, in the rest of the world by force, as the pharaohs of this world illegalize churches.

This is where we are at the time of writing: the interval of waiting "a little longer." We are not at the climax of this hatred. Nearer the end, and after the beginning of the birth pangs, Jesus warns,

> "They will deliver you up to tribulation and kill you, and you will be hated by all the nations because of my name. And then many will fall away, and they will betray one another, and hate one another. Many false prophets will arise and deceive many. And because lawlessness is increased, the love of the many will grow cold. But if you endure to the end, you will be saved. And this gospel of the kingdom will be proclaimed throughout the world as a testimony to all the nations. Then the end will come."

Because of man's alienation from God, good news can seem like bad news, and warnings of impending wrath are as hard to hear as they are to deliver. They provoke only more hostility.

A little later Jesus counsels, "If anyone says to you, 'Look, here is the Christ!' or 'There he is!' do not believe it. For false Christs and false prophets will arise and perform great signs and wonders, so as to lead astray, if possible, even the elect." This warning, similar to that at the beginning of his discourse, concerns Jews and Christians alike at the end of the age. False prophets and signs will add to the deception, the pressure to follow Judas will be intense, and the elect will be desperate for news that the Messiah has come.

And when he opened the sixth seal, I looked, and there was a great earthquake, and the sun became black like hair sackcloth, and the full moon became like blood, and the stars of heaven fell to the earth as when a fig tree sheds its unripe fruit on being shaken by a gale, and the heaven disappeared like a scroll being rolled up, and every mountain and island was moved from its place. And the kings of the earth, the great ones, the generals, the rich, the strong, every slave and free man, hid themselves in the caves and among the rocks of the mountains, calling to the mountains and the rocks, "Fall on us and hide us from the face of the one seated on the throne and from the wrath of the Lamb, for the great day of his wrath has come, and who is able to stand?"

Because the events heralded by the trumpets in chapters 8 and 9 are omitted, we come immediately to the point where the door of salvation is closed (Gen 7:16, Matt 25:10, Luke 13:25). A sevenfold cascade of portents answers the martyrs' prayers. Persecution ceases because the Church has been removed from the earth (1 Thess 1:10).

"Immediately after the tribulation of those days the sun will be darkened, and the moon will not give its light, and the stars will fall from heaven, and the powers of the heavens will be shaken" (Matt 24:29–31). The failure of sunlight recalls the 3 days of darkness before the death of Egypt's firstborn and the 3 hours of darkness when Christ himself experienced desolation. The light of the world hides his face. The Church's reflection of the light is reddened by the blood of martyrs. This is the first time that wrath is mentioned in Revelation, and it is attributed to the Lamb. Men hide in terror.

"Star" before the age of astronomy can be any heavenly body except the Sun and the Moon. Here the stars denote meteoroids, which are non-luminous. Stars proper will disappear progressively, like a scroll being rolled up (Isa 13:10, 34:4) or as if sackcloth, the garb of lamentation, were being drawn over them (Isa 50:3).

In our generation, we understand what it means for stars to fall from heaven. In 2005 NASA was mandated to detect and track potentially hazardous asteroids orbiting near Earth. So far, more than 25,000 near-Earth asteroids have been detected, ranging from a few meters in size to several kilometers. In 2018 funds were announced for the construction of two observatories to survey space above the southern hemisphere.

According to the standard account of origins asteroids are left-overs from the natural formation of the solar system. In this century we have photographed them at close quarters and even retrieved samples, adding to the information gleaned from meteorites. But they have failed to confirm the account. Most of the smaller bodies have turned out to be "rubble piles," aggregations of rocks and dust produced when larger bodies collided with one another and shattered. Larger bodies are either also rubble piles or the remains of planets which, shortly before their explosion, differentiated into crust, mantle and core, with correspondingly "stony," "stony-iron" and "iron" compositions. At the time of the Flood-Cataclysm, the "windows of the heavens were opened" (Gen 7:11) and through them asteroids rained down, instruments of God's wrath. Craters produced by their impacts on the Moon are still visible.

"The powers of the heavens will be shaken" in Matthew recalls Isaiah 34:4 (Gk: "All the powers of the heavens will melt," Heb: "All the host of heaven will rot away"). Prophecy speaks not of the humanly predictable approach of one stray asteroid, but of a strong wind or gale suddenly dislodging many. A strong wind in outer space can only be an intensification of the solar wind that continually streams from the Sun's corona, such as the spurt of gas that erupted from the far side in July 2012.

"We have been lucky that we have not been hit by a really big event," said Juha-Pekka Luntama, head of the European Space Agency's space-weather team. "We will be hit eventually, the question is, when?"

These things will not be chance events. They were foreseen by Israel's prophets, whose words, no longer sealed, have been preserved so that we on whom the end of the ages has come may take heed.

The sun also darkened when the Assyrians overran Samaria. An earthquake shook the hills, and men wished that the hills would fall on them (Hos 10:8, Amos 8:8f). So did the inhabitants of first-century Jerusalem when judgement came (Luke 23:29f).

Isaiah spoke of a future day when the whole earth would quake:

> In that day men will cast
> > their idols of silver and idols of gold
> which they made for themselves to worship
> > to the moles, and to the bats,
> so that they can enter the clefts of the rocks
> > and the gaps in the crags,
> away from the terror of Yahweh
> > and from the splendor of his majesty
> > when he rises to make the earth tremble. (2:20f)

> I will make the heavens tremble
> > and the earth will be shaken out of its place,
> at the wrath of Yahweh of hosts,
> > in the day of his fierce anger. (13:13)

> The windows from above are opened
> > and the foundations of the earth tremble.
> The earth is utterly broken,
> > the earth is split apart,
> > the earth is violently shaken.
> The earth staggers like a drunkard
> > and totters like a hut. (24:18–20)

Jeremiah was mainly concerned with contemporary Judah, but he too got a glimpse. When he looked, the heavens were dark, and the earth was formless and void of life, as before the first day of creation:

> I looked at the mountains, and behold, they were quaking
> > and all the hills swayed.

> I looked, and behold, there was no man,
> and all the birds of the air had fled. (4:24–25)

Joel spoke of the end in these terms:

> For the day of the LORD is near
> in the valley of decision.
> The sun and the moon have become dark
> and the stars have withdrawn their brightness.
> The LORD will roar from Zion
> and utter his voice from Jerusalem,
> and the heavens and the earth will quake.

And Habakkuk:

> He stood and rocked the earth;
> he looked and made the nations tremble,
> and the eternal mountains were shattered,
> the everlasting hills sank low.

Even the heavens will be shaken. God's wrath culminates with the stars of heaven falling to the earth like unripe figs (which would not normally drop) and with a "great earthquake such as has not occurred since man was on the earth."

The words are not intended as poetic fiction, and the events will not be entertainment confined to a screen in one's living room.

THE 144,000 AND
AN INNUMERABLE THRONG

Revelation 7. Where are the 12 tribes of Israel today? Why are 144,000 called out from them? And what is the great multitude now seen before the throne?

After this I saw four angels standing at the four corners of the earth, controlling the four winds of the earth so that no wind might blow on the earth or on the sea or against any tree. And I saw another angel coming up from the rising of the sun, bearing the seal of the living God, and he cried with a loud voice to the four angels to whom it was given to harm the earth and the sea, saying, "Do not harm the earth or the sea or the trees until we have sealed the servants of our God on their foreheads." And I heard the number of the sealed, 144,000, sealed from every tribe of the sons of Israel:

> *12,000 from the tribe of Judah sealed,*
> *12,000 from the tribe of Reuben,*
> *12,000 from the tribe of Gad,*
> *12,000 from the tribe of Asher,*
> *12,000 from the tribe of Naphtali,*
> *12,000 from the tribe of Manasseh,*
> *12,000 from the tribe of Simeon,*
> *12,000 from the tribe of Levi,*
> *12,000 from the tribe of Issachar,*
> *12,000 from the tribe of Zebulun,*
> *12,000 from the tribe of Joseph,*
> *12,000 from the tribe of Benjamin sealed.*

THE FOUR ANGELS GIVEN authority to damage the planet are different from the ones about to sound the trumpets, but they will be active at the same time. After the sealing is finished, huge storms will blow up. While this is the only mention of them in Revelation, storms feature prominently in descriptions of the last days (Ps 50:3, Isa 4:6, 25:4, 29:6, 30:30). As they worsen, there will be "anguish of nations in perplexity, of noise of sea and surge, of people fainting with fear and anticipation of what is coming upon the world" (Luke 21:25f). The "rising of the sun" is a Hebraism meaning "east," the direction from which God comes (Isa 60:1, Ezek 43:2).

The tribes are those descended from the twelve sons of Israel (the name God gave Jacob), omitting Dan and counting Joseph as two tribes through his sons Ephraim and Manasseh (Josh 14:4). These two were born to Joseph when he was in Egypt, whom Jacob blessed as if they were Joseph's immediate sons. Although Manasseh was born first, Jacob pronounced a greater blessing upon Ephraim, who is here listed as carrying on the name of his father. "His offspring will become a fullness of nations," Jacob prophesied (Gen 48:19). If the blessing was fulfilled, it can only have been partially, for the tribes Ephraim and Manasseh rejected God, and eventually he rejected them. Dan is omitted from the list because the tribe persistently worshiped a carved image (Judg 18:30f) and was omitted from the genealogies (1 Chr 1-7). It is not, however, debarred from finally inheriting the land (Ezek 48:1).

The first and last-named tribes, Judah and Benjamin, along with most of Levi, survive to the present day. They are the Jews, so named after their territory Judah or (in Latin) Judaea, which was named after the tribe. Their ancestors lived there from the Conquest c. 1400 BC until their exile in 586 BC, when Nebuchdrezzar deported those who lived in the cities to Babylonia; the agricultural poor remained. After 50 years some of the exiles returned; the rest remained in Babylonia and subsequently spread to other parts of the Near East, where, having finally learned not to worship idols, they kept their ethnic identity (Esth 3:8, Acts 2:9-11). After the first and second revolts against the Romans those in Judaea were also exiled. Although some today can reasonably claim to descend from the tribe of Levi, genealogies going back to specific tribes were lost when the Temple was destroyed. Over the past 100 years many Jews have migrated to the land. Nonetheless, more still live in other parts of the world—chiefly the United States—than in Palestine itself. It is remarkable that the Jews retain their identity at all.

As a single kingdom, Israel existed for little more than a century. Solomon, Israel's third king, was succeeded in 931 by Rehoboam. At his

accession ten of the tribes (counting Ephraim and Manasseh separately
and not counting Levi) broke away from Judah and Benjamin to form a
separate, northern kingdom named Israel, distinct from Judah. Their first
king was Jeroboam, from the tribe of Ephraim. A few years into his reign
he abandoned Judah's Jerusalem-centered religion, built two new religious centers, and persuaded Israel to identify Yahweh with a golden calf.
Objecting, most of the Levites in Israel went over to the house of David.

Israel's king Jehu (841/40–814/13 BC) prostrating himself (worshiping) before
the Assyrian king Shalmaneser III. Above is the winged disk of the Sun and the
star Venus, symbol of Inana/Ishtar. Black Obelisk, British Museum.

Israel continued until Assyria conquered the kingdom. In 732
Tiglath-pileser annexed the land belonging to the tribe of Naphtali,
immediately north of the Sea of Galilee, and deported the population to
Assyria (2 Kgs 15:29). Then in 721, "in the ninth year of Hoshea [king
of Israel], the king of Assyria captured Samaria. He carried Israel away
into Assyria and placed them in Halah [N Iraq] and on the Khabur,
the river of Guzana [in NE Syria], and in the cities of the Medes [NW
Iran]." (2 Kgs 17:6) These deportees were chiefly the tribes of Ephraim
and Manasseh. In their stead the Assyrians brought in people from other
parts of the empire, rendering the dispossession irrevocable, and the territory became an Assyrian province, named Samaria after Israel's former
capital. In New Testament times the inhabitants were called Samaritans.
The territory of the tribe of Issachar was also annexed—hence Jacob's
prophecy that Issachar would become a gang of slaves (Gen 49:15).
Some of the Israelites fled to the southern kingdom and became part of
Judah. Anna, for example, the woman who recognized the baby Jesus as

the Messiah when he was presented at the Temple, belonged to the tribe of Asher. Those who had been deported to Assyria and beyond merged with the Gentiles. New Testament references to "the twelve tribes in the Dispersion" (Jas 1:1, 1 Pet 1:1, Acts 26:7) were largely notional, since by then most of them no longer existed.

"Israel" in the prophecies may refer either to the whole nation of Israel (even Judah alone where Judah represents the whole nation) or to the northern kingdom distinct from the southern; usually the context makes clear which. In Ezekiel's vision of the valley of dry bones, some 150 years after the Assyrian deportations and 11 years into the Babylonian Exile, God said, "These bones are the whole house of Israel." He promised that he would raise the Israelites from their graves and place them in their own land. "Judah and the children of Israel associated with him" would be re-united with "Joseph and all the house of Israel associated with him." They would no longer be estranged, but one king would rule them all.

God drove the northern tribes out of the promised land because they did not wish to be set apart as his own people, distinct from the nations around them (2 Kgs 17:15). To abandon Yahweh was necessarily to lose their identity, and that over time is what happened. No prophets followed them into exile, and we have no evidence that the exiled tribes ever came back. "Joseph and all the house of Israel associated with him" in Ezekiel's vision therefore refers to the northern tribes before they merged with the Gentiles.

Despite the fate suffered by the northern kingdom, Judah proved to be even more adulterous. Why, then, did God allow some of the Jews back to the land? And if he still had a purpose for them, why did he apparently have no further purpose for the rest of Israel?

The prophet Hosea (or Hoshea, a contraction of Yehoshua, "Yah saves," as also, in reverse, was Isaiah) addressed these questions just before the fall of the northern kingdom. He warned that the kingdom was about to be terminated. Owing to their spiritual adultery God would cease to regard them as his own people. Yet in days to come,

> The number of the children [lit. sons] of Israel will be like the sand of the sea, which cannot be measured or numbered.
>
> And in the place where it was said to them, "You are not my people," it will be said to them, "Children of the living God." And the children of Judah and the children of Israel will be gathered together, and they will appoint for themselves one

head. And they shall come up from the earth, for great will be the day of "God Sows." (Hos 1:11)

God had promised Abraham that he would multiply his offspring "as the stars of heaven and as the sand that is on the seashore" (Gen 15:5, 22:17). Though similar, the similes are not the same. Israel had become as numerous as the visible stars already by the time they entered Canaan (Deut 1:10), but—allowing for hyperbole—they never became as numerous as the sand of the sea. The promise still awaited its time. The first part of the prophecy referred to future descendants, those who would come into the promise through faith in the Messiah (Rom 4:16–18); only after losing their ethnic identity would the children of Israel increase beyond number. The rest of the prophecy referred to a time still more distant, when the pre-exilic descendants of Israel would be reunified with Judah after rising from the grave. The place where they were told, "You are not my people," was the land of Israel. It was from there, and from the countries to which the exiles were deported, that they would be resurrected (Jer 23:7f). They would not be so populous that they could not be numbered. Rather, "I will set them in their land and multiply them" (Ezek 37:26); "I will sow the house of Israel and the house of Judah with the seed of man and the seed of beast" (Jer 31:27).

Paul cites the first half of the Hosea passage in confirmation that God has called people "not only from the Jews but also from the nations" (Rom 9:24–26). The antithesis is no longer Judah and Israel, but Jew and Gentile. The children of Israel and the nations amongst whom they intermarried are treated as one and the same. They become sons of the living God by receiving the gospel (1 Pet 1:1–2:10). Paul advances the same antithesis later in his letter, when he says:

> I do not want you to be ignorant of this mystery, brothers: . . . a hardness has affected Israel in part, until the fullness of the nations has come in. And thus all Israel will be saved, as it is written: "Out of Zion will come the Deliverer; he will banish impiety from Jacob."

The sense is that spiritual blindness has affected part of Israel, not that partial spiritual blindness has affected all Israel. There is an ordained period when the Jews, apart from the minority who believed, must be "enemies of God for your sake." But when the harvest of Gentile souls is complete, then the Messiah will come; he will lift the blindness and save the whole house of Israel. He will raise them from the dead.

Hosea enacted God's relationship with Israel by marrying, on his instructions, a woman who habitually committed adultery. Eventually he divorced her. However, after drawing the parallel with himself, God told Hosea to love her and take her back. So the prophet did. Then he writes,

> The children of Israel will dwell many days without king or prince, without sacrifice or pillar, without ephod [a totemic version of the high priest's garment] or household gods. Afterward the children of Israel will return and seek Yahweh their God and David their king, and they will fear Yahweh and his goodness in the latter days.

In the latter days—an unspecified period near the end of history—they will seek the true God and remember his covenant with David, their king before they seceded.

Gentile believers are grafted into the olive tree and share its root (Rom 11:17). Previously they were alienated from the polity of Israel; now, being reconciled to God, they are fellow citizens with them (Eph 2:12–19), a "company of nations" alongside the nation of Israel proper (Gen 35:11, Amos 9:12, Rom 4:17). So "Israel" now has a wider sense than the genealogically defined tribes, which no longer exist as such. The 144,000 from every tribe of Israel are Gentiles, even the 12,000 from Judah.

Since the tribes are notional, so presumably is the number of 12,000 attributed to each, though the total may be actual. As in Gideon's (Judg 7:3–6) and Elijah's day (1 Kgs 19:18), the total is relatively small. Not everyone is chosen—they are chosen "from" the tribes (similarly 5:9), believers who fear God rather than man, who worship him as creator of heaven and earth, and who sigh and groan at the abominations being committed. The seal is equivalent to the blood daubed on Israel's doorposts and lintels at the Exodus. It implies protection against natural as much as supernatural evil, and anointing for a special purpose. The role of these servants is to prophesy about the one who is coming. Like the seventy that Jesus sent ahead into every city and town, they will heal the sick, preach a message of repentance, and tell the people, "The kingdom of God is near." Their adversaries will be powerless to contradict them, for the Holy Spirit will tell them what to say.

"These are ones who have not defiled themselves with women," John is told (14:4). It is not simply that Christ has made them pure in this respect, but they have kept themselves pure. Since the Bride is the whole

Church, male and female, the emphasis on male purity may not necessarily mean that only men are signified. Like him, they are unmarried and without children and therefore free to follow wherever he leads. This can be costly, for he does not always lead where we wish to go. They fulfill what Joel said, that God will pour out his Spirit on all flesh in the last days, on male and female servants alike, and they will prophesy.

> And I will show wonders in the heavens above
>   and signs on the earth below,
>   blood, and fire, and columns of smoke.
> The sun shall be turned to darkness
>   and the moon to blood.

So there will be one final push. Like the apostles at Pentecost who prophesied to the Jews before their day of wrath, like John the Baptist, they will urge people to be saved from this crooked generation (Luke 3:7, Acts 2:40, Rom 2:9). Their prophesying to the rest of the world, including the Jewish Diaspora, will be at the same time as the two witnesses prophesy in Jerusalem, for it is during the trumpets that the latter bear witness. After three and a half years they will be martyred.

After these things I looked, and behold, a great throng which no one could number, from every nation and tribes and peoples and languages, standing before the throne and before the Lamb, clothed in white robes, and with palm branches in their hands. And they cry with a loud voice, "Salvation to our God who sits on the throne, and to the Lamb!" And all the angels stood around the throne and around the elders and the four living beings, and fell on their faces before the throne and worshiped God, saying, "Amen! Blessing, and glory, and wisdom, and thankfulness, and honor, and power, and strength to our God for ever and ever! Amen."

And in answer one of the elders said to me, "These clothed in the white robes: who are they, and where have they come from?" And I said to him, "My lord, you know."

And he said to me, "These are the ones coming out of the great tribulation. They have washed their robes and made them white in the blood of the Lamb. Therefore they are before the throne of God, and minister to him day and night in his temple; and he who sits on the throne will shelter them. They will hunger no more, nor thirst any more, nor will the sun, nor any heat, beat down on them; for the Lamb in the midst of the throne will shepherd them, and he will lead them to fountains of waters of life. And God will wipe away every tear from their eyes."

In his first vision of heaven John saw myriads of angels but only twenty-four human beings. Now he sees an innumerable multitude from every nation, like the sand of the sea, in contrast to the 144,000, who can be numbered. On Mount Horeb the Israelites washed their garments in water (Exod 19:10). On Mount Zion the Gentiles wash their clothing in the blood of the Lamb. That is enough to gain them access to the throne. The unexpected tense of "they cry" is dramatic present, a shift common in classical literature. "Salvation to our God" reiterates the declaration in Psalm 3:8 and Jonah 2:9, "belongs" understood. The palm branches celebrate the victory of the one who rode into Jerusalem to purchase that salvation (John 12:13).

Thlipsis, tribulation, occurs 45 times in the New Testament, mostly in non-apocalyptic contexts. It occurs with "great" in two other places (Matt 24:21 and Rev 2:22), and with "the great" only here, referring to the persecution and natural disasters that all believers will have to go through. The tribulation is in progress as the elder speaks. Although some will survive, many—more than can be counted—will be killed, both existing believers and new ones who have responded to the preaching of the 144,000. At the last trumpet they will rise.

> For you have been a stronghold to the poor,
>   a stronghold to the needy in his distress,
>   a shelter from the storm, a shade from the heat. (Isa 25:4)

On the heavenly Mount Zion he will prepare for all peoples a sumptuous banquet (Isa 25:6–8).

> He will swallow up death for ever,
>   and Lord Yahweh will wipe away the tears from all faces.

Having suffered the famine, drought, storms and stifling heat that accompany the first three trumpets—there is no suggestion of martyrdom here—they will suffer no more. God will shelter them (*skenwsei ep' autous*, lit. his tent will be over them) and soothe their sorrows. Some of the words come from a prophecy relating to Israel (Isa 49:10), but they apply equally to them. The Lamb will be their shepherd and lead them through the valley of the shadow of death to waters of rest.

An elder explains the vision, for in due time the multitude will join the elders. The tenses are significant: the cleansing of their souls occurred in the past, their service in the temple is continuous present, and the time when they will suffer no more is future. Ministering (*latreia*) has the religious sense of serving in worship, distinct from serving in other ways (*douleia*). "You shall worship the Lord your God and him only shall you serve." The New Testament singles out constant fasting and prayer (Luke 2:37, 1 Tim 5:5), which takes place spiritually in the sanctuary of God in heaven (Heb 4:16), much as sacrifices were performed in the earthly temple. More generally, it is devotedly to seek and do the will of God in daily life (Rom 12:1).

The vision of the 144,000 and the great multitude is a vision of mercy, and relates to the period of the trumpets. It thus steps out of the sequence of the six seals that culminates with the wrath. The promise of an end to suffering connects with the point later in the narrative when the promise is fulfilled (Rev 21), after the opening of the seventh seal. Silence for half an hour marks the transition to the trumpets.

THE SIX TRUMPETS

Revelation 8–9. Fire is cast on the earth, then asteroids. From below emerge hordes of demons. Although the gospel has been made known, most people refuse to repent and continue to worship darkness.

And when he opened the seventh seal, there was silence in heaven for about half an hour.

And I saw the seven angels who stand before God. And they were given seven trumpets. And another angel came and stood at the altar with a golden censer, and he was given much incense to add to the prayers of all the saints at the golden altar before the throne. And the smoke of the incense, with the prayers of the saints, went up from the hand of the angel before God. And the angel took the censer and filled it with fire from the altar and cast it on the earth. And there occurred sounds, and thunder, and lightning, and an earthquake.

"HOUR," A PREGNANT WORD in Revelation, refers to the "hour of trial that is coming on the whole world" (3:10), the "hour of his judgement" (14:7). Chronologically what should follow is the advent of Christ, so that the opening of the seventh seal marks the completion of the wrath described with the sixth seal. However, this is not described until chapter 19. The hour is split, and a new series introduced which details the great tribulation between the fifth and sixth seals, the silence broken by sounds and thunder.

The whole planet stands before its Maker while unseen angels prepare destruction, just as they did when he put an end to idol-worshiping Jerusalem. In Ezekiel's vision six angels passed through the city, beginning at the Temple, and killed whoever did not have a protecting mark on his forehead (Ezek 9). Then another angel took burning coals from between the cherubim and scattered them over the city. This was six years before its destruction. The angels dramatized the fact that the ultimate agent of destruction was God, not the army whose arrowheads archeologists have recently been unearthing from the ashes. Something similar is now building up, only on a larger scale.

The earthly Temple had two altars: one for sacrifice, located outside the building, and one for incense, located within (Exod 40:5). They were made of acacia wood, the former overlaid with bronze, the latter with gold. References to "the" altar (e.g. Matt 23:35) were to the altar for sacrifice, visible to all. A wood fire burned on it continually for burnt offerings. There was also a fire on the inner altar, where the high priest burned incense morning and evening, figuratively sending forth the fragrance of the presence of God. Once a year, on the day of atonement, he filled a censer with coals from the fire, spread a cloud of incense over the mercy seat and sprinkled it with goat's blood. Since the sacrifice of Christ's own blood, there is only one altar in heaven, the altar of gold. There we offer ourselves as living sacrifices in praise (Heb 13:15), thanksgiving (Ps 116:17) and good works (Rom 12:1, Heb 13:16). It is also where prayers are received, foremost the prayers of the martyrs.

An angel renders their supplications fragrant by mixing them with incense. They are not ritualistic, and they do not go unheard. In response the angel takes some of the fire and scatters it on earth. "Sounds, and thunder, and lightning"—previously phenomena emanating from the throne—are effects of the fire hitting the atmosphere. The text suggests that the angel's action also causes an earthquake (seismos—the Greek word lacks "earth-").

Fire is the prime instrument of judgement at the end of the age. Peter regarded the fire of Rome in AD 64 and the ensuing martyrdom of its Christians by crucifixion and burning at the stake as a prefiguring of the end. Almost his parting words were these:

> Heavens existed of old, and an earth constructed by the word of God out of water and through water, through which [heavens and earth ("which" is plural)] the then world was deluged with water and perished. But the present heavens and earth are stored up by his word for fire, being kept until the day of judgement and destruction of the wicked.

The first world of human beings was destroyed by means of the heavens and earth themselves, i.e. by asteroids raining down from above and water erupting from below. So also the present world will be destroyed: from above by the Sun and from below by a planet-shaking convulsion.

> With a roar the heavens will pass away, and celestial bodies will burn and disintegrate, and earth and the works on it will be burned up.
> Since then all these things are being dissolved, what sort of people ought you to be in holy conduct and godliness, waiting for and hastening the arrival of the day of God, when heavens will be set on fire and disintegrate, and celestial bodies will melt as they burn!

The celestial bodies (*stoicheia*) are asteroids that break apart and catch fire as they enter the atmosphere. Peter has in mind Isaiah 34:4, echoed again in Revelation 6:13f.

Other passages that describe the earth being burned up include this from near the end of Isaiah's book:

> "Behold, Yahweh will come in fire
>   and his chariots like the whirlwind,
> to render his anger in fury
>   and his rebuke with flames of fire.
> For by fire Yahweh will enter into judgement
>   with all flesh, and by his sword,
>   and those slain by Yahweh will be many."

And the closing words of the entire Old Testament:

> "For behold, the day is coming burning like an oven, and all the arrogant and all evildoers will be stubble. And the day that is coming will set them ablaze, says Yahweh of hosts, so that it leaves them neither root nor branch."

Likewise the testimony of Jesus himself: "They were eating, drinking, buying, selling, planting, building, but on the day Lot went out from Sodom, fire and sulfur rained from heaven and destroyed them all. So it will be on the day when the Son of Man is revealed." (Luke 17:28f) "I came to cast fire on the earth, and would that it were already kindled!" (Luke 12:49) The fire will be a kind of baptism (Luke 3:16), cleansing the earth in the same way as water cleansed the earth in the days of Noah (1 Pet 3:21).

Trumpets were sounded before the fall of Jericho, the first city that God judged after Israel moved in to possess the land of Canaan. Each day seven priests walked round its fortified wall, blowing their trumpets, while the ark of the covenant followed them and the men of war marched in front and behind. On the seventh day they walked round the city seven times, the priests blowing their trumpets with each circuit. Then the people gave a great shout and the wall fell down—presumably in an earthquake related to the quake that had dammed up the Jordan days earlier (Ps 114:3f). The city was burned, along with everything in it (Josh 6:24).

> The destruction was complete. Walls and floors were blackened or reddened by fire, and every room was filled with fallen bricks, timbers, and household utensils; in most rooms the fallen debris was heavily burnt.[1]

At the close of the age the seven angels march, so to speak, round the great city that is global civilization, "Babylon the Great." It too will be felled by an earthquake and burned with fire.

And the seven angels who had the seven trumpets got ready to blow them.

The first blew his trumpet, and there was hail and fire, mixed with blood, and these were cast on the earth. And a third of the earth was burned up, and a third of the trees were burned up, and all green grass was burned up.

The trumpet that sounded when God summoned Israel to meet with him at Mount Sinai was not a man-made instrument blown by a man. It sounded from above, amidst cracks of thunder, lightning, thick cloud and erupting fire. Whether the sound this time will be audible is not stated; possibly it will.

"Earth" (*ge*, Heb. *erets*) can mean the whole planet (as in Gen 1:1), the land distinct from the sea (Gen 1:10), a particular land (e.g. Judah in Zeph 1:2f), the surface of the land (Rev 5:13) or the people living on the earth or land (Hab 2:20). In the preamble to all seven trumpets it signifies the whole planet; here in verse 7 the focus is on the land, especially its trees and its grass (*chortos*, as in Gen 1:11 LXX). "A third of the earth" suggests an intensification of the disasters brought on a fourth of the earth in 6:8; some of the trees perish, but the grass everywhere is consumed. The first four trumpets affect in turn the land, the sea, the sources of fresh water and the atmosphere: the entire biosphere.

A proximate natural cause does not exclude an ultimate supernatural cause. Though willed by God, the disasters are natural phenomena.

---

1. Kenyon, *Excavations at Jericho*, 370.

Since men have not believed what is written about him, the invisible power on the throne manifests his anger by touching what is visible. Hail and fire were the seventh of the plagues (in the sense of "calamity"—*plegē* literally means "stroke" or "blow") visited upon Egypt before the Exodus. Hail denotes a shower of rock and, where the context mentions fire but rules out rocks ejected from a volcano, suggests blazing meteoroids (as in Josh 10:11). However, the fire here is thrown onto entire continents: clearly not lightning, for which there is a separate word. The only source of fire external to the planet is the Sun.

In recent decades we have come to understand how fire might be cast on the Earth. For reasons still not understood, the Sun's atmosphere—its corona—is some two hundred times hotter than its surface: at least 1,000,000 degrees C. The corona is thus extremely energetic and continually sending forth a wind of superhot plasma: charged particles, electrons and protons that blow through space at speeds up to 1000 km per second. Spurts of such material are called coronal mass ejections. The most violent produce shock-waves capable of disrupting electric power grids and disabling satellites, the things on which the functioning of civilization now depends. One such ejection, known as the "Carrington Event," occurred in 1859 and caused telegraph systems to fail. Those of May 1921, March 1989 and July 2012 were of similar magnitude.[2]

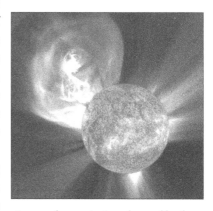

A coronal mass ejection observed by the SOHO spacecraft on 27 February 2000 (image of the sun superimposed).

The aurora borealis, along with its counterpart in the southern hemisphere, is the effect of the solar wind interacting with the Earth's atmosphere. During the most energetic storms, aurorae— like emerald-dominated rainbows—can be seen from pole to equator, accompanied by eerie sounds.[3] The thunder and lightning are the effect of the charged particles penetrating much lower than they normally would. That the solar wind could trigger earthquakes was once thought

2. Eastwood et al., "Impact of Space Weather," 206–18.

3. Amery, "People who Claim to Hear the Northern Lights."

implausible but now has statistical and theoretical support,[4] a remarkable validation of the biblical vision.

Revelation suggests at least two great mass ejections, one occurring at the first trumpet, and one when the fourth bowl is poured on the Sun. Shock waves depress the magnetosphere and impair its ability to deflect the particles, so that their energy heats up the lower atmosphere and scorches the earth. The shock waves also dislodge the asteroids and meteoroids that float in space near the earth. Hurricanes caused by the sudden heating whip up the sea, batter coastal cities and uproot trees. In the heat, lightning sparks wildfires, power cables melt, roads buckle, rivers become strings of islands (Isa 42:15). The trees and grass stand for vegetation generally, but particularly the seed-bearing kinds that provide food; botanically speaking, rice, wheat (*chortos* in Matt 13:26), barley, oats and corn are all species of grass. So famine will be one consequence of the fires (7:16) and drought another (Joel 1:17–20). Having been forewarned, readers should stock up.

Some of the global warming experienced in recent decades may be due to an increase in solar radiation; most of the rest is due to the increase in greenhouse gases in the atmosphere[5] brought about by our profligate consumerism. Half the world's rainforests as at 1960 have been destroyed, and at the current rate of destruction there will be none left in another sixty years. In June 2021 temperatures in Canada broke their previous record by 4–11° C, peaking at the village of Lytton at just under 50°; the following day Lytton caught fire. Were it allowed to run its course, the warming would wreak its own judgement. The solar mass ejections bring to a head by another mechanism what we have brought upon ourselves.

The coronavirus was so named (in 1968) because its spikes resembled the ejections of hot gas periodically seen on the Sun's corona. It too presages the day. SARS-CoV-2 came as a bolt out of the blue, but the virus was a natural one modified in the lab so as to maximize transmissibility; man's God-like ability to re-configure the genetic code was exercized for evil rather than good. As it spread around the world, mathematical modelers, psychologists, medical scientists, journalists, politicians

4. Chen et al., "Geomagnetic Storms and Global Earthquakes," 1270; Marchitelli et al., "Solar Activity and Large Earthquakes," 11495.

5. Connolly et al., "Temperature Trends," 131–98. The respective contributions are as yet unquantifiable. If solar radiation has increased, this may itself be indicative of future turmoil.

worked together to stoke mass panic, and in response, civilization shut down, gave its power and authority to "the prince of the power of the air" (Eph 2:2)—surely the reality behind today's radio, television and internet. Believing the threat to be apocalyptic, electorates surrendered everything, even authority over their bodies. "You have saved our lives; we will be slaves to Pharaoh." Masks were like spiritual veils, vaccination—injection of the genetic instructions for making the spike protein—like receiving the mark. Although the vast majority of those infected recovered, hardly anyone thought about the one who endowed man with his amazing immune system. Even churches shut their doors.

To those with eyes to see, the first trumpet will make it clear that the hour of trial has begun. They will urge people to understand where we are in history and read the Apocalypse for themselves, but the saints will be hated because of their message. Now justifiably terrified, the State will impose measures even more extreme than those imposed in reaction to the virus. The gospel will be outlawed as needlessly adding to the terror.

The second angel blew his trumpet, and ˊsomethingˋ like a great mountain, burning with fire, was cast into the sea, and a third of the sea became blood. And a third of the creatures in the sea died that had life, and a third of the ships were wrecked.

The first plague to afflict Egypt was the turning of the Nile to blood. A bloom of red algae caused by the fall-out of nutrient-rich ash from a volcanic eruption—that of Thera/Santorini, or from the Harrat Rahat area east of the Red Sea—consumed the dissolved oxygen in the water, so that all fish died and the water was poisoned.[6] The Egyptians had to dig for water.

As with the world's forests, industrial high-tech trawlers have been turning vast areas into ecological wilderness, to say nothing of the pollution from plastic and the cruelty of fish farms. This time the burning mountain is an asteroid, and it does not merely fall, it is actively thrown. Many animals will have already died on land, but John expressly mentions marine animals. Like their terrestrial counterparts they are living souls, more than just highly organized molecules. A third of the 50,000 merchant ships on the ocean either sink or become unusable, to say nothing of cruise ships and smaller craft, and undersea cables. The capacity to transport food, petroleum and other goods across the world is

---

6. Humphreys, *The Miracles of Exodus*; Trevisanato, *The Plagues of Egypt*.

crippled. Many mariners lose their lives. Coastal cities, towns and villages are overwhelmed by tsunamis.

In the ages following the Cataclysm asteroid impacts were not infrequent, the most famous being the impact at the end of the Cretaceous period which left a crater 190 km in diameter off the coast of Mexico. Only recently have we acquired sufficient geological knowledge to understand what Revelation is describing,[7] and the technological ability to turn it into mass entertainment. But this disaster is for real.

The third angel blew his trumpet, and a great star fell from heaven, burning like a torch, and it fell on a third of the rivers and on the springs of the waters. The name of the star is Wormwood. And a third of the water became wormwood, and much of mankind died from the water, because it had been made bitter.

The star (*aster*), an asteroid or comet, disintegrates on entering the atmosphere and showers the earth with toxin, possibly some form of cyanide since this is a common constituent of comets. Wormwood is proverbial for bitterness (Jer 9:15 RSV) and the name here prophetic (along the lines of Jer 20:3); it will not be the astronomical name, if it has one. Rivers, lakes and reservoirs become undrinkable. Men and animals die in large numbers.

The fourth angel blew his trumpet, and a third of the sun was struck, and a third of the moon, and a third of the stars, so that a third of them should be darkened and a third of the day should not shine, and the night likewise.

The specific mention of the sun, moon and stars rather than simply the heaven evokes the fourth day of Creation and thereby underlines the magnitude of what is happening. Partly obscured by earth-enveloping clouds of dust, the heavens foreshadow the coming Day of the Lord, "a day of clouds and thick darkness" (Isa 60:2, Joel 2:2, Amos 5:20, Zeph 1:15). Hebrew has various words for darkness (Isa 8:22–9:2). "Thick darkness" (one word) is particularly associated with the dwelling of God and with the final day of reckoning. At Mount Sinai God spoke to the people "out of the midst of fire, cloud and thick darkness" (Deut 5:22). In David's vision "he bowed the heavens and came down; thick darkness was under his feet" (Ps 18:9). Thick darkness was the penultimate plague of the Exodus, again presumably the effect of an ash cloud. Here,

---

7. Alvarez, *T. Rex and the Crater of Doom.*

since the first four disasters are all triggered by the solar wind, the cause
is probably the dust and vapor thrown up by another dislodged asteroid,
this time hitting the land. Deprived of the Sun's heat, the earth cools.
Murder, looting, and rape follow.

The heavens—long a source of wonder, and never more so than in
the age of the Hubble Space Telescope—become a source of terror. But
the door is not closed. There is still time to repent.

And I looked, and I heard one eagle say with a loud voice as it flew
overhead, "Woe, woe, woe to the inhabitants of the earth, at the sound of
the other trumpets that the three angels are about to blow!"

Each disaster is worse than the one before. Following the last, even
birds are rare (Jer 4:25, Zeph 1:3), though eagles will be among the birds
feeding on the flesh of God's enemies when they are defeated (Matt
24:28). One of them flying above the devastation—or perhaps it is an
angel?—announces that three woes are yet to precede the full force of
his wrath. Man's understanding of reality acknowledges only the natural,
and interprets even consciousness, his sense of self and of being alive,
as reducible to electricity, but he will be made to understand that there
exists a supernatural realm, below him if not above.

And the fifth angel blew his trumpet, and I saw a star fallen from
heaven to earth, and he was given the key to the shaft of the abyss. And
he opened the shaft of the abyss, and out of the shaft rose smoke like that
of a great furnace, and the sun and the air were darkened by the smoke of
the shaft. And out of the smoke came locusts onto the earth, and they were
given power like that of the earth's scorpions. And they were told not to
harm the grass of the earth or any green plant or any tree, but rather those
of mankind who did not have the seal of God on their foreheads. And it was
given, not that they should kill them, but that they should torment them for
five months. And their torment was like the torment of a scorpion when it
stings a man. And in those days men will seek death and fail to find it. They
will long to die, and death will flee from them.

Stars in the visible world (8:12) correspond to angels in the invisible;
also to the host of the redeemed, who will be like angels when they are
glorified (Gen 15:5, Job 38:7, Dan 12:3, Luke 20:36, Rev 1:20). The star
here is an angel long since cast out of heaven. The abyss (lit. "bottomless")
is the infernal region called Tartarus, in Hebrew Abaddon (Job 31:12). It
connects with the surface world through a volcanic shaft (as indicated by

the furnace simile, cf. Exod 19:18). Volcanic ash renews the darkness of the fourth trumpet.

Originally the abyss was a subterranean region of water, called the great deep (Gen 1:2 and 7:11, LXX *abussos*). After the Cataclysm, around the end of the eon called the Hadean, it was filled by the newly molten material of the upper mantle, and deviant angels were confined there pending the day of judgement (Gen 6:4, Jude 6). Wherever the gospel transforms society, communication with the abyss is suppressed, but now it is opened up. The locusts emerging from the smoke recall the eighth plague before the Exodus, noxious examples of the insects created on the fifth day of Creation, but these do not eat vegetation (grown back since the first trumpet); they are invisible demons, with power to torment.

The reality of the distinction between saved and unsaved becomes apparent. Those who have the Holy Spirit, God's seal of ownership (2 Cor 1:22), are not protected from physical disasters but are protected from the demons. The torments of the fifth and sixth trumpets give a foretaste of Gehenna (Matt 13:42), which will certainly not be less terrible than the torments about to be inflicted. Nonetheless those tormented will seek death rather than turn to God and call on the name of his son to drive away the demons.

And in appearance the locusts were like horses prepared for battle. And on their heads were what looked like crowns of gold, and their faces like human faces. And they had hair like women's hair and teeth like those of lions. And they had breastplates like breastplates of iron, and the sound of their wings was like the sound of many horse-drawn chariots rushing into battle. And they have tails and stings like scorpions, and in their tails is their power to harm mankind for five months. They have a king over them, the angel of the abyss. His name in Hebrew is Abaddon, and in Greek, Destroyer.

The description evokes a terrible invading army. In Joel's prophecy, locusts are sent to plague Judah because they have neglected to offer grain and drink offerings and acknowledge that God is the source of fruitfulness; therefore he destroys the harvest and brings drought on the land. Interwoven with the account of devastation is a vision of the final day. Gradually that day becomes the dominant theme:

> And I will show wonders in the heavens above
> and signs on the earth below,
> blood, and fire, and columns of smoke;

> the sun will be turned to darkness
> and the moon to blood,
> before the day of the Lord comes,
> the great and terrible day.

The locusts become symbolic of a human army that invades the land and sells its people into slavery, until God enters into judgement with the invaders. In Revelation the locusts are demonic, resembling warhorses that merge with their belligerent riders, and the plague strikes at the same time as Israel is occupied. They afflict everyone who does not acknowledge that God made the natural world and its goodness.

> They do not say in their heart,
> "Let us fear Yahweh our God,
> who gives the rains of autumn and spring in their season
> and keeps for us the appointed weeks of harvest."
> (Jer 5:24)

Abaddon in Hebrew means "Destruction," translated into Greek as *Apollyon*, Destroyer, the equivalent of Tartarus. Only here does Scripture reveal that the place is ruled by an angel. The demons torment others before they themselves are tormented.

The first woe has passed; behold, two woes are yet to come.

And the sixth angel blew his trumpet, and I heard one voice from the four horns of the golden altar before God say to the sixth angel who had the trumpet, "Release the four angels who are bound at the great river Euphrates." So the four angels, who had been prepared for the hour, the day, the month and the year, were released to kill a third of mankind. And the armies of the horsemen numbered two hundred million; I heard their number. And this was the appearance of the horses and their riders in the vision: their breastplates were fiery and hyacinthine and sulfurous, and the heads of the horses were like lions' heads, and fire, smoke and sulfur came out of their mouths. From these three plagues a third of mankind was killed, by the fire, smoke and sulfur coming out of their mouths. For the power of the horses is in their mouths and in their tails, for their tails are like snakes, having heads, and by them they harm.

The four angels were formerly cast out of heaven and chained. On being released, they bring up a vast horde of demonic quadrupeds. Fire, smoke and sulfur suggest natural phenomena, with "hyacinthine" referring to the blue glow of igniting sulfuric gases, but these emanations issue from their mouths. Notwithstanding previous echoes of the Exodus, they are the first afflictions to be called plagues. They come from the planet's fiery interior, and the power to kill is supernatural. Having been tormented for five months, a third of mankind die: 2.6 billion people. Much as one would like to say that the fraction applies to just a part of the earth, the number of horsemen—indeed, armies—does not justify a mitigating view, and John says that he heard correctly. The punctiliousness of the whole paragraph regarding number is also corroborative. The preceding catastrophes are all global in scope, and most probably this one is. Worse is to come (Isa 13:9–12, 10:23):

> Behold, the day of the LORD comes,
>   cruel, with wrath and fierce anger,
> to make the earth a desolation
>   and to destroy its sinners from it.
> For the stars of the heavens and their constellations
>   will not shine their light;
> the sun will be darkened at its rising
>   and the moon will not shed its light.
> "I will punish the world for its evil
>   and the wicked for their iniquity;
> I will put an end to the arrogance of the haughty,
>   and the pride of the ruthless I will lay low.
> I will make men rarer than fine gold,
>   and mankind than the gold of Ophir."

The Lord Yahweh of hosts will make a full end, as decreed, in the midst of all the earth.

And the rest of mankind, who were not killed by these plagues, did not repent of the works of their hands so as not to worship the demons and the idols of gold and silver and bronze and stone and wood which cannot see nor hear nor walk. And they did not repent of their murders, nor of their drug-taking, nor of their fornication, nor of their thefts.

After the destruction of a third of the planet's vegetation, a third of its marine life and a third of its freshwater life, a third of mankind is killed: a plague more horrific than the slaughter of Egypt's firstborn, on top of the throng, too great to number, that dies from hunger and thirst (7:9). At the start we are not told why all this has to be. Now we learn that it is to see whether anything can break the addiction to buying and owning things, and evaluating life in relation to them; whether anything can cause man to see that the good of his soul is not to be found in idols.

Prophets explain what the plagues mean. "You knew that your pursuit of pleasure was destroying the planet, yet you carried on, regardless of generations yet unborn. So God is taking away what we, his stewards, cared so little to keep. Do you not see that these calamities were prophesied?" Not all are killed, despite not having the seal of God on their foreheads. Those that remain are more hardened than ever. The word "repent" occurs four times after the letters to the churches, twice here and twice in relation to the bowls of wrath, each time in the negative.

"The" demons refers to all demons, including those previously below ground and those unwittingly worshiped as gods, whether in Africa, Asia or the atheistic West. "Drug-taking" translates *pharmakeia*, in the ancient world the use or dispensing of drugs to induce hallucinations or abortions. The taking of mind-altering narcotics frequently leads to demon possession. "Sorcery" or "occultism" would also be a viable translation, and in the modern context might include any technology that transports voices and images into the living room, entertaining and deceiving; for these too come from the prince of the authority of the air. The first commandment is to have no other gods before him who made heaven and earth, the sea and everything in them. All forms of immorality (murder, fornication, theft, covetousness) are symptoms of alienation from the true God, and ultimately to refuse to worship him is to worship other spirits. By this stage they have indeed taken over the world.

The Two Witnesses
and the Last Trumpet

Revelation 10–11. Gentiles will again occupy the land of Israel, while two prophets teach the Jews about their Messiah and testify against the world. After three and a half years they are killed and rise again.

And I saw another mighty angel coming down from heaven, wrapped in cloud, and the rainbow was on his head, and his face like the sun, and his feet like pillars of fire, and holding in his hand a little scroll, open. And he set his right foot on the sea and his left on the land, and he cried with a loud voice, like a lion roaring. And as he cried, the seven thunders also gave voice. And as the seven thunders spoke, I was about to write. And I heard a voice from heaven say, "Seal what the seven thunders have spoken, and do not write it down." And the angel whom I saw standing on the sea and on the land raised his right hand to heaven and swore by him who lives for ever and ever, who created the heaven and what is in it, the land and what is in it, and the sea and what is in it, that no more time would be given, but in the days of the trumpet to be sounded by the seventh angel, the mystery of God would also have been fulfilled, as he announced to his servants the prophets.

WHEN JOHN SAW JESUS Christ at the beginning of the book, he hardly recognized him, so terrifyingly different was he from the man he knew in his youth. Here Jesus seems even more distant. It is left for us to recognize who he is, by the enveloping cloud (1:7), "the" rainbow (an attribute of the throne of God, 4:3), the sun-like radiance of his face (1:16), the fire extending even to his feet (as in Ezekiel's vision), his voice like a roaring lion's (5:5). The details are not incidental: they allude to the phenomena that will precede and accompany his appearance when he comes down "with a shout of command, with voice of archangel and with trumpet of God." "Mighty angel" (first at 5:2) seems to be another term for archangel.

The continual cry of God's suffering people was "How long, O Lord?" Straddling sea and land and swearing by the God who lives for ever, this same angel swore to Daniel that all the wonders revealed to him, including the resurrection, would be accomplished when the shattering of their power had come to an end, and now he says, "There will be no more delay." The text also evokes Hosea's words concerning the northern kingdom (11:10f):

> Behind Yahweh they will walk.
>> He will roar like a lion when he roars.
> And his sons will come trembling from the west,
>> they will come trembling like birds from Egypt
>> and like doves from the land of Assyria.
> And I will settle them in their houses,
>> declares Yahweh.

As with the seven spirits, the seven thunders are a kind of divine plural rather than successive claps. John is forbidden to disclose the message, apparently because time has run out; the six trumpets of warning have passed and he must mentally seal what he has heard. What the angel cries is also not recorded, but he roars along with the thunder, Father and Son together. As in the gospels, the voice from heaven is the voice of God, which can itself seem like thunder (Ps 18:13, John 12:29).

The mystery of God, which goes back to the Creation, is about to be realized. The world's wise will continue to assure us that there is no Creator. They will continue to maintain that the universe of two trillion galaxies arose from a "singularity" the size of a pea, that the power to move at will can be reduced to the properties of atoms, that DNA is a program without a programmer and therefore, if we do wonder at the wonders of Nature, we must do so unthinkingly. But God is God, and his purpose will be fulfilled. In the Old Testament the word "mystery" occurs only in Daniel, and refers to the king of Babylon's dream about how all human kingdoms would be terminated by the kingdom of the Messiah. In the New Testament the word is used variously, but "mystery of God" appears only once elsewhere, referring simply to Christ (Col 2:2). "Also" signifies that in the days (plural) during which the seventh trumpet will sound all remaining prophecy will be fulfilled.

The seventh trumpet is not blown until 11:15. The three and a half years during which the two witnesses prophesy, encompassed by 11:1–14, fall within, not after, the period of the trumpets. Accordingly, while the second woe is clearly that of the penultimate trumpet (8:13), the woe does not pass until the end of their prophesying.

And the voice that I heard from heaven spoke to me again, saying, "Go, take the little scroll that is open in the hand of the angel standing on the sea and on the land." So I went to the angel and said to him, "Give me the little scroll." And he says to me, "Take, and eat it up; it will make your stomach bitter, but in your mouth it will be as sweet as honey." And I took the little scroll from the hand of the angel and ate it up. And it was as sweet as honey in my mouth. And when I ate it my stomach became bitter. And he says to me, "You must again prophesy about many peoples and nations and languages and kings."

The small edible scroll (*biblaridion*, diminutive of *biblion*) recalls the ministry of Ezekiel, which began with a vision of the divine glory similar to that inaugurating John's prophecy. After the vision, Yahweh handed him a scroll filled with lamentation and woe; it was sweet as honey in his mouth, but when he rejoined the exiles to whom he had to deliver the message he experienced bitterness. The ingesting and digesting of the scroll metaphorically enacted what prophecy was: assimilating and speaking the words of God, then writing them down. The same hand now gives John a scroll.

Peoples and nations have already been the subject of chapters 6–7. In this third allusion to Genesis 10–11 "kings" is substituted for "tribes," a reminder that God multiplied man's language in opposition to the first king. Chapter 11 concerns Jerusalem's occupation by the nations. Chapter 12 speaks of a Jewish king who will rule all nations. Chapter 13 concerns a Gentile king who will exercise authority over every tribe and language and nation in opposition to his yet-to-come Jewish counterpart. Chapters 15–19 concern the judgement of the nations.

And I was given a rod-like reed, and told, "Rise, and measure the temple of God and the altar and those who worship in it, and exclude the court outside the temple; do not measure it, for it was given to the nations, and they will tread the holy city for forty-two months."

Ezekiel, in the last part of his book, saw "a structure like a city" and within it the house of God, including an altar. An angel showed him

round the building, and as he went he measured each part, to empha-
size in specific, physical terms (as in Jer 31:38–40 and Zech 2:1–5)
that Jerusalem would recover from its destruction. God would set his
throne and habitation there for ever, in the midst of his people. In AD 70
Jerusalem was destroyed a second time. Despite this apparent negation,
John is to understand that the vision seen by Ezekiel will come to pass.

As rebuilt by Herod, the Temple precincts were divided into four
courts. The three nearest the Temple were reserved for the priests, for
Jewish men, and for Jewish women. Surrounding them was a court open
to the Gentiles. The Temple proper, *naos*, consisted of an outer Holy Place
(*hagia*) and, behind a curtain, the inner Holy of Holies (*hagia hagiwn*).
The Temple as a whole, courts and building, was the *hieron*.

Much eroded relief on the Arch of Titus, Rome, showing prisoners of war being
paraded through the city after Jerusalem's destruction in AD 70. On their shoulders
they carry the golden menorah and silver trumpets of their beloved Temple, while
behind them Romans carry placards that probably bore the names of the cities they
conquered. Two and a half centuries later Rome became itself the bearer of the light.

In Revelation, references to the temple are always to the heavenly
dwelling. Just as there is only one altar, so there is only one temple, and
those redeemed by the blood of Jesus worship there (Heb 10:19–22).
Indeed, they are the temple (1 Cor 3:16f), and in the sense of measuring
someone by a standard (2 Cor 10:12), it is they who are measured. The
court outside represents the holy city (Dan 9:24) surrounding the earthly

temple area. The nations about whom John has been told to prophesy will occupy Jerusalem for three and a half years, the "time, times and half a time" during which Daniel was told a blaspheming king would oppress the Jews before his dominion was taken away and the kingdom given to them.

Near the end of his ministry Jesus warned that a day would come when the city would be surrounded by armies and Judaea's inhabitants fall by the sword and be led captive out of the land. Jerusalem's encircle-ment would be a sign that its devastation, or desolation (*eremwsis* can mean either), was near. These would be "days of vengeance, to fulfill all that is written," following which Jerusalem would be "trodden by the nations until the times of the nations" were fulfilled (Luke 21:24). Was this, as some interpret, a reference to the revolt against the Romans in AD 67–70? Many were slaughtered, others were deported and sold as slaves, and Jerusalem laid waste. In the reign of Hadrian the city was rebuilt, from which time the city was ruled by non-Jews until the Arab-Israeli War of 1948, when Israel became a state and the western part of Jerusalem came under Jewish control. In 1967, following another war, Israel took over the eastern part.

But the interpretation has its problems. For one thing, the Temple Mount remains in Muslim hands, and more than a third of the popula-tion is Arab: Gentiles still tread the city. Another is that Jesus had already foretold the events of AD 70 (Luke 19:41–44). The present passage is part of a longer discourse that parallels the discourse in Matthew 24:1–35, and there the subject is the events leading up to his return. In both gospels the discourses consist of five sections, of which the section about Jerusalem is the third. In Matthew's account:

> "So when you see the abomination of desolation as spoken of by the prophet Daniel standing in the Holy Place (let the reader understand), then those in Judaea should flee to the hills. Whoever is on the rooftop must not go down to take anything out of the house, and whoever is in the field must not turn back to take his cloak. Alas for those who are pregnant, and for those who are nursing infants in those days! Pray that your flight may not be in winter, or on a sabbath. For then there will be great tribulation such as has not been from the beginning of the world until now, no, and never will be."

Since the reference to Daniel would have meant nothing to Gentile readers, Luke omits what Jesus said about the abomination of desolation. Instead, he fills the section with details omitted by Matthew. Two elements remain identical: the warning that those living in Judaea should flee to the hills and the warning that women slowed down by their children would be particularly vulnerable.

"Vengeance" is a key word in Old Testament prophecy, and refers primarily to the retribution God will exact on his enemies in the last days (e.g. Deut 32:43, Isa 34:8). "Trodden" (from *patew*) is another key word. While it links with "trampled" in Daniel 7:7 and hence with the destruction by the Romans, it also links with the vision in this chapter. Speaking about the end, Zechariah says, "I will make Jerusalem a trampled stone for all the nations: every one that tramples on it will mock it, and all the nations of the earth will gather against it" (Zech 12:3 LXX, where the verb is *katapatew*, "tread down"; also in the Peshitta text). "Times of the nations" verbally links with the "time, times and half a time" in Daniel 7 and 12 and Revelation 12:14, again referring to the end. For these reasons, it seems better to interpret Luke 21:20–24 as referring to a crisis yet to occur.

The events are to fulfill "all that is written." That the land will be resettled but then come under Gentile occupation before the Messiah returns is clear from many Old Testament prophecies besides Daniel:

Deuteronomy 4:30, 32:36

> When you are in tribulation, and all these things come upon you in the last days, you will return to Yahweh your God and obey his voice.

> Yahweh will vindicate his people and give comfort to his servants when he sees that their power is gone and there is no one [to help], bondman or free.

Isaiah 10:24, 9:4f, 14:3f, 30:26, 49:21 (and 24–26), 52:2–5

> Be not afraid of Assyria [Iraq] when he strikes you. . . . For the yoke of his burden and the staff of his shoulder, the rod of his oppressor, you have broken as on the day of Midian. For every marching boot in the tumult, and garment rolled in blood, will be burned as fuel for the fire.

> In the day that Yahweh gives you rest from your pain and your turmoil and the hard labour which was forced upon you, you will take up this chant concerning the king of Babylon.

The light of the moon will be as the light of the sun, and the light of the sun will be sevenfold, as the light of seven days, in the day when the Lord binds up the brokenness of his people and heals the wound of his blow.

Shake yourself from the dust, arise, take your seat, O Jerusalem; loose the bonds from your neck, O captive daughter of Zion. For thus says Yahweh: "You were sold for nothing, and you shall be redeemed without money." For thus says Yahweh the Lord: "My people went down at first into Egypt to dwell there, and finally Assyria [Iraq] oppressed them. And now what have I here?" declares Yahweh, "My people are taken away for nothing. Their rulers mock," declares Yahweh, "and all day long my name is blasphemed."

Jeremiah 30:6–8 (and 9–11)

Why then do I see every man with his hands on his stomach like a woman in labour, and every face turned pale? Alas. Great is that day; there will be none like it. It is a time of distress for Jacob. But he will be saved out of it. And it shall come to pass in that day, declares Yahweh of hosts, that I will break his yoke from off your neck and burst your bonds, and foreigners will no more enslave him.

Ezekiel 34:12, 27

As a shepherd seeks out his flock when he is among his sheep that are scattered, so will I seek out my sheep, and I will rescue them from all the places where they are scattered, on a day of cloud and thick darkness. . . . And they shall know that I am Yahweh, when I break the bars of their yoke, and deliver them from the hand of those who enslaved them.

Joel 3:1–3

When I reverse the captivity of Judah and Jerusalem, I will gather all the nations and bring them down to the Valley of Jehoshaphat. And I will enter into judgement with them there on account of my people and my heritage Israel, whom they scattered among the nations. They divided up my land, and cast lots for my people, and have given a boy to prostitution, and sold a girl for wine to drink.

Micah 5:5f

And he will bring peace when Assyria comes into our land and treads in our citadels. And we shall raise against him [the invader] seven shepherds and eight leaders, and they will shepherd [rule] the land of Assyria with the sword, and the land of Nimrod at its entrances. And he will deliver us from Assyria when he comes into our land and treads within our borders.

Zechariah 9:10, 16, 14:2f

I will cut off the chariot from Ephraim [northern Israel] and the war horse from Jerusalem. . . . On that day Yahweh their God will save them.

I will gather all the nations against Jerusalem to battle, and the city will be taken and the houses plundered and the women raped. And half of the city will go into exile, but the rest of the people will not be cut off from the city.

The Jews were expelled from their land because they had rejected their Messiah (Luke 19:27, 44, 20:16). They still have not accepted him, even though their return in the years up to and after 1948 cannot be construed as other than providential, and God was clearly with them in the wars of 1967 and 1973. He has therefore not granted them absolute title to the land. Indeed, he seems to have denied them control of the Temple Mount precisely to prevent the rebuilding of the Temple. Moreover, the Palestinians who were living there before them also have land rights. "The one law shall apply to the native and to the stranger who sojourns among you" (Exod 12:49).

The nations and kings that conquer Israel will be a confederation of Muslim nations. As we have seen in the way the self-styled Islamic State of Iraq and Syria treated Christians and Yazidis, they will sell the Jews into slavery, kill them, rape them, lay their cities waste, and send them out of their land. Western nations will be unwilling or unable to intervene (Isa 63:5).

"And I will give to my two witnesses, and they will prophesy for 1260 days, clothed in sackcloth." These are the two olive trees and the two lampstands that stand before the Lord of the earth. And if anyone would harm them, fire issues from their mouth and consumes their enemies, and if anyone would harm them, thus must he be killed. These have authority to shut the heaven, so that no rain falls during the days of their prophecy, and

*they have authority over the waters to turn them into blood and to strike
the earth with every kind of plague, as often as they will.*

The olive trees and lampstands recall the one lampstand and two
olive trees that Zechariah saw after waking from his previous vision. In
design the lampstand was the same as the gold menorah in the outer
part of the Tabernacle, whose seven lamps were like the seven "eyes of
Yahweh, ranging through all the earth." But in Revelation there are two
lampstands, and the prophets themselves are sources of divine light.
When Zechariah asked what the olive trees were, he was told, "These are
the two sons of oil that stand by the Lord of all the earth."

The two witnesses are dressed in the garb of mourning (Joel 1:13). The
fire issuing from their mouths is metaphorical but of deadly effect. They
have power comparable to that of Moses (Exod 7–10) and Elijah (1 Kgs 17,
2 Kgs 1), God's representatives in the two great contests with Satan's representatives, Pharaoh king of Egypt and Ahab king of Israel. They also stand
for the Law and the Prophets, which close with these words:

> "Remember the law of my servant Moses, its statutes and judge-
> ments, that I commanded him at Horeb for all Israel. Behold,
> I will send you Elijah the prophet before the day of Yahweh
> comes, the great and terrible day. And he will turn the hearts of
> fathers to their sons and the hearts of sons to their fathers, lest I
> come and strike the land with total destruction."

Moses and Elijah appeared at Jesus's transfiguration to bear witness to
who he was. The disciples with him were drowsy, "heavy with sleep," and
initially, like the rest of Israel, they did not see his glory (cf. Isa 29:10, Jer
31:26). He charged them not to tell anyone what they had seen until he
had risen from the dead. Perplexed, they asked him, "Do not the scribes
say that Elijah must come first?" He confirmed Malachi's prophecy.
"Elijah does come first and he will restore all things." But it was also true
he had already come in the person of John the Baptist: not that John was
a reincarnation of Elijah but that he had come in Elijah's spirit and power
(Luke 1:17).

So it will happen that two men will appear in the power and spirit
of these two prophets. They will bear witness for the same length of time
that Elijah stopped rain from falling in the reign of Ahab (1 Kgs 17:1,
Luke 4:25). They will call upon the Jews to wake from their sleep (Zech
4:1, Isa 52:1) and give heed to what is written (Isa 8:20). They will recall
the ten commandments of Moses, including the commandment not to

bow down before the image of anything or anyone in heaven or on earth; for there is only one image of God. They will point out the large stone which Joshua set up at Shechem, modern Nablus, as a witness of Israel's renewal of the covenant before he dismissed them each to his inheritance (Jos 24:26). God had told Moses, "I will raise up for them a prophet like you from among your brothers." Yeshua, they will explain, was that prophet, the one whom they pierced. They will warn that the glorified Messiah is coming to gather the wheat into his barn and burn the chaff with fire. They will open up the words of the book of Daniel. In response, many will hear (Isa 29:18) and "purify themselves and be made white and be refined" (Dan 12:9f). They will be gathered when the other saints are gathered and sit with Abraham, Isaac and Jacob at the great banquet in heaven. The remainder will find themselves shut out of the kingdom, banished to the darkness about to envelop the earth (Isa 8:22, Matt 8:12).

The prophets have power over all parts of the natural world. Like Elijah, they have authority to cause drought and, like Moses, authority to poison the waters and afflict the earth with multiple plagues (1 Sam 4:8 confirms the allusion). As in Malachi 4:6, "earth" could mean "land" or the whole planet. The context of the holy city suggests land, for the purpose of the plagues is to bear down on the beast. On the other hand, some details suggest the confrontation is being played out on a bigger, even global, stage. The possibilities are not mutually exclusive: Elijah may be speaking primarily to Israel, Moses to the Gentiles. That perhaps is why, at the end of Malachi, only Elijah is mentioned as sent to Israel.

And when they have finished their testimony, the beast that rises from the abyss will make war on them and conquer them and kill them, and their corpse `will lie` on the street of the great city that is spiritually called Sodom and Egypt, where also their Lord was crucified. And for three and a half days some from the peoples and tribes and languages and nations look at their corpse and refuse to let their corpses be placed in a tomb. And the inhabitants of the earth rejoice over them and make merry and will send presents to one another, because these two prophets tormented the inhabitants of the earth.

The beast is a Satan-inspired individual who leads an alliance of ten national leaders (Rev 13). The inhabitants of the earth are those who do not worship in heaven's temple but consider earth their home (cf. John 3:31). Because they refuse to repent, the prophets call forth torments on them, namely the demons released with the fifth and sixth trumpets. The beast is powerless to harm or silence the prophets until their testimony is over. "Make war" implies a campaign against more than two persons; in parallel occurrences of the phrase the people warred against are the saints (the Jews, 13:7) and those who bear witness to Jesus (Christians beyond Palestine who reinforce the testimony of the two prophets). Their mission accomplished, the two witnesses in Jerusalem (Luke 13:33) and the 144,000 witnesses in the streets of "the great city" are killed. Gentile-occupied Jerusalem where Christ was crucified is part of the archetypal great city. The city is called Sodom because of its pride, complacency and homosexuality (Ezek 16:49f) and Egypt because of its idol worship and persecution of the saints. The martyrs are spiritually one body, the body of Christ (Acts 9:5, 1 Cor 12:13) that lies dead on the city's one street. Some will be crucified, as Christians were in first-century Judaea (Matt 23:34) and in Nero's Rome; some will be beheaded (20:4). Those who are of the earth will rejoice.

And after the three and a half days a breath of life from God entered them, and they stood on their feet, and great fear fell on those watching them. And they heard a loud voice from heaven say to them, "Come up." And they ascended to heaven in the cloud, while their enemies watched. And at that hour there was a great earthquake, and a tenth of the city fell, and seven thousand individuals were killed in the earthquake. And the rest became fearful and gave glory to the God of heaven.

It is not true to state that the biblical writers all counted inclusively, so that Sunday was the third day after Friday. The Greeks and Romans counted inclusively (Luke 9:28, Acts 10:30), the Hebrew writers, along with Jesus himself, non-inclusively, as we do (Matt 17:1, Mark 9:2). Thus the 40.5 years of David's reign were rounded down to 40 years, not up to 41 (2 Sam 5:4f); Jehoiachin's reign of 3 months 10 days was rounded down to 3 months, not up to 4 (2 Kgs 24:8, 2 Chr 36:9). Concerning his own resurrection, Christ was explicit: "Just as Jonah was three days and three nights in the belly of the whale, so will the Son of Man be three days and three nights in the heart of the earth" (Matt 12:40). "After three days I will rise" (Matt 27:64, Mark 9:31). "On the third day" (Matt 27:64, Hos 6:2) therefore means on the third day after his death. When the chronology of Passion Week is reconciled with the days of the week corresponding to them in the calendar, it is apparent that he was crucified on the morning of Thursday 6 April, AD 30, and rose again before dawn on

Sunday 9 April.[1] The two and a half days in the grave corresponded to the two and a half years of his ministry, beginning from the year that began in the seventh month of AD 27 and overlapping with John's ministry, which began AD 26. "Behold, I cast out demons and perform cures today and tomorrow, and the third day I finish" (Luke 13:32).

The two prophets' coming back to life completes their testimony. Just as the testimony of John the Baptist and Jesus Christ continued for three and a half years, so does theirs. Just as the Father raised the Son from the grave after two and half days, so he raises them after three and a half days, one day for each year of ministry. And just as Christ ascended to heaven in a cloud while others looked on, so do they. Their resurrection attests that their testimony is true, for as with the Lamb, in their mouth no deceit is found (Isa 53:9, Rev 14:5).

Despite funeral sermons to the contrary, the Bible does not say that believers go to heaven the moment they die. They are raised corporately, on an appointed day, and nature manifests the event. When Jesus rose from the dead, an earthquake split the rocks, and the saints in Jerusalem rose with him out of their tombs. Another quake shakes Jerusalem as the martyred witnesses rise. Those not killed by it fear God and glorify him by repenting. The resurrection of other believers, and subsequently of all Israel, is yet to come.

The words "A breath of life from God entered them, and they stood on their feet" bring to mind Ezekiel's description of the day when all Israel will rise:

> So I prophesied as I was commanded. And as I prophesied, there was a sound, and behold, an earthquake, and the bones came together, bone to its bone. And I looked, and behold, there were sinews on them, and flesh came upon them, and skin covered them. But there was no breath in them. Then he said to me, "Prophesy to the breath. Prophesy, son of man [or Adam], and say to the breath, Thus says Yahweh the Lord: Come from the four winds, O breath, and breathe on these slain, that they may live." So I prophesied as he commanded me, and the breath came into them, and they lived and stood on their feet, a very, very great army.
>
> Then he said to me, "Son of man, these bones are the whole house of Israel. Behold, they say, 'Our bones are dried up, and our hope is lost; we are indeed cut off.' Therefore prophesy, and say to

---

1. Nisan 1, the first day of the year, was fixed by the sighting of the crescent new moon. In AD 30 it fell on March 24 ±1.

them, Thus says Yahweh the Lord: Behold, I will open your graves
and raise you from your graves, O my people. And I will bring
you into the land of Israel. And you shall know that I am Yahweh,
when I open your graves, and raise you from your graves, O my
people. And I will put my spirit within you, and you shall live, and
I will set you in your own land." (Ezek 37:7–14)

At last God will fulfill his four-thousand-year-old covenant with
Abraham to give to his offspring the land from the Nile to the Euphrates
(Gen 15:18), briefly fulfilled under David and Solomon inasmuch as all
kings accepted their suzerainty (1 Chr 13:5, 2 Chr 7:8, 9:26). The prophets
repeat the promise numerous times, the psalms express the hope of
resurrection numerous times. He will fuse the tribes of the northern and
southern kingdoms to make them one again (Jer 3:18, Ezek 11:14–17,
37:22). He will roar like a lion, heaven and earth will quake (Joel 3:16),
and his sons will come trembling from the west, from Egypt, and from
Assyria. He will gather the descendants of Israel from among the peoples
and bring them back to their land, as Moses himself predicted (Deut
30:1–10). How can the promise be fulfilled for all generations except by
such a resurrection? And what can the reversal of their captivity mean
but reversal of their imprisonment in Sheol (Isa 42:7, 49:9, 52:2), as Paul
too foresaw (Rom 11:15)? Jews in the Diaspora have lived and died away
from the promised land for two and a half millennia; the northern tribes
do not even exist as a distinguishable entity. While they lived, they did
not receive what was promised.

"Breath," "wind" and "spirit" in Ezekiel's prophecy are all the same
word, *ruach*, the same as denotes the Spirit of God (Gen 1:2). Without
the spirit which God breathes into a child as he knits its parts together in
the womb (Job 10:11f) the body is lifeless, just as Adam's body was lifeless. How can any believer assent to the doctrine that spirit is a form of
matter? Rising from the dead, will he be content with the reconstitution
of flesh and bones? Are we just atoms obeying the laws of physics?

The resurrection of the martyred prophets in "the" cloud—the last
mention of a cloud was at 10:1—is a sign to the enslaved and exiled Jews
that their forefathers also are about to rise, though the bowls of wrath
must come first.

> He will raise a signal for the nations
>   and assemble the outcasts of Israel,
> and the dispersed of Judah he will gather
>   from the four corners of the earth. (Isa 11:12)

> In that day a loud trumpet will be blown, and those who were lost in the land of Assyria [Israelites of the northern kingdom] and those expelled in the land of Egypt [the Jews of the Diaspora, e.g. Jer 44:8] will come and worship Yahweh on the holy mountain at Jerusalem. (Isa 27:13)

> He will send out his angels with a loud trumpet call, and they will gather his elect from the four winds, from one end of heaven to the other. (Matt 24:31)

This is the call prefigured by the sounding of the trumpet in the year of jubilee, on the day of atonement (Lev 25:9), after the trumpets on the first day of the month (Lev 23:24). Liberty was to be proclaimed throughout the land.

> "I will say to the north, Give up,
>   and to the south, Do not withhold;
> bring my sons from afar
>   and my daughters from the end of the earth,
> everyone who is called by my name,
>   whom I created for my glory." (Isa 43:6f)

> "The days are coming, Yahweh declares, when it shall no longer be said, 'As Yahweh lives who brought up the children of Israel from the land of Egypt,' but 'As Yahweh lives who brought up the children of Israel from the north country and out of all the countries where he had driven them.' For I will return them to their land that I gave to their fathers." (Jer 16:14f)

Note the sense of being raised in the verb "brought up." "From the depths of the earth you will bring me up again" (Ps 71:20). This is not a prophecy about Jews "making aliyah" at their own initiative. The curse being spent, he himself will bring them into the land (Deut 30:3–5). He will make a new covenant with them, different from the covenant which they broke when they first came out of the wilderness. Not that the Law will be abrogated, but that he will indwell them through his Spirit and write his Law on their hearts (Deut 30:6, Jer 31:31–34).

In polytheistic societies the title "God of heaven" designated the supreme deity whose throne was in heaven, father of the pantheon. He was worshiped as such in Uruk before the priestess Inana took over his temple and granted Nimrod kingship as though on his behalf. Biblical occurrences of the title are therefore mostly where the speaker is a

Gentile, or speaking to Gentiles (e.g. Dan 2:37). Men finally acknowledge his existence.

The second woe has passed; behold, the third woe is coming soon.

And the seventh angel blew his trumpet. And there were loud voices in heaven, saying, "The kingdom of the world has become ˊthe kingdomˋ of our Lord and of his Christ, and he shall reign for ever and ever."

The first woe was the demonic locusts that emerged from the abyss at the fifth trumpet to torment mankind. The second came with the sixth trumpet: two hundred million demonic horses that killed a third of mankind. The third is Jesus Christ. Other references to his coming soon are explicit: three times before this allusion (2:5, 2:16, 3:11) and three times after (22:7, 22:12, 22:20). Whoever is left on the earth will wail.

The seventh angel is like the "man clothed in linen" that Ezekiel saw putting a mark on those who grieved over Jerusalem's abominations. Distinct from the other destroying angels, he had a writing case at his waist, apparently to record their names in the book of life. Then he took burning coals from under God's throne and scattered them over the city. The day of judgement was life for one group, death for another.

"Of our Lord and of his Christ" maintains the distinction between God and his anointed (cf. 12:10, 17). But in contrast to vv. 4 and 8, "Lord" here is God; the Lord God reigns through his anointed. "Loud voice" occurs nine times before this second of Revelation's three central statements, and nine times after it. Now, just once, the phrase is plural. Having been found worthy to receive all kingship, Christ takes up his rule. The heavens exult.

Ultimately there is only one kingdom, and by right it belongs to its Creator. The moment arrives when he asserts that right. There will cease to be disputes over who owns Kashmir, or Tibet, or Crimea, or Zimbabwe, or Northern Ireland. His reign begins with the resurrection, before he pours out his wrath.

> The Lord himself will descend from heaven with a shout of command, with voice of archangel and with trumpet of God. And the dead in Christ will rise first. Then we who are alive, who remain, will be caught up together with them. (1 Thess 4:16f)

> For the trumpet will sound, and the dead will be raised imperishable, and we shall be changed. For this perishable body must put on the imperishable and the mortal put on immortality. (1 Cor 15:51–53)

These references to the last of the seven trumpets are examples of what Paul received by way of visions and revelations (2 Cor 12:1). Believers will not escape the drought, the famine, the persecution, but on the last day of the present age the living will join the dead in one great resurrection of the righteous. "Gather to me my faithful ones, who made a covenant with me by sacrifice" (Ps 50:5)—by the sacrifice provided. The long-awaited Bridegroom has come for his Bride. Left behind are those who did not choose eternal life, who said, "There is no God," "I am not religious," "I will consider it some other time." More are left behind than one might assume, including half-hearted believers (Matt 6:24, Rev 3:16). Trumpets have announced the king's coming. The gospel has been proclaimed to all. It is now too late to remember what friends had told them, "Flee from the wrath to come."

And the twenty-four elders who sat on their thrones before God fell on their faces and worshiped God, saying, "We give thanks to you, Lord God, the Almighty, who is and who was, for you have taken your great power and reigned. And the nations were wrathful, and your wrath came, and the time for the dead to be judged, and for paying the wages of your servants the prophets and the saints and those who fear your name, the small and the great, and for bringing to corruption the corrupters of the earth."

"Prophets" refers to the 144,000, distinct from "saints." "Wages" (*misthos*) conveys the idea of an employment contract, though "reward" fits some contexts better (e.g. Matt 5:12)—we are slaves who will be paid. "Corrupters of the earth" brings to mind the state of the antediluvian world: "The earth was corrupt before God, and the earth filled with violence.... All flesh had corrupted its way on the earth." The *dia-* in *diaphtherw* intensifies the verb so as to mean "corrupt utterly, in every way." Worshiping idols and abusing the mandate to subdue the earth and have dominion over the animals, we pollute the oceans, destroy rain-forests, burn up the earth's accumulated coal and oil in a few generations, farm animals in concentration camps as if they were not living beings and drive countless species to extinction. By our sexual promiscuity we have desecrated the image of God. Enraged, God will purge the earth of its desecrators.

And the temple of God in heaven was opened, and the ark of his covenant was seen in his temple. And there occurred lightning, and sounds, and thunder, and an earthquake, and great hail.

The trumpets section is rounded off with a vision of the temple reminiscent of the vision which introduced it (8:3–5). But instead of the altar we see the ark of the covenant. At 15:5 we return to the same moment, the opening of the temple to let out the angels bearing bowls of wrath. The phenomena are effects of geomagnetic storms brought on by coronal mass ejections, which will be greater still in the period of wrath. The earthquake in the earlier vision (8:5) corresponds to the earthquake just before the last trumpet (11:13). This second one (11:19) corresponds to the earthquake when the last bowl is poured out (16:18), hence the reference to "great hail," linking with 16:21. "He will cause his majestic voice to be heard and his descending arm to be seen, in raging anger and a flame of devouring fire, with cloudburst and storm and hail" (Isa 30:30).

> Fire goes before him
> > and burns up his adversaries all around.
> His lightnings light up the world;
> > the earth sees and trembles.
> The mountains melt like wax before Yahweh,
> > before the Lord of all the earth. (Ps 97:3–5)

According to 2 Maccabees, Jeremiah removed the ark from the Temple and hid it in a cave on Mount Nebo just beyond the promised land. It was to remain hidden until, in remembrance of his covenant, God should gather his people and bring them into the land. It was therefore not among the booty that Nebuchadrezzar took from the Temple in 586 BC (2 Kgs 25:14–16). The ark, we may suppose, still exists somewhere, just as its counterpart in heaven still exists, a reminder that God has pledged himself eternally to Israel, the living nation as well as the dead. While those unconvinced by the two witnesses will not be among the saints taken up to meet the Lord and must live through the tribulation yet to come, they will not be abandoned.

The Woman, the Man
and the Dragon

Revelation 12. A vision of the Serpent, the second Eve and the second Adam. At this central point in the book, the vision alludes to key events in history, notably the birth of the child who would crush the Serpent's head, the Christianization of Europe and the return of Jews to their ancestral land.

And a great sign appeared in heaven: a woman clothed with the sun, and the moon under her feet, and on her head a crown of twelve stars. And being pregnant, she cries out in travail and torment of giving birth.

THE IMAGERY EVOKES THE originally created sun, moon and twelve planets of the solar system, of which one purpose was to act as signs. The sun rises in front of the constellation Virgo while the moon lies below it, portending a birth of cosmic significance. But the sign is a vision, affording an insight into the spiritual world, not a configuration of actual heavenly bodies. The woman, unlike the goddess worshiped by Israel in Jeremiah's day (Jer 44:15–19), is the true "queen of heaven." She is the Jerusalem above, mother of those who are born from above (Ps 87, Gal 4:26). In Joseph's dream the sun symbolized Jacob, the planets his twelve sons, and the moon Rachel, his beloved second wife (Gen 37:9).

Rachel died while she was in labor for Benjamin, Jacob's youngest son. About the time of Jerusalem's siege and conquest by the Babylonians, the whole nation was compared to a woman in labor (Jer 4:31, Mic 4:9f):

> I heard a voice as of one who was sick,
>> distress as of one bringing forth her firstborn,
>> the voice of the daughter of Zion.
> Gasping for breath, she stretched out her hands,
>> "Alas for me! I am fainting before murderers."

Her travail resulted only in wind; she accomplished no deliverance for the earth (Isa 26:17f). More national suffering will accompany the birth of this first child, begotten from above.

And another sign appeared in heaven. And behold, a great red dragon, with seven heads and ten horns, and on his heads seven diadems. And his tail drags a third of the stars of heaven, and he cast them to the earth.

Ostensibly the dragon is the constellation Draco. In Greek, *drakwn* was another word for snake, like the English word serpent. The corresponding word in Hebrew was *tannin*, though this had a broader range, more like "amphibian reptile." When Moses threw his staff on the ground (Exod 4:3) it became a *nahash*, or snake; when it was thrown in front of Pharaoh it became a *tannin* (Exod 7:10, LXX *drakwn*), which in context must mean a crocodile. In Ezekiel (29:3, 32:2) the Pharaoh is himself called a *tannin*. *Nahash* and *tannin* are also interchangeable in Isaiah 27:1, where they refer to the final manifestation of the dragon.

Since appearing as a legged snake or dragon in the Garden of Eden, Satan has acquired many heads, indicating his sovereignty over the kingdoms into which the post-Cataclysm world eventually divided. As interpreted here, the seven heads symbolize the successive empires that impinged on Israel and/or its land: Egypt, Assyria, Chaldean Babylonia, Medo-Persia, Greece and Rome, plus the successive caliphates of Islam. The ten horns are a confederacy of ten kings or kingdoms yet to arise.

Originally there were twelve planets (*asteres planetai*, wandering stars). Early on, four of the planets exploded. The millions of fragments that astronomers call the Main Asteroid Belt, between Mars and Jupiter, was the result of the nearest explosion; other fragments dispersed further, and some struck the Earth, mostly during the Cataclysm but also with less frequency after it, leaving the 190 known craters that pockmark today's terrestrial crust. The physical events had their counterparts in the invisible realm. The stars cast to the Earth are angels that left their celestial habitation to copulate with women and were subsequently cast into the abyss (2 Pet 2:4). After the Cataclysm some of the angels still in heaven encouraged men to worship them, and in return men received power to rule as kings.

The first such potentate was Uruk's En-merkar, Nimrod, who united Mesopotamia's cities into a single state. His name survives in Iraq as Nimrud, the local name for the ruins of ancient Calah, which he founded. Another such, three millennia later, was Antiochus IV, king of a Hellenic empire that stretched from Turkey to Iran and south as far as Palestine. He was bent on promoting Hellenism throughout the empire, and like some earlier potentates he claimed to be a deity—indeed Zeus himself, the God of heaven—in human form. In 168 BC, after a successful campaign to add Egypt to his empire, a Roman delegation confronted him outside Alexandria and forced him to back off. It was a bitter humiliation. He retreated to Palestine to quash a rebellion there, massacred tens of thousands and sold as many more into slavery. In 167 he plundered and burned Jerusalem, forbade observance of the Torah on pain of death and ordered the population to worship idols. On the 15th day of the month Kislev (1 Macc 1:54) he erected a statue of Zeus in the Temple, the foretold "abomination that makes desolate" (Dan 8:13f, 11:31, 12:11). The Jews again revolted. After a three-year struggle they prevailed, and on the 25th of Kislev the Temple was rededicated (1 Macc 4:52f), the interval between the abomination and the rededication being the foretold "2300 evenings and mornings" (alluding to Exod 29:38f) during which the twice-daily sacrifice would be suspended. Elsewhere Antiochus will have destroyed many indigenous cults and thereby overthrown the angel-worship that they represented (Deut 32:8, 17, Ps 89:5–7, 1 Cor 10:20). Daniel says of him: "He grew great, even to the host of heaven . . . and cast down some of the stars and trampled on them" (Dan 8:10).

When Eve found herself deceived, God said to the Serpent:

> I will put hostility between you and the woman
>   and between your offspring and her offspring.
> He shall smite your head,
>   and you shall smite his heel.

Adam understood that Eve would be the "mother of all living," notwithstanding their common death sentence. Through the bearing of children life would continue, and the prophecy suggested grounds for hope. The Serpent would have spiritual offspring of his own (Matt 13:38, John 8:44), but one of the woman's sons would deal the Serpent a fatal blow, albeit at a cost.

And the dragon stood before the woman about to give birth, so that when she should bear her child he might devour it. And she gave birth to a son, a male, who is to shepherd all the nations with a rod of iron. And her child was caught up to God and to his throne. And the woman fled into the wilderness, where she has a place prepared by God, so that she may be nourished there 1260 days.

As an individual, the child-bearing woman is Mary. Every birth is a moment of wonder, for a new life is fashioned in the hidden womb of creation while the mother does nothing but await her time. But this child is especially significant, being the one promised from the beginning and promised again to Abraham (Gal 3:19), David (2 Sam 7:12), Isaiah (Isa 9:6, 49:1) and Jeremiah (Jer 23:5f). Therefore the child addressed her not as "Mother" but as "Woman" (John 2:4, 19:26), the archetypal mother. He was not only a son of Adam or like a son of Adam, his father was God himself (Ps 2), his sex highlighted because spiritual authority lies with the male, not the female (1 Tim 2:13f, Eph 5:23). For the same reason, the Passover lamb had to be a male.

When emissaries from the neighboring Parthian empire arrived in Jerusalem inquiring after "the one born king of the Jews," people knew they were seeking the long-awaited Messiah, the descendant of David who would restore Israel's independence. Herod, the incumbent king, was half-Jew, half-Edomite, and not from David's line; the Romans had granted him the kingship as a reward for helping to oust Antigonus, the king installed by the Parthians when they briefly controlled Judaea. Thus the magi were hinting at Parthian support in the event that the Jews should rise up against the Romans.

The situation was delicate. Jerusalem's population had no desire to disturb the present political accommodation, and Herod was fretting over who should succeed him within his own family, having recently murdered three of his sons on suspicion of plotting against him. Although no believer in Scripture himself, he summoned the theologians and asked them if they could help the magi with their quest: where did the Prophets say the Messiah would be born? "Bethlehem," they replied, referring to Micah, "David's birthplace." They saw no reason to keep the information secret, and they knew what he had in mind. Micah continued (5:3f),

> Therefore he will give them up until the time when she who is in travail has given birth and the remnant of his brothers turn back toward the children of Israel. And he will stand and shepherd his flock in the strength of Yahweh, in the majesty of the name of Yahweh his God. And they will abide, for now he will be great to the ends of the earth.

The Messiah would give Israel up until he came a second time. Then the daughter of Zion would bring forth many children, brothers of the firstborn. The sons of Israel would be raised, and be reunited with the surviving remnant of Judah, one flock.

"Rod" in Psalm 2, quoted here, is a shepherd's staff, but made of iron, not wood. The king as shepherd of his people was a common trope in the Ancient Near East, as witness the crook and flail that the Pharaoh gripped against his chest in statues. "Rod" is therefore also sometimes translated "scepter" (e.g. Gen 49:10, Ps 110:2). He would judge between many peoples and arbitrate over powerful nations far and near (Mic 4:3). Yahweh himself would be Israel's shepherd (Gen 48:15, Ezek 34).

Herod told the magi to look for the child in Bethlehem and report back. But they went home another way, avoiding the capital. Furious at being humiliated, Herod had every male infant in and around Bethlehem slaughtered: no price was too heavy for ensuring his dynasty remained unchallenged. But he was too late: Mary and Joseph had fled to Egypt. Not long afterwards Herod died and the family returned to Nazareth, Mary's home town. People forgot about the magi.

Forty days after his resurrection, the Son of David ascended to heaven. As it was written: "Sit at my right hand, until I make your enemies your footstool" (Ps 110). The "until" remains in the future. In the meantime there was to be terrible suffering. Losing patience with the harsh rule of the Romans, the Jews rebelled. In AD 70 Titus laid siege to the capital and five months later leveled it. In a subsequent revolt the Romans slaughtered more than half a million of the inhabitants. They "devoured and crushed; they trampled the remnant with their feet" (Dan 7:19). According to Ezekiel's foretelling of the calamity, a third of the population perished in Jerusalem, a third were struck down in the rest of the country, and a third were scattered abroad (Ezek 5:1–12, cf. Zech 13:8). For Israel, the world of exile beyond the promised land was a wilderness.

And war arose in heaven. Michael and his angels warred with the dragon, and the dragon warred, and his angels, and did not prevail, and place was no longer found for them in heaven. And the great dragon was thrown, the ancient serpent who is called the Devil and Satan, the deceiver of the whole world—he was thrown to the earth, and his angels thrown with him. And I heard a loud voice in heaven say, "Now has come the salvation and the power and the kingship of our God and the authority of his Christ, for the accuser of our brothers has been thrown down who accuses them day and night before our God. They have conquered him by the blood of the Lamb and by the word of their testimony, and they did not love their lives unto death. Therefore rejoice, you heavens and you who sojourn in them! Woe to the earth and the sea, for the Devil has come down to you in great fury, knowing that he has little time!"

In the new world Satan continued to have access to God as one of his sons and was free to malign the righteous to his face (Job 1:6). God had limited his own power to the extent that Satan and the other world-rulers in heaven (Eph 6:12) could only be expelled if defeated by fellow angels, and the power to do that depended, firstly on the victory of his firstborn over Satan (Luke 10:18, John 12:31) and secondly on the willingness of Christ's followers to bear witness to him, at the cost of their own lives.

When John received the vision, the Church was less than 70 years old and being persecuted; the prophecy that Satan and his angels would no longer be worshiped as gods was far from fulfillment. The authority and glory of all the kingdoms of the world belonged to him (Luke 4:5f, 2 Cor 4:4). Yet over the course of the millennium the vision came to pass. In Europe especially, the gospel fell on fertile ground. Many believed, and passed on the message, despite threats to desist or die. By holding fast to the word of God and the testimony of Jesus, Christians themselves overthrew the Devil. Even the Roman Emperor became a convert. Whoever knows nothing of this should read *The Blood of the Martyrs* by Leigh Churchill or *The Triumph of Christianity* by Rodney Stark or (for a more sociological focus) *The Conversion of Europe* by Richard Fletcher.

The declaration that the kingship of God and of his Christ had come does not mean that the earth was now in harmony with heaven, but simply that public worship of pagan gods had ceased. Once, all the kingdoms of the world were Satan's to offer to the Son if he would but abase himself before him. Now they were no longer entirely his. Across Europe, national and tribal leaders acknowledged the superiority of the new religion and urged, sometimes compelled, their people to do likewise—a top-down process that was the reverse of the early Church's growth. Even if few individuals understood the heart of Christianity, nations began to worship the true God, including nations around the periphery such as the Vikings and Magyars that had long plagued Christian Europe. Denmark began to convert in the reign of Harald Bluetooth (c. 958–c. 986), Norway in the reign of Olaf Tryggvason (995–1000), Sweden in the reign of Olof Skötkonung (c. 980–1022), Hungary in the reign of Stephen I (c. 975–1038), Kievan Rus in the reign of Vladimir the Great (c. 948–1015), all around the turn of the millennium.

Angels are involved in the struggle between good and evil (Ezek 28:12–17, Dan 10:13). In the Ancient Near East, as elsewhere, every nation had its own god: the Babylonians Marduk ("Bel"), the Moabites Chemosh, the Tyrians Melqart and so on, gods commonly lumped together by the biblical authors under the name Baal, or "Lord." These were angels, sons of God (Deut 32:8, Ps 82) exercising spiritual power through the nation's king. People worshiped the gods on the understanding that in return they would make the land fecund and protect them from their enemies. When Yahweh chose Israel and said to her, "I will be your god," he put himself at the same level—an entirely characteristic decision not to force himself on the world. Maker of heaven and earth, he was the national god of only one nation, worshiped only by her. She had to know by faith that he was in fact God of gods and king of all the nations (Isa 37:16).

"Warred" indicates a longer conflict than "fought" (ESV, NIV). Michael is the angel of the Jews (Dan 12:1), but under God, not seeking worship for himself. Jesus Christ is the one angel (as depicted in Rev 1:13, 10:1, 14:14, 18:1 and 20:1, probably also 7:2) who has authority to rule the earth.

"Rejoice, you heavens and you who sojourn in them!"—the angels above and the holy ones below, spiritually seated in the heavens (Heb 12:22). All previous occurrences of "heaven" have been singular. Now, this once, the noun is plural. Angels and saints are invited to rejoice because their brothers have conquered. Specifically they have conquered Satan. This is the last of the three central statements in Revelation, and it is intimately linked to the other two (5:5 and 11:15). It is also central in relation to, on the one hand, the preceding visions of the cherubim and the innumerable throng who are in the presence of God "day and night" (4:8, 7:15) and, on the other, the subsequent descriptions of the Devil, the beast and his worshipers who are tormented "day and night" (14:11, 20:10). Satan is no longer allowed to poison heaven with his words of slander. His defeat and his ejection from heaven mark a turning-point in history, but he does not give up. His knowledge that the opportunity (*kairos*) to go on deceiving and slandering is limited only intensifies his hatred. He expresses his fury in war and bloodshed.

When the dragon saw that he had been thrown down to the earth, he pursued the woman who had given birth to the male. And the woman was given the two wings of the great eagle, so that she might fly from the

presence of the serpent to the wilderness, to her place, where she is nour-
ished for a time, and times, and half a time. And out of his mouth the
serpent cast water like a river after the woman to carry her away. And the
earth helped the woman, and the earth opened its mouth and swallowed
the river that the dragon cast out of his mouth. And the dragon was angry
with the woman and went off to make war on the rest of her offspring, on
those who keep the commandments of God and have the testimony of Jesus.

Anti-Jewish feeling in Europe and Russia grew as a consequence of
the spread of Christianity, because the Jews would not convert. That they
survived at all after nineteen hundred years of homelessness and persecution is due to God. The hostility is Satan's.

The hostility came to a head with Hitler's attempt to exterminate
the Jews in the Second World War, not only in Germany but wherever
he conquered. Millions were slaughtered. But in 1948 Palestine was
designated their national homeland, a place of refuge. They flew from
the wilderness of the world at large (v. 6) to the place reserved for them
(v. 14). "The two wings of the great eagle" recalls the first Exodus (Exod
19:4) and indicates a great distance. Many settlers arrived by aeroplane.

Jews from Yemen at the Rosh HaAyin immigrants camp in 1950
(National Photo Collection, Israel).

The Old Testament repeatedly speaks of a second Exodus when
Israel will be restored to the land. However, the land will not rightfully

belong to her until the Messiah comes to give it. He himself will bring them back (Isa 60:21, Jer 16:15). The Jews were driven from their land two thousand years ago because they did not recognize him. Even today few recognize him, and most Jews in Israel, according to a poll, describe themselves as either not religious or convinced atheists. Vision and prophet are still sealed up. The conditions for rightful possession remain unfulfilled, and therefore the land is part of the wilderness, Jerusalem part of the great city.

Jesus told his disciples, "From the fig tree learn its lesson: as soon as its branch becomes tender and puts out its leaves, you know that summer is near. So also, when you see all these things [the signs of his coming], you know that he is near, at the doors. Truly, I say to you, this generation will not pass away until all these things have taken place." The fig tree symbolized Judah, planted within the vineyard of Israel so that it might bear fruit (Joel 1:7, Luke 13:6–9). He had cursed the physical tree because it was barren. As Jeremiah said, "there are no grapes on the vine, or figs on the fig tree, and the leaves have withered" (Jer 8:13). It was to bear little fruit even after the apostles had dug manure into the ground (Luke 13:8). Though still green at the time he spoke, it would dry up (Luke 23:31), be cut down (Luke 13:9) and the kingdom given to a nation bearing its fruits, namely those abiding in the true vine (John 15:1–5). But there would come a time when the stump would sprout and again put forth leaves.

Luke (21:29–33) tells the parable slightly differently from Matthew (24:32–34). Here Jesus's disciples were to look for when "all the trees" put forth new growth, as well as the fig tree. Since trees symbolized nations (e.g. Ezek 17:24, 31:4), he was saying that the nations around Israel would become sovereign states all about the same time. Iraq gained independence in 1932, Lebanon in 1943, Syria in 1946, Jordan in 1946, Libya in 1951, Egypt in 1953. Saudi Arabia became a unified state in 1932.

Jesus would return before the generation beginning with the rebirth of the Jewish state had died out. Can that be far away? But first, Jerusalem will be surrounded by armies and once more come under Gentile occupation. The inhabitants should flee, for their houses will be plundered and half of them be sent into exile, along with the rest of the country. The strange phrase "time, times, and half a time" comes from Daniel, with reference to how long the Jews would be oppressed by a foreign ruler just before the end. Analogous to the "seven times" during which Nebuchadrezzar lost his mind (Dan 4:16), it is approximately equal to the

1260 days during which two men speaking in the power of Moses and Elijah feed the population with the Word.

The torrent of water is a reference to the wars of 1967 and 1973 (a common metaphor, Ps 124, Isa 8:7f, Jer 47:2, Dan 9:26, 11:10). Furious that Israel survived these wars, the Devil turns to make war on the rest of the woman's offspring, the followers of Jesus. One focus of attention was Iran, which in 1951 wrested ownership of its oil back from Britain and two years later fell to a US- and British-backed coup. Islamic nationalism, culminating in the revolution of 1979, was a reaction to the West's interference. Since then, Iran has been infecting the whole region with hatred of Israel and Christianity. So has its rival, Saudi Arabia. The United States' retaliation for the attack on the World Trade Center, directed against Iraq, which was not involved, only added fuel to the flames. Christian communities that had lived harmoniously with their neighbors for centuries became identified with the West and embroiled in civil wars between Muslim and Muslim. In Syria and Iraq, killing and migration have all but eradicated the Church.

In Europe the Accuser does not need to be coercive, for the Church pretends that there is no war and has no notion that the time is short. She makes love with the great prostitute that is under judgement, appearing in many respects more like her than like the Bride clothed with linen, bright and pure. As in the Middle East, she too is a shrinking remnant.

Rev 12	History	Date
5	Promise concerning Eve's offspring	
4	Sons of God mix with human beings	
4	Cataclysm	
1	Jacob and his family	c. 1700 BC
2	Persecution of Jews under Antiochus	168–164 BC
5	Christ's nativity and ascension	4 BC–AD 30
6	Jews' expulsion from Judaea	70, 135
7–11	Europe's Christianization	to c. 1000
13	Sporadic persecution of Jews	c. 1000–1945
14	Jewish migration to Palestine	1948–
15–16	Arab-Israeli wars	1967, 1973
17	Persecution of Christians	
14	Jews fed the word of God 3½ years	
5	Christ's rule over all the nations	

Table 6. Events alluded to in Revelation 12 in chronological order.

Although numbered the twelfth of 22 chapters, chapter 12 comes exactly half way through the Greek text and, as Table 6 shows, encapsulates the whole of history, from Creation to Christ's millennial reign. Chapter 13, describing the two beasts, returns to the period covered by chapter 11, describing the two witnesses.

The Two Beasts

Revelation 13. Detail regarding the power that occupies Israel for three and a half years. A second Antiochus rises at the head of an alliance of Middle Eastern states and all his subjects bow down before his statue.

And I stood on the sand of the sea. And I saw a beast coming up from the sea, with ten horns and seven heads, with ten diadems on its horns and blasphemous names on its heads. And the beast that I saw was like a leopard, and its feet like a bear's, and its mouth like the mouth of a lion. And to it the dragon gave his power and his throne, and great authority. And one of its heads was as slaughtered to death, and its fatal wound was healed. And the whole earth marveled after the beast. And they worshiped the dragon, because he gave his authority to the beast, and they worshiped the beast, saying, "Who is like the beast, and who can war against it?"

THE FIRST SENTENCE ENDS chapter 12 but more properly begins chapter 13. The appearance of the beast follows Satan's going off to war against those who have the testimony of Jesus.

Composite beasts were not uncommon in ancient iconography, and go back to Uruk times.[1] A fertility god fights with a feline monster having seven heads and serpentine necks on a Mesopotamian plaque dating to the mid 3rd millennium BC. Texts from Ugarit in northern Syria attribute seven heads to the sea-monster Litan. In a myth about the origin of seasons, Baal, son of El (God), defeats the monster, but in revenge Mot (Death) swallows Baal into the maw of the underworld and thereby causes drought in the land, until Baal's sister brings him back up and fruitfulness is restored. Babylon's god Marduk was another such

---

1. Lewis, "Lion-Dragon Myths," 28–47.

The god Ninurta wounding one of the seven heads of a leopard-like monster, flames streaming from its back, c. 2400 BC. Bible Lands Museum Jerusalem.

figure. In these myths the crucial question was, "Who will go and slay the dragon? Who is to be king?"

Being among the animals created at the beginning (the *tanninim* of Gen 1:21), scaly amphibians such as Litan/Leviathan were not entirely imaginary. Their association with the demonic derived from the tradition about a legged serpent in the primeval garden and the belief that he would ultimately be opposed by one of God's sons. Babylon's Gate of Ishtar was decorated with images of a venomous composite beast with two horns, front legs like a lion's and rear legs ending in talons. The images made visible a spirit whose power to harm, it was thought, could be invoked against the city's enemies. The belief that morally ambiguous, potentially maleficent spirits could be controlled for good lay at the heart of pagan worship. They were real, and John describes composite beasts issuing from the abyss during the fifth and sixth trumpets.

Although it has heads and horns like the dragon, the beast is distinct from it, and evokes the four beasts that Daniel saw coming up from the great deep (Dan 7:2). In Daniel's vision the beasts represented kings and hence the kingdoms they embodied. The first was like a lion, symbolizing Nebuchadrezzar's empire, the second like a bear, symbolizing Cyrus's empire, the third like a leopard, symbolizing Alexander's empire: respectively Babylonia, Medo-Persia and Hellenistic Greece. Then came visions in which Daniel saw a beast not likened to any known beast of prey. It also symbolized a kingdom, and it had ten horns, representing kings, as in John's vision. Presently there rose up an eleventh horn among them.

The fourth beast was terrifying in its violence, with teeth like iron and claws of bronze; it devoured the whole land, and crushed the remnant under its feet. Historically, the next empire was Rome, which defeated the last remaining part of the Hellenistic empire, Egypt, in 31 BC. In response to a revolt, Rome brutally destroyed what remained of Palestine's Jewish population in AD 135. It therefore seems securely identifiable as the fourth beast. Daniel's vision depicted the succession of empires as they affected Palestine, omitting the period after 135 when there were no Jews there. In the 5th century, the western half of the Roman empire disintegrated and converted to Christianity, losing its beast-like quality, and subsequently most of its eastern half, which was also Christian, fell piecemeal to crusading Muslims. Thereafter small numbers of Jews drifted back. Large-scale immigration did not take place until after 1920. According to the vision, Jews would be back in Palestine when the ten horns appeared.

The beast in Revelation 13 is a composite of the first three beasts in Daniel but mainly like a leopard. In terms of geography its kingdom is therefore the lands once occupied by Alexander's empire, which stretched from Greece to Afghanistan and south as far as Egypt, swallowing up the Chaldean and Persian empires. Extensive though it was, this territory was considerably smaller than that controlled by the Roman empire. Hence if the Roman empire is the fourth beast in Daniel's vision, the ten kings must arise from it after its demise. There is also no implication that the beast's territory necessarily embraces all the lands in Alexander's empire. The mention of feet like a bear's and mouth like a lion's ties in with the claws and teeth in the vision of the fourth beast. If Rome was the power that trampled on the remnant and devoured the land, the seven-headed beast here will be intent on doing the same.

Psalm 74 speaks of God crushing the "heads of Leviathan" in the Red Sea, and Isaiah 27 speaks of Yahweh's punishing Leviathan at the time of Israel's resurrection. However, neither of these works is a point of reference in Daniel's vision, or in John's, who is unlikely to have had knowledge of the Leviathan myth. The seven heads in particular are new, and their meaning has to be explained (17:9–12):

> The seven heads are seven mountains on which the woman is seated; they are also seven kings, five of whom have fallen, one is, the other has not yet come, and when he does come he must remain a little while. The beast that was and is not, it is an eighth but belongs to the seven, and it goes to destruction. And the ten horns that you saw are ten kings who have not yet been given kingship.

The heads have a dual significance. As the location of the woman, they represent seven hills or mountains, which can hardly be other than the well-known seven hills of Rome: she is western Europe, Christian successor of the Roman Empire, but now apostate. As part of the beast, the heads represent seven kings or kingdoms. The only clue to their identity is that the sixth is contemporary with John and the seventh lies in the future. From the perspective of nineteen centuries later, the reference must be to kingdoms or empires rather than kings, for there have been numerous kings since John's time. The sixth is therefore the Roman Empire. Given that the prophecy relates to the Jews, God's elect, the seventh must be the Muslim empire, a succession of caliphates that controlled Jerusalem after the Romans, from AD 637 to 1099 and again from 1187 to 1917. Within a generation of Mohammed's death, himself a great warrior, Muslims had conquered the same territory as that once occupied by the Seleucid and Ptolemaic parts of Alexander's empire, plus all of Arabia. Collectively, these caliphates differed from previous empires in that their desire for world domination was inspired as much by religion as by personal or national ambition, and that religion was monotheistic. With prophetic authority it taught that all the Earth should be brought by force under the dominion of the one God Allah, and Allah had no son. Muhammad, not Jesus, brought the final revelation of God. God had abrogated his purposes for Israel in order to found the Ummah, not the Church, and was to be worshiped at Mecca, not Jerusalem. The Ottoman Empire—the last caliphate—was defeated in the First World War and dismembered in 1920 under the Treaty of Sèvres.

The beast "was, and is not." It is both the embodiment of successive imperial powers through the ages, as represented by the seven heads, and an eighth empire that will constitute the revival of the head that had an apparently fatal wound. It is also a man, embodying just the eighth. As such, he appears to be the reincarnation of an earlier king, who when

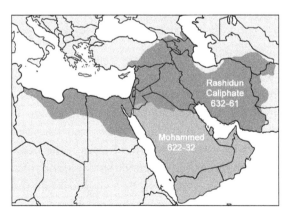

Territory conquered by Arab Muslims in the first decades of their new religion.

alive was head of one of the empires before the sixth. At his death, he was thrown into the abyss (11:7), the spiritual equivalent of the sea (13:1).

The eighth empire is an alliance of ten rulers. Daniel indicates that their leader will come to power after the other ten and put down three of them; initially he does not have a territory of his own. He is the end-time counterpart of the Seleucid king Antiochus IV, who ruled the countries known today as Turkey, Syria, Lebanon, Jordan, Israel-Palestine, Iraq and Iran, also Egypt for a time, and he displays the same hatred of God's people as Antiochus did. All these countries are dominantly Muslim, but not at present politically united.

The dragon is Satan. He is pictured in chapter 12 with the same number of heads and horns as the beast, but there the diadems crown the heads rather than the horns, because the kings symbolized by the horns have not yet come into being. Strictly, the beast is a kingdom, but some of the description suggests a worshiped individual. No mere figurehead, in this head of state is invested the whole power of the kingdom, and that power comes from Satan himself (cf. Luke 4:6), Satan being quite capable of possessing a man whose thoughts and desires align with his (John 13:27).

And it was given a mouth speaking great things, and blasphemies. And it was given to it to exercise authority for forty-two months. And it opened its mouth to blaspheme against God, blaspheming his name and his tabernacle, those who sojourn in heaven. And it was given to it to make war on the saints and conquer them. And it was given authority over every tribe and people and language and nation. And all the inhabitants of the earth will worship it, those whose names have not been written in the book of life of the Lamb who was slaughtered from the foundation of the world.

If anyone has an ear, let him hear. If anyone is to be taken captive, to captivity he goes; if anyone kills with sword, with sword he must be killed. Herein is the endurance and the faith of the saints.

The saints are the Jews (e.g. Ps 85:8, Dan 7–8), sanctified because God has made them holy by virtue of his election; in the New Testament the term is extended to those sanctified by faith in the Messiah. If John specifically means Christians, he clarifies: "those who keep the commandments of God and have the testimony of Jesus." The beast wages war against the Jews in the land of Israel, conquers them, and rules over them for three and a half years (Dan 7:25). Britain, Russia and the United States—the powers that dictated terms at the end of the Second

World War—have neither the will nor the ability to interfere, for their economies have been ruined by the disasters heralded by the trumpets.

To a modern reader "every tribe and people and language and nation," like "all the inhabitants of the earth," appears to mean literally the whole world, as it does in other parts of Revelation. However, "all" and "every" are sometimes used in contexts where a modern reader would want a less absolute phrase, as when Paul states that the gospel "has been proclaimed in all creation under heaven" (Col 1:23, cf. Luke 2:1, John 12:32, Acts 2:5, 11:28). In Daniel, which provides the most relevant analogue, "all peoples, nations and languages that dwell on all the earth" denotes every people group within the empire (Dan 6:25). The phrase could mean the same here, with reference to the ten states that form a confederation or caliphate. Alternatively, the beast's authority could be so great amidst the global chaos that it unifies all God-haters under his headship. Events will clarify one way or the other.

Like Antiochus and like emperors after him, the beast exalts himself (speaks great things, Dan 7:11, 11:36) and claims to be God in human form. He blasphemes the name of God, Jesus. Similarly, Paul warns about "the son of destruction, who opposes and exalts himself against every so-called god or object of veneration, so as to sit towards [*eis*] the temple of God, demonstrating that he himself is divine" (2 Thess 2:4). Many have inferred that Jerusalem's Temple will have been rebuilt by this time, but Paul's prophecy, obscure though it is, refers to his sitting not in (*en*) the temple but in its direction. Moreover, "temple of God" (*naos tou theou*, confusingly translated "God's temple" in other contexts) always has a spiritual meaning in the New Testament, referring either to Christ (Matt 26:61) or to his Church (e.g. 2 Cor 6:16). In the corresponding passage here the term is "tabernacle" or "tent" (*skenē*) but the meaning is the same. God's dwelling is equated with those who, although they have not yet risen, spiritually sojourn (*skenountas*) with him, contrasted (as in 12:12) with those who dwell on earth.

"The foundation of the world" is the creation of the world in six days, as Hebrews confirms when it says "his works were finished" from that juncture, were Genesis 2:2 by itself not clear. Some translations position the phrase "from the foundation of the world" so that it refers to the writing of one's name in the book of life, contrary to the Greek word order. The sacrificial slaughter of the Lamb was part of God's plan from the beginning (Gen 3:15, Matt 25:34), and its actualization at the end of the ages embraced all the dead back from the beginning (1 Pet 3:18–20).

The beast is given power by the dragon, but that power is not unlimited, as the phrase "it was given" emphasizes (six times in this chapter). His supremacy will not last long, and in the meantime the saints should not repay violence with violence. The words echo Jeremiah's when he prophesied that his compatriots would go into exile (Jer 15:2, 43:11), but without the note of judgement. His warning about dying by the sword is modified so that it echoes Jesus's warning about not resorting to the sword (Matt 26:52). Jesus was once taken captive himself and exemplified the best response. Only when he himself unsheathes his sword will the Jews be free to retaliate.

And I saw another beast, coming up from the earth. And it had two horns like a lamb, and it spoke like a dragon. It exercises all the authority of the first beast in its presence and makes the earth and its inhabitants worship the first beast, whose mortal wound was healed. And it performs great signs, even making fire come down from heaven to earth in front of people. And it deceives the inhabitants of the earth by the signs it was given to perform in the presence of the beast, telling the inhabitants of the earth to make an image for the beast that was wounded by the sword and lived. And it was given to it to give breath to the image of the beast, so that the image of the beast might even speak and cause those who would not worship the image of the beast to be killed. And it causes all—both the small and the great, the rich and the poor, the free and the slave—to give themselves a mark on their right hand or on their forehead, so that no one can buy or sell unless he has the mark, the name of the beast or the number of its name. Herein is wisdom. Let him who has understanding calculate the number of the beast, for it is a man's number, and his number is 666.

If the first beast represents the military power of the caliphate, the second represents its religious power. Its rising out of the earth suggests that its power is chthonic. Possibly its two horns symbolize the leaders of the two main branches of Islam, Sunni and Shia—thus a Grand Imam and a Grand Ayatollah. Putting aside their long-standing differences, they promote worship of the caliph as "the Mahdi," the one expected to bring justice on earth before the Day of Judgement. He may even be reported to have been killed and have risen from the dead. The New Testament takes a different view. In Paul's words, the arrival of the lawless one will be "by activity of Satan, with all power and false signs and wonders, and with all wicked deception for those who are perishing, because they refused to love the truth and so be saved" (2 Thess 2:9f). Jesus spoke in the same terms: "False messiahs and false prophets will arise and perform great signs and wonders, so as to lead astray, if possible, even the elect" (Matt 24:24). Even when done in his name, signs and wonders by themselves are not proof of God's approval (Deut 13:1–3, Matt 7:22).

The preaching of the two witnesses during the same three and a half years is therefore not in a spiritual vacuum. Like the sorcerers of Egypt, the second beast also has supernatural power. The descent of fire is presumably lightning. Many will be persuaded to disregard God's second commandment and worship the beast's image, just as Nebuchadrezzar, on pain of death, required "all peoples, nations and languages" to worship his image (Dan 3:4–7). Although the statue is in one place, people can worship it simply by turning in its direction and bowing down, wherever they are. It is even endowed with breath or spirit (same word, *pneuma*), in contrast to the lifeless artifacts people are accustomed to venerating. Satan wants everyone to worship him, and they do that, ultimately, by abasing themselves before a visible image. The image represents God, the second beast tells them; God is indeed angry, and this is the way to placate him. Most Jews—those remaining in the land—will not bow down, even though death is the consequence. Even some Muslims will not, for their religion too forbids idol worship.

In 167 BC Antiochus caused desolation in Jerusalem by identifying Yahweh with Zeus and sacrificing a pig in the Temple. Daniel foretold a similar provocation at the end of the age (Dan 9:27), as did Jesus, citing Daniel. "When you see the abomination of desolation standing in the holy area, then let those in Judea flee to the hills. . . . For then there will be tribulation such as has not been the like since the beginning of creation" (Matt 24:15, Mark 13:19). The "holy area" (*topos hagios*) designates the site of the former Temple, where the Al-Aqsa Mosque and Dome of the Rock now stand. "Abomination" is circumlocution for a worshiped idol (2 Kgs 23:13). The statue is set up towards the end of the 1260 days which conclude with the killing of the two witnesses in Jerusalem and the 144,000 witnesses in the rest of the world. When John next looks, the 144,000 are on Mount Zion in heaven. The tribulation is the ensuing wrath of God.

With so much agricultural production destroyed, food will be in short supply and will need to be rationed. The marking of the right hand or forehead conjures up the specter of a cashless society in which the right hand or forehead is implanted with a microchip. The technology is already being adopted in some countries, for limited uses. Right-handed people receive the chip in/on their left hand (and not yet on the fore-head). Whether this is what Revelation has in view remains to be seen. Certainly, increasing use of contactless payment hastens the day when cash will be abolished. In the absence of cash, everyone becomes locked into digital banking, and that system can then dictate the terms on which it is accessed; anyone who does not subscribe to certain "values" can be locked out. China is already a cashless society, and since most transac-tions are by mobile phone, it tracks those transactions. In the West, like-wise, financial institutions are closing the accounts of organizations they disapprove of. Facilitated by individuals' increasing willingness to cede autonomy as well as by technological advances, surveillance systems are growing ever more sophisticated, and totalitarianism—the total control of speech and behavior by a godlike State—is becoming the norm. One cannot say with confidence that the totalitarianism depicted in Revelation will be restricted to the Middle East.

The statue is the Satanic counterpart of the image through which God has always made himself visible. Hagar saw his form when she saw the "angel of Yahweh" (Gen 16:7–14). In conversing with him, Moses regularly beheld that form (Num 12:8). Ezekiel saw it in his vision. Just as we have borne the image of the man of dust, so at the resurrection we shall bear the image of the man of heaven (1 Cor 15:49). Therefore it is right to bow down before him (Matt 2:2, Rev 5:8). It is not right to worship any other man or his image.

To be clear: man's body takes after God's body, not an ape's. In believing that man descends from other primates and primates from flying lemurs and tree shrews, we are bowing, spiritually, before the image of a beast. We are accepting a belief system that denies that man was in existence "from the beginning of creation," that the original human form was that of God walking in the garden and that the incarnate Son was fully human as well as fully God. Man is like the other animals only inas-much as his body comes from the ground and God breathes into him as into them the breath that gives it life (Gen 6:17). God's animating spirit does not pass down through the genes and it is not a product of evolu-tion; it comes to an individual directly. In Darwinism there is no spirit. The theory does not begin to account for life.

The mark is the Satanic counterpart of the invisible seal of the Holy Spirit (Ezek 9:4, Eph 4:30). Apparently it consists of either the beast's name or a number representing him, adding up to 666 (one gets at the number by counting). People are advised under no circumstances to accept the mark, for it is a stamp of ownership. Instead, we should internalize the word of God (Deut 11:18f, Heb 8:10):

> You shall lay up these words of mine in your heart and in your soul, and you shall bind them as a sign on your hand, and they shall be as frontlets between your eyes. You shall teach them to your children, talking of them when you sit in your house, and when you walk by the way, and when you lie down, and when you rise.

His words are more precious than gold. If parents do not pass the truth of a living faith to their children, their children will fall away.

The Harvest of the Earth

Revelation 14. A vision of the 144,000 resurrected, three messages from heaven, the earth harvested, and the winepress of God's wrath outside Jerusalem.

And I looked, and behold, the Lamb, standing on Mount Zion, and with him 144,000 who had his name and his father's name written on their foreheads. And I heard a sound from heaven like the sound of many waters, and like the sound of loud thunder. And the sound I heard was like lyre-players playing on their lyres. And they sing a new song before the throne and before the four living beings and the elders, and no one could learn the song except the 144,000 purchased from the earth. These are the ones who did not defile themselves with women, for they are virgins. These are the ones who follow the Lamb wherever he goes. These were purchased from mankind as first-fruits for God and for the Lamb, and in their mouth no falsehood was found, for they are blameless.

Mount Zion, distinct from the western hill of that name in present Jerusalem, was the site of the Temple. It is mentioned only here, and signifies the place of God's dwelling-place in heaven, in new Jerusalem, before he reigns on earth (Heb 12:22). "I have set my king on Zion, my holy hill" (Ps 2:6). Martyred because of their testimony, the 144,000 are temporarily in heaven with him. They are a new presence before the throne. The comparison with "many waters" suggests that they come from the nations (Isa 17:12), not therefore from the twelve tribes of genealogically defined Israel. No longer needing the protection of God's seal, they instead bear his name on their foreheads and his son's name (which is the same—"written" in the Greek is singular). It is a sign that they are owned by God, the reward for having conquered (3:12). Like the twenty-four elders and all who will have conquered (15:2), they are given

186

a lyre—the instrument of David—so that they praise with hands as well as voices. Their song is known only to them, just as those who conquer are promised a name known only to them. The many others purchased for God will learn the song when they have been raised, but the 144,000 are the first. "From" (*apo*) the earth/mankind indicates separation from (earth/mankind are not sellers).

Israel was commanded to observe three festivals through the year: the Feast of Unleavened Bread, the Feast of First-fruits, and the Feast of Ingathering (Exod 23:14–17). The Feast of Unleavened Bread began with the Passover, when Israel was to kill and eat a male one-year-old sheep or goat without blemish. On this and the next seven days their bread was unleavened, in remembrance that when God rescued them from slavery they left in haste. The lamb was not a sin offering as such but a whole-body substitution. Israel belonged to God because he had redeemed them, and the price paid was the blood of the animal killed in their place (Exod 12:13). All life came from him and belonged to him; therefore every male that opened the womb had to be redeemed (Exod 13:12).

The Passover was the only animal sacrifice that every Israelite household had to make. They internalized it by eating it, and eating it all. Apart from the peace offering, other sacrifices were either burned to ash or, in part, consumed by the priests. Grain and other offerings were made on the day following, including a sheep or goat of the same description as the Passover offering. This animal did make atonement (Num 28:17–23). Sin still needed to be atoned for notwithstanding the Passover.

On the day after the first sabbath following Passover, the priest waved the sheaf of the first-fruits before God and repeated the offerings. In AD 30 that day coincided with the day Christ rose from the tomb, for he was the sheaf of the first-fruits (1 Cor 15:20). When he rose, he also led others out of the depths, both from Hades and from Tartarus, who thus became the assembly of the firstborn in heaven (Matt 27:52f, Eph 4:8, Heb 12:23). These were the first-fruits of the spiritual harvest prefigured in the week-long Feast of First-Fruits, seven weeks after the waving of the sheaf (Jas 1:18, cf. Jer 2:3). The feast celebrated the completion of the grain harvest. In the following months the trees were harvested, beginning with the vines.

Finally came the feasts of the seventh month. On the first day trumpets were blown; they announced a new beginning, in which the year would begin on the seventh month rather than the first. On the tenth day Israel again made atonement. On the fifteenth day they celebrated the end of the harvest. Having gathered from the threshing floor, vineyard and orchard, they were instructed to take the branches of palms and other trees, make booths (*sukkot*) with them, and rejoice. The week-long festival was therefore also called the Feast of Booths or Tabernacles (Lev 23:34).

The Day of Atonement was the one day in the year when the high priest was permitted to enter the Holy of Holies. After expiating his own guilt, the priest took two goats. The one he slaughtered, sprinkling its blood on the incense altar outside the curtain and on the mercy seat inside the curtain. Although its prophetic significance was not explained, it prefigured the day when the Messiah would shed his own blood and enter the tabernacle "not of this creation" to mediate a new covenant for the nation (Heb 9:11–26). They were to humble themselves, because the blood was an atonement for their souls (Lev 16:29, 17:11). The other goat the priest did not kill. Instead, he confessed the people's sins and all their transgressions and laid them on the animal's head; then he sent it into the wilderness. Again, although the significance was not explained, the goat enacted how God would drive Israel out of the land for rejecting their Messiah.

Moses was alone when he received the Law at the top of Mount Sinai. After writing it down, he descended the mountain to read it to the people. They bound themselves to it in a ritual solemnized by blood. Then he went up again to receive the hewn tablets of rock which God had engraved with the essence of their obligations. He remained there more than five weeks. Tested by his absence, the people became impatient and made themselves a golden calf, as if an idol could represent the creator of heaven and earth; they sacrificed to it, worshiped it and danced before it. Eventually Moses came down, and when he saw them celebrating, he was seized with fury and smashed the tablets. The idol was prophetic, for five centuries later Jeroboam persuaded the northern tribes to split from the house of David. In place of the temple in Jerusalem he set up two golden calves, one at Dan and one at Bethel, telling the tribes to worship them as Yahweh (1 Kgs 12). The sanctuary platform at Dan can still be seen. Moses' wrath foreshadowed God's wrath. But Moses also said, "Perhaps I can atone for their sin." So God made a second set of tablets and thereby foreshadowed the re-acceptance of Israel under a new covenant, when he would write his law on their hearts (Deut 10:1–16, 30:6, Jer 31:31–37). The generation baptized into Moses died without entering the promised land; the generation after them entered under Joshua (1 Cor 10:2), crossing into the land by the same river as the disciples of Jesus would one day be baptized in. Indeed, the disciples were baptized at the same location, at present-day Al Maghtas, opposite Jericho. "Jesus" is simply the Greek spelling of "Joshua."

The nation was to observe the rites at one location only (Deut 12:1–27). For over 300 years that place was Shiloh. Then David brought the Tabernacle to Jerusalem, the new capital, and that city became the central place of worship, and in Solomon's reign the Tabernacle was replaced with a stone building. Three decades later, the northern tribes seceded from Judah and reverted to paganism. So did the southern tribes. Like their Canaanite neighbours, they erected pillars of Baal on every high hill and wooden Asherahs under every green tree, and looked to promote fertility by fornicating and sacrificing before them (1 Kgs 14:22–24). The Temple itself was closed for a time. Only after a long period of abeyance did Hezekiah (727–c. 686 BC) restore centralized worship. Meanwhile the book of Deuteronomy, which set out the covenant as renewed under Joshua, was completely forgotten and only resurfaced when another king ordered the Temple to be repaired, shortly before the Exile (2 Chr 34:14f). The one festival that probably was kept throughout was the Feast of Ingathering. Even then, its deeper significance, reminding the Israelites that they were forced to live in the wilderness before they came into their inheritance, did not register until after their return from Babylon (Neh 8:17). The requirement to read out the Law every seventh year during the Feast was also not observed: it had been commanded in the very book that had gone missing (Deut 31:10–13).

Like the other rites, the Feast of Ingathering, or Tabernacles, had prophetic significance, for a time would come when the Jews would again find themselves in the wilderness, living in tents as refugees. That is why Peter, not knowing what he was saying, offered to make tents for Moses and Elijah at Christ's transfiguration. The two witnesses were to instruct the Jews about their Messiah before he came in glory. He himself would then lead the Israelites into the land and bring them into the bond of the covenant. He would thresh and glean them one by one (Isa 27:12).

So far as Gentile believers are concerned, the first-fruits are the 144,000, and the main harvest the resurrection of those who have died in Christ since his first coming, including those who perish during the great tribulation. (In 2 Thess 2:13 the correct reading is *ap' arches*, "from the beginning," not *aparchen*, "first-fruits.") When the kingdom of

Platform at Tell Dan, northern Israel, where Jeroboam erected a gold calf and told his subjects this was the god that had rescued them from Egypt. Ashlar stonework was characteristic of royal architecture of the period (1 Kgs 7:9).

God comes, survivors of his wrath will be required to keep the Feast of Tabernacles (Zech 14:16–19), for then they will be in the same interim position as Israel was after the Exodus: they will have received and begun to practice the Law (Isa 2:3), but they will not yet have entered his promised rest (Heb 3:7–4:10). They will enter his rest, if at all, only at the general resurrection.

Feast	NT/OT refs.	Israel	Gentiles
Passover	1 Cor 5:7	Christ's death	
First-fruits	1 Cor 15:20	Christ's resurrection	144,000
Trumpets	Rev 8–9		Final warning
Main harvest	Matt 13:24–30, Rev 11:15	Resurrection of the righteous	Resurrection of the righteous
Day of atonement	Ezek 16:59–63, 20:43	Banishment; eventual reconciliation	
Jubilee (Yr 50)	Isa 27:12f, Zech 9:14, Isa 61, Matt 24:31	Resurrection and return to the land	
Feast of Booths	Zech 14:16–19 Rev 21:24–22:2		Millennial reign

Table 7. The prophetic significance of Israel's festivals (Lev 23–25).

And I saw another angel flying overhead, with eternal good news to deliver on those who were seated on the earth, and on every nation and tribe and language and people, saying with a loud voice, "Fear God and give him glory, because the hour of his judgement has come, and worship him who made the heaven and the earth, and sea and springs of water."

"Another" suggests that the eagle of 8:13 was in fact an angel; conversely, "flying" suggests an eagle (nowhere else in the Bible are angels portrayed with wings). Both images are non-literal. "Those seated on the earth" are the inhabitants of Babylon the Great, named for the first time in verse 8. The good news delivered "on" them—as coming from above, and contrasting with the wrath about to be poured on the earth—is eternal inasmuch as it was in view before the foundation of the world (Gen 3:15, 4:4), and it has effect back to the beginning. Since the gospel announces the coming of the king, it expires once the kingdom arrives. An angel makes the appeal because the 144,000 are on Mount Zion in heaven.

Whatever the Church may say, Scripture says that we should fear God (Eccl 12:13, Prov 1:7, 19:23, 2 Cor 5:11, 7:1, 1 Pet 2:17). All humanity should obey the gospel and worship him, for he is the Creator and the judge of our souls (Ps 33:8f):

> Let all the earth fear the Lord;
> > let all inhabitants of the world be in awe of him.
> For he spoke, and it was;
> > he commanded, and it stood.

Why be afraid of him if everything came into existence by itself? The proper response on entering his presence is to fear him, as the disciples did when he spoke to the sea (Mark 4:39); it is to glorify him by the amending of our lives. What the angel proclaims is itself the gospel, in summary. The Holy Spirit comes to convict the world concerning sin, righteousness, and judgement (John 16:11). Whoever is inwardly convicted and believes in the Son will not be condemned.

How can people understand that God has a son, unless they first recognize that there is a God? And how can they recognize that God exists unless they see him in the things he has made? Speaking about the gospel, Paul says (Rom 1:18–21),

> In it . . . is revealed the wrath of God from heaven against all impiety and unrighteousness of men who possess the truth in unrighteousness, because what can be known about God is manifest, for God has made it manifest to them. For since the

> creation of the world his invisible attributes—his eternal power
> and divinity—are perceived by understanding what has been
> made, so as to leave them without excuse; because although they
> knew God, they did not glorify him as God or give thanks to
> him, but became futile in their thinking.

The gospel begins with the assertion that men know the truth that God
created the world, even though they deny it. The truth is obvious, and
has been ever since the Creation (for the world was peopled from the
beginning). It only ceases to be obvious when one wilfully shuts him out.
Unrighteousness, intellectual darkness, and wrath then follow.

> Therefore God gave them up in the desires of their hearts to
> impurity, to dishonouring their bodies among themselves,
> because they exchanged the truth about God for a lie and
> venerated and served what was created alongside him who
> created it . . . For this reason God gave them up to dishon-
> ourable passions. Their women exchanged natural relations for
> unnatural ones, and the men likewise gave up natural relations
> with women and burned with lust for one another, men
> committing shameless acts with men.

With its dogma of the "theory of evolution," scientific atheism has
led our own society down the same path. Tolerating no opposition, its
priests tell the peoples of the earth, "We have examined the evidence and
discovered that the appearance of design is only appearance; believe our
testimony, not what you see. Do not worship an illusion." They contradict the second of the two most fundamental laws of physics in order to
claim that molecules have a natural tendency to self-assemble into forms
ever more complex. They ignore the fossil record, which shows plant and
animal phyla appearing suddenly—animals not until five-sixths through
the record, terrestrial plants still later—in order to portray all organisms
as genealogically linked. Contrary to our experience of ourselves and
how we relate to others, they say that there is no such thing as a soul: our
ideas, atheistic as well as religious, are the products of atoms that know
nothing about truth; our sense of free will is a self-affirming illusion. So
the western Church, not wishing to seem futile in its thinking, has gone
along with the denial of spirit and of the witness of God in creation, and
ingested a heresy of the first order, a corruption of the gospel itself. She
cannot believe that the wisdom of God and the wisdom of man might
be in conflict. She is ashamed of his words. Unresisted by those who
were appointed to champion a God-given understanding of reality, the

corruption of society inevitably follows. Those who believe that Nature brought itself into being end up worshiping a human version of Nature, an Asherah-like sex-goddess.

"Heaven" can refer to one of three places: the firmament containing the solar system (Gen 1:8), the face (Gen 1:20) of the firmament where birds fly, or the "heaven of heavens" (Gen 1:1, 1 Kgs 8:27, Ps 148:4) beyond the solar system. "Earth" denotes the land, distinct from the sea (Gen 1:10). Springs or fountains are singled out because in the first world there was no rain; instead, water oozing up through springs from the great deep kept the earth moist and supplied the water for lakes and rivers (Gen 2:6, 7:11, Prov 8:24).

And another, a second angel, followed, saying, "Fallen, fallen is Babylon the great, who made all the nations drink from the wine of her raging fornication."

"Raging" renders adjectivally the noun *thumos*, which denotes strong emotion, usually anger. "Fornication" translates *porneia*. The root word, *pornē*, means a female prostitute, that being the only social category for an unmarried woman who regularly lay with a man. *Pornos* is the corresponding male (1 Cor 5:9, 6:9). *Porneia* refers to all copulation outside marriage (John 8:41, 1 Cor 5:1, 7:2), not just adultery (Heb 13:4) and sodomy (Jude 7). Again, the western Church has almost given up on insisting that the sexually impure will not inherit the kingdom. The identity and fall of Babylon the Great are dealt with in chapters 17–18. Mention of the city's fall here functions like the prophetic finger that interrupted Belshazzar's feast as he drank with his lords, wives and concubines and praised its gods. Babylon's days are numbered and about to end. That is now part of the gospel's message.

And another angel, a third, followed them, saying with a loud voice, "If anyone worships the beast and its image and receives a mark on his forehead or on his hand, he himself will drink from the wine of the fury of God, served unmixed in the cup of his wrath. And he will be tormented with fire and sulfur before the holy angels and before the Lamb. And the smoke of their torment goes up for ever and ever. And they have no rest, day and night, the worshipers of the beast and its image, and whoever receives the mark of its name."

Everyone will have to decide: lukewarmness, or agnosticism, will not be an option. Either we worship God or we worship his adversary.

The fire, smoke and sulfur refer to both the natural afflictions of the impending wrath and the demons released at the sixth trumpet, for they have not gone away.

"The smoke of their torment goes up for ever" ironically recalls the smoke of the incense going up before God (8:4). It is also an allusion to Isaiah 34:

> For the Lord has a day of vengeance,
> > a year of recompense for the cause of Zion.
> And its [Edom's] wadis will be turned into pitch
> > and its dust into sulfur,
> > and its land will become burning pitch.
> Night and day it will not be quenched;
> > its smoke will go up forever.

The phrase is repeated in 19:3, where the smoke is that of ruined, tormented Babylon the Great. As with Sodom and Gomorrah (Gen 19:28, Jude 7), there will be no rebuilding of the city. The torment takes place on the surface of the earth and lasts for the limited time preceding its fall.

Angels are mentioned many times in the New Testament but described as holy elsewhere only once, where Jesus says that he will come with the holy angels in glory, not humility. Then he will be ashamed of whoever is ashamed of him and his words (Luke 9:26). "Having no rest, day and night" is an echo of the incessancy with which the cherubim proclaim that God is holy (4:8), with the twist that the lack of rest is now the consequence of pain and anguish.

One last time the first angel urges the world to accept God's mercy, because, as the second warns, judgement of the world's civilization is imminent, and as the third warns, individuals who worship his adversary may expect no mercy. To fall into the hands of the living God is a fearful thing.

Herein is the endurance of the saints, those who keep the command-ments of God and the faith of Jesus.

The comparable phrase in 13:10 refers to the Jewish saints. Here the saints are defined as those who hold to the faith of Jesus, referring to those still alive, distinct from the 144,000. Christians too must be stead-fast, for life will be hard. If we endure to the end, we will be saved: we will gain our souls (Luke 21:19). We should pray that we have strength to endure, remembering the example of our Savior (Heb 12:2f). God's commandments will remain important (Matt 5:19f, I Cor 14:37) and faith will carry us through.

And I heard a voice from heaven say, "Write: Blessed are the dead who die in the Lord from henceforth." "Yes," says the Spirit, "that they may rest from their labours. Their works follow them."

"A voice from heaven" is God (e.g. Matt 3:17, Rev 11:12), even when it speaks of him in the third person (Acts 11:9, Rev 21:3). In English, to "bless" means to pronounce his favour on a person, the opposite of curse or blaspheme; to "be blessed" means to enjoy his favour. In Greek the concepts are distinct: *eulogetos* (verbally blessed) and *makarios* (enjoying God's favour). The word here is *makarios*, as elsewhere in the book (*eulogia* in 5:12f and 7:12).

The instruction to write down the blessing adds emphasis to the assurance. Many in the last three and a half years will be killed because of their faith, but they must hold fast to the promise that their diligence will be recognized and their works rewarded. Unlike those who worship the beast, they will finally enjoy God's rest.

And I looked, and behold, a white cloud, and seated on the cloud one like a son of man, with a golden crown on his head, and a sharp sickle in his hand. And another angel came out of the temple, crying with a loud voice to the one seated on the cloud, "Send forth your sickle and reap, for the hour to reap has come, for the harvest of the earth is dried up." So he who was seated on the cloud swung his sickle over the earth, and the earth was reaped.

The description "like a son of man" identifies the reaper as Christ (1:13). He wears a victor's crown, and the cloud suggests that he is the same as the angel at 10:1. The parallelism of the two harvests, in which one angel bearing the authority of God instructs another, also suggests he is an angel.

The first-fruits—the 144,000 who prophesied about the wrath and the kingdom—are already in, after which comes the main harvest. In the parable about the wheat and the darnel, the good seed is the sons of the kingdom and the darnel the sons of the evil one. They are harvested together at the conclusion of the age (Matt 13:36–43, Luke 3:17). The type of crop here is not stated, but it is *exeranthė*, withered, even though reaped at the right time. The same word is used to describe the seed that fell on rocky ground and was scorched in the sun (Mark 4:5f), the fig tree cursed because it bore no fruit (Mark 11:20f), and the vine branches gathered and burned because they became detached from the stem (John 15:6); also the waterless Euphrates (Rev 16:12). "The hour to reap" is the "hour of judgement" (v. 7), which for the sons of the evil one is a time of woe (11:14). Though implicit in the sounding of the seventh trumpet, the harvesting of the sons of the kingdom is not described.

And another angel came out from the temple in heaven, he too holding a sharp sickle. And another angel came out from the altar, having authority over the fire, and he called in a loud voice to the one who had the sharp sickle, "Send forth your sharp sickle and harvest the clusters of the vine of the earth, for its grapes are ripe." So the angel swung his sickle across the earth and harvested the vine of the earth and threw it into the great winepress of the fury of God. And the winepress was trodden outside the city, and blood flowed from the winepress up to the horses' bridles, for 1600 stadia.

The image is of a single vine. The grapes are *ekmasan*, ripe, the word pointedly not used of the previous crop. While again one expects a positive meaning, the tree is "the vine of Sodom" (Deut 32:32); it is rooted in the earth, not the man from heaven, and bears bad fruit. The angel with authority over the fire is the angel that cast fire on the planet at the beginning of the trumpets (8:5) and, as before, another angel performs the reaping. Who treads the winepress is not stated, but in reality the acts of reaping and treading are the same. This is the Day of the Lord that culminates the period of wrath.

The slaughter is not global but concentrated "outside the city." According to Joel (3:2, 3:14), the enemies of Israel will gather in the Valley of "Jehoshaphat," an unknown place name meaning "Yahweh has judged," close to Jerusalem.

> Let the nations be roused and come up to the Valley of Jehoshaphat, for there I will sit in judgement against all the surrounding nations.

> Send forth the sickle,
>   for the harvest is ripe.
> Come, descend,
>   for the winepress is full.

As in Revelation, the harvesting sickle brings down judgement. Isaiah 34 confirms the magnitude of the bloodbath:

> Draw near, you nations, to hear,
>> and give heed, you peoples!
> Let the earth hear, and all that is in it,
>> the world, and all that it brings forth.
> For the Lord's wrath is against all the nations
>> and his fury against all their armies.
> He has devoted them to destruction,
>> he has given them over to slaughter.
> Their slain will be thrown out,
>> and a stench will rise from their corpses,
>> and the hills will dissolve with their blood.

There is further slaughter to the south-east, when the land of Edom (the descendants of Esau, Gen 25:30) becomes burning pitch (Isa 34:5–9, 63:1–4):

> Who is this who comes from Edom,
>> in stained garments from Bozrah,
> glorious in his apparel,
>> bearing down in the greatness of his strength?
> "It is I, speaking in righteousness,
>> mighty to save."
> Why is your apparel red,
>> and your garments like his who treads in the wine-vat?
> "I have trodden the winepress alone,
>> and from the peoples no one was with me;
> I trod them in my anger
>> and trampled them in my wrath;
> their juice spattered my garments
>> and I have defiled all my attire.
> For the day of vengeance is in my heart,
>> and the year when I redeem has come."

This is the "banquet of God" described in chapter 19, where the language is equally gruesome, and reveals that the treader is Jesus Christ. The hyperbolically depicted scale of the bloodshed recalls the carnage at the end of the Bar Kochba Revolt, when the Romans "went on killing until their horses were submerged in blood to their nostrils."[1] God tramples the surrounding nations because they have trampled Jerusalem. He comes to redeem Israel because "they have scattered them among the nations and divided up my land."

---

1. Jerusalem Talmud, Ta'anit 4:5.

One thousand six hundred stadia is about 184 miles: if we take the number at face value, the carnage cannot be confined to the Jezreel valley or valleys around Jerusalem. It is vengeance against all the nations that rejoiced at Israel's ruination and hoped to possess the land for themselves (Ezek 36:5). Bozrah was the ancient capital of Edom, its location still evident from the name of the village next to its ruins, Basira in southern Jordan. It lay on the Kings' Highway 40 miles north of Mount Seir. As the crow flies, 1600 stadia is the distance from Mount Seir to Megiddo (16:16). It is possible to imagine armies stationed at intervals between these points along the rift valley. If the measurement is hyperbolic, the meaning remains that the land will be drenched in blood (Isa 34:7).

THE SEVEN BOWLS OF GOD'S FURY

Revelation 15–16. Wrath is poured out on the world with a mighty hand and an outstretched arm, culminating in the Day of the Lord.

And I saw another sign in heaven, great and wondrous: seven angels with seven plagues—the last, for with them the fury of God is finished.

THE FIRST SCOURGES TO be designated plagues were the fire, smoke and sulfur, both natural and supernatural, which came with the sixth trumpet, expressly three in number. The seven last plagues bring the total to ten, as in the time before the Exodus. While the trumpets also signal God's fury, these judgements are worse, and Israel will not be delivered from its oppressor until the tenth plague.

And I saw what seemed like a glass sea mingled with fire, and those conquering, from the beast and from its image and from the number of its name, standing on the glass sea holding lyres of God. And they sing the song of Moses, servant of God, and the song of the Lamb, saying,

> *"Great and wondrous are your deeds,*
> > *Lord God, the Almighty!*
> *Just and true are your ways,*
> > *King of the nations!*
> *Who should not fear you, Lord,*
> > *and will not glorify your name?*
> *For you alone are sinless;*
> > *for all nations will come and bow down before you;*
> > *for your righteous acts have been manifested."*

The glass sea, seen in John's first vision of heaven, represents the waters that overwhelmed the antediluvian world. Additionally it now represents the sea in which the Egyptian army perished but the Israelites passed through unharmed.

> Was it not you who dried up the sea,
> the waters of the great deep,
> who made the depths of the sea a way
> for the redeemed to pass over?
> And the ransomed of the LORD will return
> and come to Zion with jubilation. (Isa 51:10f)

"Conquering from [ek] the beast" is grammatically clipped, the verb of motion omitted. They conquer because they refuse to bow before the image of the beast or receive his mark, even on pain of death. Therefore the sea is solid to them and, like the 144,000, they are safe in heaven. They have passed through the waters and walked through the fire (Isa 43:2). Perhaps we are reminded of the multitude from every nation standing before the throne (7:15), but these are Jews, and they are dying as martyrs.

The Pentateuch records two songs: one in which Moses celebrated Yahweh's triumph over Pharaoh (Exod 15) and one in which, just before Israel entered the promised land, he foretold the nation's prosperity, unfaithfulness, exile and final deliverance (Deut 32). The song of triumph is in mind. As God's servant and as though he were God himself (Exod 14:31, 7:1), Moses inflicted misery on a country that had made Israel's life a misery. The Lamb too was God's servant (Isa 52:13, Mark 10:45). He inflicts judgement on the beast-Pharaoh, and those who have conquered share in his victory, seeing no distinction between him, the Lord, and the Lord Almighty. They sing from a position the other side of death. It is from there they observe God's judgement of his enemies.

Some of the words come from Jeremiah (Jer 10:1–16), who avers that because Yahweh created heaven and earth it is folly to worship wooden images. The redeemed of Judah rejoice, and amplify their sound with lyres (citharas—also 5:8, 14:2). It is an interim state, for when Christ returns, they will return with him. All the nations will make the journey to Mount Zion and bow the knee before the Almighty (Ps 22:27, 65:2, 86:9, 102:22, Isa 45:23, 66:18, 23, Jer 3:17, 16:19, Zeph 2:11, Zech 14:16).

And after these things I looked, and the temple of the tabernacle of the testimony in heaven was opened, and out of the temple came the seven angels with the seven plagues, dressed in pure, bright linen, and with golden belts around their chests. And one of the four living beings gave to the seven angels seven golden bowls full of the fury of God who lives for ever and ever. And the temple was filled with smoke from the glory of God and from his power, and no one could enter the temple until the seven plagues of the seven angels had ended.

The vision connects with the end of chapter 11, where the temple opens to reveal the ark of the covenant and there follow the lightnings, sounds, thunderings, earthquake and heavy hail that will punctuate the final period. Like the Tabernacle, the Temple in Jerusalem was the earthly representation of God's dwelling-place, and it had the same design. Both consisted of a sanctuary partitioned by a curtain or veil. Within the inner sanctuary or tent was "the ark of the testimony" and within the ark were the tablets inscribed with the ten commandments, bearing witness to the covenant. The inner sanctuary, the Holy of Holies, was therefore called the tent of the testimony. (In Hebrew "Tabernacle" meant "dwelling-place" and "tent" was a separate word; in the New Testament *skenē* was the word for both.) The sanctuary on the outer side of the veil contained the bread and the shining lamps of the menorah, symbolizing his daily presence and light. In due time, the Word "became flesh and tabernacled amongst us" (John 1:14). Christ's body was the temple of God because it housed his Spirit (John 2:21), and he became the bread and the light. After his ascension those who participated in his body and spirit continued the testimony as they took his word from Jerusalem to the ends of the earth.

Like him (1:13), the angels wear belts of gold (the emphasis in Greek being on what the belts are made of). Their golden bowls once held the prayers of the saints (5:8); now they hold the wine of God's wrath. The door of the temple closes as the angels leave, and after the loud voice telling them what to do, silence falls, to complete the hour's silence begun at the seventh seal. As when Christ was crucified, his eye will not spare; he will show no pity.

"Fury" is *thumos*, a stronger word than *orgē*, wrath or anger. We have emotions because we are made in God's likeness and he has emotions. He who made the world is no impassive bystander. But anger is rarely good, and we should not be overcome by it, just as he continually exercises *makrothumia*, patience (Rom 2:4). He does not will that anyone should perish but that all should repent. Were it not for that patience, we should have died the moment we became acquainted with evil. Judgement is deferred to the end of life and to the end of the age. "I did not come to judge the world, but to save the world" (John 12:48). But ultimately judgement must come.

The wrath of God has a double meaning. First, it refers to the punishment of death (Rom 4:15, 7:9f), because in Adam all die; we are by nature children of disobedience (Eph 5:6) and therefore of wrath (Eph 2:3, Col 3:6, John 3:36). "All our days pass away under your wrath" (Ps 90:9). A ruler who imposes the just sentence of death for a crime exacts the wrath of God on his behalf, for the sentence is the same (Rom 13:4); it is the fate of every soul at the resurrection who does not obey the truth but unrighteousness (Rom 2:5–8). Whoever is justified by the blood of Christ will be saved from wrath (Rom 5:9).

Second, it refers to a moment in history when there will be "tribulation and distress for every human soul that does evil, the Jew first and also the Greek." For the Jews, this came to pass in the Jewish-Roman wars. More than a million lost their lives, including many in AD 70 who had congregated in Jerusalem to celebrate the Passover; the remaining population of Judaea was enslaved and deported.[1] In their pursuit of national independence the Jews brought these calamities upon themselves. Ultimately, however, they came from God. The Jews had rejected God, so he rejected them, having warned about the consequences often (Ezek 5:1–13, Zech 13:8, Mal 4:6, Matt 21:32–41).

In advance of the appearing of the Messiah, John the Baptist too warned about the wrath to come (Luke 3:7, 3:17). It would come upon Jews and Gentiles alike. Elsewhere it is described as the time of their "visitation" (Luke 19:44, 1 Pet 2:12), and Jesus briefed his disciples about both episodes. It is now the turn of the Gentiles. The boils on the skin, the extreme thirst, the intolerable heat anticipate in the land of the living the subsequent fate of the wicked, when they rise from the dead and are thrown into the lake of fire. Those in Israel who have not resisted the beast will also suffer; the Lord will wash them clean by "a spirit of judgement and a spirit of burning" (Isa 4:4).

And I heard a loud voice from the temple telling the seven angels, "Go and pour out the seven bowls of the fury of God onto the earth."

The seven seals, the seven trumpets and the seven bowls all have the same structure, 4 + 2 + 1. So do the days of creation. During the first four days God formed the environments of the earth, during the fifth and sixth he created the animals to live in them, and on the seventh he rested. The trumpets and bowls of wrath describe the undoing of creation—this precious, wonderful world.

---

1. Josephus, *Wars of the Jews*, 6.9.3; Cassius Dio, *Roman History*, 69.12.1–14.3.

	7 days of creation	7 seals	7 trumpets	7 bowls of wrath
1–4	Light, water, land, sun	Four horsemen	Land, sea, water, sun	Land, sea, water, sun
5	Animals of air and water	Persecution	Demonic locusts	Darkness
6	Animals of the land	Day of vengeance	Demonic horses	Armageddon
7	Sabbath	Silence	Redemption	Destruction

Table 8. The three sets of seven in Revelation compared with the seven days of Creation.

God looks down to see if there are any who seek after him. All have corrupted themselves; all have turned away. With the seeing eye and the hearing ear, with his belly and his genitalia, man enjoys everything that God has given him, but the wealthier he becomes, the greater the sense that he owes it all to himself. The more he understands scientifically about nature, which he freely acknowledges to be wondrous, the less he sees God and the more he believes in his own intellectual power. He shows no gratitude. He shuts him out, refusing to worship the one who made the heaven and the land and sea and springs of water, even to acknowledge his existence. The vineyard of Europe is no longer producing fruit.

Although it seems unthinkable that God would destroy what he has made, we have been polluting and destroying it ourselves. According to the most realistic projections, by 2100 the amount of CO_2 in the atmosphere will be twice what it was in 1900. As forests burn and temperatures rise, floods, hurricanes, wildfires, plant and animal extinctions become more frequent and we return to the instability that prevailed before the Pleistocene. By casting fire on the earth, God concentrates into a few months the devastation that was beginning to happen anyway. Man learns that the creation cannot be taken for granted. One by one the bowls of wrath are poured onto land and sea, the bodies of drinking water, the sun and the air.

So the first went and poured out his bowl onto the earth, and a noxious and evil sore came on the people who had the mark of the beast and worshiped its image.

In the sixth plague of the Exodus, the boils that broke out on the skin were caused by a fine air-borne dust—volcanic ash, to judge from the mimetic heavenward tossing of soot from a furnace (Exod 9:9, 19:18). The pouring of the bowl onto the earth from above the earth likewise indicates a physical cause: possibly an increase in X-ray and ultraviolet radiation arising from the weakening, if not collapse, of the planet's magnetic shield, exacerbated perhaps by volcanic dust and by destruction of the ozone layer. The sores are a mark corresponding to the beast's mark. Given that the bowl is poured out globally, the implication is that people everywhere will have received the mark, not just in the Middle East.

And the second poured out his bowl onto the sea, and it became blood, like a corpse's, and every living soul died that was in the sea.

The judgement of the second trumpet was restricted to a third of the ocean; now the whole ocean is affected. The blood of dead animals discolors the surface. Again the physical cause is not stated, but one possibility is heat-induced hypoxia, an intensification of the "marine heatwaves" that have already become common.

And the third angel poured out his bowl onto the rivers and onto the springs of water, and they became blood.

In the catastrophe of the third trumpet, only a third of the rivers were polluted. The implication is that the judgement has become total. "I make the rivers a desert; their fish stink for lack of water and die of thirst. I clothe the heavens with blackness and make sackcloth their covering" (Isa 50:2f). Reservoirs dry up, and rivers and springs choke with corpses.

And I heard the angel of the waters say, "Righteous are you, who is, and who was, sinless one, for thus you have judged; for they poured out the blood of saints and prophets, and you have given them blood to drink. They are worthy of it."

And I heard the altar say, "Yes, Lord God the Almighty, true and just are your judgements!"

One angel has authority over sea and land (10:2), another over the fire (14:18), another over the waters. The angel does not address God as "he who is to come" because he has come, with his appearance at the seventh trumpet (11:17).

God's concept of justice is not fundamentally different from man's. "As you have done, so shall it be done to you; your recompense shall return on your head" Obad 15). "By the judgement you judge by, you will be judged, and with the measure you measure with, it will be measured back to you" (Matt 7:2). The beast and his associates polluted the land with the blood of the saints and the 144,000 prophets; in return God gives them blood to drink. Righteousness and justice are interrelated, because right action and the penalty for not acting rightly have to do with following or breaking God's law; the nouns translate the same word, *dikaiosunė*. From the altar the long-suffering martyrs voice their approval: God at last grants them justice (Luke 18:7). "They are worthy" is an ironical echo of the acclamation of the Lamb in 5:9.

And the fourth poured out his bowl on the sun, and it was given to it to scorch men with fire. They were scorched by the great heat, and they reviled the name of God who had power over these plagues, and did not give him glory by repenting.

The sun is the light of the world. Without it there would be no photosynthesis, no oxygen therefore, no food. It rises on the evil and good alike, and life depends on it. Spiritually, the Son of God is the light, the sun of righteousness that shines on all the world. His eyes are like a flame. Who can look into them?

The fire is part of the torment warned about (14:10f), directed chiefly against those who associate themselves with the beast. If previously only implied (8:7), the sun as it spews forth superhot plasma is now explicitly the source of fire. It is no longer beneficent. The atmosphere heats up, plants are reduced to tinder and wildfires multiply. Men are aware that God is the ultimate cause of their tribulation, but unlike Job, who was also afflicted with "evil sores" despite his innocence, they curse God. It is the only retaliation left to them. They do not give him blessing and honour and glory (5:13). Repentance glorifies God through being an acknowledgement of his justice and holiness.

And the fifth poured out his bowl on the throne of the beast, and his kingdom became dark. And they gnawed their tongues in pain and reviled the God of heaven because of their pain and their sores, and they did not repent of their deeds.

The light is taken away. Clouds of volcanic smoke and ash envelop the empire, the other part of the torment warned about. Day turns to night (6:12), the stars vanish and the moon does not shine (Isa 13:10). God seems utterly remote. In the outer darkness men gnash their teeth, gnaw their blaspheming tongues and go on blaspheming, notwithstanding the pain.

And the sixth poured out his bowl on the great river, the Euphrates. And its water was dried up to prepare the way for the kings from the rising of the sun. And I saw out of the mouth of the dragon and out of the mouth of the beast and out of the mouth of the false prophet three unclean spirits, like frogs. For they are demonic spirits, performing signs that go out to the kings of the whole world to gather them for battle on the great day of God the Almighty. ("Behold, I am coming like a thief! Blessed is he who is vigilant and keeps his garments, lest he go about naked and be exposed to shame.") And he gathered them at the place that is called in Hebrew Armageddon.

The scorching heat dries up the Euphrates, the future boundary of Israel, and prepares the way for the kings to take the land, just as the Jordan became dry for Joshua. Evidently earthquakes have destroyed the bridges. As at 7:2, "from the rising of the sun" means "from the east," but in Greek "of the sun" can be omitted; the point of including it is ironic, for the sky is dark, and it is Christ—associated with the sun at 1:16 and 10:1—who will rise from the east (Matt 24:27) and for whom a way is to be prepared (Isa 40:3). The invisible dragon, the "son of destruction" and the falsely prophesying "beast with two horns" (13:11) are the earthly counterparts of God the Father, his Christ and Christ's two Spirit-anointed witnesses.

The great day is the "Day of Yahweh" foreseen by the prophets (e.g. Isa 13:1–16, 24:21–23, Joel 2:31, Zeph 3:8, Mal 4:1, 2 Pet 3:12), equivalent to the "day of vengeance"—lasting years—which in the 6th century BC was visited upon Egypt, Philistia, Tyre, Moab, Ammon, Edom, Syria, Arabia, Elam and eventually Babylon itself, after the kingdom of Judah was judged (Jer 46–51, Ezek 25–32, Zeph 2). Those countries were the "whole world" at that time (Jer 25:26), hostile to Israel then and hostile now. Presumably their descendants are the "whole world" whose leaders are persuaded by supernatural signs to gather at Armageddon, the hill (Heb. *har*) that marks the site of ancient Megiddo. Although they congregate there, it is not necessarily where the final battle will take place, and other texts indicate that the battle will be at Jerusalem. Jerusalem poses no threat after three years of foreign occupation. Rather, the kings await the imminent arrival of the Messiah himself. Mocking, they expect to defeat him by force, just as when Sennacherib king of Assyria came up against Jerusalem in the reign of Hezekiah and mocked.

"Behold, I am coming like a thief!" repeats the warning given to the church at Sardis. The interruption is as unexpected as the event itself.

While it is true that the Day will come like a thief (1 Thess 5:2, 2 Pet 3:10), the Lord likens himself to a thief, plundering the house of the strong man. The Day can also refer to the moment when he takes his own. It is either the day of rapture or the subsequent day of wrath. "Know this, that if the master of the house had known the time of night when the thief was coming, he would have been vigilant and not let his house be broken into." (Matt 24:42f) Jesus exhorts us to be ready, lest we be stripped bare.

And the seventh poured out his bowl on the air, and a loud voice came from the temple, from the throne, saying, "It is done!" And there occurred lightning, and sounds, and thunder. And there was a great earthquake, such as has never been since man was on the earth, so great was that mighty quake. And the great city split into three parts. The cities of the nations fell, and God remembered Babylon the Great to give her the cup of the wine of the fury of his wrath. Every island fled, and mountains were not to be found. And great hailstones about a hundred pounds weight come down from heaven on mankind. And they reviled God for the plague of the hail, because its plague is very great.

The voice of God breaks heaven's silence. Lightning, noises and thunder have been going on intermittently since the first trumpet, but with this last bowl, poured on the troposphere, the solar storms producing these effects intensify. The earth and its works are burned up, in accordance with the "wrath of God from heaven" revealed in the gospel (2 Pet 3:10, Rom 1:18). The threshing-floor is purged.

The singling out of the earthquake and hail for particular description confirms that all the phenomena in the list are real. Earthquakes occur when tension is released between tectonic plates. Most originate near the surface, all are local, and the shallower their origin, the greater the damage. A global earthquake could be triggered only by something deeper, involving movements in the outer core of the planet, the same kind as generate its magnetic field. In the last thirty years the rate at which magnetic north has shifted across the surface has accelerated from 0–15 km to 50–60 km per year, but apparently slowing now. The shift is linked to accelerating movements in the core, but exactly what is happening there remains unknown. The earthquake is the same as caused mountains to crumble when the sixth seal was opened.

The waters roar and foam, mountains and islands sink into the heart of the sea, all the foundations of the earth are shaken (Ps 46, 82:5, 97:4f). Whereas the first "great city" was the tripartite conurbation of Resen,

Nineveh and Calah (as it had become by the 8th century, Gen 10:12, Jonah 3:2f), now it is global—the cities of Eurasia, Africa and America—and it splits apart.

> "As you looked, a stone was cut out by no human hand and struck the image on its feet of iron and clay, and broke them in pieces. Then the iron, the clay, the bronze, the silver and the gold together were broken in pieces and became like the chaff of the summer threshing floors; and the wind carried them away so that no place could be found for them." (Dan 2:34f)

It has happened before, when Berlin, Hamburg, Coventry, Stalingrad, Tokyo, and many other cities were all but obliterated. Men will look at the mountains and every tall building as it collapses and cry, "Fall on us, and hide us from the wrath of God!" (6:16) The heavens also shudder (Joel 3:16, Hag 2:6). The hailstones are meteors, for a hundred pounds weight (lit. "talent") is far heavier than any frozen rain pellet, and ice would be incongruous in the midst of fierce heat. "Stars" fall on the earth like figs shaken by the wind.

With that the wrath of God is finished (15:1), as it finally was for Jesus (John 19:30). The words "there was a great earthquake" are the same as in Matthew's account of the resurrection. The convulsion that brings down Babylon the Great will also bring up Israel's dead (Ezek 37:7).

The following chapters (17–19) reveal the character of Babylon the Great and utter a lament for her fall. The army of the beast and his prophet is reduced to carrion, while those attending the marriage of the Lamb feast and rejoice.

BABYLON THE GREAT

Revelation 17. A prostitute seated on the beast: her identity and destiny.

And there came one of the seven angels who had the seven bowls, and he spoke with me, saying, "Come here, I will show you the judgement of the great prostitute who is seated on the many waters, with whom the kings of the earth have fornicated, and from the wine of whose fornication the inhabitants of the earth have become drunk." And he carried me away in spirit to a wilderness, and I saw a woman seated on a scarlet beast that was full of blasphemous names and had seven heads and ten horns. And the woman was clothed in purple and scarlet and gilded with gold and jewels and pearls, holding in her hand a golden cup full of abominations. And I saw the uncleanness of her fornication, and on her forehead a name written, a mystery, "Babylon the Great, mother of prostitutes and of earth's abominations." And the woman was drunk from the blood of the saints and from the blood of the witnesses of Jesus.

THE WRATH OF GOD climaxes with the fall of Babylon the Great. Now, in another excursus, one of the avenging angels takes John to a personification of the city. "Many waters" is a set phrase from the Old Testament (Heb. *mayim rabbim*, variably translated in Bibles as "many," "great," "mighty" or "abundant waters"), signifying surface or underground rivers (Ezek 17:5) or the open sea (Isa 23:3). The "many waters" of the Euphrates that flowed through ancient Babylon (Jer 51:13) fed a network of canals. More pregnantly, the phrase connotes death and chaos (Ps 18:16, Ezek 26:19), with reference to the deep that covered the earth when it was formless and lifeless (Gen 1:2); "great" in "great deep" (Gen 7:11) being the singular form of *rabbim*. More figuratively still, the waters signify the nations that surrounded and always threatened to overwhelm Israel (Ps

144:7, Isa 17:12f, Hab 3:15). Purple and scarlet were expensive dyes associated especially with royalty. "Uncleanness" refers to the sexual stains that besmirch her fine clothing.

Seated queen-like above the waters, Babylon the Great is not a single city but civilization as a whole. It is the fruition and culmination of the first imperial city, its lineage traceable from Babel to the empires of its Assyrian and Babylonian successors through to the empires of Persia, Greece, and Rome. It is the city of man as opposed to the city of God, located in unfruitful wilderness. The mother of the appointed heir of all things also lives in that wilderness (12:6), but for her it is a place of exile, not domicile. As throughout Revelation, "the inhabitants of the earth" contrast with those whose minds are set on the things above (Col 3:2). "The saints" are the Jews.

Being a prostitute, the woman rejects the restraints of marriage. Virginity prior to the 20th century was implied in the very word for an unmarried woman: Hebrew *almah* (so Isa 7:14), Greek *parthenos*, Latin *virgo*. It was not the foremost meaning because it was taken for granted. The equivalent English word, "maid" or "maiden," has dropped out of currency as a result of virginity's ceasing to be the norm. Since the Second World War there has been a social revolution, an undoing of the created order itself, and it has been catastrophic: not only for its undermining of the family and traditional ideas of parenthood, with the State filling the vacuum, but because to copulate outside marriage is knowingly or unknowingly to spurn God and listen to the Serpent. That very act makes one his subject. "When you eat of the fruit you will not surely die. Your eyes will be opened, and you will be like God, knowing good and evil." Innocence melts away, and now one keeps God at a distance (Gen 3:1–8). This is perhaps the chief reason why today old and young, male and female, are impervious to the gospel, supposing they ever get to hear it. Atheism rationalizes away the guilt.

They have been seduced by the intoxicating sense of participating in life's mystery, the thrill of defying God with impunity and liberating oneself from his moral laws. Even the oldest generation can hardly remember anything different. It must seem odd to read Baroness Trumpington reminiscing, without any Christian belief, "We really were awfully pure. None of us went to bed with anybody. You didn't do it. The boys tried, of course, but no, we weren't brought up that way." That was in 1943. Today State programs of sex education are eroticizing the psychological development of children from the age of five.

We see then why the symbol of the prostitute is so apt. Sin is infidelity towards our Maker, causing us to want to hide our nakedness, and fornication is the wilful repetition of that infidelity in the domain of procreation, which is God's power of creation delegated to the creature. "Against you, you only, have I sinned and done what was evil in your sight," confessed David after his adultery. Advanced though it is in technology and scientific knowledge, Western civilization—portrayed as a woman rather than a beast because it once knew God—has reduced itself to an obsession with sexual intercourse and erected around it an entire counter-religion, an entire philosophy of personal identity, rights and self-fulfillment. Self-gratification is valued more highly than bringing up a family. Even motor cars are marketed with images of sexual Eden.

The nature of earth's abominations is not specified, though Leviticus and Deuteronomy mention several. The bloodguilt of the woman recalls Ahab's adulterous wife who, inspired by those with whom she communed by witchcraft, murdered the prophets and other servants of Yahweh (2 Kgs 9:7–22). "Mother of prostitutes" is a reference to the practice of "sacred marriage" that originated in 4th-millennium Babylonia. Inana, purportedly the daughter of the God of heaven (or Anu, Sumerian for heaven) but actually a woman, stole Anu's kingship by lying with his high priest, and she then gave it to Nimrod by lying with him. On her death she was deified as the queen of heaven, whereupon her priestess assumed the role. The ritual of marriage was repeated annually, and subsequently imitated by peoples beyond Babylonia. In Canaan, Inana's equivalent was the goddess Asherah and her role taken by sacred prostitutes. By Manasseh's reign the cult had penetrated to the very heart of Israel (2 Kgs 21:7, 23:7).

Being the original prostitute, the woman is the first civilization as well as the last. Like Inana, she drinks from the golden cup of a religion she has spurned, pouring into it filth that she herself would have regarded as an abomination a hundred years ago. She sits on a beast similar to the beast in chapter 12 in color and similar to the beast in chapter 13 in respect of its blasphemous names. Christian faith decays as Islam within Europe grows. Islam covers its women and disapproves of homosexuality, but is happy to fornicate with unbelievers, the *kuffaar*. The prostitute is happy to fornicate with Islam. In the final days the West will hate those who disturb the peace with the gospel. It will seek to silence their witness by killing many of them, and take delight in the slaughter. Their blood will be like wine.

It is Islam—a geopolitical power distinct from the people in its grip—that has destroyed the Church in Syria and Iraq, provoked in part by Western military interventions. Iran is overtly hostile towards the West but tolerates a substantial Christian population in its midst so long as Farsi-speakers remain loyal; those who share the gospel are imprisoned and beaten. Saudi Arabia is covertly hostile. It holds it a capital offense for a Muslim to convert to Christianity, tolerates no church buildings on its soil and spreads its Wahhabi brand of jihadism throughout the world. But it supplies oil to the West and buys its arms, so the US government overlooks the fact that 15 of the 19 hijackers involved in the World Trade Center attacks were Saudis. Similarly, Britain's government refuses to publish its finding that Saudi Arabia was funding and promoting jihadism in Britain. Britain once played a part in the rise of Wahhabism,[1] and regards Saudi Arabia as a friend and ally.

Until the 20th century, the majority of Christians lived in Europe and North America; hence the majority of Christian martyrs also lived in those countries. Of those, the greatest number—many millions— were members of the Orthodox Church, killed in the decades following the Russian Revolution. The "blood of the saints" refers to the Jewish Holocaust.

And I marveled greatly when I saw her. And the angel said to me, "Why did you marvel? I will tell you the mystery of the woman, and of the beast carrying her, with its seven heads and ten horns. The beast that you saw was, and is not, and is to rise from the abyss and go to destruction. And the inhabitants of the earth whose names have not been written in the book of life from the foundation of the world will marvel when they perceive the beast that was, and is not, and will arrive.

"Herein the mind that has wisdom. The seven heads are seven mountains on which the woman is seated; they are also seven kings, five of whom have fallen, one is, the other has not yet come, and when he does come he must remain a little while. The beast that was and is not, it is also an eighth but belongs to the seven, and goes to destruction. And the ten horns that you saw are ten kings who have not yet received kingship, but will receive authority as kings for one hour together with the beast. These are of one purpose, and give their power and authority to the beast. These will make war on the Lamb, and the Lamb will conquer them, for he is Lord of lords and King of kings, and those with him are called, and chosen, and faithful."

---

1. Curtis, *Secret Affairs.*

A Babylonian portrayal c. 1600 BC of the goddess Inana with horned cap, standing on two lions and, below them, the mountains of Aratta. The owls symbolize nocturnal spirits, while Inana's owl- or eagle-like talons show that she too is to be feared. (British Museum, digital restoration of a damaged original.)

Wisdom is needed to interpret the vision, just as Daniel needed divine wisdom to interpret Nebuchadrezzar's dream of a colossus. The heads have a double significance, one relating to the woman (who sits on them) and the other to the beast (whose heads they are). In the first aspect they suggest the seven hills of ancient Rome, consistent with the woman's representing European civilization, successor of Rome. (Vatican Hill is not one of the seven.) In Nebuchadrezzar's dream (Dan 2), the third kingdom after his own was the Roman Empire, which morphed into a divided kingdom, the final one before the kingdoms were all smashed by an everlasting kingdom. Rome was eponymous for the empire it founded, controlled and epitomized. Peter apparently referred to Rome as Babylon in his first letter.

The other significance of the heads is that they symbolize seven kings. Kings can denote kingdoms as well as rulers, and in Daniel's vision of four beasts the concepts are interchangeable (Dan 7:17, 23). In relation to the kingdoms which dominated the Levant at various times, the heads are Egypt, Neo-Assyria, Neo-Babylonia, Medo-Persia, Greece, Rome and

Islam, although during Islam's ascendancy the Jews were exiled from the land. All are manifestations of the underlying power that is Satan, the dragon with seven heads and ten horns. From the long perspective that sees Christ as having come at the end of the ages, the 1192 years of Islamic rule between AD 637 and 1917 are not incompatible with "a little while" (ESV's and NIV's "only" before the phrase is unwarranted). The caliphate yet to come will constitute a short-lived eighth empire of ten states. They will reign for "one hour," which does mean only a short while, and make war on the saints (13:7), eventually on the Lamb himself. But although the beast will initially prevail, the kingdom of God will be theirs and will supplant every earthly kingdom. The beast does not see that behind the saints' apparent helplessness is one who, having already conquered, sits far above all rule, authority, power and dominion. At the end of the age he will conquer his enemies by force.

The scarlet beast has the same number of heads and horns as the red dragon (12:3). In relation to the dragon, it amounts to an eighth head, an eighth kingdom or empire, and since all the other empires are defunct, the dragon and this last empire are pictured as identical. As an individual, the beast is the man at the head of this union. He "was, and is not, and will arrive"—a phrase mimicking what was said about God (4:8), for indeed he will claim to be God. His former incarnation was Antiochus IV. He rises from the abyss, the abode of demons. When he comes again, he will be present for a time, then return to the abyss (19:20). That is why Paul calls him the "man of sin, the son of destruction." The world marvels at the beast, it seems, because he has come back to life (also 13:12).

And he says to me, "The waters that you saw, where the prostitute is seated, are peoples and throngs, nations and languages. And the ten horns that you saw, they and the beast will hate the prostitute, and will cause her to be laid waste, and naked, and will eat her flesh and burn her up with fire. For God has put it into their hearts to carry out his purpose, and to be of one purpose, and to give their kingship to the beast until the words of God are fulfilled. And the woman that you saw is the great city that has kingship over the kings of the earth."

"Peoples and throngs, nations and languages" is the last variation of the phrase at 5:9. Having lost their genealogical identities, the tribes of the earth are merely urban crowds, albeit still divided by language. Over the past two centuries the proportion of the world's population living in urban areas has increased from less than 10% to more than half;

by another definition, to more than three quarters. The great city (11:8, 16:19, Gen 10:12) unites the earth as if all its cities were one. The kings of the earth over which it has kingship (cf. v. 14) are distinct from Europe, although as a political entity Europe is itself a kingdom (v. 18).

The woman is first pictured seated on the waters, subsequently on the beast, indicating perhaps that she has not always been seated on the beast or been a prostitute. In recent decades we have already seen something of this spiritual and political re-alignment, but it is a bad move, for the beast will be no friend. She is condemned to repeat Israel's delusion (Jer 4:30, Ezek 16:15–40):

> And you, in your devastation,
>> what do you mean by dressing in scarlet,
>> by adorning yourself with ornaments of gold,
> by enlarging your eyes with paint?
>> In vain you beautify yourself.
> Your lovers despise you;
>> they seek your life.

Despite her professions of love, the ten kings and the beast hate the woman. Ironically, their unanimity of purpose—and note that the woman too will submit to the beast's authority if "their" in v. 17 includes her—is what God also has in mind. Because of her association with the beast, they will cause her to be stripped of her scarlet finery and be eaten and burned like a sacrifice to demons. "Laid waste" (*eremwmenos*) has the same root as the words "wilderness" (*eremos*) and "desolation" (*eremwsis*): what was metaphorically characterized as wasteland becomes literally wasteland (Ps 46:8, Isa 24:12, Mic 7:13) in consequence of the devastation brought down by the final bowl of wrath. The fulfilled words of God are those quoted from the Old Testament in the next chapter.

THE FALL OF BABYLON THE GREAT

Revelation 18. Fulfilled prophecies concerning ancient Babylon, Jerusalem and Tyre give grounds for believing that the days of modern civilization are numbered.

After these things I saw another angel coming down from heaven, having great authority, and the earth was illumined from his glory. And he cried with a mighty voice, "Fallen, fallen is Babylon the Great! She has become an abode of demons, and a prison of every unclean spirit, and a prison of every unclean and hated bird. For all the nations have drunk from the wine of her raging fornication, and the kings of the earth have fornicated with her, and the merchants of the earth have got rich by the power of her luxury."

AS AT 10:1, THE angel must be Jesus Christ himself, for only his glory is destined to illumine all the earth and fill the rebuilt Temple. "My glory I will not give to another" (Isa 48:11)—except, that is, to his firstborn (John 17:22). He, Jesus, is the glory of Yahweh (Heb 1:3), a person (Zech 2:8), the one who dwelt among his people Israel and will dwell among them, who will fulfill what is written in Isaiah (40:4f, 60:1):

> The uneven ground shall become level,
>   and the rough places a plain.
> And the glory of the LORD shall be revealed,
>   and all flesh shall see it together.

Mountains crumble, the planet lights up, and everyone sees the brightness, from one horizon to the other.

> Out of Zion, the perfection of beauty,
>   God shines forth.
> Our God will come, and not keep silent.

> Fire will devour before him,
> and around him storms will rage. (Ps 50:2f)

Thick darkness will be followed by blazing light, as when the sun stood still and large stones fell from heaven and the nation took vengeance on its enemies (Josh 10:13). The moon will be as the sun, and the sun's light sevenfold (Isa 30:26, Zech 14:7). All who serve images will be put to shame (Ps 97:6f).

"Fallen, fallen is Babylon the great!" echoes Isaiah's pronouncement on ancient Babylon (Isa 21:9). The city is the antitype of the abode of God, and as with ancient Edom and Babylonia (Isa 34:10ff, Jer 51:43), demons and unclean birds (Lev 11) inhabit the place. Incantations from Babylonia speak of demons flitting around like birds, which may be the metaphor here, but the explanatory "for" suggests that the birds are nations (Dan 4:14) and they have introduced unclean religions into the city. The largest mosque in the western world by land area is the Mosque of Rome. Strasbourg's is not far behind. Demons have returned to the house that was swept clean and brought with them spirits more evil than themselves. The sense is not that they are captives; rather they hold the city captive.

Isaiah's prophecies date to the second half of the 8th century BC, when, apart from eleven years of independence under Merodach-Baladan (Marduk-apla-idinna, 721–710 BC), Babylon was a vassal of the Assyrian Empire. In what could hardly have been an extrapolation of the contemporary situation, Isaiah predicted that one day Judah would be deported to Babylon (Isa 39:6f, 47:6), after which God would bring up the Medes to avenge himself on the city and Judah would return. He predicted its fall three times: in chapter 13, chapter 21 and chapter 47. In the second prophecy, Elam—which in Belshazzar's third year was part of the Babylonian empire (Dan 8:2)—was pictured laying siege alongside Media.

Part of Isaiah's message was that only God had the power to foretell such things (46:10f):

> declaring the end from the beginning
> and from of old things not yet done,
> saying, "My counsel shall stand,
> and all my pleasure I will do,"
> calling a bird of prey from the east,
> the man of my counsel from a distant land.

Some of the events lay in the near future, some further off. In the first prophecy the fall of the Chaldean city (the Babylon renovated by Nebuchadrezzar) was interleaved with that of its modern-day counterpart, so that Isaiah 13:9–13, at a minimum, remains to be fulfilled. The second prophecy appears to relate solely to the Chaldean city. The first part of the third prophecy (47:1–7) relates to the Chaldean city, the second part (47:8–15) solely to the unfulfilled future. John quotes extensively from this second part. (Such conflation of the near and distant future was common, the judgements being foretastes of the final Day: compare the mixed prophecies of Joel 2 and Zeph 1.)

Left: Aerial view of the base of Babylon's ziggurat (the many times rebuilt "tower of Babel"). The trench projecting forwards marks the position of the ascending stairway. Right: Interpretative drawing of the upper part of stele MS2063 in the Schøyen Collection. The cuneiform epigraph reads "E-temen-an-ki, ziggurat of Babylon"; above is the ground-plan of the surmounting temple.[2] The stele celebrates the restoration of the building by king Nebuchadrezzar, shown standing.

Ancient Babylon was guilty primarily on account of her idolatry (Jer 50:38). As in other Mesopotamian cities, a terraced ziggurat stood in the center, on the same site as the original tower. It was called in Sumerian the *E-temen-an-ki*, "House of the Foundation of Heaven and Earth." At the summit stood a temple representing the heavenly dwelling of Marduk, "king of heaven and the underworld." From there a stairway descended to a terrace half-way down, representing the earth at ground level, while subsidiary stairways led up to the terrace from the underworld, the earth's

2. George, "A Stele of Nebuchadrezzar," 153–69.

"foundation." The ziggurat also supported shrines for the land's other deities. Opposite was a second building, the *E-sag-ila*, where Marduk resided as Babylon's king. As throughout the ancient world, the human king was the god's viceroy.

Some 180 years after Isaiah, the predictions referring to the Chaldean city came to pass. The "bird of prey from the east" was Cyrus, commander of the Medes and Persians and later the Elamites, who had changed sides.[3] Isaiah even predicted his name (Isa 44:28). Persia lay to the east, but as we know from his crossing the river Diyala on the way, he approached Babylon from the north (Jer 50:3). A successful battle outside the walls was followed by a long and frustrating siege, until the invaders hit on the idea of diverting the river that flowed through the city. Once the channel was drained, they were able to walk into the capital by night while the unsuspecting leaders were feasting, drunk with wine (Herodotus I, 191, cf. Isa 21:5, 44:27, Jer 51:39, Dan 5). Supposedly impregnable Babylon was captured with ease, on October 18th, 539.

For millennia, the nations had drunk the stupefying wine of Babylon's idolatry. Eventually God made them drink the stupefying wine of his wrath, as his agent Nebuchadrezzar conquered city after city. "All the kingdoms of the earth" in this context were the kingdoms of the Middle East. A few decades later Babylon herself was made to drink (Jer 25:15–26).

The city was captured intact. While slaughter must have been widespread, it was not immediately reduced to a wasteland, and indeed immediate destruction would not have helped the Jewish exiles there. In 521, Babylon rebelled but was recaptured after a seventeen-month siege. Another unsuccessful revolt took place in 484, following which its defenses and some of its temples were destroyed. Decay was gradual. In 331 Alexander the Great demolished the ziggurat, but the *E-sag-ila* was restored and remained in use for two centuries or more.

Sudden destruction is reserved for modern Babylon. The charge against her is that she is promiscuous and a lover of fine living, and has persuaded the rest of the world to adopt the same materialist view of life. Her carnality and affluence exert great power. The world's business tycoons grow rich by her—we might say, obscenely rich. In addition, she has blood on her hands. So the angel testifies that history will repeat itself, only on a larger scale. Just as the fall of the ancient city was prophesied and came to

---

3. Waters, "Cyrus and Susa," 115–18.

pass, recorded for our sakes as much as Judah's, so will the fall of today's megalopolis.

The metaphor describing the woman's passionate lust and God's passionate anger is apt, for Europe produces, exports and consumes more wine per head than any other region. Having drunk to satiety from her own cup, Europe will drink from his. So will all worshipers of the beast (14:10).

And I heard another voice from heaven, saying,

> *"Come out of her, my people,*
>   *lest you participate in her sins*
>   *and in her plagues you share;*
> *for her sins have been glued together as far as heaven,*
>   *and God has remembered her iniquities.*
> *Pay her back as she herself has paid back*
>   *and render double for her deeds;*
>   *in the cup she has mixed mix double for her.*
> *As she glorified herself and lived in luxury,*
>   *in like measure give her torment and mourning,*
> *since in her heart she says,*
>   *"I sit a queen, no widow am I,*
>   *and mourning may I never see."*
> *For this reason her plagues will come in a single day,*
>   *death, and mourning, and famine,*
> *and she will be burned up with fire,*
>   *for mighty is the Lord God who judged her."*

The prophetic voice is God's. His warning to come out of her repeats the warning of Isaiah and Jeremiah (Isa 52:11, Jer 51:45): the people of God must dissociate from a culture that stands condemned, or they will suffer the same fate. Babylon's sins are glued together like bricks glued with tar (Gen 11:3f); her judgement has reached up to heaven higher than her towers. He declares, "I am God, and there is none other" (Isa 46:9). She thinks to herself, "I am, and there is none other. I shall not sit a widow or know the loss of children." (Isa 47:8)

God appeals to the Church. Insofar as Babylon controls her and tells her what to say and think, she must break free, sanctify herself and hold fast to what he says in his Word. How many even know of this appeal in the Bible? How many accept that God has the power as well as the will to bring this comfortable world to an end? How many understand that his indictment of apostate Jerusalem in the book of Jeremiah applies equally to us, that he still demands faithfulness of his people?

The angels with the seven bowls are told to pay back "as she herself paid back." When she retaliated, she did so disproportionately, as Lamech boasted he had done (Gen 4:23f). Perhaps the most flagrant example was the decision to drop an atomic bomb on Nagasaki. President Truman boasted, "The Japanese began the war from the air at Pearl Harbor. They have been repaid many fold. . . . The basic power of the universe, the force from which the sun draws its power, has been loosed." Another example was the havoc wreaked on Afghanistan and Iraq for the attack on the World Trade Center.[4]

Much will be required of those to whom much has been given. When David lay with another man's wife, God said to him, "I will take your wives from before your eyes and give them to your neighbor, and he will lie with your wives in broad daylight. You did it secretly; I will do this in front of all Israel." In his judgement God took into account David's circumstances and how much he already knew of God and repaid him double. Justice requires that the punishment be greater than the suffering caused, otherwise the guilty party suffers no more than the victim. So it will be in the final judgement. Europe, Russia and America cannot say that they did not know about God and his righteousness.

Disaster comes suddenly, by quake and by fire, by the power of the earth and the power of the sun.

And the kings of the earth, who fornicated and lived in luxury with her, will weep and wail over her when they see the smoke of her burning, standing far back for fear of her torment, and saying, "Woe, woe, the great city, Babylon the mighty city! For in a single hour your judgement has come."

And the merchants of the earth weep and mourn for her, because no one buys their cargo anymore: cargo of gold, and of silver, and of precious stones, and of pearls, and of fine linen, and of purple, and of silk, and of scarlet, and every aromatic wood, and every article of ivory, and every article of costly wood and of bronze and of iron and of marble, and cinnamon, and cardamom, and incense, and myrrh, and frankincense, and wine, and oil, and fine flour, and wheat, and mules, and sheep, and of horses, and of carriages, and of bodies and souls of men.

4. Crawford, "Human Cost of Post-9/11 Wars," "$6.4 Trillion Cost of Post-9/11 Wars."

And the fruits which your soul desired are departed from you, and all the sumptuousness and the splendor are destroyed from you, and they will be found no more.

The merchants who got rich from her will stand far back for fear of her torment, weeping and mourning, saying, "Woe, woe, the great city that was clothed in fine linen, purple and scarlet, and gilded with gold, and jewels, and pearls! For in a single hour all this wealth has been laid waste."

And all shipmasters and seafarers and mariners and all who traded on the sea stood far back and cried seeing the smoke of her burning, saying, "What compared with the great city?"

And they threw dust on their heads and cried, weeping and mourning, saying, "Woe, woe, the great city, in which all who had ships at sea grew rich by her wealth! For in a single hour she has been laid waste." Rejoice over her, heaven, and the saints, and the apostles, and the prophets, for God has passed your judgement on her!

The future tense becomes past as the pronouncement is fulfilled. "Clothed in fine linen, purple and scarlet, gilded with gold, jewels and pearls" echoes the previous description of the personified city (17:4). Her "torment" refers to the torment inflicted by the demons of the fifth and sixth trumpets, climaxing with the pain and anguish of the destruction itself. "Woe" (*ouai*) has the sense of "alas." Those who have profited by her watch from afar, implying that some places will escape devastation. "Kings of the earth," a frequent term in the Old Testament, could refer to kings of cities as well as nations. It is one of the many echoes of Ezekiel's prophetic lament over Tyre, principal city-state of Phoenicia (Ezek 26–28). Tyre was a fortified island off the coast of Lebanon, linked to a sister city on the mainland, Old Tyre, a little to the south. By its maritime trade it had enriched both itself and other kingdoms. It had applied its wisdom and understanding to making money, saying to itself, "I am God; I sit where the gods dwell, in the heart of the seas." But its self-assurance was a delusion, and God vowed to bring it down. Nebuchadrezzar conquered Old Tyre soon after conquering Jerusalem. Although he failed to capture its offshore stronghold, despite a 13-year siege, two and a half centuries later Alexander the Great captured it by building a causeway to the island with rubble from the old city. This must have been what Ezekiel was referring to when he spoke of men purposefully laying Tyre's stones, trees and soil in the midst of the waters. Alexander's army was the final wave of the "many nations" that hurled themselves against the city.

Supposedly impregnable Tyre was ruined, 2000 of its men were crucified, the remaining population made slaves. As with Babylon, fulfillment of the vision tarried but eventually came to pass.

At the moment it seems inconceivable that this present world should meet a sudden end. Mortal though we are, we think that our way of life will continue forever, while its comforts inure us against the thought that it might not. Our civilization encompasses the whole earth; even China has merged with it. The merchants of the earth have got rich by its trade. They invest in the real estate of London, New York and Berlin, they buy up football clubs, they educate their children in the West's schools and universities.

Today, we don't have ziggurats in the center of cities; we have skyscrapers, dwarfing the once dominant steeples, serving Mammon and glorifying man. The fall of the Twin Towers was a sign.[5]

> For the Lord of hosts has a day
>   against all that is proud and lofty,
> against all that is lifted up,
>   and it will be brought low . . .
> against all the lofty mountains
>   and against all the uplifted hills,
> against every high tower
>   and against every fortified wall . . .
> And people will enter the caves of the rocks
>   and the holes of the ground,
> away from the terror of the LORD
>   and from the splendor of his majesty,
>   when he rises to make the earth tremble.

Because countries are now interdependent, we speak of "the global economy." Modern economies depend on continually stimulating consumers to covet more and buy more, storing or throwing away what they bought the year before. If consumption is not increasing year on year, the state reduces taxes, loosens credit and itself borrows more in order to stimulate growth. But a person's life does not consist in the abundance of his possessions. When monotheism drove out polytheism, men ceased to worship idols. Scientific atheism having driven out monotheism, artefacts again dominate consciousness; the wonders of technology eclipse the wonders of created nature. Machines and gadgets endowed with artificial intelligence promise to liberate, but in fact enslave, so that men

5. How it happened remains unclear: see ae911truth.org, Hughes, "9/11 Truth".

"worship at a new shrine"[6] and growing covetousness—idolatry in new guise—along with fornication, impurity and bad desire, becomes the reason wrath is coming on the world (Col 3:5f).

The list of goods, mostly luxury items, is a modification of Ezekiel's list of Tyre's imports, with the addition of carriages, marble and wooden articles, and omitting the countries that supplied them. The list ends with the bodies and souls of human beings: slaves are trafficked as well as animals. By implication, all this wealth is at the expense of human suffering and exploitation. Do we too measure ourselves in terms of how much wealth we have, what we call our "standard of living"? It is not how God measures us. The comparison with Tyre is apt, for over 90% of the world's goods are transported by sea. Much of what we enjoy is on the backs of forced labor beyond our shores.

The Church was founded by the apostles and prophets. The word "apostle," from the verb *apostellω*, meaning to send, implied someone who had seen Jesus (1 Cor 9:1) and had special authority to act as his witness and perform signs (2 Cor 12:12). The first apostles were the twelve disciples, later joined by others (Acts 14:14, Gal 1:19), and the prophets were their contemporaries (Acts 11:27, 13:1, 15:32, 21:10, Eph 3:5, 4:11f). The prophets' role was to encourage the fledgling Church and confirm the apostles' witness at a time when the New Testament had either not been written or was not widely known. Many were martyred (1 Thess 2:15). Today, speaking under inspiration is rare, though not unknown. More importantly, the gospel of the kingdom is itself a prophetic message.

The apostles and prophets addressed here are the 144,000 (cf. 11:18), counterparts of those sent to Jerusalem before her destruction in AD 70 (Luke 11:49). Like the other saints, they are with the angels in heaven, and they rejoice because their prayers have been answered. Columns of smoke from the rubble answer to the incense rising from the altar. The time foreseen by Moses has come (Deut 32:43):

> Rejoice with him, you heavens,
>   bow down to him, all you gods,
> for he will avenge the blood of his children
>   and take vengeance on his adversaries.

And one mighty angel took up a stone like a great millstone and threw it into the sea, saying, "Thus with violence will Babylon the great city be thrown down, and let it be found no more. And let the sound of lyre-players

6. Roberts, *History of the World*, 818.

and singers and pipers and trumpeters be heard in you no more, and
craftsmen, of whatever craft, be found in you no more, and the sound of a
mill be heard in you no more, and the light of a lamp shine in you no more,
and the voice of bridegroom and bride be heard in you no more! For your
merchants were the great ones of the earth, for all the nations were deceived
by your sorcery. And in her was found the blood of prophets and saints, and
of all the slaughtered on the earth."

Jeremiah was told to tie a stone to the document recording his prophecy against Babylon and throw it into the Euphrates, a sign that thus would Babylon sink and never be rebuilt (Jer 51:63). Ezekiel was told that Tyre too would sink under the waves and never be rebuilt. Jesus said, "Stumbling-blocks are sure to come, but woe to the one through whom they come! It would be better for him if a millstone were hung round his neck and he were thrown into the sea than that he should cause one of these little ones to stumble." The vision of the millstone is implicitly an indictment of how the great city corrupts even its children. Exposed to pornographic imagery in films, music videos, magazines and the internet, children are becoming sexually aware at an ever earlier age, with consequential depression, mental illness, sexual disease and sexual violence that the State then counters through the education system, teaching "values" that only add to their premature awareness. Society is corrupt from top to bottom.

The dirge is adapted from Jeremiah's pronouncement of doom upon Judah and surrounding nations (Jer 7:34, 25:8–10). If one wishes to update the cultural references, the prophecy is speaking of guitarists and orchestras, of manufacturers, of flour mills and electric lights, of everything that typifies normal life. The people of Judah said to themselves, "He will not do anything. Disaster will not come upon us; we shall not see sword and famine." But they did see sword and famine, and just as Jerusalem fell, so will the civilization built on the foundations of Christianity. "If the vision tarry, wait for it," said Habakkuk, "it will surely come." "They were eating, drinking, marrying, being given in marriage, until the day Noah entered the ark and the cataclysm came and destroyed them all."

The mention of drug-dealing, *pharmakeia*, is shocking after the evocation of innocent normality. The word comes from Isaiah's third prophecy concerning Babylon, where it means "sorcery," but again we should note the two explanatory "for"s. The city falls because its merchants, its billionaire magnates, have become "the great ones of the earth" (2 Sam

7:9) and they have become great through deceit In the modern world pharmaceutical companies are among the greatest deceivers.[7] They are also among the most profitable: the fines incurred by Johnson & Johnson and Pfizer alone since 2000 total $25 billion, a small fraction of their profits.

Babylon the Great is likened to three archetypal cities: Babylon, on account of her idolatry, Tyre, on account of her pride, Jerusalem, on account of her adultery. She is the unnamed city or cities in Isaiah's vision of a devastated earth. Although some identify her with the Roman Empire, or the Roman Church, neither of these has the characteristics of all three cities. She is the civilization of all the earth.

The whole planet is depopulate and desolate (Isa 24:6–13, 26:5, Mic 7:13). The lofty city is suddenly cast to the dust, reduced to a wasteland. The few remaining inhabitants are scorched. Merry-making has ceased.

> For thus will it be in the midst of the earth
>   among the nations,
> as when an olive tree is beaten,
>   as at the gleaning when the grape harvest is done. ...
>
> Come, my people, enter your chambers
>   and shut your doors behind you;
> hide yourselves for a little while
>   until the fury has passed by.
> For behold, the LORD is coming out from his place
>   to punish the inhabitants of the earth for their iniquity,
> and the earth will disclose its blood
>   and no more conceal its slain. (Isa 26:20f)

Murder is the undoing of God's purpose in bringing a soul into being. After Abel's murder, God said to Cain, "What have you done? The voice of your brother's blood is crying out to me from the ground." By the time of Noah, the earth was filled with violence. At the end of the present age, vengeance, deferred till now, will be exacted as if for all the righteous blood shed since Creation, not only in the final generation, just as it was when Jerusalem suffered retribution after she killed the prophets sent to her.

The blood of prophets and saints includes that of Christians in the period from Nero to Diocletian, the blood of the saints who gave up their lives in the conversion of Europe, the blood of murdered Waldensians,

---

7. Gøtzsche, *Deadly Medicines;* Kendrick, *Doctoring Data;* VAERS data as analyzed by Craig Paardekooper; Obomsawin, "Immunity, Disease and Vaccination."

the blood of Protestant reformers such as Jan Hus and William Tyndale, the blood of the Huguenots, the blood of Jews massacred during the Black Death in 1348–50 and in the Ukraine in 1648–1656 and 1919, the blood of the 6 million Jews murdered during the Second World War in Poland, the Baltic States, Germany, Austria, Bohemia, Moravia, Slovakia, Croatia, Greece, the Netherlands, Hungary, Byelorussia, Ukraine, Belgium, Yugoslavia, Romania, France, Bulgaria, Italy and Russia, as well as the blood of the 144,000 who prophesied. Only God has a full account.

"All the slaughtered of the earth" includes the millions of Greek, Assyrian and Armenian civilians massacred by the Ottomans during and after the First World War, the more than 15 million killed by Communists in the Soviet Union, the more than three hundred thousand Serb civilians tortured or otherwise killed by the Ustashe in Croatia during the Second World War, the 2 million or more Polish civilians killed by the Germans following their invasion, the untold millions killed by Communists in China and Cambodia, and the millions killed in the Congo, Sudan, Rwanda and Angola, to say nothing of soldiers killed in war. Previous centuries also have their roll calls.

The slaughtered also include innocents killed in the womb. Fornication gives rise to babies, and the babies are not always wanted. As in pre-Christian societies, in such circumstances modern society claims the right to kill, long after the first trimester in which most miscarriages occur, with hospitals cremating or simply incinerating the bodies. One in four pregnancies worldwide and three in ten in Europe end in abortion, amounting to more than 56 million a year,[8] though most abortions are within the first trimester. The rate is higher in Europe because marriage and family are less valued. One of the gravest charges brought against Jerusalem was that "you took your sons and your daughters, whom you had borne to me [God], and these you sacrificed to them [the idols] to be eaten. Was your fornication so small a matter that you slaughtered my children and gave them to the fire for them?" (Ezek 16:20f) Immolation was a convenient solution to the problem of babies born out of wedlock. Psalm 106 says that in so doing Israel sacrificed to demons.

8. Sedgh et al., "Abortion Incidence between 1990 and 2014," 258–67.

The Marriage Feast
and the Banquet of God

Revelation 19. The Bride prepares for her wedding. The Bridegroom prepares by slaughtering his enemies with his sword, their flesh a banquet for vultures.

After these things I heard what seemed like the loud voice of a great throng in heaven, saying, "Alleluyah! The salvation and the glory and the power of our God! For his judgements are true and just; for he has judged the great prostitute who was corrupting the earth with her fornication, and has avenged the blood of his servants from her hand." And a second time they cried, "Alleluyah! Her smoke goes up for ever and ever."

And the twenty-four elders and the four living beings fell down and worshiped God who is seated on the throne, saying, "Amen. Alleluyah!" And a voice came from the throne, saying, "Praise our God, all his servants and all who fear him, the small and the great."

THE THRONG OR CROWD (*ochlos*) is not identified, and John only hears them, but their words evoke the great throng emerging from the great tribulation (7:10, 12). The salvation ascribed to God and the Lamb is now manifest in the smoke of Babylon's burning. Elsewhere other reasons have been given for the judgement (9:20f, 18:3) but here they are twofold: the great city has corrupted the earth's inhabitants through her promiscuity, and she has brought about the deaths of God's apostles and prophets. The verb *phtherw*, corrupt, has a less comprehensive sense than *diaphtherw* (11:18). "From [*or* by, *ek*] her hand" appears to govern "blood" rather than "avenge," with "shed" or "dripping" omitted (cf. 15:2). The smoke from her ruination goes up like that of Sodom and Gomorrah (Gen 19:28), examples of "eternal fire," irreversible destruction (Jude 7).

This is the third time that God's judgements have been declared just and true (15:3, 16:7), and the declaration has to be made, because we do not naturally assent to the destruction or perceive that it is just. It troubled Abraham, who only a few years earlier had rescued the citizens of Sodom from their enemies. "Will you sweep away the place and not spare it for the fifty righteous that are in it? Far be it from you to do such a thing, to kill the righteous with the wicked, so that the righteous fare as the wicked! Shall not the Judge of all the earth do what is right?" (Gen 18:22–25) God said he would not destroy the city even if there were only ten righteous in it, and went out of his way to rescue Abraham's nephew and his family before the fire came down.

"Alleluyah" occurs nowhere else in the New Testament. It is straight Hebrew, and as such echoes the psalms' exhortations for all to praise Yah (the older name of Yahweh)—all Israel, all the nations, even all creation. The psalms climax with the cry. But the circumstances are different. The rejoicing is a response to the previous exhortation that all the inhabitants of heaven should rejoice (18:20), and rounds off the revelation of the seven last plagues that began with the similar song at 15:3f. As before, fear of God is commended. Those who praise him, however, need not fear.

And I heard what sounded like a great throng, like the sound of many waters, and like mighty thunder, saying, "Alleluyah! For the Lord God the Almighty has reigned. Let us rejoice, and exult, and give him glory, because the marriage of the Lamb has come, and his wife has made herself ready, and it was given her to clothe herself in fine linen, bright and pure. For the linen is the righteous acts of the saints."

And he says to me, "Write this: Blessed are those who are invited to the marriage feast of the Lamb." And he says to me, "These are the true words of God." And I fell down at his feet to worship him. And he says to me, "Don't do that. I am a fellow servant with you and your brothers who have the testimony of Jesus. Worship God." For the testimony of Jesus is the spirit of prophecy.

The great throng is the numberless multitude at 7:9, plus all the others who are raised at the last trumpet, plus the 144,000 whose sound was compared to the sound of many waters and loud thunder at 14:2: all the saved; the bride herself. As at 11:17, "has reigned" means "has become king," beginning from the last trumpet. "Rejoice" is frequently combined with "exult/be glad" (e.g. Ps 68:3, Isa 61:10, Matt 5:12).

"Wife" is *gunė*, woman. In conjunction with the possessive adjective "his," it means "wife," just as *aner*, man, with the possessive means "husband." "Bride" would be *numphė*. Hebrew thinks in the same way: wife and husband each belong to the other. So the bride belongs to the Lamb and the Lamb to the bride. Made from plant fiber rather than hair or skin (cf. Gen 3:21), fine linen (one word in Greek) is especially the dress of kings, high priests and angels. On her it represents righteous acts, the "fruit of righteousness" that faith produces (Heb 12:11) rather than imputed righteousness (1 Cor 1:30). From the material provided she makes the garment herself (cf. Isa 61:10, Eph 2:10), proof that she has "put on the new man [*anthrwpos*] created after the likeness of God" (Eph 4:24). In 15:4 "righteous acts" refers to what God himself has done: this is the extent to which the woman is exalted! By contrast, the fine linen of Babylon the Great betokens a spurious morality.

The pure white linen is her wedding garment. The saints, comprising one body, will be married to the Lamb, whom John the Baptist announced to the world as the bridegroom, himself the bridegroom's friend (John 3:29). The metaphor is enlarged upon in the parable about the ten maidens and in another about the wedding which a king held for his son (Matt 22:2–14). Many were invited to the feast, but the first invitations were declined.

> Again he sent other servants, saying, "Tell those who are invited, 'See, I have prepared my dinner, my oxen and the fatlings have been sacrificed, and everything is ready. Come to the wedding.' " But they took no notice and went off, one to his farm, another to his business, while the rest seized his servants, abused them and killed them. On hearing this, the king became angry and despatched his army. He destroyed those murderers and burned their city. Then he says to his servants, "The wedding feast is ready, but those invited were not worthy. Go therefore to where the highways led into the city and invite to the wedding as many as you find." And the servants went out into the highways and gathered everyone they found, both evil and good.

Invitations go out first to the Jews, then to the Gentiles. To receive one is a privilege, for they come from the king, the occasion is one of joy, and admission is free. In the end—at the point when "everything is ready"—few even among the Gentiles accept. Most consider the affairs of their daily lives more important and make their excuses (Luke 14:18–20). Some persecute, even kill, the king's messengers. In his wrath, God destroys their city by fire. Instead, and this is after the city is burned, the poor, crippled, blind and lame come into the kingdom, those whom the gospel of grace did not reach and who had nothing in this life. "The hungry he filled with good things, the rich he sent away empty"—the prophetic past tense referring to the future. The hope of the poor will not perish forever (Ps 9:18, 113:7f, Isa 29:19).

There were several stages to a Jewish marriage in ancient times. A man who wished to marry went to the woman's father, agreed a price, and paid it (Gen 34:12). Then the couple entered into a binding covenant with each other, similar to the medieval practice of handfasting. A cup of wine was shared to seal the vows, and the man gave his bride gifts. From that point they were betrothed and legally married and any dissolution of the relationship required a divorce (Matt 1:19). The groom then returned to his father's house where he lived and prepared additional quarters for her. When all was ready, he went with his friends to his wife's house at a time unknown to the bride and either he or a friend acting as forerunner gave a shout to announce his arrival. Usually this happened at night, so that both she and her bridesmaid friends needed to have lamps trimmed and filled with oil. On the man's return with his bride, the couple consummated the marriage, celebrated for seven days and concluded with a feast.

So, having prepared a place for her, Christ has taken his betrothed to himself and the marriage is celebrated (though the wedding itself is not described) at the feast he looked forward to when he said to his disciples, "I will not drink again of the fruit of the vine until that day when I drink it new with you in the kingdom of the Father." Paul saw the significance:

> Husbands, love your wives, as also Christ loved the church and gave himself up for her, that he might sanctify her, having cleansed her by the bathing of water, in word, so that he might present the church to himself glorious, without stain or wrinkle or anything such, but that she might be holy and without blemish. Thus should husbands love their wives as their own bodies. He who loves his wife loves himself. For no one ever hated his own flesh, but nourishes and cherishes it, just as Christ does the church, because we are members of his body, from his flesh and from his bones. "Therefore a man shall leave his father and mother and cleave to his wife, and the two shall be one flesh." This is a great mystery, and I am saying it refers to Christ and to the church. (Eph 5:25–32)

It is indeed a great mystery. God created Adam on the third day, before vegetation (Gen 2:5) and before the animals. On the same day he planted a garden—a *paradeisos*—and after putting the man there, he caused to spring up every tree that was good for food, including the tree of life and the tree of the knowledge of good and evil. But the man was alone. On the sixth day God brought to him every bird and animal of the field so that he could name them and thereby confirm his dominion over them. But when Adam looked for a suitable counterpart among them, none was found, and he felt incomplete. So God put him to sleep and out of his side fashioned woman, and brought her to him. Adam was the first human son of God. His awaking prefigured Christ's resurrection from the tomb in the garden, and the creation of Eve the birth of the Church. The wound in Christ's side was like the cut that God made in Adam's side. We eat his flesh and drink his blood as a sign that we are part of him. In due time the Father will present the woman pure and spotless to his son, who purchased her and loved her as his own flesh—for so she was—and the two will become one.

The Song of Songs is a poem about the love of a betrothed woman for her future husband, and about his love for her. The metaphors evoke an orchard.

> As an apple tree among the trees of the forest,
>   so is my beloved among the young men.
> With great delight I sat in his shadow,
>   and his fruit was sweet to my taste.
> He brought me to the house of wine . . .

She herself is a walled garden; a sister and yet a bride. She longs for him, she is sick with love. He came to her garden while she was dreaming:

> My beloved put his hand to the latch
>   and my heart yearned for him.
> I arose to open to my beloved
>   and my hands dripped with myrrh,
> my fingers with liquid myrrh
>   on the handles of the bolt.
> I opened to my beloved,
>   but my beloved had turned and gone.

In the dream the watchmen of the city beat her. Although Solomon brought her into his chambers, her heart was elsewhere. Solomon is not her beloved. While he wishes to add this comely woman to the queens and concubines he already has, her heart is pledged to a shepherd, and in his eyes she is perfect. He is ready to take her:

> How beautiful and pleasing you are,
>> my love, with all your delights!
> Your figure is like a palm tree
>> and your breasts like its clusters.
> I said I will climb the palm tree,
>> I will take hold of its fruit . . .

And she is ready to give her love. But still he has not presented himself. He is still in his own garden. She waits for him with longing.

Kings in the Ancient Near East planted gardens next to their palaces in imitation of the tree garden planted in Eden. In Persia the enclosure was called a *pairi-daeza*. The biblical texts mention several, including the garden enjoyed by the king of Judah (2 Kgs 21:18, 25:4). Reliefs from Ashurbanipal's palace at Nineveh, on the Tigris, depict waterways running through the orchard, and inscriptions have him boasting of animals collected from across the empire and kept in his grounds. With conscious reference to the primeval tradition of all mankind, the enclosure symbolized Eden in the midst of uncultured wilderness; the king was the man entrusted by God to look after the garden,[1] and the animals corresponded to those brought to the man to see what he would name them. Ritual lion hunts represented the king exercising his dominion

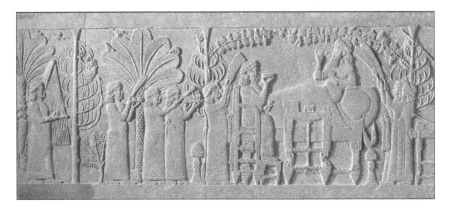

Relief of Ashurbanipal (669–631 BC) with his queen, north palace at Nineveh. In his left hand he holds a lotus, the plant of life. The couple enjoy wine made from the vines above them while a harpist entertains and attendants cool the air and bring platters of bread. On the tree in front of the harpist hangs the head of Teumman, king of Elam (British Museum).

1. Widengren, *The King and the Tree of Life*.

over creation. On the occasion of his defeating his enemies, he would hold a banquet in the garden, sit on his throne and drink the fruit of the vines growing there, while his wife celebrated opposite and musicians played on harps and tambourines. On one relief the decapitated head of the king of Elam hangs from a tree. Attendants offer loaves of bread.

The feast that the Lamb lays on for his bride is not only a marriage feast, but a celebration of victory over his enemies. The bread and wine of the eucharist—a full meal originally—give a foretaste of that banquet following the wheat harvest on the one hand (Matt 13:30) and the grape harvest on the other (Rev 14:19). After Abraham's defeat of the kings of the East, he and Melchizedek, king of Salem, also celebrated with bread and wine. "You have laid before me a table in the sight of my enemies," said David. "My cup overflows."

The "he" in "he says to me" is the angel who has been John's guide from the beginning, up to now neither seen nor heard. Seeing him at last, John prostrates himself, but the angel objects, for he serves alongside God's human servants. Only one angel has ever been worthy of worship, namely the angel Joshua saw (Jos 5:14). Like "the faith of Jesus" (14:12), "the testimony of Jesus" refers to both our testimony about him and that which he himself bore about the kingdom and the Father (John 5:31–37). Either way, to bear that testimony is to be a prophet, for the gospel is prophetic.

And I saw heaven opened, and behold, a white horse, and its rider, called faithful and true, and in righteousness he judges and wars. His eyes were like a flame of fire, and on his head many diadems, and he had a name written which no one knew but himself, and he was clothed in a garment dipped in blood, and his name was called The Word of God. And the armies of heaven, dressed in fine linen, white and pure, were following him on white horses. And from his mouth issues a sharp sword with which to strike the nations, and he will shepherd them with a rod of iron. And he treads the winepress of the fury of the wrath of God the Almighty. And on his garment and on his thigh he has a name written, King of kings and Lord of lords.

Unlike the man on a white horse in chapter 6, the rider is a named individual. But the picture is similarly militaristic, and contrasts with the same rider's entry into Jerusalem two thousand years ago. He is the commander of the army of Yahweh (Matt 25:31), going forth to rescue as in the day when Israel was pursued by the chariots of Egypt (Exod 15:1–18). He is called the Word of God, faithful and true, because it was he who inspired Scripture, who spoke through the prophets, and appeared as the Word in visions (e.g. Gen 15:1, 1 Sam 3:21). The Lion of Judah has been roused (Isa 31:4).

The words from Psalm 2 have been quoted twice before (2:27, 12:5). The kings of the earth take their positions against the Lord God and his anointed, while he looks down and laughs. The time of salvation for the nations has passed, and his name is no longer Yeshua ("salvation," or "Yah saves"); he cannot now be personally known and his name called upon, though his own will know it (3:12). The weapon in his mouth is the power to strike and kill (Num 22:31, Isa 27:1, 30:27, Rev 2:23). "I kill and I make alive, and there is none that can deliver out of my hand" (Deut 32:39). His garment is dipped in blood from treading the wine-press already described, and about to be described again.

In reverse order, "King of kings and Lord of lords" reiterates the Lamb's title at 17:14. It is written on the part of the body where the sword was strapped (Ps 45:3). The first man known to have called himself King of kings was Tikulti-Ninurta I, who reigned over Mesopotamia in the late 2nd millennium BC. The statement was factual enough, for the kings were chiefly rulers of cities, over which the supreme king ruled as emperor. Later examples include Nebuchadrezzar, head of the Babylonian empire (Ezek 26:7), and Artaxerxes, head of the Persian empire (Ezra 7:12). "Lord of lords" was also a common title and sometimes combined with "King of kings," as in this designation of the king of Assyria at the begin-ning of the 1st millennium: "Tiglath-pileser, strong king, unrivalled king of the universe, king of the four quarters [of the earth], king of all princes, lord of lords, chief herdsman [shepherd], king of kings." The titles could be applied to gods as well as kings, because gods ruled as kings. In 1 Timothy the double title is applied to God, "whom no man has seen or can see."

The people who settled Mesopotamia in prehistoric times found a lush, well-watered land that seemed like the Eden of their traditions. They named its major rivers after the original Tigris and Euphrates, and the upper part of Mesopotamia after the original Assyria (Gen 2:14). Kingship, they said, had come down to them from heaven, enabling God to rule by proxy. Over time the number of cities grew, each of which had its own god, and each god was assigned a distinctive function in the cosmos and a place in the growing genealogy of gods; but the king of Babylon's ultimate destiny, as a kind of second Adam, was to subdue and unite the whole earth. Passing orally from one generation to the next, the tradition about the first world underpinned the new ideology. But it was distorted. In truth, Mesopotamia was not the promised land. Babylon with its artificial mountain was not the city of God. The legitimate King of kings was yet to come.

And I saw an angel standing in the sun, and he cried with a loud voice to all the birds flying overhead, "Come, gather for the banquet of God, to eat the flesh of kings, the flesh of captains, the flesh of mighty men, the flesh of horses and their riders, the flesh of everyone, both free and slave, small and great." And I saw the beast and the kings of the earth with their armies gathered to make war against the rider on the horse and against his army. And the beast was captured, and with it the false prophet who had performed in its presence the signs by which he had deceived those who received the mark of the beast and worshiped its image. The two were thrown alive into the lake of fire that burns with sulfur. And the rest were killed by the sword that issued from the mouth of the rider on the horse, and all the birds filled themselves with their flesh.

An angel stands in front of the sun so that the sky is dark (as at 16:10, the same point in time). Like "all the nations of the earth" in Zechariah 12, everyone "small and great" refers to everyone in the nations surrounding Israel. They have laid Israel's cities waste and exiled their inhabitants; they have captured the city of the Great King and sent half its inhabitants into exile, enslaved them, killed them. The Devil has assured them of his power by signs and wonders. They are therefore confident that they can defeat the King, when he comes.

The banquet (*deipnon to mega*, literally "great dinner") takes place at the same time as the feast (*deipnon*) that celebrates the son's marriage. In the prophecy to which this vision alludes Ezekiel describes the meal as a sacrifice, as if the horses, charioteers and warriors were sacrificial rams, lambs, goats and bulls. "You shall be filled at my table," God tells the scavengers (Ezek 39:20). If this is not bad enough, the oxen and fatlings in the parable about the wedding of the king's son suggest the same metaphor: the slaughter of these armies is part of the celebration. Much as in the Ashurbanipal relief, "Every stroke of the appointed staff that Yahweh lays on them will be to harps and tambourines" (Isa 30:32).

> The sword of Yahweh is sated with blood;
> > it is gorged with fat,
> with the blood of lambs and goats,
> > with the fat of rams' kidneys.

> For Yahweh has a sacrifice in Bozrah,
>> a great slaughter in the land of Edom.
> Wild oxen shall fall with them,
>> and steers with the mighty bulls. (Isa 34:6f)

The sacrifice is an act of ritual annihilation (Isa 34:2), as of people pronounced to be anathema (Deut 7:2). It will take place on the mountains of Israel (Ezek 39:17).

This is the final day of vengeance (Isa 34:8, 61:2, 63:4) which Moses foretold at the outset:

> "I will take vengeance on my adversaries
>> and repay those who hate me.
> I will make my arrows drunk with blood,
>> and my sword will devour flesh." (Deut 32:41f)

Psalm 110, referred to more than any other psalm in the New Testament, begins with God saying to his son, "Sit at my right hand until I make your enemies your footstool. The staff of your might Yahweh sends from Zion." It ends by declaring that the son

> will crush kings on the day of his wrath.
> He will execute judgement among the nations,
>> he will fill [their territory] with corpses,
>> he will crush their head on the great earth. (Ps 110:5f)

Their head is the beast, the offspring of Satan. The offspring of the woman will smash their forces like a potter's vessel.

A great chasm will split the Mount of Olives from east to west (Zech 14:4), presumably in the same earthquake that brings down Babylon the Great. He will come

> with thunder and earthquake and great noise, with whirlwind
> and tempest and flame of devouring fire. And they will be like a
> dream, a vision of the night, the multitude of all the nations that
> fight against Ariel, all that fight against her and her stronghold
> and oppress her. (Isa 29:6f)

God will strike Jerusalem's assailants with a plague, so that their flesh rots and they panic and fight each other (Zech 14:12f, Hag 2:22). Then all the nations will see his glory (Ps 97:6).

He will lead the Jews exiled in Egypt, Iraq and elsewhere back to the land of their inheritance (Isa 11:11). They will take part in the day of vengeance (Obad 18, Mic 4:13, 5:8, Zeph 2:9, Zech 12:6, Mal 4:3).

> And they will swoop on the shoulder of the Philistines in the west. Together they will plunder the sons of the east, Edom and Moab. They will stretch out their hand, and the sons of Ammon will obey them. And Yahweh will annihilate the tongue of the Sea of Egypt, and wave his hand over the River with his scorching wind and strike it into seven channels, and lead across in sandals. And there will be a highway for the remnant of his people that remains in Assyria, as there was for Israel in the day that he came up from the land of Egypt. (Isa 11:14–16)

The Euphrates will dry up when the sixth bowl of God's wrath is poured on the river; the Nile likewise (Isa 19:5–7, Zech 10:10f). His liberated people will cross its parched bed in the same manner as their forbears crossed the Red Sea when a strong wind cleared a path for them.

The contrast between the marriage feast and the banquet on the mountains of Israel is similar to that in the parable about the rich man and Lazarus. Lazarus personifies those who are left on the margins, who must wait for comfort. He finds himself next to Abraham in the abode of the blessed, not because he heard the gospel but because he had nothing in this life. The anonymous man who feasted every day ends up in a place of torment, equivalent to the surface of the earth in its time of wrath.

The Beginning and the End
of the Kingdom

Revelation 20. The Devil is put away. The saints come to life and reign on earth with Christ for 1000 years. Then some of the nations rebel but are defeated. The rest of the dead are raised and judged.

And I saw an angel coming down from heaven, holding the key to the abyss and a great chain in his hand. And he seized the dragon, the ancient serpent who is the Devil and Satan, and bound him for a thousand years and threw him into the abyss, and shut and sealed it over him so that he should no more deceive the nations until the thousand years had ended. After this he must be released for a little while.

In chapter 9 a fallen angel opened the abyss to release demonic locusts. Another angel now shuts the abyss, locking the Devil and his fellow angels in and locking the demons back in. Having been cast out of heaven, the Devil is also barred from the earth. He has fallen as far as it is possible to fall.

This is the third time that John sees an angel coming down from heaven (also at 10:1 and 18:1). All three are manifestations of Jesus Christ, who came down from heaven. "How can someone enter a strong man's house and plunder his goods, unless he first bind the strong man, and then he will plunder his house?" Jesus was speaking of himself, for only he has the keys to the underworld and authority to imprison the Devil (1:18). Having won that authority on the cross, it seems inconceivable that he would delegate the act.

Until now, the god of this world has blinded the minds of unbelievers (2 Cor 3:14–4:4). With his removal, "the veil that is woven over all nations," including the Jews, will be swallowed up (Isa 25:7). The earth will be full of the knowledge of the Lord (Isa 11:9).

He deceives believers too, alas. There are three schools of thought regarding the thousand years: pre-millennialism, a-millennialism and post-millennialism. Pre-millennialism holds that Christ will return at the start of the thousand years. As attested by Papias (c. 120), Justin Martyr (c. 150) and Irenaeus (c. 175), pre-millennialism was the earliest understanding of the Church, and is the view accepted here. Later theologians argued against it, among them Origen (c. 220, the first to teach "the eternal generation of the Son"), Eusebius (c. 300) and Augustine (c. 400). A-millennialism rejects the idea that Christ will reign on earth in his own person, for whatever length of time. Ostensibly the 4th-century Nicene Creed is a-millennialist, implying that there will be only one resurrection and saying nothing about the kingdom of God except that it will have no end; the so-called Apostles' Creed does not speak of the kingdom of God at all. Post-millennialism, where distinguishable from a-millennialism, holds that Christ reigns on earth through his Church and Christianity will continue to spread until the Church has brought all nations under his rule; after that he will return, but to judge, not to reign. Naive, and exegetically perverse, the view is contradicted not least by the contemporary world's increasing hostility to the gospel. That the Devil continues to be a free agent on earth is surely evident, if one recognises his existence at all. Only when he has gone will the nations cease to deceive themselves and be deceived. Darwinism, Mohammedanism, Hinduism, Buddhism, Marxism will all be as chaff that swirls from the threshing floor.

Doubt that Christ's reign on earth will last for a thousand years is doubt that Scripture means what it says, since Revelation, supported by Papias and others, is explicit on the point. Papias must have passed on John's own understanding, and while John could not have understood everything he saw, he knew when he was being shown symbols and when not. He would have corrected his hearers if their understanding had been wrong. The thousand years, as a true number, asseverate God's absolute sovereignty over the timing, a sovereignty that is clear from Christ's ascending to the throne of his father exactly 1000 years after Solomon, son of David, ascended to the throne, in 971 BC. God foretells what he brings about, working all things according to the counsel of his will (Isa 46:11).

With him a thousand years is as a day, and a day as a thousand years (Ps 90:4, 2 Pet 3:8). Some infer from this that the days of Creation each represent a thousand years of history. However, Moses in the psalm is contrasting our brief lifespan with God's eternity. Peter is emphasizing God's patience, not making a statement about the age of the Earth, which is much older than 6000 years. Nonetheless, it may not be entirely misguided to think along these lines. Only the first few chapters of the Bible are devoted to the antediluvian world, because that world no longer exists and its history is therefore of limited significance. The emergence of dry land on the third day prefigured a renewal of the creation. Cleansed by the waters of baptism (1 Pet 3:21), the deluged earth re-emerged (Gen 1:9, 8:13) and, as we know from geology, a new igneous crust replaced what was destroyed. That same day God planted a garden on the earth. Correspondingly, in the second half of the 4th millennium the colonizers of Mesopotamia began to cultivate a new Eden. Their cities united to form a kingdom, but God confounded their language and forced some of them to spread abroad; the earth divided into many kingdoms. Since man's earlier history is a blank apart from the genealogy of Genesis 10, that must be the event that marks the beginning of the present age.

Day	1000 yrs	Genesis 1	History
3 = 1	3rd BC	God plants a garden of trees and forms Adam to look after it.	The first states after Gen 11:8: Sumer, Elam, Egypt, India, China, Crete.
4 = 2	2nd BC	He makes the Sun, the Moon and the 12 planets.	Jacob, Rachel and their 12 children (Gen 37:9).
5 = 3	1st BC	He creates marine and flying animals, including *tanninim*.	Gentile nations (Dan 7–8, Hab 1:14, Acts 10:12).
6 = 4	1st AD	He creates land animals. He forms woman and gives her to the man.	The Church called into being from the side of the last Adam (1 Cor 15:45, Eph 5:31f).
7 = 5	2nd AD	He rests the seventh day.	The Church established in Europe.
8 = 6	3rd AD	The man and the woman are given dominion over the animals.	Christ and his bride exercise dominion over the nations (Ps 8:6, Heb 2:8).
9 = 7			God's unending sabbath rest (Heb 4:9). The new heaven and earth.

Table 9. A typological interpretation of the days of Creation, counting them afresh from when the history of the new world begins.

Empires and nation states in Scripture are expressly likened to the trees God planted in his garden. As one empire was uprooted, another rose in its stead. First-millennium Assyria was a cedar of once unequalled height and beauty, supplied by many waters and giving shelter to all the birds (peoples and tribes). Then God dried up its waters and cut it down at the hands of the Chaldeans; it went down to join the other trees in Sheol (Ezek 31). Israel in one place is likened to a terebinth (Isa 6:13), in another to a vine, a seedling grown in the nursery of Egypt. After clearing the land of Canaan of its wild plants, God transplanted Israel there so that it might grow and bear fruit (Ps 80:8, Jer 2:21) but the vine degenerated and became good only for firewood (Isa 5:1–7, Ezek 15). Therefore, Jesus provided another vine, himself, joined to whom his disciples would not be unfruitful. In another simile, God's kingdom was compared to a mustard tree. Beginning with the smallest of seeds, it would eventually grow bigger than any other tree and even shelter birds in its branches (Mark 4:32), like empires before it (Ezek 31:6, Dan 4:12). In the growth of Christianity we can see this coming to pass, in a limited way. But complete fulfillment awaits the millennium (Ezek 17:22–24). Only then will all the trees know that Jesus is Yahweh.

Marine animals were created on the fifth day. The sea and the animals living in the sea also symbolized the Gentile world. Men were like fish (Hab 1:14–17), at the mercy of the potentate who caught them in his net for food. The king of Egypt was like a dragon, *tannin*, in the Nile and the seas (Ezek 29:3, 32:2). Insofar as they symbolized nations, terrestrial animals too were occasionally associated with water (Ps 68:30). Although the analogy is not perfect (terrestrial animals were not created until the sixth day), the fifth day thereby links with the 1st millennium when Israel came into contact with many Gentile nations: Assyria, Babylonia, Medo-Persia, Greece, as well as its immediate neighbours. A beast was any kingdom that did not acknowledge Yahweh, God of Israel, to be the ultimate ruler (Dan 4:25), and although Babylonia, Medo-Persia and Greece were visualized as terrestrial beasts, they came up from the sea (Dan 7:2f). At the start of the next millennium, the Church sprang from the side of the second Adam. The apostles came to understand that the quadrupeds of the earth, the beasts, the crawling animals, and the birds of the air (Acts 11:1–18, echoing the language of Genesis 1) were no longer to be considered unclean, if God had made them clean. Gentiles were to be part of his kingdom.

And I saw thrones, and people sitting on them, and judgement was given them, and 'I saw' the souls of those beheaded for the testimony of Jesus and for the word of God, and whoever did not worship the beast or its image and did not receive its mark on their forehead and hand. And they lived, and reigned with the Christ for a thousand years. The rest of the dead did not live until the thousand years had ended. This is the first resurrection. Blessed and holy is he who has a share in the first resurrection. Over these the second death has no authority, but they will be priests of God and of Christ, and they will reign with him for a thousand years.

There are two resurrections: the resurrection of whoever is in the new man, Christ, and the resurrection of whoever is in the old man, Adam: the "resurrection of life" at the end of the present age and "the resurrection of judgement" at the end of the thousand years. The period inbetween is "the age to come" (Matt 12:32, Eph 1:21), by definition a finite period. "Judgement" can be ambiguous in English. Sometimes it means the process of arriving at a judgement (*krisis*), i.e. a trial, sometimes "verdict" (*krima*), and sometimes "condemnation" (*krisis*, *krima* or *katakrima*); the Greek words can also be ambiguous. In John 5:29 the word is *krisis*.

The soul is the essence of a person. Since God has a perfect memory of who we are, and nothing is impossible for him, he is able to recreate us and clothe us with an incorruptible body. He contains the sum of all human souls, and more.

John sees those to or for whom judgement (*krima*) is given. The phrase recalls the coming of the Ancient of Days, when Daniel sees thrones being placed, as yet unoccupied (Dan 7:9), and judgement being given for the saints after three and a half years of oppression (Dan 7:22, 26f). God alone delivers the verdict; no court is involved (*pace* modern translations). He has vindicated his people and therefore they sit on thrones. Singled out are those beheaded because of their witness (predominantly Gentiles) and those killed because they refused to associate themselves with the beast (perhaps predominantly Jews). Nothing is said about the book of life, for they all have life. Therefore whoever accepts death rather than deny his name will gain far more than he loses. The rest of the dead remain unconscious.

This, in its fullness, is the kingdom to which the gospel has always pointed (Matt 7:21–23, 25:34, Luke 22:18). The nations of the world become the kingdom of God and of his Christ. Drawn from every part of humanity, the saints take up the positions reserved for them by the elders and serve Christ as his viceroys: blessed (the inaugural beatitudes now realized) and holy (all sin removed). Even the least are greater than those born in the present world. All receive the gift of eternal life (Matt 20:1–16) but each is rewarded according to what he has done with his talent money (Matt 16:27). One person can be called greatest and another least, even then, by reason of the differing honors bestowed. "Well done, good and faithful servant," they will hear. "You have been faithful over a little; I will set you over much. Enter into the joy of your master." He will set them "over all his possessions." They will repair the cities laid waste and inhabit them, together with the survivors (Isa 61:4–9). They will judge in the sense of administering justice (Exod 18:22, Luke 19:17, Rev 2:26).

Paul upbraids the church at Corinth: "Do you not know that the saints will judge the world?" (1 Cor 6:2) "When Christ our life is manifested, then you too will be manifested with him in glory" (Col 3:4, Zech 14:5, 1 Thess 3:13, Jude 14). Returning with Christ, the saints inherit the earth (Matt 5:5, Rom 4:13, 1 Cor 3:22). They will literally reign.

The Lord will come back to the Mount of Olives in the same way as he departed from it (Acts 1:11). Seated on his throne, he will make the survivors of his holocaust assemble before him and separate them into two groups (Matt 25:31–46). Those who treated his persecuted brothers kindly will also inherit the kingdom, even though they did not know him (Matt 10:40f); those who looked only after their own interests will be cast into "the eternal fire prepared for the Devil and his angels." The angels that had accepted worship from the peoples of polytheistic religions will join the angels already imprisoned (Isa 24:22). In different terms the parable about the harvest describes the same thing.

> Just as the darnel is gathered and burned up with fire, so it will be at the conclusion of the age. The Son of Man will send his angels, and they will gather out of his kingdom all causes of sin and all who live lawlessly, and throw them into the furnace of fire. There, there will be weeping and gnashing of teeth.

The furnace is the lake of fire and sulfur, a smoking lava-filled chasm that the New Testament calls Gehenna. The name derives from the Hebrew *Ge Hinnom*, Vale of Hinnom, the valley on the south side of Jerusalem where the most reprobate offered sacrifices to the fire-god Molech, even their own sons and daughters (2 Kgs 17:17, Jer 7:31, Ezek 23:37). Molech, whose name meant "King," was ruler of the demonic underworld, the equivalent of Abaddon. Judah's kings Ahaz and Manasseh also burned their sons as offerings in the valley.

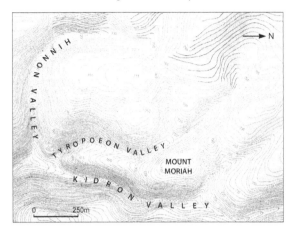

Topography of ancient Jerusalem. Mount Moriah is Mount Zion, where the Temple was situated. The Mount of Olives lies east of the Kidron Valley (freebibleimages.org).

Misleadingly translated "hell" in some versions, Gehenna was almost the first thing Jesus taught about. It was a place to avoid at all costs, for into it the unrighteous would be cast headlong and their bodies and souls destroyed in it (Matt 5:22–30, 10:28). The sentence would be irrevocable: the maggots that destroyed the body would not die; the fire that destroyed the soul would not be quenched (Matt 3:12, Mark 9:44). He himself would be the one pronouncing sentence (Luke 12:5).

The lake does not exist at the present time. It will be kindled (Isa 30:33), burning as far as lowest Sheol (Deut 32:22). The "mountains will melt under him and the valleys split open, like wax before the fire, like waters poured down a slope" (Mic 1:4). Christ—"whose fire is in Zion and his furnace in Jerusalem" (Isa 31:9)—will stand on the Mount of Olives as it splits from east to west, the fissure destroying the Al-Aqsa Mosque and Dome of the Rock that dominate Mount Zion today, west of the Mount of Olives. The surrounding hills and valleys will be flattened, whereas Mount Zion will become the highest of the mountains (Isa 2:2, 40:4, Zech 14:10). It is here that the king of all the earth will set his throne.

The lake will be a place of torment and regret. Justice requires that there be some penalty for sins that are not forgiven. In the parable about Lazarus, the rich man who wore fine clothes and ate fine food every day found himself in agony, for Abaddon's infernal fire had penetrated up to Hades. We ask God, "Forgive us our sins, as we forgive those indebted to us." If we do not, he will not (Matt 6:15). He will deliver us to torment: not for ever, and not necessarily in Gehenna, but until the debt of unforgiveness is paid (Matt 18:34). If we have wronged another and not reached a settlement, the debt will have to be paid to the last penny (Matt 5:26); the same applies if we have wronged God (Luke 12:58f). The pastor who neglects to prepare his flock for the Lord's coming will receive a beating, light or severe depending on how much the neglect was wilful (Luke 12:42–48); he will be saved "as through fire" (1 Cor 3:15). We get a good idea of how God will measure out retribution by considering his law, for the justice exemplified there is unlikely to be different from that administered at the last judgement (Matt 5:17–7:12). Whether finally saved or destroyed, those who are punished will not rise until the second resurrection. Where there is forgiveness, there is no condemnation, no punishment—that is why the gospel needs to be heard. The gospel is about forgiveness of sins.

"Eternal" (*aiwnios*, lit. "age-long") and "for ever and ever" (*eis tous aiwnas twn aiwnwn*, lit. "to the ages of the ages") do not necessarily mean "time without end." Moses provided for a slave in certain circumstances to be bound to his master "for ever," not meaning to all eternity but until one of them died (Exod 21:6). Jeremiah warned that a fire would be kindled "that will burn for ever," referring to the day when the Babylonians would destroy Jerusalem's palaces and temple; the fire would not be quenched (Jer 15:14, 17:27). When the destruction came, Jerusalem was ruined "for ever" (Ps 74:3). Habakkuk spoke of the "everlasting mountains" at the same time as prophesying that they would be shattered and levelled, foreseeing a time when God would shake the nations and the mountains be laid low (Hab 3:6). Christ will reign "for ever and ever" (11:15), and the saints with him (22:5), until he has put all his enemies under his feet (1 Cor 15:25). Jude spoke of the angels being kept in "eternal" chains (v. 6), apparently "for ever" (v. 13). But they are eternal, age-long, "until the judgement of the great day." Nor was the fire that destroyed Sodom and Gomorrah "eternal"—go to the the south-eastern Dead Sea and you won't see any fire where the cities were. As an example of what awaits the ungodly, they were turned to ashes (2 Pet 2:6). It was the effects of the fire that were perpetual; the cities were never rebuilt. Even their ruins have never been found.

Everything depends on context. When the context is the everlasting life that comes from God, the meaning is "for all eternity," and we know this because of the assurance that whoever accepts salvation will never die (John 11:26). Where the context is torment in the lake of fire, other scriptures categorically state that the final penalty of sin is destruction

(Deut 7:10, Ps 9:5f, 73:27, Matt 7:13, John 3:16, Phil 3:19, 2 Thess 1:9), even for the Devil (Heb 2:14).

Man's soul is not immortal. In the beginning, God formed his body from the dust of the ground. Only after God breathed spirit into his nostrils did he become a living soul. Like every animal, he had a dual nature, physical and spiritual. So with subsequent generations: when an infant grows in the womb, it is God who forms the body and endows it with life, as he realizes in time what he preordained (Ps 139). Man was given the opportunity to become immortal, but the serpent deceived Eve, and through her, Adam. In the act of eating what was forbidden, he internalized evil so that he knew what evil was from within; his body knew that it was naked, that it was "laid bare to the eyes of him who holds us to account" (Heb 4:13), and immediately he feared his Maker. He was permanently changed. So he was barred from the tree of life, he grew old, and in time his corrupted spirit was taken away; he returned to the dust. Terrible though the penalty was, it was not vengeful. Had everlasting torment been the consequence, it would have been a penalty no substitutionary atonement could have satisfied, "for then he would have had to suffer repeatedly since the foundation of the world" (Heb 9:26). The justice of God would have been a travesty of justice.

The logical opposite of eternal life is permanent extinction, not eternal life in another place (conceived of, somehow, as a state of being destroyed but never attaining destruction). Death occurs when body and spirit are severed, the one returning to the dust from which it came, the other returning to God (Eccl 12:7). That is what the word means. Some theologians draw a distinction between "physical death" and "spiritual death," as if the body could live apart from the spirit, but the Bible knows nothing of such a distinction. Pain will be suffered for a time; that is clear from the crucifixion; but ultimately there is only one kind of death: the loss of life. There are two deaths only in the sense that the first is provisional, the second irrevocable.

Although "the payback of sin is death" and therefore all must die, we do not die as soon as we sin, just as Adam did not immediately die. The judgement that now matters is not the judgement that God pronounced on the flesh, in the garden, but the judgement following death (Heb 9:27), relating to what we do in the years allotted to us in our state of reprieve. Death does not have to be the final sentence. The gospel brings the judgement into the here and now so that the punishment for wrongdoing can be anticipated, before it is too late (John 3:18f). The penalty has been paid, so that whoever repents will not be hurt by the second death. Those who reject the offer of eternal life will find the second death merely a confirmation of the first. They will forfeit the life they had on loan.

And when the thousand years are ended, Satan will be released from his prison and go out to deceive the nations at the four corners of the earth, Gog and Magog, to gather them for battle, their numbers like the sand of the sea. And they went up over the breadth of the earth and surrounded the camp of the saints and the beloved city. And fire came down from heaven and consumed them, and the Devil who deceived them was thrown into the lake of fire and sulfur where both the beast and the false prophet were. And they will be tormented day and night, for ever and ever.

"When the thousand years are ended" implies, of course, the specific number of years stated. Satan is released in order to draw out the last dregs of evil in one last purge. Gog is the leader of the Magog nation (Gen 10:2), the people of the western and eastern steppes prophesied about in Ezekiel (38:1–39:16). He will assemble a great army, comprising central Asians, Iranians, Sudanese, Libyans and the peoples around the Black Sea. He will attack Israel at a time when the land is restored from war (the war of Rev 13:7) and all its people have returned to it (Ezek 38:8). Even though the Great King himself is there and rules with a rod of iron, these nations will conspire to attack the apparently defenseless country and plunder it. They are interested in its silver and gold! But they will be destroyed by a great earthquake, volcanic eruptions, and a hail of stones. It will take seven months to bury the dead. For seven years the people of Israel will use the weapons left behind to make fires.

"The camp of the saints and the beloved city" refers to Jerusalem in the midst of the earth (Ezek 38:12). At first, the camp lay at some distance from the Tabernacle and, because of the golden calf, God was unwilling to go up with Israel into the promised land. But when Moses offered to atone for their sin, God changed his mind; he renewed the covenant and the Tabernacle was put in the middle of the camp (Num 2:2). Later the Temple replaced the Tabernacle. To define what was "outside the camp," a notional camp area centered on the Temple extended beyond the city's boundary (Heb 13:11). "Camp" suggests temporary residence, for only when all enemies have been subdued will there be a new earth. That, finally, will be the promised land.

From what point the Devil, the beast and the false prophet begin to be tormented is not stated—possibly not until the end of the thousand years. There comes a time when the demons are also tormented (Matt 8:29). Contrary to folklore, Scripture nowhere says that the Devil himself does any tormenting.

And I saw a great white throne and him who was seated on it, from whose presence the earth and the heaven fled, and no place was found for them. And I saw the dead, the great and the small, standing before the throne of God, and books were opened. And another book was opened, that of life. And the dead were judged by what was written in the books, according to their works. The sea gave up the dead that were in it, and Death and Hades gave up the dead that were in them, and they were judged, each according to their works. And Death and Hades were thrown into the lake of fire. This is the second death, the lake of fire. If anyone was not found written in the book of life, he was thrown into the lake of fire.

The same phraseology is applied to Earth and the physical heaven as to Earth's islands and mountains on the great Day (16:20). "Fled" means they vanished. "No place was found for them" means they ceased to exist; they "passed away" (Matt 24:35). "The earth" is the whole planet, "heaven" the whole universe. At the same time the sea and the subterranean regions give up their dead. "Death" is metonymous for Tartarus, where angels and men from before the Cataclysm are confined. In the Old Testament Tartarus and Hades are commonly paired (e.g. Prov 15:11, 27:20) and, retrospectively, this understanding of "Death and Hades" also applies at 1:18, where, in contrast to 20:1, "keys" is plural: one key for each place. Christ revealed himself to the antediluvians before his resurrection (1 Pet 3:19, Rom 10:7) and whoever responded to his word rose with him. The souls remaining are judged. After that, the two prisons will be consumed along with the earth containing them.

Paul wrote (1 Cor 15:21–26):

> For since death came by a man, resurrection of the dead also came by a man. For as in Adam all die, so also in Christ will all be made alive. But each in his own order: Christ the first-fruits, then at his arrival those who are of Christ, then the end, when he delivers the kingdom to God the Father, after he has abolished all rule and all authority and power. For he must reign until he has put all his enemies under his feet. The last enemy to be abolished is death.

It will take a thousand years to accomplish the full obedience of the peoples. He will reconcile all things to himself (Col 1:19) and restore all things (Matt 19:28, Acts 3:21), including the devastated earth. During that time people will still be born and die. At some indeterminate time after the thousand years, sea and land will yield up the souls who died in them and the old earth will pass away. The great throne is that of God himself. But when the dead come before it, the voice they hear and the face they see is Jesus Christ, for all judgement has been given to the Son and he sits on the throne (John 5:22, Acts 10:42, 17:31).

The question whether an individual is granted eternal life (here put negatively, "thrown into the lake of fire") is determined according to what he has done. A record has been kept of his life, and it is reviewed. There is also one other book, the book of life, which humanity has always known about (e.g. Exod 32:32, Dan 12:1). While relevant also to the first resurrection, the book is mentioned only in connection with the second. The register is not blank, nor is its title now "the book of death." Some are appointed to eternal life; some not.

It may come as a surprise to find that at the general resurrection men will be judged according to their works, and that not all will be condemned. But this is the answer to the familiar question, "What about those who have never heard the gospel?"

> "Nothing is beyond your understanding . . . O God, the great one, the mighty one, whose name is Yahweh of hosts, great in counsel and mighty in action, whose eyes are open to all the ways of the sons of man, to give to each according to his ways and the fruit of his deeds." (Jer 32:19)

This is not to be read as God condemning all humanity before AD 30 to destruction or everlasting torment. The judgement that brought condemnation to all men (Rom 5:16) was death. But there is also a judgement after death.

> "Though I say to the righteous that he shall surely live, yet if he trusts in his righteousness and does iniquity, none of his righteous acts shall be remembered, but in the injustice that he has done he shall die. Again, though I say to the wicked, 'You shall surely die,' yet if he turns from his sin and does what is just and right, if the wicked restores the pledge, gives back what he has stolen and walks in the statutes of life, not doing iniquity, he shall surely live; he shall not die. None of the sins he has committed shall be remembered against him. " (Ezek 33:13–16)

"Then he will answer them, saying, 'Truly, I say to you, as you did not do it to one of the least of these, you did not do it to me.' And these will go away into eternal punishment, but the righteous into eternal life." (Matt 25:45f)

"An hour is coming when all who are in the tombs will hear his voice and come out, those who have done good to a resurrection of life, and those who have done bad to a resurrection of judgement" (John 5:29).

[He] will render to each according to his works: to those who by steadfastly doing good seek glory and honour and immortality, eternal life, but to those who seek their own interest and do not obey the truth but obey unrighteousness, fury and wrath.... For when Gentiles, who do not have the law, do by nature what the law requires, they are a law to themselves, despite not having the law. They show that the work of the law is written on their hearts, their conscience adding its witness and between the two their thoughts accusing or also defending them. (Rom 2:6–15)

The occasion on which all who are in the tombs hear his voice and come out is the second resurrection, not the first. Then those who have done good will rise to eternal life.

Faith and works are not antithetical. Paul's commission was to call the Gentiles to "repent and turn to God, doing works worthy of repentance" (Acts 26:20). Righteousness and faith go hand in hand. An individual is righteous if he believes that there is a God who is good and who rewards those who seek him (Heb 11:6), and he walks by that light, even though he stumble (Prov 24:12–16, John 3:21). God justifies him even though he does not know of the Saviour whose sacrifice enables his justification. Abraham's faith was that God was good and would honour his promise of an heir.

Was not Abraham our father justified by works when he offered up his son Isaac on the altar? You see that faith was working along with his works, and faith was completed by the works. The scripture was fulfilled that says, "Abraham believed God, and it was reckoned to him as righteousness." And he was called a friend of God. You see that by works a person is justified and not by faith alone. (Jas 2:21–24)

This was before Christ came into the world, and it applied to all who sought to live by the light God gave them. While in absolute terms "no one living is righteous before him" (Ps 143:2), for "all have sinned and fall short of the glory of God" (Rom 3:23, 5:12), Psalms and Proverbs abound with references to the righteous. Job knew that he had a Redeemer, and that at the last, in his own flesh, he would see God (Job 19:25–27). Simeon also knew. Zacchaeus was saved because he met Jesus and repented, even though Jesus had not yet paid for his sins.

God says, "The soul that sins shall die," referring to the soul that persistently does what is wrong, and referring to the second death, not the first (Ezek 18). But he remembers mercy in the midst of wrath, for he knows that we are flesh. When Abraham asked God, "Will you indeed sweep away the righteous with the wicked? Shall the Judge of all the earth not do right?" the reply was not that his concept of justice was flawed, or that no one on earth was righteous. God destroyed Sodom because all its population was wicked, except Lot, who was righteous (2 Pet 2:7f) albeit far from perfect. On the other hand, he did not destroy every city in the plain, nor the other cities in Canaan, though he would do once their wickedness had come to fruition.

In the Old Testament, God's saving of a person or family in this life was an indication that he would save them also at the resurrection. Those saved included Rahab the prostitute, Naaman the Syrian and, when Nebuchadrezzar brought God's wrath on Judah, the daughters of Jonadab and the country's poorest (Jer 35:18f, 39:10). When Jonah, a man from an insignificant town in northern Israel, prophesied to Nineveh that it would be overthrown, he performed no sign to testify that he came from God. Yet God considered his message sufficient; and the Ninevites repented. So he reversed his decision, and not only for this life. Jesus told his hearers, "The men of Nineveh will rise up at the judgement with this generation and condemn it, for they repented at the preaching of Jonah— and see, something greater than Jonah is here" (Matt 12:41). Even many from the land of Sodom and Gomorrah will receive mercy, despite being judged in the flesh (Ezek 16:53, 1 Pet 4:6).

The gospel is good news, because it makes known the truth that God is good, and he has mercy on those who acknowledge their sin and repent. It is only bad news for those who say, "Let us drink and be merry, for tomorrow we die," who have heard and rejected the word of life, who are materially rich (for though they have more, they give less), who appear to be godly but shun the Holy Spirit, who are defiled by persistent fornication, homosexual relations, dishonouring of parents, occultism, hatred, jealousy, ingratitude, fits of anger, deceit, blasphemy, stealing, covetousness. It is only bad news for those who live by a moral law of their own making, opposed to God's law. The charge sheet includes most people in the West. Much is expected of those who have been given much. Some say, "Prove to me that God exists and I will believe," not seeing that even if someone came to them from the dead they would not believe. Or must he raise someone from the dead in every generation in order to answer that challenge? They are under judgement and in no position to make demands. The onus is on them to seek him, not on God to show himself. There has never been an age that had more proof of God.

It is Christ's death that enables God to judge men according to their works, even though all are guilty. In the light of his holiness sin will be exposed, admitted, and punished. It will not be a matter of good works outweighing bad in a pair of scales (Ezek 33:13), though they may mitigate. He will take all circumstances into account, in accordance with what he has told us about himself, that he is "compassionate and gracious, slow to anger, . . . taking away sin and transgression but unwilling to clear the guilty" (Exod 34:7)—guilty because they have not asked him to take away their guilt. He does not condemn a soul simply because he was born at the wrong time. Paul told the Athenians, "The times of ignorance God overlooked, but now he orders all men everywhere to repent" (Acts 17:30, Rom 3:25). Whoever fears God and does what is right is acceptable to him (Acts 10:35). The crippled, the blind and the lame, and those who care for them, will also inherit. Those who turn their backs on the gospel exclude themselves, whereas those who have no roof above their heads he compels to come in. There are many places at his table, and his house must be filled (Luke 14:23).

> The LORD releases the prisoners;
>> the LORD opens the eyes of the blind;
>> the LORD lifts up those who are bowed down.
> The LORD loves the righteous;
>> the LORD watches over the foreigners.
> The widow and the orphan he embraces,
>> but the way of the wicked he makes crooked. (Ps 146)

The prisoners are the dead. Who cannot see that this is a psalm about the resurrection? Lazarus was a sinner, like everyone else. But God took no notice of his sin. His life was blighted by hunger and disease, but after death he was comforted. Saif ul-Malook is a Muslim lawyer who risks death by defending Christians in Pakistan accused of blasphemy. God will receive him too.

THE HOLY CITY JERUSALEM

Revelation 21–22:5. The city that God has prepared for those who love him. Its gates are open, and the nations who have survived the wrath live by its light.

And I saw a new heaven and a new earth, for the first heaven and the first earth have gone, and the sea is no more.

THE REPLACEMENT OF THIS present world is the last event in the Bible. The Sun will not, as scientists say, get hotter and hotter until the oceans boil. It will not, 5 billion years from now, become a red giant, engulfing the planets Mercury and Venus. Long before then, the heaven will vanish like smoke (Isa 51:6).

> Formerly you founded the earth
> and the heavens were the work of your hands.
> They will perish, but you will endure;
> they will all wear out like a garment.
> You will change them like a robe, and they will pass away.
> (Ps 102)

Just as the original heaven and earth were his direct handiwork—they did not form by themselves over billions of years—so God will speak the new universe into being by his word (Isa 65:17). He will change the old for the new, just as the soul will be given new clothes. Then the new heaven and earth will endure for ever, along with Israel's offspring (Isa 66:22). But, "there will be no more sea."

In the first world the sea, or seas, was the deep beneath the land; the land was founded upon the seas (Exod 20:4, 11, Ps 24:2, referring to the world as originally constituted). The seas were also surface bodies of water surrounded by land, like the Great Lakes of North America, their water welling up from the deep. It was these that teemed with marine creatures

(Gen 1:20–22). At the onset of the Cataclysm the pillars collapsed, so that the deep erupted through and overwhelmed the land. The interconnected oceans that surrounded the continents as they re-emerged were maintained by a different water cycle. In the declaration that God created the sea there is no sinister connotation (10:6 and 14:7).

Some suppose that the sea will be destroyed because it is where the beast came from (13:1), but the sea in that context is a metaphor, not a real place of evil. The metaphor can hardly be reason for abolishing the literal sea, any more than the false prophet's rising out of the earth (13:11) would be reason for abolishing the literal earth. The crashing of waves, the cry of gulls, the smell of stranded seaweed, the crunch of pebbles, the unseen creatures that crawl and swim and burrow: who would wish them gone?—to say nothing about the sea as a source of food. Rather, in the new creation there will be no abyss, no boundless ocean, no anglerfish imaging the demons of the abyss. Inasmuch as he will cast all our sins into the sea (Mic 7:19), there will be no sin.

And I saw the holy city, new Jerusalem, coming down out of heaven from God, prepared as a bride adorned for her husband. And I heard a loud voice from heaven saying, "Behold, the tabernacle of God is with men, and he will sojourn with them, and they will be his peoples, and God himself will be with them, their God. And he will wipe away every tear from their eyes. Death will be no more; neither will there be mourning, or crying, or pain anymore; for the former things have gone."

Jerusalem (a dual in Hebrew, *Yerushalayim*) has a double reference, earthly and heavenly (Gal 4:25f). Both cities are holy, for "Yahweh will inherit Judah as his portion in the holy land and will again choose Jerusalem" (Zech 2:12). The new Jerusalem is personified as a bride, and her descent from heaven is related twice. The first time, she personifies the redeemed of both the first and second resurrection. The city is settled on a new earth in which righteousness dwells and there are no unrighteous. The former things having passed away, God makes all things new. The second time (v. 10), the vision sets forth the significance of the city for the nations around it. John is taken to a mountain—elevated Mount Zion—and there sees the redeemed of the first resurrection descending to the present earth. The first vision anticipates the newness that the second moves towards.

The principal inspiration for the passage is Isaiah 25:8 and 65:17–19. The latter verses announce the new creation as Jerusalem's assured destiny. Jerusalem will be created a place of great joy. Restored to their land, the people of Israel will again build houses, enjoy the fruit of their labor and bear children. Wolves and lions will no longer prey on other animals. God will dwell on Mount Zion and wipe away men's tears. Longevity will increase to what it was before the Cataclysm, so that a man dying aged 100 will be considered young. Eventually, God will swallow up death itself.

His intention has always been to make the nations his own (Ps 2:8, 82:8, Isa 56:7f, Luke 2:32). "Peoples" is therefore plural, and the promise that Israel would be his people and he their God (Exod 6:7, Jer 24:7, Ezek 11:20, Zech 8:8) is expanded. He erects his tent/tabernacle (*skenē*) in the midst of all humanity, for "many peoples will join themselves to Yahweh on that day" (Ezek 37:27, Zech 2:10–12, 8:3). God comes in the company of the redeemed out of heaven—their temporary refuge—to the peoples on earth, and sojourns (*skenwsei*) there with them.

God, Moses told Israel before foretelling their unfaithfulness, is perfect in all his ways; he is a God of faithfulness and without injustice (Deut 32:4). He alone is good, and everything good comes from him. Nonetheless he has created a world that has been blighted ever since the eighth day by evil, in order that we may distinguish good from evil (Gen 3:22). In the life to come, our knowledge of him will be informed by the knowledge gained in this world of what he is not, for there are qualities—such as courage, patience, truthfulness, justice—which can only be experienced in an imperfect world where good is postponed, or hidden, and evil has to be opposed.

> I form light and create darkness;
> > I make well-being and create evil. (Isa 45:7)

> He has made everything for its purpose,
> > even the wicked for the day of trouble. (Prov 16:4)

It is he who subjected the creation to death, consigning all human striving to futility (Rom 8:20). It is he who determines if a man is mute, or deaf, or blind (Exod 4:11). In the story about Job, Satan is given permission to strike everything Job has. After losing all ten of his children in a storm, Job accepts this natural disaster as God's prerogative to take back what he has given. "Shall we accept good from God and not accept evil?" God makes these disclosures in order that we may grapple with them, in life as well as in theology. There is comfort in knowing, amidst the darkness, that he is in control. But the knowledge that God allowed it, even willed it, can also augment the pain. Somehow we are to entrust our souls to the very person responsible for our suffering (1 Pet 4:19).

The last judgement is the vindication of God's justice following the injustice which vitiates this world. He wipes the wicked from the face of the earth (Gen 6:7); the sins of the penitent he wipes from remembrance (Ps 51:9, Acts 3:19), and finally he wipes away their tears. The verb is *exaleiphw*, in Hebrew *machah*, denoting complete erasure. It is an act of tenderness, the obverse of his justice and the vindication of his love. He wipes our faces the way a mother comforts her child. Having made us creatures susceptible to pain, and having been its ultimate cause—to test, to discipline, to purify, or for no reason that we can discern—he himself wipes the tears away, he who once also mourned, and wept, and was tortured. It is specifically a promise for Israel, on the day God saves her from her enemies (Isa 25:8–10). "He binds up the brokenness of his people, and heals the wound of his blow." "He will gather the lambs in his arm."

God has created us for pleasure and for joy.

> So we do not lose heart. Though indeed our outer man is wasting away, yet our inner is being renewed, day by day. For the momentary lightness of our affliction is working out for us an eternal weight of glory surpassing every superlative.
>
> (2 Cor 4:16f)

The present creation has many pleasures, and at his right hand there are pleasures for evermore (Ps 16:11). In his presence there is fullness of joy, his joy and ours, and one day we will enter it (Matt 25:21). Sorrow and sighing will flee away. So we wait for that day.

> *And he who was seated on the throne said, "Behold, I am making all things new." And he says, "Write, for these words are trustworthy and true." And he said to me, "It is done! I am the Alpha and the Omega, the beginning and the end. To the thirsty I will give from the spring of the water of life without payment. He who conquers will inherit these things, and I will be God to him and he will be a son to me. As for the cowardly, and faithless, and abominable, and murderers, and fornicators, and drug-dealers, and idolaters, and all liars, their share will be in the lake that burns with fire and sulfur, which is the second death."*

Progressive transformation leads towards the completely new. The creation will be delivered from its bondage to decay. The corruptible will put on the incorruptible and the mortal put on immortality. Somehow, he will give us back the Eden of our childhood: the innocence, the freshness of perception in the light of which everything is wonderful, the simplicity of feeling, the sense that here is our home, the place where we are totally loved. If we must become like children to enter the kingdom, will we not actually be like children? Childhood and adulthood will be reconciled.

"It is done" previously announced the end of God's anger (16:17) and implicitly a new beginning for humanity. Finally, at the end of the millennium, God's purpose in creating heaven and earth many ages ago will have been accomplished.

Water is essential for life. Earthly Jerusalem had a natural spring, but it was outside the walls (2 Chr 32:3), and spiritually she was dry. She needed a spring of living water, Yahweh himself (Jer 2:13). On the great last day of the Feast of Tabernacles Jesus cried, "If anyone thirsts, let him come to me and drink." On the day he is revealed such a spring will open for Jerusalem, washing away sin and uncleanness (Joel 3:18, Zech 13:1).

Let the reader remember the promises for each one who conquers (Rev 2–3). And here is an eighth: "I will be God to him and he a son to me"; he will inherit the covenant promises given to Abraham (Gen 12:7) and to David (2 Sam 7:14). To believe that God exists is of no account. What matters is that we should desire him, and that he should choose to be our God: the greatest privilege, the greatest blessing. To those who courageously and faithfully overcome the world he gives his whole self, embracing them as sons and daughters.

And there came one of the seven angels who had the seven bowls full of the seven last plagues, and he spoke to me, saying, "Come, I will show you the Bride, the wife of the Lamb." And he carried me away in spirit to a great mountain, and showed me the holy city Jerusalem, coming down out of heaven from God, having the glory of God, her radiance resembling a precious jewel, like diamond, crystalline, and with a great, high wall, with twelve gates, and at the gates twelve angels, and names inscribed of the twelve tribes of the sons of Israel, to the east three gates, to the north three gates, to the south three gates, and to the west three gates, and the wall of the city having twelve foundations, and on them twelve names of the twelve apostles of the Lamb.

And he who spoke with me had a golden reed with which to measure the city, and its gates, and its wall. The city lies foursquare, its length the same as its width. And he measured the city with the reed at 12,000 stadia.

Its length and its width and its height are equal. He also measured its wall:
144 cubits, a man's measure being an angel's. And the structure of the wall
was diamond, and the city pure gold, like clear glass. And the foundations
of the wall of the city were adorned with every kind of jewel: the first foun-
dation diamond, the second sapphire, the third agate, the fourth emerald,
the fifth onyx, the sixth carnelian, the seventh chrysolite, the eighth beryl,
the ninth topaz, the tenth chrysoprase, the eleventh jacinth, the twelfth
amethyst. And the twelve gates twelve pearls, each of the gates being of one
pearl, and the street of the city pure gold, like pellucid glass.

This second vision of Jerusalem is introduced, like the vision of
Babylon the Great, by one of the angels who poured out wrath on the
earth, as if the plagues are not to be forgotten. Both cities are portrayed as
female: one a prostitute, the other a pure bride (both the names and the
common noun for city, *polis*, are grammatically feminine, so "it/its" could
be translated "her"). One is seated on waters representing the nations of
the earth, in a wilderness; the other originates from heaven and comes to
rest on a mountain. One is adorned with gold, jewels and pearls; the other
is actually composed of gold, jewels and pearls—her beauty internal, not
merely external.

Isaiah draws a similar contrast:

> "We have a strong city;
>   he makes salvation our walls and rampart . . .
> For he has humbled those who dwell on the height;
>   the lofty city he lays low,
> lays it low to the ground;
>   he casts it down to the dust." (26:1–5)

> "For the mountains will depart
>   and the hills shake,
> but my love will not depart from you
>   and my covenant of peace will not be shaken.
> Afflicted one, storm-tossed, not comforted,
>   behold, I set your stones in antimony
>   and lay your foundations with sapphires.
> Of diamond I make your pinnacles
>   and your gates of carbuncle,
>   and all your walls of precious stones.
> All your children shall be taught by the LORD,
>   and greatly shall your children prosper. (54:11–13)

The angel with the measuring stick brings to mind both the prophecy of Jerusalem under occupation (11:1f) and Ezekiel's final vision (Ezek 40:2f). Ezekiel was transported to a high mountain in the land of Israel, where he saw a "structure like a city," not named until the end of the book. Evidently it is the Jerusalem that John sees. But the descriptions are different, not least in respect of the dimensions. Ezekiel's city is 4500 cubits or 1.5 miles square, consistent with a literal signification, whereas a city extending in every direction 12,000 stadia (around 1400 miles) is absurd, understood literally. But the number still holds. Centered on Jerusalem, an area with those dimensions would reach from the Black Sea to the Red Sea and from the Mediterranean to the Persian Gulf, encompassing Greece, Asia Minor, Iraq (ancient Assyria and Babylonia), Phoenicia, Syria, Jordan and Egypt, all the nations and empires that Old Testament Israel came into contact with except Medo-Persia. The significance is that they now are included in God's kingdom. "His rule will be from sea to sea, and from the River"—the Euphrates—"to the ends of the earth" (Zech 9:10).

> In that day Israel will be the third with Egypt and Assyria, a blessing in the midst of the earth, whom the LORD of hosts has blessed, saying, "Blessed be Egypt my people, and Assyria the work of my hands, and Israel my inheritance." (Isa 19:24)

The wooden measuring stick indicates that Jerusalem will be rebuilt physically, the golden measuring stick that it will be rebuilt spiritually (Isa 28:16f).

The city also extends into heaven, its cubic shape like the holy of holies in Solomon's Temple (1 Kgs 6:20). But the entire city is now his sanctuary, and is gold all the way through, not just overlaid with gold. John avoids saying that the city was "built," or "made." God's residence is not a building but a newly created people (1 Cor 3:17, Eph 2:22), a vast multitude. Babylon's walls were made of brick, Jerusalem's of stone, the walls protecting new Jerusalem, figuratively, of adamantine. As with the twelve tribes at 7:5–8, the exact nature of the stones does not matter. The Bride's jewels are the gems in the high priest's breastplate of judgement, engraved with the names of Israel's twelve sons. They symbolize an imperishable, heavenly splendor.

Yahweh chose Jerusalem even from birth, a foundling abandoned in the field (Ezek 16). He waited for the child to grow to womanhood. When the time was right for love, he washed her (the ritual cleansing before marriage, Exod 19:10), spread his garment over her (similarly Ruth 3:9) and covered her nakedness. He entered into a covenant betrothing her to himself. As wedding gifts he clothed her in fine linen and silk, adorned her with gold and silver, and set a tiara on her head. But she used her sumptuous raiment to rig up the booth of a prostitute; she turned the gold and silver into images and solicited the favors of the Philistines, the Egyptians, the Assyrians, the Babylonians: adulterous spiritually and fornicating literally. She became even worse than the peoples she lived amongst, including Sodom. "Can a maiden forget her ornaments or a bride her attire? Yet my people have forgotten me, days without number," he lamented. So, instead of consummating the marriage, he divorced her and brought on her the full force of his anger—he who had saved her from perdition. Nonetheless, in the last days he would remember his covenant. He would cleanse her again and give her a new heart. Then she would gladly call him husband.

> I will betroth you to me for ever. I will betroth you to me in righteousness, and in justice, and in love, and in compassion. I will betroth you to me in faithfulness. (Hos 2:19)

In Israel's idolatrous and syncretistic religion Yahweh already had a wife, the Canaanite goddess Asherah. The nation never supposed that in the latter days, after many years of exile they themselves would become his consort.

The Gentiles were formerly alienated from the polity of Israel, but them too Christ washed. We share the citizenship of the city with the people he chose first (Eph 2:12–22), for it was with the house of Israel that Jesus made a new covenant (Jer 31:33, Matt 15:24). The twelve foundations of the city symbolize Israel's sons; the twelve gates through which the righteous nation enters bear their names (Ezek 48:30–34). The apostles themselves were Israelites. There is no separate Gentile bride.

Only a little earlier, earthly Jerusalem had been laid waste and its inhabitants driven out. "Surely Yahweh has forsaken us," they said. But he had not.

> "See, I have engraved you on the palms of my hands;
>   your walls are before me continually.
> Your builders make haste;
>   your destroyers and those who laid you waste
>   go out from you.
> Lift up your eyes and look around:

> they all gather, they come to you.
> As I live, declares the LORD,
>   you shall put them all on as an ornament
>   and bind them on as a bride does.
> For your waste and desolate places
>   and the land of your destruction
> will now be too narrow for your inhabitants,
>   and those who swallowed you up will be far away.
> The children of your bereavement
>   will yet say in your ears:
> 'The place is too narrow for me;
>   make room for me to dwell there.'
> And you will say in your heart:
>   'Who has borne me these?
> I was bereaved and barren,
>   exiled and put away,
>   but who has begotten these?' " (Isa 49:16–21)

"These" are Israel's resurrected children: the people who did not live in faithfulness. When God raises them from their graves, he will restore their skin, their flesh and their bones and give them a new spirit (Ezek 11:19, 37:7–14). But they will not at this stage be immortal; they will not ascend to heaven or be part of the bride coming down from heaven. He will raise them up (Isa 49:6) and in so doing "reverse their captivity," and lead them back to the land of Israel (Jer 29:14). He will say to the prisoners, "Come out"; to those who lie in darkness, "Appear!" He will enter into judgement with them in the "wilderness of the peoples," face to face, as he did with their forefathers in the wilderness of Sinai (Ezek 20:34–38, 34:20–22). They will pass under his rod and walk along a highway of holiness from which rebels and transgressors will be excluded (Isa 35:8–10, 40:3).

> They will feed along the ways;
>   on all the bare heights they will pasture.
> They shall not hunger or thirst,
>   nor will the desert or sun strike them.
> For he who has compassion on them will lead them
>   and by springs of water he will guide them.
> And I will make all my mountains a road,
>   and my highways shall be raised up. (Isa 49:9–11)

The landscape is wilderness, but physical springs and rivers will open for them, as in the first Exodus (Isa 30:25, 35:6f, 41:18, 43:19f; Jer 16:14f). He will gather the remnant of Israel from the farthest parts of the earth, among them the blind, the lame and the pregnant (Jer 31:8f, Mic 4:6f, Zeph 3:19f).

> Then the eyes of the blind will be opened
>> and the ears of the deaf unstopped;
> then the lame man will leap like a deer
>> and the tongue of the mute sing for joy. (Isa 35:5f)

This is not a vision of what Jesus was to do at the time of John the Baptist. Rather, his works prefigured the day when he would come in vengeance against Israel's enemies (Isa 35:4), save the nation and heal those leaping from the grave (Mal 4:2), as he hinted when he added the raising of the dead to Isaiah's prophecy (Luke 7:22). He is still the "one who is to come."

The raising of Israel's dead is likened to a birth (Mic 5:3). Suddenly the barren woman brings forth an entire nation:

> "Before she was in labor she gave birth;
>> before her pangs came on she produced a male.
> Who has heard such a thing?
>> Who has seen these things?
> Shall a land go into labor in one day?
>> Shall a nation be brought forth all at once?" (Isa 66:7f)

The outcasts of Israel and the dispersed of Judah, living and dead, will be re-united. Those who were driven out of the land will be carried on horses and other forms of transport, laden with silver and gold. The nations themselves will bring them (Isa 14:2, 60:9, 66:20). Angels will gather those overseas, so that no Jew will be left among the nations (Matt 24:31, Ezek 39:28). Arabs who lived in the land will also have an inheritance (Ezek 47:22f).

He will give to Abraham's descendants the land he promised them in his first covenant, from the Negev to northwestern Syria, as far east as Damascus and the river Jordan (Gen 15:18–20, Josh 13:2–6, Ezek 47:13–21). "I will bring them to the land of Gilead and Lebanon, till there is no room for them" (Zech 10:10). Although the territory occupied previously was small, because the nation was small, "You have increased the nation; . . . you have enlarged all the borders of the land" (Isa 9:3, 26:15, 54:2f, Mic 7:11). So the land will be divided among the twelve tribes anew, including this time an allotment for the Levites. God's dwelling will be in the midst of Levi's allotment, and the priests who minister (22:3) will be specifically Zadok's resurrected descendants. Created for his glory (Isa

43:7), the Israelites will bear the name of God on their foreheads, and no longer bear it in vain (Exod 20:7).

They will marry and have children (Ezek 44:22, 37:26, Isa 65:3). Boys and girls will play in the streets (Zech 8:5). Their lives will be like a watered garden (Num 24:6, Jer 31:12). They will fill out their days, but nonetheless die at the end of them (Isa 65:20).

And I saw no temple in the city, for the Lord God the Almighty is its temple, and the Lamb. And the city has no need of the sun or the moon to shine on it, for the glory of God gave it light, and its lamp is the Lamb. And the nations will walk by its light. And the kings of the earth bring their glory and honor into it. And at no time will its gates be shut, for there will be no night there. They will bring the glory and the honor of the nations into it. And nothing common may enter it, nor anyone who does what is abominable or false, but only those who are written in the Lamb's book of life.

The earthly temple was only a shadow of the heavenly things (Heb 8:5). Therefore there will be no physical temple as such, for the *naos* is Christ (John 2:19), and the whole earth will be filled with his glory. He will fill all in all. The building in Ezekiel's vision is simply called his house, or holy place (*hagion*). A house there will certainly be, as Isaiah also says:

> It shall come to pass in the latter days
>   that the mountain of the house of the LORD
> shall be established on top of the mountains
>   and be lifted up above the hills.
> And all the nations will flow to it
>   and many peoples will come, and say:
> "Come, let us go up to the mountain of the LORD,
>   to the house of the God of Jacob,
> that he may teach us his ways
>   and we may walk in his paths."
> For out of Zion shall go forth the law,
>   and the word of the LORD from Jerusalem. (2:1–3)

The Gentiles will walk by the light that the city shines spiritually. The Lamb will shine like the sun, the glory of Yahweh rise upon Jerusalem like the dawn (Isa 60:1f). With a lesser light the Law looked forward to the Lamb and now looks back.

Do not be misled by Paul's polemic against self-righteousness. The Torah with its commandments and its requirement that our inability to keep the commandments be covered by sacrifice is good (Ps 19:7, Rom 7:12). When the physical house comes back, so too will the law.

> He will not grow faint or be dismayed
> until he establishes justice on the earth
> and the coastlands wait for his law. (Isa 42:4)

> "Do not think that I have come to abolish the Law or the Prophets; I have not come to abolish but to fulfill. For amen I say to you, until heaven and earth pass away, not one iota or one dot will pass from the Law until all is accomplished." (Matt 5:17f)

A few years before the Babylonians destroyed it, the glory quit the Temple. Now he will again fill the building (Ezek 43:1–5). "This is the place of my throne and the place of the soles of my feet, where I will dwell in the midst of the children of Israel for ever." God's house and the king's house will be one, because God will be the king.

When, and by whom, the house will be built is not stated. In a passage whose opening lines (Isa 60:1–3) are often misapplied to the first advent, Isaiah again describes the return of Zion's sons and daughters, then adds: "The glory of Lebanon will come to you, the cypress, the plane-tree and the pine, to beautify the place of my sanctuary," suggesting it will be built only after Christ's return and after Lebanon has been reforested.

His kingdom having come, reconciliation will no longer be a matter of appropriating by faith the righteousness revealed in the law and in the gospel. The age of the gospel will be over.

> From new moon to new moon,
> and from sabbath to sabbath,
> all flesh shall come to worship before me,
> declares the LORD. (Isa 66:23)

Once a year, the tribes of the earth will go up to Jerusalem to keep the Feast of Tabernacles, even the Egyptians (Zech 14:16–18). "Yahweh will make himself known to the Egyptians, and the Egyptians will know Yahweh in that day and worship with sacrifice and offering" (Isa 19:22). All must offer sacrifice (Zech 14:21), for sin will still need to be atoned for. At the direction of David their prince (Ezek 34:24, 45:17) and of the designated priests (44:15–41, Isa 66:21, Jer 33:21) even Israel must offer (Ezek 45:16f, 20:40, Mal 3:4), being still capable of sin. "Because of your palace at Jerusalem kings will bring gifts to you" (Ps 68:29, 96:8, Isa 60:11). Kings will still be ruling over nations, subject to the saints. "The treasures of all the nations shall come in, and I will fill this house with glory," as he said on the final day of the feast (Hag 2:7). It will be a house of prayer for all the peoples (Isa 56:7). The earth's kings will no longer be enemies of God, nor war with each other (Ps 46:9, Isa 2:4). Rather, they will acknowledge that he alone is worthy to receive power, and riches, and wisdom, and might, and honor, and glory, and blessing. The nations are the ingathering envisaged by the feast, welcomed in order that they too may have life. They include the poor, the maimed, the blind and the lame among the survivors (Luke 14:21), even the wicked (Matt 22:10). "Common" has the sense of "unsanctified" (Ezek 44:23, Acts 10:13), for not everyone will be admitted. The wicked must come in repentance.

The Sumerian King List opened, "When kingship came down from heaven, the kingship began in Eridu." The kingship shifted from one city to another, until a great king unified the country and chose Babel, the "gate of God," as his capital (Gen 10:10). Its builders erected there a terraced pyramid, symbolic of a great mountain, and the gate at the top gave the city its name. Through it the gods walked down to the earth. But the kingship was illegitimate, a usurpation of what belonged to God. Babylon was not the City of the Great King and not at the center of the earth. Later, Jacob dreamt of a stairway on which angels ascended and descended. When he awoke, he said in awe, "This is none other than the house of God, and this is the gate of heaven." Stairways branched half way down the building like the arms of a cross, a prefiguring of the true stairway between heaven and earth (John 1:51).

"Will God indeed dwell on the earth?" Solomon exclaimed. "The heaven and the heaven of heavens cannot contain you—how much less this house that I have built!" The heaven was the firmament containing the sun, the moon and the planets, within the envelope of water whose frozen remains we call the Oort Cloud (Gen 1:14–16, Ps 148:4), the origin of the long-period comets. It was created as God separated the waters below from the waters above and thereby stretched out the space inbetween (Gen 1:7f, Isa 42:5, Jer 10:12). The heaven of heavens was the space beyond the firmament, containing what subsequently became the stars of the Milky Way and, as we now know, countless other galaxies. As with "water," the Hebrew word for "heaven" (*shamayim*) was a dual; whether to translate as singular or plural is therefore a matter of choice. The duality goes back to the language's origin and reflects the duality of the heavens/waters themselves. Unlike Sumerian, the Afro-Asiatic language family of which Hebrew was part went back to Creation.

Jerusalem's temple was not so much God's palace as his footstool (Ps 132:7, cf. 2 Chr 9:18). In relation to the whole land and still more the peoples of all the earth, his throne stood in heaven. Heaven was like a tent which God made for himself (Ps 19:4, 104:2).

> He it is who sits above the circle of the earth,
> its inhabitants like grasshoppers;
> who stretches out the heaven like a curtain
> and spreads it like a tent to dwell in.

The nations were as nothing before him, like a drop from a bucket. The whole earth was his footstool; the entire heaven was his throne (Isa 66:1, Ezek 1:26).

The physical heaven was a representation of the "greater and more perfect tent" which was God's spiritual habitation (Heb 8:2, 9:11). In the beginning the solar system was illumined by an ultraluminous quasar (Gen 1:3). All galaxies began as ultraluminous super-energetic globes of fire. Later the quasar nearest us shot out jets that condensed into stars, forming the spiral arms of our present galaxy, while the remnant collapsed to leave a supermassive black hole. The primeval earth had no need of the sun to give it light, though the sun—less powerful then—still shone. The quasar represented the glory of God. In the new world the sun represented that glory, running his course "like a bridegroom going out

NGC 1365, one of the largest galaxies known. Early on, when the speed of light was much faster, the nucleus ejected two arms of ultra-condensed gas which caused it to spin. Over time the rate of spin slowed and the arms became a bar. It is thought the Milky Way looks similar, except that the center is now dark.

from his chamber." In the age to come, as we have glimpsed already in our hearts, the face of Jesus Christ will be that light.

And he showed me a river of water of life, bright as crystal, flowing from the throne of God and of the Lamb, in the middle of its street; and on either side of the river a tree of life producing twelve fruits, each month yielding its fruit, and the leaves of the tree for healing of the nations. And there will be no curse any more. And the throne of God and of the Lamb will be in it, and his servants will minister to him. And they will see his face, and his name will be on their foreheads. And night will be no more. They will need no lamp, or light of a sun, for the Lord God will illumine them. And they will reign for ever and ever.

First the physical, then the spiritual (1 Cor 15:46). In the beginning God planted a garden, in the midst of which was a tree of life, and a river flowed there. Like the tree of the knowledge of good and evil, it was an ordinary tree; its life-giving property inhered in his word. But man ate from what was forbidden, forfeiting eternal life, and God expelled him. In the new Jerusalem there is again a tree, and a river. The way to them is no longer barred.

As in the great city (11:8), only the central street is mentioned. The river running down it flows from the throne of God and of the Lamb— still one throne, but now on earth—because "just as the Father has life in himself, so he has granted the Son to have life in himself." And there is a tree on either bank. Spiritually, the tree is the stake on which our Lord was crucified (1 Pet 2:24), the apple tree among the trees of the forest (Song 2:3), the true vine.

> His delight is in the law of Yahweh,
> and on his law he meditates day and night.
> He is like a tree planted by streams of water
> that yields its fruit in its season,
> and its leaf does not wither. (Ps 1)

As the nations eat from the fruit of the tree, their lives will be prolonged (Prov 3:16–18); as they apply its leaves, they will be healed of their diseases. There will be no more condemning to ritual annihilation (Zech 14:11), as there was at the banquet of God (Isa 34:5) and as there was when Jerusalem (Isa 43:28, Jer 25:9, Mal 4:6) and modern Babylon (Jer 50:21-26) were destroyed.

In physical reality too there will be a river, flowing from the south side of the temple eastward and providing water for every kind of fruit tree (Ezek 47:1ff). It will get progressively deeper, emerging at the valley north of the Dead Sea (Joel 3:18), by Jericho. The Dead Sea will become fresh, and fishermen standing on its shores will fish there. As when Moses struck the rock at Meribah, the source will be an aquifer tapped by the great earthquake. On every mountain and hill there will be streams of water.

One might also venture an allegorical interpretation, given that the cubits measured along the river might be a measure of time (Matt 6:27). A thousand years after the first Temple was built the waters of life were only ankle-deep; a thousand years later, knee-deep; a thousand years later, waist-deep; in the millennium to come they will be deep enough to swim in (Ezek 47:3–6). The fish in the river will be caught in the nets of the kingdom, as all the nations are brought in. Alternatively the deepening signifies the progress of Christ's rule during the millennium itself, for "of the increase of his government there will be no end." Since the river is for all, the waters, physical and spiritual, will flow west as well as east (Zech 14:8).

When Israel entered the promised land, they were commanded to follow the ark at a distance of about 2000 cubits. The Lord of all the earth went into the river—the waters of death—before them, just as Jesus was to do before they entered permanently into their inheritance (Mark 1:9, 10:38). The ark stood on dry ground in the midst of the Jordan, and so all Israel crossed.

He who planted and uprooted Israel will plant them again, in their own land (Jer 31:28, 32:41, Ezek 17:23, Amos 9:15). He will take them from the dust of the ground, breathe his spirit into them, and set them in the land where he himself will dwell. He will make Zion's wilderness like the primeval garden (Isa 41:19, 51:3, Ezek 36:35) and make it his sanctuary. The walls of the holy of holies, lined with cedar and carved with cherubim, palm trees and flowers, pointed to the future rather than the past. This is the paradise that Paul was given a glimpse of, and which was promised to the rebel crucified next to Jesus. We ourselves have a glimpse of it whenever we raise our eyes to search for the blackbird hidden in the foliage, singing as from another world.

"Truly, you are a God who hides himself, O God of Israel," Isaiah interjected (45:15). He hid his face because of Israel's sins (59:2), and because of our sins he still does. But there were also other reasons. Understanding that our parent's instructions really were for the good, having the freedom to make mistakes and learn from them without fear of chastisement, becoming parents ourselves—these are elements of growing up. How would man repay that gift of freedom? Would he become like God in wisdom and holiness and compassion for the unfortunate, simply by moral evolution? Would wars cease? Would he still believe in goodness in the face of brain tumors, leprosy, mosquitoes, in the face of evidence that the Creator, if he existed, might not be good? Or would he curse?

God revealed himself for a time, then went away. Instinctively, we, knowing our nakedness and his holiness, hide ourselves as much from him as the other way round. But he will hide himself no more. The pure in heart will see him face to face, not dimly. At last we shall look into the eyes of the one who made us. We shall know him fully, even as he knows us.

Concluding Words

Revelation 22. The final words of Jesus, the angel, John and the Bride.

And he said to me, "These words are trustworthy and true. And the Lord God of the spirits of the prophets has sent his angel to show to his servants what must happen speedily. And behold, I am coming soon. Blessed is he who keeps the words of the prophecy of this book."

As in the first chapter, the speaker is not named, but "I am coming soon" tells us who it is. The message is urgent and will be repeated two more times. The certainty of his coming, previously symbolized by the reaper with the sharp sickle and the warrior on a white horse, is stated in plain words: there is no scope for evasion.

"Faithful" and "trustworthy" translate the same word, *pistos*. Combined with "true," it appears twice in relation to Jesus himself (3:14, 19:11) and twice in relation to the words that he speaks and John writes down (21:5, 22:6). The living and written Word are equally trustworthy. This needs stressing, because the mind, conditioned as it is to the natural and every-day, finds the content of Revelation difficult to stomach. Will the earth and man's works on it really be burned up? Will demons really torment men for five months? Will the glorified Jesus really reign in Jerusalem, in his own person? The speaker reiterates what John stated at the beginning (1:1–3), adding that the prophecy comes from the same God who commanded and controlled the spirit of every prophet when he prophesied. Elsewhere he is called "the God of the spirits of all flesh" (Num 16:22), the source of the life animating every living creature (Job 12:10, 34:14). Being prophetic, the message consists precisely of its carefully chosen words, which the reader should take to heart.

I, John, am the one who heard and saw these things. And having heard and seen, I fell down to worship at the feet of the angel who showed them to me. And he says to me, "Don't do that. I am a fellow servant with you and your brothers the prophets, and with those who keep the words of this book. Worship God."

And he says to me, "Do not seal the words of the prophecy of this book, for the time is near. Let the wrongdoer still do wrong, and the filthy still be filthy, and the righteous still do right, and the holy still be holy."

The apostle vouches for what he has heard and seen. Because of the wondrous things revealed since he last spoke with his guide, he is again moved to prostrate himself, and again he is rebuked. Those who serve by sharing the gospel (19:10) and honouring the prophecy have the same status as the angels. We must worship the one who begot us all.

Angels appear in the Apocalypse more than in any other book, giving us insight into the unseen. They perform the Father's will, and do not sin. God could have created a world inhabited only by angels, for sinlessness is not incompatible with the freedom to choose evil. But instead he created a world alongside heaven, inhabited initially by just one couple, creatures of flesh who would become as numerous as the angels by the innate, autonomous power of procreation. Man knew neither good nor evil, and flesh veiled the world of spirit. Satan, having free access to the garden, was tempted by the opportunity to interpose himself between God and man and become God himself. He became evil in the very act of tempting another to commit evil.

And what was the message that man listened to? "You can be like your Maker, even if you do not heed his words." God had set before him just one prohibition, devoid of moral content except that he had said it. "I was once alive apart from the law, but when the commandment came, sin came, and I died." Sin consisted in not acting in accordance with his words and listening to another voice. Man got to know evil, and since he was now excluded from God's presence, he had to learn what good was by resisting evil (Gen 4:7), and that involved suffering. Angels learned by observing God's response and obeying his commands.

Initially there was no separation between earth and heaven, and no underworld. After man's transgression God continued to live on earth; there could be no kings, therefore, claiming authority in his absence. But his sanctuary was closed off. Angels, being his sons, had spiritual bodies in his likeness, just as human beings had physical bodies in his likeness. Women conceived children by them, and men became increasingly violent. Instead of resisting evil, they succumbed to it. So there came a point when the earth was corrupt beyond saving, and God withdrew, destroying the planet's surface by the fragments of other destroyed planets. What remained of the first world was subducted into the now molten mantle, which thereby became the underworld.

Many ages passed, man multiplied, and the earth renewed itself. Eventually, in a land flowing with milk and honey God planted a people of his own and established in their midst, as before, a dwelling-place. In 592 BC he withdrew a second time (Ezek 11:23), ascending to heaven from the Mount of Olives. In the reigns of Augustus and Tiberius he dwelt among them again, this time as a man, revealing to them his grace and truth, so that they might dwell not only with him but in him. When he finally returns, the saints will also return, in bodies of the resurrection. They will live among human beings that continue to be flesh and blood.

> "Those who are counted worthy to attain that age and the resurrection from the dead neither marry nor are given in marriage; nor can they die anymore, for they are equal to angels and are sons of God, being sons of the resurrection." (Luke 20:35f)

They will no longer be male and female (Gal 3:28), because there will be no more reproduction. As at the beginning, the female will be in the male, one body, just as male and female, both, are in the image of God (1:13), and God is "he," not "she." We shall be like the firstborn Son himself, even in his glory (1 John 3:2f, 2 Thess 2:14). In a sense not envisaged by the Serpent, we shall be like God, and cease to know sin. Meanwhile, in this mortal body we seek to be like him now, together growing up into him who is the head (Eph 4:13–15).

Christ came down from heaven in order to raise us up. He divested himself of his glory and became for a little while lower than the angels. Perfected by his sufferings, he re-entered heaven on our behalf. So he will lead many sons to glory and not be ashamed to call them brothers, for they will be his brothers (Heb 2:10–17, Matt 25:40, 28:10, Luke 8:21, John 20:17). That is the significance of our being called sons of God. Together with the angels, we shall be "heirs of God, joint heirs with Christ, if indeed we suffer jointly, that we may also be glorified jointly" (Rom 8:17).

"The sufferings of the present time are not to be compared with the glory that is to be revealed for us" (Rom 8:18). But glorification, I infer, is a subsequent stage, awaiting the new heaven and earth:

> For those whom he foreknew he also predestined to be conformed to the image of his son, that he might be the firstborn among many brothers. Those whom he predestined he also called, and those whom he called he also justified; those whom he justified he also glorified. (Rom 8:29–30)

It is in heaven that "the righteous will shine like the sun in the kingdom of their father" (Matt 13:43), "like the stars" (Dan 12:3, Gen 15:5). The kingdom of the Father is in heaven, where the new earth will be, and comes after the kingdom of the Son (1 Cor 15:24). In the meantime, Revelation opens up what, in the books of Daniel (12:4) and Isaiah (29:11), was once under seal. Until the predestined end, events must take their course (Dan 12:9f), for the darnel will continue to grow alongside the wheat. Individuals will continue to be measured by their moral choices, not their intelligence, or creativity, or pleasing appearance.

"Behold, I am coming soon, and my wages with me, to pay to each as his work deserves—I, the Alpha and the Omega, the first and the last, the beginning and the end."

Blessed are those who do as he commands, so that they will have the right to the tree of life and may enter the city by the gates. Outside are the dogs, and the drug-dealers, and the fornicators, and the murderers, and the idolaters, and everyone who loves and practices falsehood.

Like the Lord God (1:8), Jesus is the beginning and the end. "For from him and through him and to him are all things." He knitted our bones and sinews together in the womb, and he will receive us when we rise. Zion is told to announce to the cities of Judah, "Behold your God!"

> Behold, the Lord—Yahweh—comes with strength,
>> his arm ruling for him.
> Behold, his wages are with him
>> and his reward before him.
> He will tend his flock as a shepherd;
>> he will gather the lambs with his arm. (Isa 40:10f)

As the Bible closes, he chooses to emphasise what he taught at the beginning of the gospel. There is a reward for those who fear and serve him (11:18). In the age to come there will be a blessing for those who act on his commandments (*poiountes tas entolas autou*). The sanctuary of his presence will not be closed off, and they will share in its benefits. (The alternative reading, *plunontes tas stolas autwn*, "who wash their robes," is a copyist's correction, prompted by 7:14.) The word *entole*, command or commandment, refers to the decalogue, but not in any narrow way. Whoever loves his neighbour fulfills the Law and will be approved. Those who break the Law, whether by flagrant acts of wickedness or by habitual dishonesty, are and will be excluded. Their lot is to be burned in the lake of fire outside the city. "Dogs" (Phil 3:2) epitomises the evildoers particularized in the list that follows, ending with a generality that encompasses them all.

"I, Jesus, have sent my angel to testify to you about these things to the churches. I am the root and the offspring of David, the bright morning star."

The Root of David has conquered (5:5), the scion whom David acknowledged as his lord (Matt 22:42), the first and the last. Like the morning star, he has risen from the womb of death's darkness, and at sunrise we shall follow, leaping from the stall like calves. Let every believer hear what the Spirit is saying to the churches.

And the Spirit and the Bride say, "Come." And let whoever hears say, "Come." And let whoever is thirsty come. Whoever desires, let him take the water of life without charge.

The Spirit and the Bride are one, using language that Laodicea in the 21st century can relate to ("wages," "reward," "without charge"). They invite whoever is attentive to their voice to join them, and say, "Come, Lord Jesus—come into my heart."

> Seek the LORD while he may be found;
> call upon him while he is near.

I testify to everyone who hears the words of the prophecy of this book: if anyone should add to them, God will add to him the plagues described in this book. And if anyone should take away from the words of the book of this prophecy, God will take away his share in the tree of life and in the holy city, which are described in this book.

Like the earlier blessing, this solemn warning—adapted from Deuteronomy 4:2 and directed, surely, towards teachers, translators and theologians—is a measure of the importance of the revelation. Why does the Church pay the book so little heed and not consider its words trustworthy? Why is she so unconcerned about the ending? Meanwhile those who suffer for the Name cry, "How much longer?"

He who testifies of these things says, "Yes. I am coming soon." Amen. Come, Lord Jesus!

"Amen" occurs by way of agreement seven times in the prophecy, as does the message that he is coming speedily. The Song of Solomon ends on the same note, the bride's cry of longing.

> The voice of my beloved!
>   Behold, he comes,
> leaping over the mountains,
>   bounding over the hills. . . .
>
> Make haste, my beloved, and be as a gazelle
>   or a young stag on the mountains of spices.

The grace of the Lord Jesus be with all the saints.

DANIEL, THE COLOSSUS
AND THE TREE

IT WAS ONLY NEBUCHADREZZAR's second year on the throne (the regnal year beginning Nisan 603 BC), but one night the king had a dream, and he wanted his wise men—the dream-interpreters, enchanters, sorcerers and astrologers—to tell him what the dream was. They answered, "O king, live forever! Tell us the dream, and we will reveal the interpretation." The king was skeptical. "If you cannot divine what I saw, you are not true mediums and your interpretations are worthless. Tell me, or I will throw you to the lions."

Dreams, planetary conjunctions, eclipses, animal entrails were all regularly interpreted in the ancient world. Nebuchadrezzar wanted to be assured that his advisers really did have access to secret knowledge. The wise men were obliged to speak frankly. "This is not reasonable. No one can reveal it to the king except the gods, and they do not dwell with mortals." A day was set for the wise men to be executed.

A few years earlier Nebuchadrezzar had deported a number of high-ranking Jews to Babylon, including a youth named Daniel. Having undergone a long program of training in Babylon's literature and arcane arts, he too was one of the king's advisers and on the execution list. He urged his friends to pray with him. In a nocturnal vision God answered their prayers and revealed the mystery. Being granted an audience with the king, Daniel told the dream.

> "You looked, O king, and there before you stood a large statue. The statue was great, extremely bright, and frightening in its appearance. Its head was of fine gold, its chest and arms of silver, its belly and loins of bronze, its legs of iron, its feet partly of iron and partly of clay. As you looked, a stone was cut out by no

human hand and struck the statue on its feet of iron and clay, and broke them in pieces. Then the iron, the clay, the bronze, the silver and the gold together were broken in pieces and became like the chaff of the summer threshing floors; and the wind carried them away so that no place was found for them. But the stone that struck the statue became a great mountain and filled the whole earth."

And this, he said, was the interpretation:

"The God of heaven has given you kingship, power, and might, and glory, and given into your hand the children of man, the beasts of the field and the birds of the heavens. Wherever they live, he has made you ruler of them all. You are the head of gold.

After you another kingdom inferior to you will arise, then a third kingdom of bronze, which will rule over all the earth. And there will be a fourth kingdom, strong as iron, because iron breaks to pieces and shatters all things. And like iron that crushes, it will break and crush all these.

And as you saw the feet and toes, partly of potter's clay and partly of iron, it will be a divided kingdom, but some of the strength of iron will be in it, just as you saw iron mixed with the muddy clay. And as the toes of the feet were partly iron and partly clay, so the kingdom will be partly strong and partly brittle. And as you saw the iron mixed with muddy clay, so they will mix with one another in marriage, but they will not hold together, just as iron does not mix with clay.

And in the days of those kings the God of heaven will set up a kingdom that will never be destroyed, nor will the kingdom be left to another people. It will break in pieces all these kingdoms and bring them to an end. It itself will endure forever, just as you saw that a stone was cut from a mountain by no human hand, and that it broke in pieces the iron, the bronze, the clay, the silver and the gold. The great God has made known to the king what shall be after this. The dream is certain, and its interpretation sure."

The astonished king prostrated himself before Daniel. "Truly your god is God of gods and Lord of kings, and a revealer of mysteries." Amongst other honors he made him ruler over the province of Babylon.

That Daniel was a historical figure seems clear from Ezekiel's holding him up as an example of righteousness (Ezek 14:12), for Ezekiel was a prophet of the 6th century and thus a contemporary of Daniel's. But did the developments foretold in the dream come to pass?

The four empires and afterward

Daniel lived long enough to witness the end of the first empire symbol-ized. A coalition of Medes and Persians conquered it while Belshazzar, its last king, was holding a feast. That was in 539 BC. At its height the Persian empire stretched from Turkey and eastern Libya to Afghanistan and Pakistan, and it continued until its defeat by Alexander. His most decisive battle against the Persians was in 331 BC, at Gaugamela, northern Iraq. On his death his empire—symbolized by the belly and loins of bronze—broke up into four kingdoms. The longest-lived of these, Ptolemaic Egypt, fell to the Romans in 31 BC. The Roman empire was the legs of iron, eventually dividing into a western and eastern part. It was bigger even than Alexander's empire, but had different borders, extending from Spain to Syria. North to south, it extended from Britain to the northern coast of Africa.

After the sack of Rome in AD 410, Rome's empire disintegrated into multiple entities, though its spiritual core—Christianity, which had supplanted paganism—remained a unifying and civilizing force. Collectively these entities amounted to a fifth, divided kingdom. The German and Gallic kingdoms retained imperial ambitions. At times they saw themselves as reviving the Roman Empire, whether as the Holy Roman Empire of Charlemagne (742–814) or the short-lived empire of Napoleon Bonaparte (1769–1821). Hitler's "Third Reich" was also conceived in these terms. After two devastating wars, the European Union was a further attempt to bring unity to western Europe, but full political and economic unity remains elusive. Symbolized by the feet of iron and clay, the European states intermingle but do not cohere. It is in their days that God will set up a kingdom that will never be destroyed.

The ram and the goat

In the third year of Belshazzar, Daniel saw a vision of a ram with two horns. One of its horns was higher than the other and came up after it, and charged westward, northward and eastward. Then from the west came a goat, with a conspicuous horn between its eyes, passing so quickly over the earth that it did not touch the ground. It overthrew the ram and grew exceedingly powerful, until its horn was broken. In its place came up four horns. An angel explained that the first animal represented the kings of Medo-Persia. In part, Daniel knew what was coming when he interpreted the writing on the palace wall in Belshazzar's final year. The second animal represented the kings of Greece, with the conspicuous horn representing the first of those kings (Alexander).

Then the angel gave details of what would happen in the days of a little horn that rose from one of the four horns: a figure identifiable as Antiochus IV, ruler from 175 to 164 of the Seleucid portion of Alexander's empire. The vision was so exactly fulfilled that some commentators have concluded it was written after the fact—an explanation first put forward by Porphyry (AD 232–305) in his work *Against the Christians*. The same logic would also apply to the book of Isaiah, who, ostensibly in the 8th century BC, prophesied the fall of Babylon and the rise of Persia under Cyrus. At that time Assyria was the dominant power in the region. Since

Seal impression found in a c. 700 BC Jerusalem midden and ascribed with high probability to the prophet Isaiah.

it is axiomatic that no one can know the future, the prophet we know as Isaiah must have been an impostor, a liar so consummate that, knowing the prophecies to be bogus, he had God expressly insisting that they were not (41:26, 44:6–8, 25f, 46:10f, 48:3).

True, but false?

It is of course a serious matter to accuse a person of forgery, even if one excuses such mendacity as "pious." In Daniel's case, the charge is buttressed by the claim that the book is historically inaccurate, chiefly in respect of two details.

One is the statement that on Belshazzar's death, and ostensibly before the reign of "Cyrus the Persian" (6:28), "Darius, son of Ahasuerus [Xerxes], by descent a Mede" received the kingdom (5:31, 9:1). Scholars have argued that this Darius is not otherwise attested. They deny the Medes a major role in Babylon's conquest and accept Cyrus's own testimony that he had previously conquered the Medes. But why would a forger have placed in this prominent position a person unknown to history? And why did Isaiah, and subsequently Jeremiah, who both lived before the fall of Babylon, prophesy that the Medes and neighbouring peoples subject to them would destroy the city (Isa 13:17, Jer 51:11, 27–28)? The questions are only the more pertinent if the prophecies originated, or were edited, after the fact.

However, it is not true that Darius is unattested. Three ancient historians come into the reckoning here: Berossus, Josephus, and Xenophon.[1] In his work *Babyloniaca*, of which only fragments survive, Berossus states that Cyrus defeated the last Chaldean king of Babylon, Nabonidus, and forced him to flee to Borsippa. After capturing Babylon Cyrus gave Nabonidus the province of Carmania, but "Darius the king took some of the province for himself." Apparently there was a king (then or subsequently) called Darius at the time of the city's fall and he had greater authority than Cyrus. Cyrus, king of Persia and commander of the attacking army, was his subordinate.

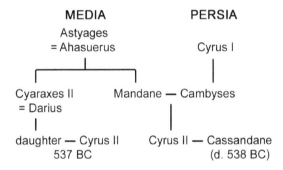

Inferred genealogy of Cyrus the Great.

It seems that Cyrus's father had formed an alliance with Media by marrying the daughter of Astyages, king of Media. Josephus says that Darius, son of Astyages, was Cyrus's relative but known to the Greeks by another name. That other name, we know from Xenophon, was Cyaraxes; Cyaraxes was the son of Astyages and became king of the Medes when his father died. "Darius," we may infer, was the throne name that Cyaraxes assumed on becoming king of Babylon, and Cyrus's mother was Darius's sister, Mandane. Many commentators on the book of Daniel have made these connections, including Jerome (AD 347–420).

Archeological documents are also supportive. A stele set up some time before the fall of Babylon in 539 BC but after Cyrus's supposed conquest of Media mentions a certain "king of the land of the Medes" alongside the kings of Egypt and Arabia as Babylon's principal enemies,

---

1. Anderson and Young, "Remembrance of Daniel's Darius," 315–23.

indicating that Media was then an independent state; it was hostile to Babylon, whereas Persia was not. In his famous cylinder inscription Cyrus accuses Nabonidus of neglecting the god of Babylon and provoking the god to look for a replacement: he presents himself as Babylon's divinely appointed liberator rather than conqueror. Significantly, Cyrus does not say he came as a friend who had conquered the Medes. Evidently he could not make such a claim, because the city knew he had not conquered the Medes.

We can therefore surmise that Darius, having, as Xenophon says of Cyaraxes, no son of his own, appointed Cyrus to be his heir and that, following the death of Cyrus's wife in 538, he sealed the arrangement by giving him his daughter in marriage. In this respect he would have followed in the footsteps of his father, who had given his daughter in marriage to Cyrus's father. Xenophon indicates that Cyrus's reign lasted 7 years, i.e. it started in 537 or 536, not 539. Only from that point did Cyrus become king of Babylon, alongside Darius, and only after Darius's death—he was already 62 in 539 BC (Dan 5:31)—did Cyrus become the ruler of both peoples. With a disregard for historical truth characteristic of despots, he erased the memory of his predecessor and wrote inscriptions claiming to have been Media's conqueror.[2] In Daniel's vision of the ram one of its horns was higher than the other and, without breaking the other, came up after it. The meaning must be that Cyrus—the greater horn—rose to supremacy without violence after Darius, and after Medo-Persia had been established.

The other detail on which the charge of historical inaccuracy rests is the reference to King Belshazzar. Prior to the mid 19th century Belshazzar was otherwise unknown, so that critics could reject Daniel's authenticity with some confidence. Then inscriptions were discovered at Ur showing that Belshazzar was the son and heir of Nabonidus, the last Chaldean king. That Daniel knew the name which history subsequently forgot was in fact evidence that Daniel lived close to Belshazzar's time! Then it was objected that Belshazzar was not a king. However, further discoveries indicated that Nabonidus had been campaigning for more than half his reign in Arabia, leaving Belshazzar, the Crown Prince, to rule in the capital as co-regent. Daniel does not mention Nabonidus as present on the night of Babylon's capture because he had fled to Borsippa. It was Belshazzar who fulfilled the prophecy that Babylon would fall during a

---

2. Anderson, *Darius the Mede: A Reappraisal*, 70.

drunken feast (Jer 51:39, 51:57). Herodotus and Xenophon both agree that the city was distracted by some such celebration.

Co-regencies were not uncommon in the ancient world. To forestall any conflict over the succession, the heir apparent would be invested with royal authority while the father was still alive and formally anointed when he died. That Belshazzar was not the only ruler is clear from Belshazzar's proclamation that Daniel, having solved the riddle of the writing, should be made the kingdom's third, not second, ruler (5:29), joint with himself and Nabonidus. Similarly, Nebuchadrezzar is described as king (1:1) at a time when, strictly, he was only Crown Prince.

Darius succeeded Nabonidus as king on the night that Babylon was captured. Israel's historians counted regnal years on a factual basis,[3] i.e. from the day of accession, so that his first year began in June/July 539 BC. He lived long enough to start organizing the empire into satrapies (Dan 6:1), and we know that his reign extended into a second year because the year is mentioned in Zechariah 1:7. Scholars have assumed that Zechariah's Darius was the one who reigned 522 to 486 BC, but this is clearly wrong, for the question is asked, "How long, O Yahweh of hosts, will you have no mercy on Jerusalem and the cities of Judah, against which you have been angry these seventy years?" The "seventy years" refer to the length of time that Jeremiah told Judah it would have to serve Babylon as vassal (Jer 29:10). The prophet urged the Jews to escape Babylon because the seventy years were about to end (Zech 2:7). Darius even lived to a fourth year (7:1), by which time the exiles had returned.

As portrayed, Daniel was a man of integrity, whom men of ill will sought to denigrate in his day just as men unsympathetic to his testimony do in ours.

> Actually, the book was written in Palestine in the mid-second century BC by an author who expected God to set up his everlasting kingdom in his own near future. . . . The original purpose of the Book of Daniel was to comfort and encourage persecuted Jews during the Maccabean revolt.[4]

Jesus considered Daniel to have been a historical person and a genuine prophet (Matt 24:15). Certainly someone is not telling the truth. Either his book is a forgery or, with its prophecies reaching all the way to the present, it is one of the most significant works in all literature.

3. Robinson, "Chronology of Ancient Israel," 89–98.

4. Sandoval, *The Failure of Bible Prophecy*, 102.

Nebuchadrezzar's second dream

Some time later Nebuchadrezzar had a dream of a tree in the midst of the earth, which grew very tall. Like Babylon's ziggurat, its top reached to heaven and it was visible to the ends of the earth. Then an angel cried, "Chop the tree down. Let his mind be changed from a man's to a beast's. Seven times must pass, until those living come to know that the Most High is sovereign over the kingdom of man, gives it to whom he will and sets over it the lowliest of men." As before, knowing that the dream must be significant, the king asked Daniel to interpret. In fact most of the meaning had been given in the dream itself. The tree represented Nebuchadrezzar. Soon the king would be banished from human company, lose his mind and live like a beast, but after seven times had elapsed, he would understand that the supreme God ruled the kingdom of man and set over it whomever he chose. So it turned out. At the end of the period he came back to his senses and praised the God of heaven, recognising that he was indeed the ultimate ruler.

However, after the dream foreshadowing the succession of future empires, this second dream is puzzling. Why seven times in particular? Was Nebuchadrezzar really the lowliest of men? Why does Scripture record the dream at all, if it adds so little to what was communicated by the first dream?

In truth the significance was more far-reaching. As Daniel said, the tree represented a kingdom, not just an individual, one whose dominion reached to the ends of the earth. In the light of Revelation, this has to be the final kingdom, Babylon the Great. The seven "times" are seven years, twice the "time, times and half a time" prophesied for Jerusalem at the end of the age. The strange circumlocution is precisely in order that we might make that connection. The period of the seven trumpets and seven bowls of wrath during which world civilization is laid low will last seven years. In the chaos people will not think or act rationally. It will begin when fire is cast on the earth and end on the great Day of the Lord when the cities collapse, probably on the last day of the feast of Tabernacles, the "great day" (John 7:37). Then the Messiah will no longer be "the lowliest of men" as when he came two thousand years ago (Isa 53:3). Ezekiel's parable of the cedar tree (17:22–24) is to the same effect.

Daniel's Seventy Years and Seventy Times Seven Years

It was the first year of Darius's reign as king of Babylon, 539/538 BC, and Daniel was reading the scroll containing these words of Jeremiah's.

> This whole land shall become a waste and a desolation, and these nations shall serve the king of Babylon seventy years. Then after seventy years are completed, I will punish the king of Babylon and that nation, the land of the Chaldeans, for their iniquity . . . and I will bring you back to this place.

The 70 years were almost up, and the question was whether God would fulfill his promise. Babylon had just fallen, but the Jews remained in exile; there was nothing on the horizon to indicate that their captivity was about to end. Daniel turned his face to Jerusalem and prayed. In answer the man/angel Gabriel avoided the issue and instead revealed what would take place much later.

In his first year as king of Babylon Cyrus issued a decree, saying,

> Yahweh, the God of heaven, has given to me all the kingdoms of the earth, and has charged me to build him a house in Jerusalem, in Judah. Let those among you who are his people go up and rebuild the house.

The writer of 2 Chronicles indicated that this marked the imminent fulfillment of Jeremiah's prophecy. However, neither he nor anyone else in the Old Testament demonstrated that 70 years had elapsed, so it is left for us to verify.

As discussed in relation to Nebuchadrezzar's first dream, Cyrus became king of Babylon in 537, when Darius, his predecessor, was still alive. In view of their existing kinship and having no male heir, Darius gave Cyrus his daughter in marriage and made him his heir and partner. In those circumstances Cyrus's accession is likely to have coincided with his formal coronation at the beginning of the Babylonian year, in April 537. His decree concerning the Jews was one of his first acts as emperor. Assuming that the return took place in the same year as the decree, they were back in their towns by October of 537 (Ezra 3:1). This would have been 390 years after Jeroboam committed apostasy (Ezek 4:4f), some time after his accession in 931 BC (1 Kgs 12:28–30). Less probably, the return took place in the following year, 536.

As a young man Daniel must have known Jeremiah, for he was among the few Jews, if not the only one, to have lived through the entire period of exile. The first exiles were hostages, Daniel included, whom Nebuchadrezzar took back with him following his capture of Jerusalem in the third year of Jehoiakim, king of Judah (Dan 1:1). Since Jehoiakim ascended the throne in September 609, the period of servitude began at some point between September 607 and September 606, 69 or 70 years before its end in 537 or 536. The writer of 2 Chronicles counted 70 years.

Another deportation took place in 597 (2 Kgs 24:10–17), an independent record of which is preserved in British Museum tablet 21946, known as the Babylonian Chronicle:

> In the seventh year [of Nebuchadrezzar, 598 BC; his eighth year by Judah's factual-year method of reckoning] in the month Kislev [Nov/Dec] the king of Babylon assembled his army, and after he had invaded the land of Hatti [Syria-Palestine] he laid siege to the city of Judah. On the 2nd day of the month Adar [16 March 597] he conquered the city and took the king prisoner. In his place he installed a king of his own choice, and received valuable tribute which he sent back to Babylon.

The king captured was Jehoiachin. Remarkably, another tablet recovered from Babylon's ruins and now in Berlin's Vorderasiatische Museum details Jehoiachin's rations. He was replaced on the throne by Zedekiah.

The final, most sweeping deportation took place in 586 BC (2 Kgs 25:8–12). After destroying Jerusalem by fire and pulling down its walls, Nebuchadrezzar

> removed those who had escaped from the sword to Babylon, and they became servants to him and his sons [i.e. successors] until the reign of the kingdom of Persia, to fulfill the word of the LORD by the mouth of Jeremiah, until the land had enjoyed its

sabbaths. All the days that it lay desolate it kept sabbath, to fulfill seventy years. (2 Chr 36:20f)

The sabbaths were a reference to the 50-year cycle of the Law of Moses,[1] the last year being a year of jubilee (Lev 25):

> "For six years you shall sow your field, and for six years you shall prune your vineyard and gather its fruits, but in the seventh year there shall be a sabbath rest for the land, a sabbath to the LORD. . . . And you shall count seven weeks of years, seven times seven years, so that the time of the seven weeks of years shall give you forty-nine years. And on the tenth day of the seventh month you shall sound the trumpet. On the Day of Atonement you shall sound the trumpet throughout your land. And you shall consecrate the fiftieth year, and proclaim liberty throughout the land to all its inhabitants."

A little later God warned the people that if they broke their covenant with him,

> "I myself will devastate the land, so that your enemies, when they settle in it, shall be appalled. And I will scatter you among the nations, and unsheathe the sword after you, and your land shall be a desolation and your cities a waste. Then the land shall enjoy all its sabbaths, as long as it lies desolate and you are in your enemies' land."

Daniel was painfully aware that this had come to pass. "All Israel has transgressed your law and turned aside, refusing to obey your voice. The curse and oath written in the Law of Moses the servant of God have been poured out on us."

So in 586 BC the land was vacated and in 537, 49 years later, some of the exiles returned to their land. In the seventh month they built an altar and offered burnt offerings on it, including the offering of the Day of Atonement, and celebrated the Feast of Tabernacles. In so doing, they inaugurated the year of jubilee. We know of two other occasions when the jubilee was celebrated. The first was in 687–86 (date inferred), when Isaiah assured Hezekiah that God would rescue besieged Jerusalem from the Assyrians and the people would eat what grew of itself for two years (the 49th and 50th years) and only sow and reap in the third year (2 Kgs 19:29f). The second was in 587 BC, when Zedekiah ordered Jerusalem,

---

1. Kawashima, "The Jubilee, 49 or 50 Years?" 117–120.

again under siege, to grant slaves their liberty. Subsequently, they changed their minds and took the slaves back (Jer 34:6–11).

The decree of seventy sevens

Gabriel's message to Daniel in 9:24–27 is a mixture of cryptic and perspicuous. The passage starts as follows:

> "Seventy sevens [weeks] are decreed about your people and your holy city, to constrain the transgression, to seal up sin, to atone for iniquity, to bring in everlasting righteousness, to seal up vision and prophet, and to anoint one most holy."

The numbers refer to years. The previously ordained period of 70 years is to be followed by another period apparently lasting 490 years.

The years are to fulfill several purposes (each one separated by "and" in the Hebrew). The first three announce an intention to deal with the enduring and seemingly insoluble problem of the transgression of God's laws, the sin in the human heart, and the guilt arising when sin causes man to transgress. These concepts are interrelated and mentioned together in God's proclamation to Moses of what his name stood for: "Yahweh, a God compassionate and gracious . . . forgiving iniquity, and transgression, and sin" (Exod 34:7). They also feature in his explanation of the meaning of the scapegoat let go on the Day of Atonement: "Aaron shall confess over it all the iniquities of the people of Israel, and all their transgressions, all their sins, and put them on the head of the goat" (Lev 16:21). They are discussed at length in Paul's letters to the Romans and Hebrews. Presumably the reference to "the" transgression is to the transgression in respect of the covenant (Isa 53:8).

"Everlasting righteousness" or justice becomes possible once iniquity is covered and justice satisfied. As Hebrews says, "By a single offering he has perfected forever those who are being sanctified." The sealing of vision and prophet refers to the cessation of prophecy and to the inability to understand what the prophets said, not least Daniel himself (Dan 12:4, 9). It was as if God had poured out on Israel "a spirit of deep sleep," so that she could not understand. God intended this (Rom 11:25–32). The "anointing of one most holy" refers to the anointing of a person. Although the noun is not specified, verse 25 refers to the coming of an anointed leader, the Messiah or Christ (which means "anointed one").

The next part of the passage reads:

"Know therefore and understand that from the going forth of
the word to restore and build Jerusalem until an anointed ruler
there will be seven sevens and sixty-two sevens. Again squares
and drains will be built, in a troubled time."

The passage is punctuated as in the KJV and NIV. The ESV ends the
first sentence after "seven sevens," so that the anointed one comes after
49 years and the period of building lasts 434 years. This is unsatisfactory
since the building phase then occupies only the second period, whereas
the word to restore and rebuild goes forth from the outset. Also, four
centuries is a long time to be building a city. "Drains" translates the word
charuwts, something incised or dug, such as a ditch.

The word to restore Jerusalem could be (i) the decree of Cyrus in
537 BC to rebuild the temple, (ii) the decree of Artaxerxes shortly before
April 458 authorising Ezra, "the scribe of the Law," to strengthen the
finances of the now rebuilt temple, to appoint magistrates and judges,
and to promote observance of the Law of Moses, or (iii) the letters of
authorization that Nehemiah received in 446 to rebuild Jerusalem's wall.
We can rule out the last option, since the wall had already been rebuilt.
Nehemiah was responding to the news that it had been pulled down and
its gates burnt. The damage was an illustration of the "troubled time"
foreseen in the vision.

As God reminded the people, the rebuilding of the temple had to be
the priority. "Is it a time for you to dwell in your panelled houses, while
my house lies in ruins?" (Hag 1:4) Likewise Isaiah's message in chapter
58 was: focus on moral restoration and restoration of the city will follow.
The phrase "restore and build Jerusalem" is therefore best understood as
referring to Ezra's mission. Reckoned by the factual method, Artaxerxes'
7th year began c. September 459 BC. Ezra went forth from Babylonia with
a letter containing his decree the following April and arrived in Jerusalem
in August (Ezra 7:9). The "square" was specifically where the people gathered to hear Ezra read out the Law (Neh 8:1) and where they heard about
the forthcoming Feast of Tabernacles. This dual effort of moral and physical restoration was destined to go on for 49 years, from 458 to 409, led
by Ezra as theologian and Nehemiah as governor. Malachi, Israel's last
prophet, wrote his book some time after 434–33, the last dated year in
the Hebrew Bible (Neh 5:14). No specific event is associated with 409 BC.

The passage continues:

"And after the sixty-two sevens, Messiah [lit. an anointed one] will be cut off, but not for himself. And the people of the ruler to come will destroy the city and the sanctuary. Its end will be with a flood, and until the end of the war desolations are decreed."

The death of the anointed one takes place after the 434 years, i.e. after AD 26. Whether this will be immediately after is unclear. The date suggests an association with either the start of John the Baptist's ministry or the start of Jesus's ministry.

Luke says that John began prophesying in the 15th year of the reign of the Roman emperor Tiberius. Tiberius's reign could have been counted either from the inception of his co-regency with Augustus or from his accession as sole ruler. The practice of Hebrew historiography was to count ordinal years from the co-regency if the new king was the principal ruler, otherwise from his sole reign.[2] Luke probably would have followed this tradition if he knew of it (the Romans counted from Tiberius's sole reign). Tiberius assumed control from October AD 11 (per Velleius Paterculus) or AD 12 (per Suetonius), when the senate made him joint governor of the provinces; by then, Augustus was seriously ill. If we take this event as the starting point, John began preaching some time between October 25 and October 27—Daniel's prophecy suggests March or August 26. Another clue is that the first Passover mentioned in the gospels came 46 years after Herod began renovating the Temple (John 2:13–20). Herod began the work in 20/19 BC, probably in the autumn, so this takes us to the year AD 27/28, with the first Passover in 28. How long this was after John began preaching we are not told. The last-mentioned Passover, the third, was in AD 30. August 26 to April 30 would equate to the 1335 days mentioned as a time of blessing in Daniel 12:12.

Being guiltlessly "cut off" evokes Isaiah's picture of a man who was stricken for his people's transgression and bore their iniquity and sin even though he had done no wrong (Isa 53). It relates to the premature death of Christ. The people of the ruler to come (the Messiah) are therefore the Jews. Although it was the Romans who destroyed Jerusalem, the Jews brought the destruction upon themselves by rejecting their Messiah and supposing that national liberty would come by armed revolt. The revolt began in 66 and ended with the fall of Jerusalem in September 70, forty years after Jesus's death (Ezek 4:6). Initially the Roman general ordered the Temple to be spared. According to Josephus, it was the Jews

2. Robinson, "Chronology of Ancient Israel," 89–98.

who set on fire the northwest approach to the Temple, in order to stop the Romans from coming nearer. The Romans then set fire to an apartment adjacent to the Temple, a conflagration the Jews made worse, until the whole Temple was destroyed. Subsequently the Romans flattened the city. "Flood" was a standard metaphor for war (Ps 124, Isa 8:8, Dan 11:10).

The prophecy concludes:

> "And he shall confirm a covenant with many for one seven, and in the midst of the seven he shall put an end to sacrifice and offering. And on the wing of abominations shall come one who makes desolate, until the ordained end is poured out on the desolator."

"He" refers to the anointed one. On 6 April AD 30 he put an end to sacrifice and offering by offering himself, three and a half years after John the Baptist. Thus the final seven began immediately after the sixty-ninth, and he was cut off in the middle of the seven. During those three and a half years he confirmed with his followers a new covenant. "This is my blood of the new covenant, which is poured out for many [key word] for the forgiveness of sins" (Matt 26:28, Mk 10:45, Isa 53:12).

The coming of one who makes desolate on the wing of abominations refers to a future person who erects an "abomination of desolation" (Matt 24:13). Similar to Nebuchadrezzar's golden image and to the image erected by Antiochus IV, the abomination will be a statue before which men must bow down and worship (Rev 13:15). The final three and half years are separate from the first three and half years (Dan 7:25, 12:7, Rev 13:5). During that final period the faith of those who hold to the testimony of Jesus will be tested. The new covenant extends over the full seven years, including the long gap of uncounted years in the middle, thus from AD 26 to the time of the end.

The fulfillment of the foretold 70 years of captivity, of the foretold 49 years during which the land would enjoy its sabbaths and, if we count from August 458 BC, of the foretold 486½ years (7 x 7 + 62 x 7 + 3½) between the coming of Ezra to instruct Judah in the old covenant and Messiah's inauguration of a new covenant all assure us that what remains to be fulfilled will be fulfilled. Moreover, the foretelling of the year of Christ's first public appearance (Luke 1:80) suggests that Scripture may also have indicated the year of his second appearance.

Appendix 1

REFERENCES TO GOD
AS CREATOR IN THE BIBLE

THE ISRAELITES UNDERSTOOD THAT they were the creation of Yahweh, the one who had created all things. He had taken their ancestor Abraham out of Sumer and led him to the land of Canaan, where his descendants became a new nation, informed by his life-giving law. While this was a different kind of creation from that with which all things began, it was still supernatural.

Yahweh worship was founded on three facts: he had created the world, he had redeemed Israel from slavery, and he had given Israel a reflection of his holiness and righteousness in the Torah. The biblical authors mention the Creation as many times as they mention the Exodus, perceiving that everything owed its existence to him and he alone had power over the weather and the womb. That is what made him God. By contrast, Baal did not create the world, did not redeem Israel, and was not holy and righteous, though he was much less demanding.

The New Testament conception was the same, but with some additions: God had created all things through Jesus Christ, believers in Christ could be redeemed from sin in a more fundamental way than was possible under the Law, and Christ was the perfect reflection of God's holiness and righteousness. In the 19th century, under pressure from the prophets of Baal in new guise, the Church began to abandon belief in God as Creator, and it became customary to talk about Providence rather than God. The Church ceased to understand who God was and forfeited much of her power as witness-bearer.

Let us not fool ourselves. If the world is the product of atoms ordering themselves through time, and if atoms themselves produce consciousness, the wise men of this world have some basis for arguing that God does not exist, for his existence then explains nothing. Some try to save the biblical testimony by arguing that evolution and creation amount to the same thing: heaven and earth were created over billions of years, and creation is therefore still going on today. However, Genesis states that the creation of the world was finished "in the beginning," and scientists themselves never speak of creation when describing natural processes. Unlike most theologians, scientists know what the word means.

To follow Baal has always been the more popular and enticing path. Just as when even three years of drought were not enough to puncture Israel's belief in his powers (1 Kgs 18), we profess belief in the Creator from one corner of our lips and belief in Nature from the other. Part of our brain tells us that man has a spirit, another that spirit is just a property of matter. We limp along on opinions that contradict each other.

It might be supposed that creation is affirmed only at the beginning of the Bible, after which it fades from view. The purpose of this Appendix is to correct that notion. The creation of heaven and earth and/or man is referred to in 15 of the 36 books of the Old Testament and in 13 of the 27 books of the New Testament. Jesus himself affirms it. Are we really prepared to say—and one day it will be to his face—that he was mistaken? The list omits references to God as father and creator of Israel, of which there are also many.

Gen 6:6f, 13—God resolves to destroy what he has made

Gen 14:19, 22—Melchizedek and Abraham alike affirm that God is the getter of heaven and earth ("get" in the sense of "produce," Gen 4:1, Deut 32:6)

Exod 4:11—he is our maker now, not only in the beginning

Exod 20:11, 31:17—the significance of the seventh day of the week

Deut 4:32

1 Sam 2:8—the metaphorical pillars of the earth express the idea that the original landmass was physically supported above discrete bodies of water

2 Kgs 19:15, repeated at Isa 37:16

2 Chr 2:12—Hiram accepting Israel's belief that Yahweh made heaven and earth

Neh 9:6—Yahweh made the heaven, the heaven of heaven with all its starry host, the earth and its animals, the seas and their animals

Job 9:8f

Job 10:8–12—he is intimately involved in the genesis of each individual (also 31:15, Ps 139:13–15, Isa 49:5, Jer 1:5)

Job 38:4–40:15—the works of the Creator are wonderful; it is foolish to question him on the basis that we know better

Ps 8:3—the heavens are "the work of his fingers": Yahweh was distinct from what he created, and formed it in the same sense as a potter forms a pot; a pot cannot form itself

Ps 19:1—the firmament is God's handiwork and declares his glory

Ps 24:2—Yahweh founded the dry land on the (subterranean) seas and (subterranean sources of) the rivers (Ps 136:6)

Ps 33:6-9—the heavens and everything in them were made by speaking them into existence; therefore we should fear him

Ps 74:12-17—God has power over creation because he created it: therefore we cry to him for help

Ps 89:11f (and 47)—heaven and earth belong to God because he created them, the thought also behind e.g. Deut 10:14, 1 Chr 29:11.

Ps 90:2

Ps 94:9—see on Exod 4:11 and Job 10:8–12

Ps 95:4-6—his hands formed the depths of the earth and its heights; see on Ps 8:3

Ps 96:5

Ps 100:3—Yahweh made us, not we ourselves

Ps 102:25

Ps 104—an entire hymn of praise to God the Creator

Ps 115:15, 124:8, 134:3

Ps 121:2—Yahweh can actively help us, much as he actively made the world

Ps 136:5-9

Ps 146:6

Ps 148:5—Yahweh created by his word of power (Ps 33, Jer 10:12)

Prov 3:19

Prov 8:25–31

Prov 20:12

Prov 30:4—God together with his son created the earth

Isa 40:26, 28

Isa 42:5—God is the origin of spirit (also Eccl 12:7)

Isa 44:24f—Yahweh the Creator formed Israel, and makes foolish the knowledge of those who think they know better

Isa 45:12, 18—Yahweh, not nature, created the earth, in order that man might live on it

Isa 48:13

Isa 51:13, 16

Isa 66:1f—re-affirmed in Acts 7:50

Jer 5:22

Jer 10:10–12, 16—as opposed to the gods that did not make heaven and earth

Jer 27:5—Yahweh made the earth with his outstretched arm, just as he had actively saved Israel in the Exodus with an outstretched arm (Exod 6:6, Deut 4:34, Jer 32:21)

Jer 32:17—Yahweh having created the world, nothing is too hard for him

Jer 33:2

Jon 1:9—what it means to be a Hebrew

Zech 12:1—cf. Isa 42:5

Mal 2:10—Creator of all mankind, Father of Israel, one God

Matt 19:4, Mark 10:6—"Have you not read that he who created them from the beginning made them male and female?"

Mark 13:19—"tribulation such as has not been the like since the beginning of creation" (even in the beginning there were people capable of experiencing tribulation)

Luke 3:38

Luke 11:50—"the blood of all the prophets shed from the foundation of the world"

John 1:3, 10

John 8:44

Acts 4:24

Acts 14:15

Acts 17:24–29—God made the world, and human beings are his direct offspring (*genos*)

Rom 1:20—his eternal power and divinity have been manifest to humanity since the creation

Rom 8:19–22

1 Cor 11:9–12

1 Cor 15:45–47—referring back to Genesis 1–2

Eph 3:9

Col 1:16

Col 3:9f—the "new man," Christ in us (1:27), contrasted with the "old man," Adam, referring back to Gen 2 (cf. 1 Cor 15:45–47, Eph 4:24)

1 Tim 2:13

Heb 1:10—affirming Ps 102

Heb 4:3—his works were finished (Gen 2:2) from the foundation of the world: hence "foundation of the world" means the six days of creation

Heb 9:26—sin, and therefore man, was in existence from the foundation of the world

2 Pet 3:5

Rev 4:11

Rev 10:6

Rev 14:7

Appendix 2

REFERENCES TO THE RESURRECTION IN THE OLD TESTAMENT

IT IS COMMONLY THOUGHT that "the Old Testament does not place any substantial hope in the afterlife. Rather, God's purposes for blessing and shalom are expected for the faithful in this life, in the midst of history."[1] According to the New English Translation, Daniel 12:2 is the "only undisputed reference to a literal resurrection found in the Hebrew Bible." N.T. Wright[2] characterises the scriptures that refer to resurrection as "covert allusions," including the one that Jesus cited (Exod 3:6), and suggests that belief in the resurrection developed only after the Old Testament canon had closed. While he accepts that the Daniel verse is not covert, in his opinion the book bearing Daniel's name is a forgery dating to the 2nd century BC, four centuries later than its apparent date. It counts for nothing that Jesus called Daniel a prophet and considered those who did not believe in resurrection ignorant of the Scriptures (Matt 22:31f).

According to Wright, pagans also had no concept of resurrection. However, his evidence simply consists of statements in pagan literature that no one had ever witnessed a dead body come to life. Like Psalm 90, these say nothing about the possibility that an individual might rise in the future or come back to life in a paradise beyond the horizon. In fact the contention that "resurrection was not part of the pagan hope" is not true. One has only to think of the almost ubiquitous practice of including material goods in graves—a practice as old as burying the dead itself.

1. Middleton, *A New Heaven and Earth*
2. Wright, *Resurrection of the Son of God*

Here is archaeologist Manfred Bietak on the Bronze Age graves (c. 1600 BC) at Tell el-Daba:

> The miniature offering vessels illustrate an interesting shift in the concept of providing the dead with the victuals they would need for their after-life. The initial tomb-offerings of food and drink would supply a man for a time but not eternally. The additional supply of miniature pottery guaranteed food forever by magical means.

Even Christians did not believe that they would rise immediately; the New Testament view was that there would be one resurrection at the end of the age.

Philosophy, the practice of asking questions independently of religious authority, began relatively late in history, in 6th-century Greece. It rapidly came to relativist, agnostic or atheistic conclusions. Christianity was revolutionary in arguing that questions of life and death could only be determined by revelation. On this basis, religion regained its place in educated society and belief in an after-life returned. Only in the 17th century did thinkers begin to question the authority of Scripture. Reasoning from matter rather than spirit, philosophy revived, and in the face of the absolutist claims of Christianity again came to relativist, agnostic and atheistic conclusions.

As regards the Old Testament, what matters is not what Israelites believed, but what God told them, whether they understood or not. The scriptures below span the whole gamut of the Hebrew Bible. Some are in the nature of covert allusions; others are plain enough. The psalms abound in assurances that one's soul is in safe keeping, even if modern translators, unsure whether the soul is a real entity, prefer to have them speak of "life" (for which Hebrew has a separate word). The prophets continually put the hope of resurrection before God's people: eventually he would fulfil his promise to "reverse their captivity" and bring them back to the promised land. Since many generations died without seeing the promise fulfilled, that could only mean that he would restore them to their land when he raised them from the grave. Heaven was never represented as the final abode of souls.

We learn from the Word incarnate how to interpret the written Word. When he said that God was God of the living, not the dead, his point was that God would hardly be worthy of worship if those who hoped in him were destined to perish. They would be no better off than those outside Israel's covenant, who were neither blessed for obedience nor cursed for disobedience. In fact we are all born with eternity in our heart,[3] believers and unbelievers alike.

Direct references and hints

Gen 4:4—Abel offered blood sacrifices because he believed in the resurrection, as did all who lived by faith (Heb 11)

Exod 32:13—the descendants of Abraham, Isaac, and Israel will possess the land forever (if the promise was only for the nation as a whole, each member of which would die, the promise was broken twice)

Exod 32:32f—the book of life (Rev 20:12)

Deut 32:39

1 Sam 2:6–8

1 Kgs 2:10, 11:43, 14:20 etc—sleeping implies waking

2 Kgs 4:18–37—the Old Testament equivalent of the raising of Lazarus, demonstrating that the dead can live again

Neh 5:19, 6:14, 13:14, 22, 29—Nehemiah's prayer that God should remember what he and his enemies have done must relate to judgement after death

Job 14:10–12—implying that man will rise when the heavens are no more (cf. Rev 20:11)

Job 14:14—"I will wait until my change [of garment] comes" (cf. Gen 45:22 etc, 1 Cor 15:51–54, 2 Cor 5:4)

Job 19:25f—*pace* Wright, the translation (ESV) is not problematic

Ps 1:6—by implication, the wicked will not perish, will not suffer the second death (cf. Ps 9:5, 68:2, 73:16–19 and Job 19)

Ps 17:13–15—"As for me, in righteousness I will see your face; I shall be satisfied when I awake in your likeness" (cf. Job 19:26 and Ps 11:7)

Ps 22:29

Ps 23:6—"I will dwell in the house of Yahweh [in his presence] forever [lit. for length of days, cf. Ps 21:4, Dan 7:9]"

Ps 27:4—the house/temple not yet built (the prayer will be answered when Ezek 44:3 comes to pass and David dines at his Lord's table)

3. Dor-Ziderman et al., "Mechanisms for shielding from existential threat."

Ps 27:13—normally "the land of the living" is the earth, distinct from Sheol under the earth, but here it is the land of the resurrected

Ps 30, written near the end of David's life—v. 3 "You brought up my soul from Sheol; you revived me from among those going down to the pit"; v. 5 "His anger [death] is but for a moment, his favor is for life"; v. 9 "What profit is there in my blood, in my going down to the pit?"; v. 12 "... forever"

Ps 34:22—Yahweh redeems the soul of his servants; none will be condemned

Ps 37:10f, 18–20, 22, 28, 29—inheriting the land, referring back to Gen 17:8

Ps 49:15—"God will ransom my soul from the hand of Sheol, for he will receive me"

Ps 65:2—cf. Ps 22:29, 86:9, Isa 45:23

Ps 69:28—the book of life (cf. Ps 87:6)

Ps 71:20, 23

Ps 73:24—i.e. receive me to God's glory at the resurrection

Ps 73:26f—"portion" connoting inheritance after death (cf. Lam 3:24); Israel inherits God and the Messiah inherits Israel

Ps 89:36

Ps 102:20—to hear the groaning of the prisoner(s), to release the sons of death (cf. Ps 79:11, 142:7, 146:7f, Isa 42:7, 61:1, Zech 9:11, Eph 4:8)

Ps 103:3–5, 17

Ps 113:7–9—"He raises the poor from the dust" (dust as in Gen 2:7, 3:19): this can hardly be said to happen in this life. Likewise, "He settles the barren [woman] in a home, a joyful mother of children" is paradoxical, since by definition a barren woman does not have children (Sarah, Hannah and Elizabeth being rare exceptions), but when Israel is raised, perhaps then the barren woman will bear children.

Ps 116:8f (cf. Ps 27:13)

Ps 118:17f

Ps 119:17, 37, 40, 50, 77, 88, 116, 144, 149, 154, 156—since we must all die, "live" must have the NT sense of John 6:57 and 1 Thess 5:10

Ps 121:7f—"he will keep your soul ... forever" (cf. Mic 4:7)

Ps 133:3

Ps 136—"His mercy [Heb. *chesed*, Gk. *eleos*] [is] for ever": meaningful only if "for ever" relates to the individual as well as the nation

Ps 142:5 (and v. 7 "Bring my soul out of prison"), cf. Ps 73.26

Ps 146:4—implying that this is not the fate of those who trust in God, also v. 7

Prov 2:19, 23:14—we all die, yet the one who learns wisdom will be saved from Sheol

Prov 3:18, 4:22, 5:5f, 8:35, 12:28, 22:4—references to life clearly not referring to this life (as for Ps 119)

Prov 10:30—evidently the wicked do dwell in the present land

Prov 11:4, 11:7, 11:19

Prov 15:24—". . . that he [the prudent person] may turn away from Sheol below"

Prov 23:18—"future" is lit. "hereafter", referring to redemption at the end of the age; also Prov 24:14, 24:20, Jer 29:11

Eccl 8:12f

Eccl 11:9, 12:14—open-ended judgement at the end of life implies that some receive eternal life (also Ps 62:12, Prov 24:12, Jer 17:10, Neh 13:14)

Isa 25:8

Isa 26:19

Isa 27:13—the dead exiles of Israel and Judah will rise

Isa 35:10—ditto

Isa 42:6f

Isa 49:6, 21

Isa 51:6, 8, 11—the inhabitants of the earth will die, but his salvation will be forever; having been ransomed (from death, permanently), those who know righteousness will come to Zion

Isa 55:3—"hear, that your soul may live": the hearer is already living, so the sense is "live forever" (so John 5:40, 20:31)

Isa 56:5–7—the promise is that the childless will do better than live after death through their children; having an "everlasting name" means having everlasting life, when God has brought them into his house (v. 7) by resurrection—cf. Ps 23:6, Isa 66:22, Rev 3:12

Isa 57:13

Ezek 18—the whole chapter (and see on Eccl 12:14)

Ezek 33:9–20—cf. Prov 4:22 etc

Ezek 37:12

Dan 7:10—"judgement took its seat, and books were opened," cf. Rev 20:12

Dan 12:1—the book of life

Dan 12:2—"sleep" as in 1 Kgs 2:10

Dan 12:13—Daniel will stand at the end of the age, after resting in the grave

Hos 1:11 (2:23)—they shall come up from the earth

Hos 6:2—on the third day (Matt 16:21) he will raise Israel and Judah up

Mic 7:7–9, also 7:19f

Hag 2:23—the resurrection of Zerubbabel after the shaking of the heavens and the earth

Mal 3:16–4:2—On a future day God will remember those whose names are recorded in his book by sparing them from destruction and making them his own

Acts 24:14f—Paul confirms that the Law and the Prophets give hope of a resurrection

Scriptures pertaining to Jesus' resurrection

1 Chr 17:11—cf. reiteration of this promise in Jer 33:26 when the dynasty is about to be terminated

Ps 16:10—"You will not leave my [David's] soul in Sheol or let your faithful one [the Messiah] see the pit," and cf. Ps 30:9 and Acts 2:31

Isa 53:10—"He shall see [his] offspring; he shall prolong [his] days"

Scriptures referring to a resurrected David

Jer 30:9f—"They shall serve Yahweh their [Israel's] God and David their king, whom I will raise up for them," where David refers to the historical David, distinct from the Messiah (Jer 23:5, 33:15)

Ezek 34:23, 37:24f—David will be Israel's "prince/king," distinct from Yahweh the Messiah (44:3)

Promises that God will reverse Israel's captivity

Deut 30:3

Jer 29:14, 30:3, 30:18, 31:1–25, 33:7, 33:26 (33:11 refers to the return from the Babylonian Exile)

Ezek 16:53, 39:25

Joel 3:1, Amos 9:14, Zeph 3:20

References

Altholz, Josef Z. "The Mind of Victorian Orthodoxy: Anglican Responses to 'Essays and Reviews, 1860–1864.'" *Church History* 51 (1982) 186–97.

Alvarez, Walter. *T. Rex and the Crater of Doom*. Princeton, NJ: Princeton University Press, 1997.

Amery, Fiona. https://www.bbc.com/future/article/20211001-the-people-who-claim-to-hear-the-northern-lights.

Anderson, Steven D., *Darius the Mede: A Reappraisal*. Grand Rapids: Steven D. Anderson, 2014.

Anderson, Steven D., and Rodger C. Young. "The Remembrance of Daniel's Darius the Mede in Berossus and Harpocration." *Bibl. Sacra* 173 (2016) 315–23.

Bietak, Manfred. *Avaris: Capital of the Hyksos, Recent Excavations at Tell ed-Daba*. London: British Museum, 1996.

Bloom, Harold. *The Revelation of St John the Divine: Modern Critical Interpretations*. New York: Chelsea House, 1988.

Brierley, Peter. https://www.brierleyconsultancy.com/where-is-the-church-going.

Caird, George B. *A Commentary on the* Revelation *of St. John the Divine*. New York: Harper & Row, 1966.

Chen, Hongyan, et al. "A Statistical Study of the Correlation between Geomagnetic Storms and M ≥ 7.0 Global Earthquakes during 1957–2020." *Entropy* 22 (2020) 1270.

Commission of the European Communities, 2001. *Making a European Area of Lifelong Learning a Reality*, Brussels.

Connolly, Ronan, et al. "How Much has the Sun Influenced Northern Hemisphere Temperature Trends? An Ongoing Debate." *Res. Astron. Astrophys.* 21 (2021) 131–98.

Crafts, Nicholas, and Peter Fearon. "Lessons from the 1930s Great Depression." *Oxford Rev. Econ. Pol.* 26 (2010) 285–317.

Crawford, Neta C. "Human Cost of the Post-9/11 Wars: Lethality and the Need for Transparency." Providence, RI: Watson Institute for International and Public Affairs, Brown University, 2018.

———. "United States Budgetary Costs and Obligations of Post-9/11 Wars through FY2020: $6.4 Trillion." Providence, RI: Watson Institute for International and Public Affairs, Brown University, 2019.

Curtis, Mark. *Secret Affairs: Britain's Collusion with Radical Islam*. London: Serpent's Tail, 2012.

Dodsworth, Laura. *A State of Fear: How the UK Government Weaponised Fear during the Covid-19 Pandemic*. London: Pinter & Martin, 2021.

Dor-Ziderman, Y., et al. "Prediction-based Neural Mechanisms for Shielding the Self from Existential Threat." *NeuroImage* 202 (2019) 116080.

Eastwood, J. P., et al. "The Economic Impact of Space Weather: Where do we Stand?" *Risk Analysis* 37 (2017) 206–18.

Gellately, Robert. *Lenin, Stalin and Hitler: The Age of Social Catastrophe*. London: Random House, 2007.

George, A. R. "A Stele of Nebuchadrezzar." In: *Cuneiform Royal Inscriptions and Related Texts in the Schøyen Collection*, edited by A. R. George, 153–69. Bethesda: CDL Press, 2011.

Gøtzsche, Peter. *Deadly Medicines and Organised Crime: How Big Pharma has Corrupted Healthcare*. Boca Raton, FL: CRC Press, 2013

Gutentag, Alex. https://www.tabletmag.com/sections/news/articles/the-war-on-reality-gutentag. *The Tablet* (2021).

Harper, Kyle. *From Shame to Sin: The Christian Transformation of Sexual Morality in Late Antiquity*. Cambridge, MA: Harvard University Press, 2013.

Harris, Sheldon H. *Factories of Death: Japanese Biological Warfare, 1932–45 and the American Cover-Up*. 2nd ed. New York: Routledge, 2002.

Hill, Clifford. *The Reshaping of Britain, Church and State since the 1960s: A Personal Reflection*. London: Wilberforce, 2018.

Hughes, James T. *Ecclesial Solidarity in the Pauline Corpus*. Eugene, OR: Pickwick, 2019.

Hughes, David A. "9/11 Truth and the Silence of the IR Discipline." *Alternatives: Global, Local, Political* 45 (2020) 55–82.

Humphreys, Colin. *The Miracles of Exodus: A Scientist's Discovery of the Extraordinary Natural Causes of the Biblical Stories*. New York: HarperCollins, 2003.

Kawashima, Robert S. "The Jubilee, Every 49 or 50 Years?" *Vetus Testamentum* 53 (2003) 117–20.

Kendrick, M. *Doctoring Data*. Caldicot: Columbus, 2014.

Kenyon, Kathleen M. *Excavations at Jericho*. Vol. 3. London: British School of Archaeology in Jerusalem, 1981.

Koester, Craig R. *Revelation and the End of All Things*. Grand Rapids, MI: Eerdmans, 2001.

Kühn, Stefan, et al. *World Employment and Social Outlook—Trends 2021*. Geneva: International Labour Organization, 2021.

Lay, Thorne. "The Surge of Great Earthquakes from 2004 to 2014." *Earth Planet. Sci. Lett.* 409 (2015) 133–46.

Lewis, Theodore J. "CT 13.33-34 and Ezekiel 32: Lion-Dragon Myths." *J. Am. Orient. Soc.* 116 (1996) 28–47.

Marchitelli, Vito. "On the Correlation between Solar Activity and Large Earthquakes Worldwide." *Sci. Rep.* 10 (2020) 11495.

Middleton, J. Richard. *A New Heaven and a New Earth*. Ada, MI: Baker Academic, 2014.

Miller, Samuel. *Letters on the Eternal Generation of the Son of God*. Andover: Flagg & Gould, 1822.

Neumark, S. D. "World Situation of Fats and Oils." *S. Afr. J. Econ.* 15 (1949) 192–203.

Obomsawin, Ray. "Immunity, Infectious Disease, and Vaccination." pennybutler.com/vaccine-lies-forever/ (2011).

Paul, Ian. *Revelation: An Introduction and Commentary*. Downers Grove, IL: InterVarsity, 2018.

Paxton, Roberto. *French Peasant Fascism*. Oxford: Oxford University Press, 1997.

Picón, Carlos A., and Seán Hemingway. *Pergamon and Hellenistic Kingdoms of the Ancient World*. New York: Metropolitan Museum of Art, 2016.

Pinilla, Vicente, and María-Isabel Ayuda. "The International Wine Market 1850–1938." In *Wine, Society and Globalization*, edited by G. Campbell and N. Guibert, 179–99. New York: Palgrave Macmillan, 2007.

Ramon-Muñoz, Ramon. "Modernizing the Mediterranean Olive-Oil Industry, 1850s-1930s." In *The Food Industries of Europe in the Nineteenth and Twentieth Centuries*, edited by D.J. Oddy and A. Drouard, 71–88. London: Routledge, 2013.

Roberts, J. M. *The Pelican History of the World*. Harmondsworth: Penguin, 1980.

Robinson, Steven J. "The Chronology of Ancient Israel Re-examined." *J. Anc. Chron. Forum* 5 (1991) 89–98.

———. "Bronze and Iron Age Chronology Recalibrated." https://www.researchgate.net

Sandoval, Chris. *The Failure of Bible Prophecy*. Victoria, BC: Trafford, 2010.

Schmidt, Wilhelm. *The Origin and Growth of Religion: Facts and Theories*. Translated by H.J. Rose. London: Methuen and Co, 1931.

———. *Primitive Revelation*. Translated by J. Baerl. London: B. Herder Book Co., 1939.

Sedgh, Gilda, et al. "Abortion Incidence between 1990 and 2014: Global, Regional, and Subregional Levels and Trends." *The Lancet* 388 (2016) 258–67.

Skambraks, Ole. https://multipolar-magazin.de/artikel/i-cannot-do-it-anymore.

Steiner, Richard C. "Does the Biblical Hebrew Conjunction -ו have Many Meanings, One Meaning, or No Meaning at All?" *J. Biblical Lit.* 119 (2000) 249–67.

Thomas, Jeremy A. *The Nation's Gospel. Volume 2 (1791–1900) Revolution to Revival*. London: Wilberforce, 2020.

Trevisanato, Siro I. *The Plagues of Egypt: Archaeology, History and Science Look at the Bible*. Piscataway, NJ: Gorgias, 2005.

Waters, Matt. "Cyrus and Susa." *Rev Assyrol. Archéol. Orient.* 102 (2008) 115–18.

Welch, John W. "Doubled, Sealed, Witnessed Documents: from the Ancient World to the Book of Mormon." In *Mormons, Scripture, and the Ancient World: Studies in Honor of John L. Sorenson*, edited by D. Bitton, 391–444. Provo, UT: FARMS, 1998.

Wenham, John. *Redating Matthew, Mark and Luke*. London: Hodder & Stoughton, 1991.

Widengren, Geo. *The King and the Tree of Life in Ancient Near Eastern Religion*. Wiesbaden: Otto Harrassowitz, 1951.

Wright, N. T. *The Resurrection of the Son of God*. Minneapolis, MN: Fortress, 2003.